American Indians
of the Ohio Country
in the 18th Century

American Indians of the Ohio Country in the 18th Century

PAUL R. MISENCIK *and*
SALLY E. MISENCIK

McFarland & Company, Inc., Publishers
Jefferson, North Carolina

ISBN (print) 978-1-4766-7997-6
ISBN (ebook) 978-1-4766-3850-8

LIBRARY OF CONGRESS AND BRITISH LIBRARY
CATALOGUING DATA ARE AVAILABLE

Library of Congress Control Number 2019057027

On the cover: An Indian of the nation of Shawanoes (Shawnee),
an Algonquian-speaking North American people
who lived in the central Ohio River Valley
© 2020 Everett Historical/Shutterstock

Printed in the United States of America

*McFarland & Company, Inc., Publishers
Box 611, Jefferson, North Carolina 28640
www.mcfarlandpub.com*

To the Native American people who made Ohio
so much richer by their presence, and also to our teachers
at Cleveland Benedictine High School, Northfield-Macedonia
High School, the University of Akron, and Bowling Green
State University, who nurtured our love of history.

Acknowledgments

Our thanks to the many research sources we were able to access, and their incredibly helpful and knowledgeable staff. These include the National Museum of the American Indian in Washington, D.C.; the Library of Congress; the National Archives; the William L. Clements Library at the University of Michigan; the Fort Lebœuf Historical Society in Waterford, Pennsylvania; the Winchester-Frederick County Historical Society in Winchester, Virginia; the Pickawillany Ohio State Historic Site in Piqua, Ohio; Fort Roberdeau in Altoona, Pennsylvania; the Fort Ligonier Association in Ligonier, Pennsylvania; the Ohio History Connection in Columbus, Ohio; the Reeves Library at the Moravian College in Bethlehem, Pennsylvania; the Fort Laurens Museum at Bolivar, Ohio; the Gnadenhütten Park and Museum at Gnadenhütten, Ohio; Cheryl McClellan of the Chardon Branch of the Geauga County Public Library; Cody Addy and Chris Kincaid at the Newcomerstown, Ohio, Public Library; and any others that we inadvertently failed to mention. Special thanks to Mr. Arthur W. Rosvanis of Upper Sandusky, Ohio, who graciously interrupted his work and took the time to help us locate several obscure Native American historical sites.

Table of Contents

Preface

This book has been a labor of love. Ever since we were children growing up in rural Northfield, Ohio, we were interested in the history of the area, primarily in that wondrous time when American Indians roamed free across the rivers and pathways that crisscrossed our marvelous state. The trans-Allegheny region, including present Ohio and western Pennsylvania, contained all the adventuresome elements of archetypal frontier America: remote outposts; hardy, resourceful and almost bigger-than-life frontiersmen; wild Indian tribes; and savage battles fought in the wilderness for possession of the magnificent territory.

The last Native Americans were gone from Ohio about a hundred years before we were born, but when we were growing up on farmland in northern Ohio, it seemed the era of the Indians was not that far in the distant past. We were constantly reminded of the Indians' existence, especially after a spring rain on a freshly plowed field that rinsed clear a myriad of flint arrowheads and other artifacts that we reverently collected in old cigar boxes. When Sally's grandfather arrived from Prague and tilled his newly purchased farm fields for the first time, the overturned soil was covered with small arrowheads, which are now part of our family treasure.

Arrowheads weren't the only remnants of the Erie, Iroquois, Shawnee, Wyandot, Lenape, Ottawa, Mingo, and other Indian nations who lived in and roamed through Ohio. When we were young, we could still find traces of old trails, along with a few of the rare, uniquely bent trail marker trees that indicated the major Indian thoroughfares. Armed with a battered copy of *Ohio Indian Trails* by Frank Wilcox, Paul trekked all over the area seeking out the old Indian pathways, often camping along them for days as he followed the trails deep through Ohio's forests. Most of all, we were entranced by the melodic names of lakes, rivers, streams, and other landmarks that reminded us that the Indians were once the masters there.

During his high school years, Paul was recognized as an expert in Native American history and was a regular guest of Jim Breslin on WEWS Channel 5 television in Cleveland, Ohio, where he discussed the Indians of Ohio and surrounding states. Sally shared Paul's interest in Native American history, and together they explored the many sites relevant to the Indians of Ohio. Even though we studied Ohio's Indians for most of our lives, while researching this book we became aware of how much more there was still to learn. We enjoyed traveling throughout Ohio, western Pennsylvania, Michigan, Indiana, Kentucky, and West Virginia, visiting the sites of old Indian villages, museums, libraries and historical societies in order to increase our knowledge of the Indians and their communities in Ohio.

During the 18th century, Ohio had several fairly permanent Indian villages and an even greater number of transient locations, which were either stopovers during relocation or a temporary camp for trading, hunting, or war. In our book, we've attempted to describe as many established Indian towns as we could find documentary evidence for. Since Indians, for various reasons, often moved from one location to another, permanence in the sense of an established village was relative. Ohio in the 18th century was very dynamic, and because of the constant wars and other factors, communities were often forced to relocate. More Ohio towns claim to have had an Indian village within their limits than was actually the case. In fact, there were some Ohio counties that did not have a permanent Indian village. We were frequently told by local residents about supposed old Indian village sites, only to learn there was no documentary evidence to support the assertion. That doesn't necessarily mean that Indians did not live there in a transient camp that was used for hunting, war, relocation, or other reasons. We respected those claims and scoured contemporary maps, journals, diaries and other accounts looking for supporting evidence. In some cases, we included the legends of those village sites even when there was scant documentation to prove they existed, and though we related the local lore, we explained there was no documentary evidence to support that an Indian village existed in that location.

It took us about two and a half years to write this book, after perhaps a decade of research, and even as we put the finishing touches to the manuscript, we found ourselves returning to different areas of Ohio to double check that our material was presented as accurately as possible.

In writing the manuscript, we experienced other challenges, which we tried to mitigate in order to make the book more readable and understandable. For example, there is no definitive spelling of Indian names for the simple reason that the American Indians of the area did not have a written language. Most Indian names were recorded by soldiers, traders, frontiersmen, and missionaries, many of whom were poorly educated, and all of whom depended on how they heard an Indian word pronounced. To further complicate matters, the French, English, and Moravian missionaries who were the most numerous white people in Ohio at the time used different letter combinations to denote guttural sounds. In an attempt to present Indian words in a way that is both reasonably accurate and readable, we've used the most common spellings; however, different sources may have several alternative spellings for each of the Indian words used here. Though we used the most common spelling of a word, when quoting a source we've used the spelling that was presented in the quote and clarified it when necessary.

In this book we regularly use the generic term "Indian" as a synonym for the indigenous peoples who inhabited the Americas prior to the coming of the Europeans. The term originated as early as 1492, when Christopher Columbus first thought he had found an alternate route to India and that the natives he encountered were Indians. The misconception was soon rectified, but the name for the people endured. Today, we tend to use more accurately descriptive or thoughtfully correct terms like "Native Americans" in the United States, or "First Nations" in Canada. However, throughout the 18th, 19th, and most of the 20th centuries, the term Indian was in common use, even by Native Americans in reference to themselves. Most of the documents cited as references in this book use the term "Indian," and we have continued to use the term for continuity.

Ohio was crisscrossed with a myriad of major trails that served as thoroughfares connecting many of the major towns within Ohio, as well as important locations beyond the borders of the present state. In addition, those trails were often linked together with many lesser pathways that were, in effect, shortcuts to areas within Ohio. We've tried to include all of the major trails, as well as some of the lesser connecting trails, but it would be impossible to describe every pathway used by Indians during the 18th century. Regarding the names of trails, most names were coined by the authors who wrote about them, such as Frank Wilcox in *Ohio Indian Trails* and William C. Mills in *The Archeological Atlas of Ohio*. There is no way of knowing what names the Indians gave the trails, but some historians surmise a trail was called by the destination of whoever traveled on it. If that were the case, a person traveling south on the Scioto Trail might call it "the trail to Lower Shawnee Town" or the trail to any one of a number of intermediate stops that may have been that person's destination. To avoid confusion, we've used the trail names commonly used by historians.

We hope this book serves as an impetus for readers to discover more about the Native American communities that were scattered throughout the state of Ohio. Ideally, someone will expand on our efforts with additional information about the Indians of Ohio during the 18th century.

PART I

The Repopulation of Ohio in the 18th Century

ONE

The Beaver Wars
or Iroquois Wars
(c. 1628–c. 1677)

Ohio Is Emptied of Permanent Settlements

During the first half of the 17th century, the Erie Indians were the dominant nation in present Ohio. The first recorded mention of the Erie was in 1624, when Huron Indians[1] told French Recollet missionary Friar Gabriel Sagard about a nation living south of Lake Erie that were called Eriehronon or Eriquehronon. In his journal, Sagard translated the name to mean "cat people," while the Huron translation is closer to "long tailed," possibly referring to the eastern puma or panther. When French Jesuit missionaries learned of the nation, they recorded their names variously as Erieehronon, Eriechronon, and Riquéronon, which they interpreted to mean "people of the panther." In subsequent writings, the terms were shortened and somewhat Gallicized to Erie.[2] However, the Erie Indians were remembered as the "Cat People" or "Cat Nation," and most French maps referred to Lake Erie as "Lac du Chat" (Lake of the Cat), and the Erie themselves as "Nation du Chat."

The Erie Indians were part of the Iroquoian language family, as were the Huron. However, the Erie felt a greater kinship and had a better relationship with the less warlike Huron than they did with the aggressively militant Iroquois Confederacy. The populous Erie nation covered a vast area that extended south from Lake Erie, according to some sources, as far as the Ohio River.[3] In breadth, the Erie homeland reached from about Lake Chautauqua in present western New York to the Great Miami River in western Ohio. Depending on the source cited, it's estimated that at their peak, the Erie numbered about 14,500.

The Erie were reputed to be fierce, warlike, and protective of their territory, although they maintained friendly relations with the Huron, who lived in the area between Lake Ontario and the Georgian Bay, centered around present Lake Simcoe in Ontario, Canada. The Huron homeland was known as "Huronia," and it was closer to the French cities of Montréal and Québec, which made the French a more logical trading partner for the Huron. The Huron also carried on a brisk trade with the Erie and acted as middlemen for the Erie in the French fur trade.

The Huron were a large and populous confederation that in the early part of the 17th century numbered between 20,000 and 40,000. However, between 1634 and 1640, Europeans brought smallpox and measles to New France, and the Huron communities became infected. With no immunity or tolerance for European viral infections, the Huron population was devastated, and it's estimated that as many as two-thirds of the Huron people died from the epidemic.

South of Huronia, the Iroquois homeland stretched across present upstate New York, from the Hudson River in the east to the Erie homeland in the west. The Iroquois called themselves Haudenosaunee, which means "people of the longhouse," and their nation was composed of the Mohawk, Oneida, Onondaga, Cayuga, and Seneca nations, stretching from east to west across present northern New York and northern Pennsylvania. They were referred to as the "Five Nations" until 1722, when they admitted the Tuscarora into the confederacy, after which they became known as the "Six Nations." Using the longhouse analogy, the Mohawk, who were the easternmost nation, were referred to as "keepers of the eastern door," and the westernmost Seneca were "keepers of the western door." The main Iroquois council fire, in effect the capital of the Iroquois Confederacy, was in the Onondaga homeland near present Syracuse, New York, and the Onondaga were referred to as "keepers of the council fire."

At the height of their power, the Iroquois numbered about 12,000 men, women and children, fewer than both the Huron and the Erie. However, their incredible organization compensated for their lesser population. According to Iroquois oral history, their form of centralized government, which was unique among American Indians, originated during the 12th century, but many historians and anthropologists believe the league was formed around 1450. At any rate, by the 17th century the Iroquois Confederacy had bonded into a cohesive and formidable force under the leadership of a Grand Council at Onondaga that was made up of representative chiefs from each of the clans of the member nations. Because of their unique form of centralized government, the League was not only unified in diplomatic interaction with their neighbors, but they presented a very cohesive and formidable fighting force in time of war.

Along with the major confederations of Erie, Huron, and Iroquois, there were smaller nations in the area, which included the Wenro or Wenrohon, Neutrals, Mahican, and Susquahannock. Of those, only the Susquahannock nation in Pennsylvania was powerful enough to challenge the Iroquois. However, the relative equal strengths of the Iroquois, Huron, Erie, and Susquahannock provided a form of equilibrium through a balance of power. The prospect of a mutually destructive war with a powerful neighbor resulted in a tenuous peace until the mid–17th century.

The factor that upset the uneasy balance of power between the major confederacies was the increasingly lucrative fur trade industry. Beaver fur was an important commodity in the European hat-making and fashionable clothing industries. The best hats were made of beaver fur felt, and the demand for beaver pelts was so great that Russian and Scandinavian beavers had been hunted and trapped almost to extinction. When Europeans penetrated the interior of North America, they found a new, seemingly inexhaustible supply of beaver pelts, and even better, the natives were eager to trap beavers and trade the pelts for the most basic, cheapest and mundane European articles, such as metal pots, knives, beads, mirrors, cloth, and anything else that could be carried into the interior. Both the Europeans and the Indians were very enthusiastic about the burgeoning fur trade, in that the Europeans could not get enough beaver pelts, and the Indians quickly became addicted to European manufactured merchandise. In the past, the Indians had trapped only enough to satisfy their family needs, but now they scoured the woodlands and streams for every fur-bearing animal they could trap in order to trade the pelts for European manufactured goods.

Initially, the French and the Dutch controlled the European fur trade in North America. The French colony of New France controlled most of the area west of the Allegheny mountains, while the Dutch colony of New Netherland extended along the east coast of

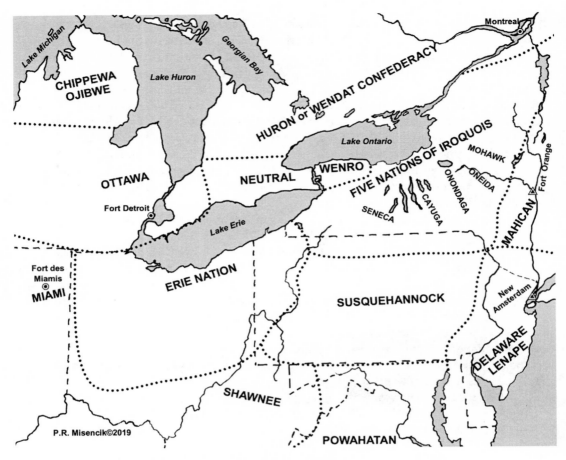

Approximate homeland areas of Indian nations around 1650.

North America from the Delmarva Peninsula to southwestern Cape Cod, encompassing all of present Delaware, New Jersey, eastern New York, and Connecticut, with outposts in Pennsylvania and Rhode Island. Being the nearest Europeans to the Iroquois homeland, the Dutch were the main trading partners of the Iroquois through Fort Orange, which was their trading post at present Albany, New York.

Within a few years, the fur trade became very competitive, and the Iroquois became increasingly aggressive in their quest to achieve and maintain a lion's share of the enterprise. However, it wasn't long before the beaver population in the Iroquois homeland was significantly depleted, and the Five Nations needed to take action if they were to monopolize the fur trade. The most expedient means of gaining a monopoly was to eliminate their competition, either by driving them off or destroying them. Either method would serve the dual purpose of gaining their neighbors' fur-producing areas and eliminating the competition. That approach was similar to the methods that bootlegger gangs in Chicago would use some 270 years later to eliminate competition during the American Prohibition era. That strategy resulted in what became known as the "Beaver Wars" or "Iroquois Wars," which were perhaps the bloodiest conflicts ever fought on the North American continent.

Since New Netherland was established as a private business venture to generate income by exploiting the American fur trade, the Dutch were among the first to realize a decline in profits from the depletion of fur-bearing animals. So, in a purely commercial sense, providing weapons to the Iroquois so they could acquire additional fur-rich territory was a sound business investment. To prevent the fur trade profits from declining, the Dutch traders at Fort Orange were eager to facilitate the Iroquois strategy by supplying the Five Nations with muskets, lead, and gunpowder. That gave the Iroquois a significant firepower advantage over their neighbors, whose primary weapons were bows and arrows, spears, and tomahawks. Until that time, the Europeans, particularly the French, had been reluctant to furnish the natives with more than a few firearms per village in order that the whites could maintain a weapons superiority. In fact, it was French policy to provide firearms only to Indians who had been baptized as Christians, because they were considered to be more reliable. Other than that, in a few instances, a small number of trade muskets were presented as ceremonial gifts to non–Christianized chiefs and important tribal leaders.

The first Iroquois land grab occurred in 1628, when they moved against the weaker Mahican Nation, whose homeland straddled the Hudson River around Fort Orange. The Mahican numbered about 3,000 men, women, and children, and they were no match for the Iroquois, who easily drove them east across the Hudson River. That not only provided the Five Nations with Mahican land, but it also placed them adjacent to Fort Orange, which facilitated the Iroquois trade monopoly with the Dutch.

Within ten years, the Iroquois sought additional lands on which to trap, and in 1638 they forced the neighboring Wenro nation across the Niagara River into Canada. The surviving Wenro fled north to Huronia, where they were absorbed into the Huron Nation.

Around 1641, the Iroquois attacked the Huron, who had become a more tempting target since the Huron population had recently been devastated by epidemics. Even so, the weakened Huron, with assistance of French troops from Montréal, were able to successfully hold off the Iroquois. One reason for the Iroquois' lack of success was an unexpected disunity among the Five Nations. In spite of their centralized government at Onondaga, individual nations sometimes acted independently. For example, while the other Iroquois nations were carrying out raids against the Huron, the Mohawk negotiated a peace agreement with the Huron. The fighting was sporadic until 1648, during which time the French attempted to broker peace between the Huron and Iroquois.

However, by 1648 the Iroquois reestablished the unified command structure that was their strength, and the Dutch began to sell firearms directly to the Iroquois, rather than through traders. That year, the Iroquois, heavily armed with modern weapons, launched a devastating winter attack against the Huron and destroyed several key Huron villages, killing and capturing hundreds. The attack broke the back of Huron resistance, and the surviving Huron abandoned their homeland. Some escaped to the north across the Ottawa River, but most fled westward toward Lake Huron, where the Ottawa Nation offered protection and prevented further pursuit by the Iroquois. The Iroquois now controlled the vast fur-rich area that once belonged to the Huron, and they also absorbed many of the Huron captives into their society.

In 1650, The Iroquois struck the Neutral Nation across the Niagara Peninsula, and by the end of 1651, the Neutrals ceased to exist. Thousands were killed or captured, and the captives were assimilated into the Iroquois.

The Erie Nation was alarmed by the destruction and dispersal of the Huron, Wenros, and Neutrals. They speculated that it was only a matter of time until they would be attacked by the Iroquois. In 1653, the Erie decided to take the initiative, and launched a preemptive strike against the Seneca, who were the westernmost Iroquois nation. The Erie had some initial successes, but in 1654, the entire might of the Iroquois Confederacy was arrayed against the Erie. At first, even with their more primitive weapons, the Erie were able to hold their own, but the superiority of modern firearms in the hands of the Iroquois turned the tide. The fighting raged for about five years, but in the end the Erie Nation was totally shattered, and the few survivors fled their homeland to be assimilated into neighboring tribes. Those who were taken captive were adopted by the conquering Iroquois to make up for their losses.

With the annihilation of the Erie, Ohio became the domain of the Iroquois by right of conquest, and for about sixty years it remained an empty forest wilderness devoid of permanent settlements. At the most, Ohio was visited by hunters from the surrounding tribes, but none wanted to arouse the wrath of the Iroquois by taking up permanent residence in their conquered territory.

The Iroquois continued their campaign of conquest after the defeat of the Erie. Next, they turned their might on their southern neighbors, the Susquahannock. Royal Governor Calvert of Maryland wanted the Susquahannock to serve as a buffer between Maryland and the aggressive Iroquois, so he formed an alliance with the Susquahannock and began to arm them. The newly armed Susquahannock were able to hold off the Iroquois during a war that continued intermittently for more than a decade, but in 1674, the Maryland authorities

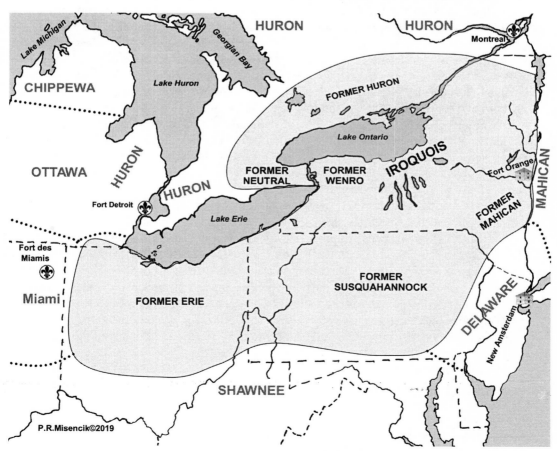

Iroquois dominion after the Beaver Wars, c. 1675.

began to grow fearful of the growing strength and belligerence of the Susquahannock. Not only did Maryland end the alliance, but Maryland militia were sent to attack and destroy Susquahannock villages, during which action several prominent chiefs were killed. The Iroquois quickly took advantage of the situation and drove the surviving Susquahannock from their lands in central Pennsylvania.

That, in effect, ended the major conflicts of the Beaver Wars, and the Iroquois emerged as the single dominant power in the northeastern woodlands. For the next century, they would decide the balance of power in the area and would be courted as allies or pressured not to take sides by both the French and English. However, that would not be easy, because as the Oneida chief Scarouady once sagely quipped, "You can't live in the woods and be neutral."[4]

Ohio stayed virtually empty of Indian settlements until the early 1700s, when tribes began to move into the area for a variety of reasons, the most significant being the loss of their homelands. The east coast was flooded with increasing numbers of European immigrants who all wanted land on which to settle. This was especially true after the Dutch capitulated and ceded their colony New Netherland to England in 1667. That gave the British an unbroken chain of colonies that stretched from present Maine to the Carolinas, and by 1732, it included Georgia. Those English colonists were hungry for land, and they rapidly

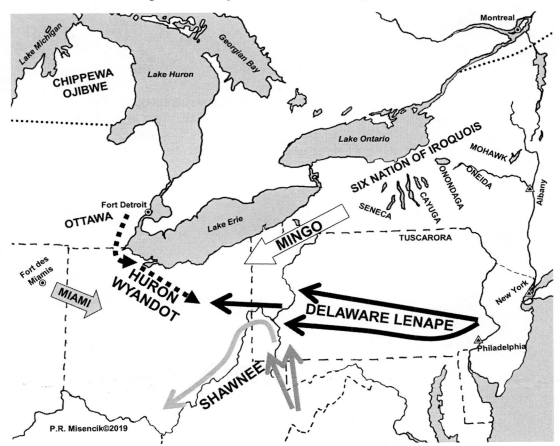

Principal migration of tribes into Ohio after the Beaver Wars.

expanded into the interior. The French and Dutch provinces were mainly financial ventures meant to generate profits through the fur trade, and there was no plan or emphasis on encouraging immigration and settlement. The British colonies were different, in that they advertised the availability of cheap land to promote and encourage immigrants, build towns and cities, and indeed expand the colonial borders deeper into the interior. The enticement of a fresh start on cheap land attracted shiploads of immigrants, and by 1740, the population of the British colonies outnumbered that of New France by a factor of about twenty to one. The non–Indian population of the English colonies was over a million people, of which about 930,000 were white and 63,000 were black. The non–Indian population of New France, on the other hand, was only about 45,000.[5]

The people in the English colonies had a voracious craving for land. After all, that's why the majority of them undertook the expensive and hazardous ocean voyage to get here. The land abutting the colonies was populated by Indian tribes who had lived there for centuries. However, most white Europeans did not recognize Indian rights of land ownership any more than they would recognize the land ownership rights of animals in the forest or the birds in the trees. In fact, many Europeans considered Indians to be something less than human, more on a par with a higher-level animal that could be exploited. As a result, the Europeans used questionable land purchases, trickery, fraud, or often simply brute force to evict the Indians from their homelands, and the constant press of white settlement forced many of the Indians across the Allegheny Mountains toward Ohio.

There were five Indian nations represented in the major migrations into Ohio that began in the early years of the 18th century. Those were the Miami; the Huron or Wyandot; the Lenape or Delaware; the Shawnee; and expatriate Iroquois or Mingo. However, it should be stressed that while they comprised the greatest numbers, they were not the only nations who settled in Ohio. Groups of other nations like the Ottawa, Ojibwe, Potawatomi, Mohican, Illinois, Kickapoo, and others moved into Ohio and established villages. That resulted in many diverse groups of Indian societies living in fairly close proximity to one another, and explains why Indian nations were spread seemingly at random throughout the state.

Two

The Wyandot and
Miami Migration into Ohio

Moves to Escape the French Fur-Trade Monopoly

At the beginning of the 18th century, Ohio was a marvelous, fertile, forested wilderness, rich with fish and game, and crisscrossed with scores of rivers and streams. Best of all for the Indians who migrated into the area, they found it virtually empty of inhabitants. Most of the Indians who moved into Ohio after the Iroquois Wars were refugees who had been forced from their traditional homelands. They had spent years being displaced from one area to another, and Ohio seemed to be a welcoming haven where they could reestablish their communities. While most of the tribes who entered Ohio had been forced from their homelands by European immigrants, there were some like the Huron who relocated to escape hostile neighbors, and others like the Miami who wanted to distance themselves from the monopolistic French fur trade and take advantage of the English competition. There were, of course, some tribes whose primary motivation was curiosity, wanderlust, and a spirit of adventure.

The five largest groups who moved into Ohio after the Beaver Wars were the Delaware or Lenni Lenape; the Huron, also known as Wyandots; the Shawnee; the Miami or Twightwees; and the Mingo. The Mingo were expatriate Iroquois who for one reason or another decided to leave the Iroquois homeland. In addition, some smaller groups including the Ottawa, Ojibwe or Chippewa, Potawatomi, and a smattering of southern Indians moved into Ohio and established their villages. It's difficult to determine which group was the first to take up residence in present Ohio in the 18th century, but most likely it was the adventuresome Shawnee, who had once lived along the Ohio River and returned sometime around 1725. They were closely followed by the Huron, Miami, Lenape, Mingo, and a smattering of other tribes. In this chapter, we'll primarily discuss the Huron/Wyandot and Miami migrations into Ohio.

After being evicted from their homeland north of Lake Ontario during the Beaver Wars, some Huron fled north toward Québec, where they settled and became known as the "Huron–Wendat Nation," or the "Eastern Huron." The remaining Huron escaped northwest to the Georgian Bay area, where they first sought refuge among a related people, the Petun or Tionontati nation, who in some sources are referred to as the "Tobacco People." The Petun and Huron combined for mutual protection and eventually became known as the "Wyandot," which was a corruption of "Wendat," the Huron name for themselves. The term Wyandot also distinguished them from the Eastern Huron, who had resettled along the St.

Lawrence River. Even though the Huron-Wyandots had abandoned their homeland north of Lake Ontario, they had not fled far enough to distance themselves from raiding Iroquois war parties, so they crossed the Detroit River and moved into the present state of Michigan. The Ottawa, Potawatomi, and Ojibwe or Chippewa people who lived in Michigan allowed the Wyandots to resettle on their lands, but the Wyandots weren't warmly welcomed. One tribal spokesman told the Wyandots, "My brothers, you are here, in the midst of a multitude of nations who do not love you, you do not understand their language. You are ignorant of their customs, and because of this, you are in a position each day to involve yourselves in evil affairs."[1] Settling in Michigan among neighbors who didn't like them was less than ideal for the Wyandots; however, the fierce Ottawa disliked the Iroquois even more, which provided the Wyandots with a measure of mutual protection against Iroquois incursions.

The Wyandots lived in that uneasy environment for several years, and in 1701, the French established a fortified post with a military garrison at present Detroit, which they named Fort Pontchartrain du Détroit, or simply Fort Détroit. The fortified trading post was the center of the French fur trade in the area from which furs were shipped to Montréal and Québec. It also had a heavily armed military garrison whose purpose was to enforce French sovereignty in New France by intimidating the Indians into compliance with the French monopoly, and also to interdict and expel English traders who entered the area.

The French at Fort Détroit became aware of the tension between the Wyandots and the other Michigan tribes, and they tried to mediate their differences. However, before any progress could be made, the relationship between the Wyandots and their neighbors took a turn for the worse. That occurred when an alliance of Ottawa, Potawatomi, and Salteurs invited the Wyandots to join them in a war against the Catawba tribes. The Wyandots balked at the prospect of involving themselves in unnecessary bloodshed, and instead negotiated a separate peace with the Catawba nation. Then they made the mistake of inviting their neighboring tribes in Michigan to join in the peace treaty with the Catawba. The alliance tribes were enraged at the Wyandots' action and completely rejected the Wyandot and Catawba peace belts. Worse yet, they accused the Wyandots of traitorously plotting to join the Catawba in a war against their alliance.

To show their disdain for the proposed peace settlement, the alliance immediately sent a war party south against the Catawba. The Wyandots, who had accepted peace with the Catawba, felt honor-bound to uphold their peace commitment, so they dispatched several warriors south to warn the Catawba of the coming attack. The Wyandot emissaries did more than just warn the Catawba; they took part in the ambush of the alliance war party. Only three of the alliance warriors escaped,[2] and when they returned to Michigan, the fragile relationship between the Wyandots and the other Michigan tribes was shattered. The French commander at Fort Détroit reported that the Wyandots were universally hated by their neighboring tribes. Once again, the French attempted to mitigate the hostility between the tribes, but their simplistic plan was to relocate the Wyandots to the St. Lawrence River near Montréal and Québec, where they would join the Eastern Huron.

The Wyandots found themselves in a quandary, because they had no consensus on the best course of action. Two of the chiefs, Sasteresty and Tayatchatin, advocated that they accept the French plan and move east; but the clan matrons, who had a prominent say in tribal decisions, joined a group of young men and women who opposed the move. Other Wyandots were in favor of attempting to repair their damaged relationship with their Michigan Indian neighbors, while another increasingly vocal group suggested they move south into Ohio.

The defection of the clan matrons caused a shift away from the older chiefs in the tribal council, which impacted the authority of Sasteresty and Tayatchatin. Two lesser chiefs, Angouriot and Orontony (c. 1695–1750) were the most vocal in advocating a move to Ohio. To counter the rising popularity of Angouriot and Orontony, and also break the influence of the tribal matrons, Sasteresty and Tayatchatin met secretly with Chevalier de Beauharnois, the nephew of the governor-general, and assured him the Wyandots would move to Montréal. They promised that the tribal council would disavow both Angouriot and Orontony if the two refused to comply. However, the old chiefs were unable to deliver on their promise, and around 1738–1739, both Angouriot and Orontony led most of the Wyandots south to establish new settlements in Ohio.

Little is known of Angouriot other than he was a chief of the Turtle Clan and a leader of the non–Christian Wyandots. As such, he was distrusted and indeed hated by Father de la Richardie, the missionary at Fort Détroit, who publicly disparaged him as the "Drunkard Angouriot."[3] Orontony, also of the Turtle Clan, was born about 1695, and received the name "Nicolas" when he was baptized in 1728 at Fort Détroit, most likely by Father Richardie. Many sources refer to him as Nicolas Orontony, or simply Nicolas.[4]

Angouriot had been among the first to speak up against the move to Montréal, and around 1738–39, he was the first to move to Ohio, taking about half the Wyandots with him. He was soon followed by Orontony with more of the Wyandot tribe. Ohio was not a completely strange land, since the Wyandot had hunted and explored the area for years following their arrival in Michigan. Some Wyandots had even crossed the length of Ohio to live with the Shawnee for a time along the Ohio River. In addition, the Wyandot and Catawba delegations had previously met near Sandusky Bay, where they negotiated their earlier peace agreement. To the breakaway Wyandot, Ohio was an uncrowded and beckoning new homeland. However, not all the Wyandot moved with Angouriot and Orontony, and those who remained near Fort Détroit were called the "hondatorinke," or the "stay-at-homes."

Angouriot and Orontony were both fiery and impassioned orators, but after the two chiefs established the villages of Junundat and Anioton on the south shore of Sandusky Bay west of present Sandusky, Ohio, Orontony began to emerge as the principal leader of the Ohio Wyandots. The Wyandots moved to Ohio to distance themselves from the hostile and aggressive Michigan Indians, but Orontony also wanted his band to take advantage of the increasingly favorable English fur trade. The Indians, like most people, were interested in finding the best bargains, and compared to what the French had to offer, English trade goods were bargains indeed.

There were several factors that gave the English a trade advantage. The burgeoning industrial revolution and the resultant superior manufacturing capabilities were considerably more advanced in England than in the rest of Europe. That allowed the English to produce goods faster and cheaper than their European neighbors. Another British advantage was the shorter and less arduous distance they had to transport merchandise. Once French ships arrived off the coast of North America, they still had to sail more than 800 miles up the St. Lawrence River to Québec or Montréal, which could only be accomplished during the eight or so months when the St. Lawrence was not frozen or filled with hazardous ice floes. Once the ships reached Montréal, merchandise had to be transported over a grueling 600-mile route past the St. Lawrence rapids, across Lake Ontario, over the Niagara portages, and then across Lake Erie by canoe or bateau to Fort Détroit. Then, the merchandise still had to be painstakingly carried by canoe or pack animal into the interior. The English, by contrast, had shorter distances and fewer logistical challenges. English colonial seaports were ice-free all year round, and the roads and trails from the major cities like Alexandria, Annapolis, Baltimore, Philadelphia, and New York into the Ohio territory were less arduous and only about a third the distance the French had to transport their goods into the interior.

Another factor that contributed to the French trade disadvantage was the conduct of unscrupulous and corrupt officials along the French supply chain. Commanders of the French forts in the interior controlled the distribution of trade merchandise, and to line their own pockets, they regularly raised prices of commodities sold to the traders, which further inflated the cost. The French traders had no choice but to pass the additional costs on to the Indians.

By comparison, English traders were not tied to frontier outposts to replenish their stock, and traders were able to obtain their goods in the towns and cities where there was sufficient competition among suppliers to keep prices competitive. Another English advantage was the sheer weight of population. In 1740, the white European population of New France was about 45,000, while the non–Indian population of the English colonies was about one million. That number was made up of about 940,000 white people and 63,000 blacks.[5] Since the European population of New France was about one-twentieth the white population of the English colonies, the French were hard pressed to counter the increasing English influence and the growing numbers of English traders among the Indians in the Ohio territory.

When the Wyandots left the Fort Détroit area, the Ottawa and other Michigan tribes were not sorry to see their troublesome neighbors go. The French, on the other hand, viewed their departure as a defection to the English, which was essentially true since Orontony wanted the opportunity to do business with English fur traders. The Indian trade with the English became even more of an issue when King George's War between France and England broke out in 1744. The bloody war, which took a heavy toll on both sides, ended in 1748 with the Treaty of Aix-la-Chappelle, which called for *status quo antebellum*, or a restoration of borders to their prewar status. The treaty did little to alleviate the tension between the French and the English, and nowhere was it more evident than on the borders of New France. But in a broader sense, King George's War was the opening conflict in the struggle between France and England for control of the North American continent.

Prior to the 1730s, French dominion of the trans-Allegheny region south of the Great Lakes was virtually unchallenged but increasing numbers of English traders began to penetrate the area and siphon off French profits from the fur trade. In 1745, English traders and some of Orontony's Wyandots erected a blockhouse called Fort Sandoské, at a peripheral Wyandot village on the north shore of Sandusky Bay south of present Port Clinton, Ohio.[6] At the same time, Orontony turned Junundat into a trading hub, and went so far as to welcome English traders. The French at Fort Détroit admonished the Wyandots to cease trading with the English, and when admonition and enticement failed, the French tried intimidation. In 1746, Orontony responded by fighting back, and after fortifying Junundat and Anioton, he began to engage in retaliatory hostilities against the French in what became known as the "Conspiracy of Nicolas," or "Orontony's Rebellion."

While the French were trying to cope with Orontony's breakaway Wyandots, they were also forced to deal with another breakaway tribe in the west. In 1715, the French built Fort St. Phillipe at Quiskakon (cut-tail),[7] the principal village of the Miami Indians at present Fort Wayne, Indiana. In some accounts, Quiskakon was also referred to as Kekionga (blackberry patch).[8] In spite of the fort's formal name, it was more popularly referred to as Fort des Miamis, and like Fort Détroit, it was meant to enforce the French fur trade monopoly among the Indians in the area, particularly the Miami. The Miami Indians at Quiskakon were also aware of the disparity between the French and the English fur trades, and after learning of Orontony's successful departure from Forth Détroit, a Miami chief named Memeskia decided to lead his band of Piankashaw Miami about eighty miles to the southwest, where he established the village of Pickawillany along the western bank of the Great Miami River near present Piqua, Ohio. As with Orontony's Wyandots, the French viewed Memeskia's move to Ohio as a defection to the English, and they began to exert pressure on the break-away tribe to return to Quiskakon to place them firmly within the sphere of French control. For some reason, the French referred to Memeskia as "La Demoiselle" meaning damselfly or young lady; however, he soon became known as "Old Briton," because of his staunch loyalty and friendship with the English traders.

The Miami people were of Algonquian stock like the Lenape and Shawnee. Although they refer to themselves by the name Mihtohseeniaki, "the people," the name "Miami" derives from "Myaamia" or "downstream people." Other tribes and some white people sometimes referred to the Miami as *Twightwee*, "sandhill crane," but it was not a name they used for themselves. Historians generally agree they came from present Wisconsin to establish a homeland in present northern Indiana, eastern Illinois, and southern Michigan. By the mid–17th century their homeland was centered near present Fort Wayne, Indiana. The Miami were composed of six major divisions, whose more common names were the Greater Miami or Crane Band, Eel River Band, Michikinkwa (Little Turtle), Piankeshaw, and Wea.

The defection Old Briton's Miamis, in addition to the Wyandot rebellion, was more than the French could stomach, and they sternly ordered Memeskia to abandon Pickawillany and return to Quiskakon. Instead, Old Briton allied himself with Orontony and joined the Wyandot in attacking the French. In the meantime, Orontony had gathered other allies, including bands of disaffected Ottawa, Potawatami, Ojibwe, and even some expatriate Iroquois.

In the autumn of 1746, Orontony ambushed a fur-laden flotilla of French-Canadian canoes bound for Fort Détroit, killing five of the voyageurs and taking their furs. In addition, they attacked Fort Détroit itself, and their constant harassment prevented the inhabitants from planting their spring crops. Old Briton's Miamis were also active in the fight, and in 1747, with the assistance of Orontony's Wyandot, they attacked Fort des Miamis at Quiskakon, and after sacking it, burned it to the ground. The fort was rebuilt the following year, in the summer of 1748.

With King George's war ongoing, the French blamed the Indians' unrest on British intrigues. In January 1748, the commander of Fort Détroit, Paul Joseph Le Moyne de Longueuil, Chevalier de Longueil, extended an olive branch in an attempt to end the uprising. He pardoned the rebel Indians and released all the Indian prisoners the French had taken. Unfortunately, his leniency earned him a reprimand from his own father, Charles Le Moyne, Baron de Longueuil, who would soon become the governor-general. The senior Longueuil informed his son that French policy was nothing less than the surrender of all "Indian murderers and malefactors"[9] who would be sent to Québec for punishment. In addition, "each tribe was to produce two British prisoners for every Frenchman they had killed."[10] The Indians were appalled by the French terms, and especially dismayed when the French refused to smoke a calumet (peace pipe) or accept a peace (wampum) belt until all of their demands had been complied with. Worse yet, when French reinforcements began to pour into Fort Détroit, it became apparent that the French were going to use overwhelming force against the rebellious Indians.

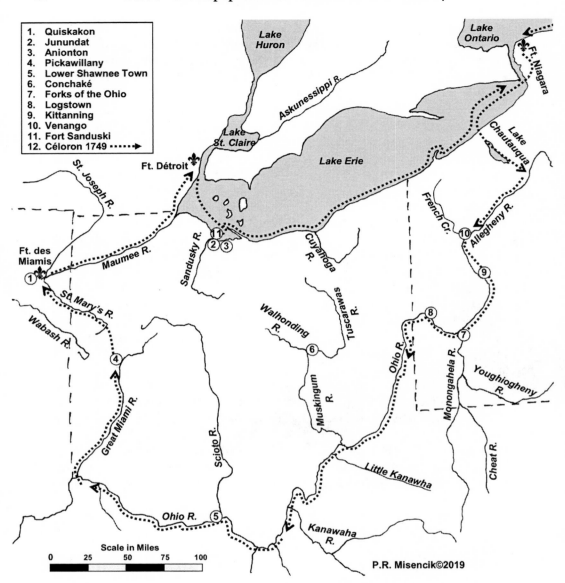

1. Quiskakon
2. Junundat
3. Anionton
4. Pickawillany
5. Lower Shawnee Town
6. Conchaké
7. Forks of the Ohio
8. Logstown
9. Kittanning
10. Venango
11. Fort Sanduski
12. Céloron 1749 ·····➤

The Ohio area between 1738 and 1750.

Some of the Orontony's allies, most notably the Potawatomi, quit the uprising and returned to their homes, where they petitioned the French for a pardon. Soon, other tribes began to waver, and it was apparent the Indian rebellion was losing steam. The choice of either surrendering to the French or engaging in a bloody and increasingly unwinnable war against regular French troops led Orontony to conclude that his only viable option was to pack up and abandon the area. In 1748, he left his villages along Sandusky Bay and led most of the Wyandot southeast about 105 miles to the confluence of the Muskingum, Tuscarawas, and Walhonding Rivers at present Coshocton, Ohio, where he established the village of Conchaké. Orontony died at Conchaké around 1750, presumably from smallpox.

With the collapse of Orontony's Rebellion, Memeskia and the breakaway Miamis also stopped fighting the French, and once again concentrated on trade. That suited the French for the time being, because they were occupied with rebuilding Fort des Miamis. However, the continued existence of Pickawillany was a worrisome liability to French authority in Ohio that could be exploited at any time by the British. It wasn't long before the French once again tried to entice Memeskia to abandon Pickiwillany and return to Quiskakon, but this time it was in the nature of a major French military force commanded by Captain Pierre Joseph Céloron de Blainville. Céleron had been ordered by the governor-general of New France, Roland-Michel Barrin de La Galissonièr, to reaffirm France's ownership of the territory by planting lead plates and posting the French royal coat of arms at principal rivers and streams around the area. Céloron de Bienville carried several inscribed lead plates and metal plaques with the French coat of arms, which he was instructed to place at the junctions where major rivers met the Ohio River. The lead plate affirming French ownership was buried and the metal plaque was fastened to a nearby tree. Céloron is believed to have buried six plates, one of which was dug up by Indians as soon as Céloron departed and delivered to the British. Two others were found in the 19th century, one of which was partially melted down for either bullets or fishing weights. The lead plates were about eleven inches long by seven and one-half inches wide. The size of the plaques with the coats of arms is not known.

In addition, Céloron's force was meant to awe the Indians into remaining loyal to the French, and also to expel English trespassers who entered the area. Céloron's expedition departed Montréal in June 1749 and traveled down the Allegheny and Ohio Rivers, skirting the eastern and southern borders of present Ohio. When they reached the Great Miami River near present Cincinnati, they followed the river north to Pickawillany. At a time when war parties seldom exceeded thirty or so warriors, the French force of 216 French and Canadian troops and about 30 Indians was the largest armed party most of the Indians had ever seen, and they were understandably shaken by what they considered a massive display of arms.

Céloron was aware of the pro–English leaning of the Pickawillany Miamis, but he was still somewhat surprised to find several English traders in the village, and many more had recently departed with their bales of furs. The French commander sent the remaining English packing and requested a council with Memeskia, but Old Briton delayed several days until suitable interpreters could be found. The council finally took place on Sunday, September 17, 1749, during which Céloron presented the Indian leaders with gifts and several peace belts. He also harangued the Indians about English perfidy and exhorted the Miamis to cease all trade with the English and expel them from the territory. The Miamis listened politely, and even appeared to endorse Céloron's criticism of the English, but the French commander was familiar with the Indians' practice of disingenuously appearing to agree out of politeness. When the French commander pressed the Miamis to abandon Pickawillany and accompany him to Quiskakon, Memeskia sidetracked the issue by claiming that it was too late in the season to relocate, but they would move back to Quiskakon in the spring. Céloron tried several more times to convince Memeskia and his Miamis to return to Quiskakon with the French force, even promising that the French troops would build cabins for Memeskia's Miamis when they arrived. Memeskia thanked Céloron for his kind words and concern for the well-being of the Miamis, but he was adamant that a move before spring was out of the question. To make matters even worse, the Indians somewhat insultingly returned the gifts Céloron had given them. The French commander had no choice but to press on without the Pickawillany Miamis. Céloron and his troops marched out on Tuesday, September 19, 1749, but since there was no water route to Quiskakon, and Céloron was unwilling to gift the expedition's canoes and bateaux to the Miamis, he had them burned before he and his men departed.

Céloron's visit with the Pickawillany Miami was the last peaceful overture by the French to try to bring Memeskia and his breakaway Miamis back into the French fold. However, the increasing popularity of Pickawillany as an English trading hub was more than the French commanders could tolerate. When Céloron returned to Québec, he gave a pessimistic report to the new governor-general, Jacques-Pierre de Taffanel de la Jonquière, Marquis de la Jonquière, concerning the challenges of maintaining French sovereignty in the Ohio region. He made it clear that his expedition alone was not sufficient to secure the exclusive allegiance of the Indians, nor deter the flood of Englishmen into the Ohio area. He reported that even the once-loyal tribes were being won over by the British and were influencing their neighbors. He mentioned the pervasiveness of the English traders, who were winning over the Indians with their inexpensive and plentiful trade goods. He added, "All I can say is that the nations of these localities are very badly disposed toward the French, and are entirely devoted to the English. I do not know in what way they could be brought back." He continued, "If our traders were sent there for traffic, they could not sell their merchandise at the same price as the English sell theirs, on account of the many expenses they would be obliged to incur."[11]

Céloron was correct in his negative assessment of the Ohio Indians, particularly the Miamis. Memeskia's break with the French was particularly ominous, because it fractured nearly a century of alliance. If allowed to continue, the French could expect further defections to the English, which would threaten their tenuous hold on New France.

The logical military move would have been to interdict the influx of English traders into the Ohio region by positioning French troops along the eastern borders of New France, but instead the governor-general chose the less costly option. The problem was that many of the advisors to King Louis XV questioned the economic and strategic value of Canada and the Ohio region. Many did not consider it worth the effort or expense to occupy and defend. The popular writer Voltaire criticized any and all initiatives to defend the area against the British. In a letter to his friend and fellow writer François-Augustin Paradis de Moncrif, Voltaire wrote, "One pities that poor human race that slits its throat on our continent about a few acres of ice in Canada."[12] Then in his 1758 novel *Candide*, Voltaire commented, "You know that these two nations are at war for a few acres of snow in Canada, and that they spend over this beautiful war more than Canada is worth."[13]

Instead of sealing off the borders of New France militarily, as they would attempt to do a couple of years later, the French decided to chastise the Indians who were trading with the English and make them a grim example for the rest of the Ohio tribes. In 1751, after learning of a visit to Pickawillany by frontiersman Christopher Gist and trader George Croghan, who was recognized as the king of the Pennsylvania traders, Governor-General Jonquière ordered Céloron, who was now commanding at Fort Détroit, to punish the wayward Miamis at Pickawillany. Céloron tried to gather a force, but after more than twenty days of unsuccessful talks with the Ottawa, Ojibwe, and Adirondack Indians, he was unable to muster a sizable war party for the punitive expedition. Several of the Adirondacks were willing to go it alone, but they were warned off by Ottawas who were friendly with the Miamis.

The following summer of 1752, about fifty Nippissings, with a scattering of Indians from other tribes, set off to attack Pickawillany, but when they reached Fort Sandoské, they encountered a band of Ottawa and Ojibwe Indians who warned them not to harm the Miamis. That caused most of the war party to return to Fort Détroit, but some continued on toward Pickawillany. However, an Ottawa woman had raced ahead and warned the village. When the raiders got there, the town was almost deserted, so in frustration the Nippissings killed and scalped a Miami man and woman before they headed back to Fort Détroit. In retaliation, the angered Pickawillany Miamis killed and scalped two unfortunate French traders who happened to be in the vicinity.

Governor-General Jonquière had died in March 1752, and Charles Le Moyne Longueuil became acting governor-general. It was the same Longueuil who a few years earlier had admonished his son for advocating leniency toward Indians during Orontony's Rebellion. Longueuil was not inclined to take half-hearted measures in dealing with the pro–British Indians, and he considered the Pickawillany Miamis to be the most flagrant and militantly pro–British of the Ohio Indians. He was determined that their chastisement would be an unmistakable warning to the other tribes that the French would no longer tolerate any shift in allegiance to the British. Longueuil ordered Céloron, who was still commanding at Fort Détroit, to make sure the job was done right this time.

Céloron selected Charles Michel Langlade to lead the force against Pickawillany, and he couldn't have chosen better. Langlade was a very effective leader with strong ties to the Ottawa. His father Augustin was a French-Canadian coureur de bois,[14] or woodsman, and his mother Domitilde was an Ottawa woman who was the sister of Nissowaquet, a notable war chief, called La Fourche (The Fork) by the French. Charles was educated by the Jesuits, but it was his mother's Ottawa culture that Charles more readily absorbed. When Langlade was ten, his uncle Nissowaquet took him as a member of a war party against the Chickasaw, and his father told young Charles, "You must go with your uncles, but never let me hear of your showing any marks of cowardice."[15] Apparently Langlade acquitted himself admirably, because he earned the respect of the Ottawa war chiefs who gave him the title Auke-wing-eke-taw-so (defender of his country).[16]

Among the Ottawa, Langlade was respected as exceptionally brave and fierce, as well as a charismatic war leader. Various writings describe him as being honest, ambitious, diplomatic, courageous, and even charming. Some descriptions, however, portrayed him as egocentric, self-serving, and having a cruel streak. He totally embraced the Ottawa culture, and around 1750, he married an Ottawa woman named Agathe, and had a son named Charles after himself.

Langlade, with the assistance of the Ottawa chief Pontiac, who was his close friend, mustered a massive war party of over 250 Ottawa, Ojibwe, and Canadian militia. They struck Pickawillany just at sunrise on Sunday, June 21, 1752, and swept through the town before the Miamis could mount much of a defense. Most of the inhabitants were killed or captured before they could escape into the woods, and among those taken were Old Briton and five English traders. Thirteen Miami warriors were killed and scalped after they had surrendered, and Old Briton and an English trader were ritually killed, boiled, and eaten. It's not certain whether Memeskia was ritually cannibalized as a sign of respect for his personal qualities, or whether Langlade's raiders meant to shock the Ohio Indians with a horrific example of what would happen to other defectors from French allegiance.

The attack completely eliminated Pickawillany as a trading center, and many of the surviving Miami meekly returned to Quiskakon. However, not all returned to French control. Many remained in Ohio and took revenge by attacking French targets of opportunity. Two months after the attack, Céloron reported from Fort Détroit that the Miamis had killed and scalped French soldiers, civilians, traders, and slaves, and he said that the Miamis were increasingly hostile and dangerous. After the attack on Pickawillany, the surviving Ohio Miamis requested military aid from the English, but when it did not materialize, most of the Miamis returned to Quiskakon and grudgingly accepted French dominance.

With the British capture of Fort Niagara in 1759 and the capture of Fort Detroit in 1760, French control of the Ohio region came to an end, and the Miami were free to establish villages in Ohio to take advantage of the British fur trade. However, they had yet to learn that the Indian lands had been the prize that went to the victors of the French and Indian War, and now the British were their new overlords.

THREE

The Shawnee Migration
into Ohio

Returning to the Ohio River

In the late 1720s, the Shawnee returned to their old homeland along the Ohio River Valley. They were believed to be the descendants of the Ohio "Fort Ancient" culture, which between the 11th and 17th centuries consisted of diverse farming societies that flourished along the Ohio River Valley from present southern Indiana to West Virginia.[1] The Shawnee belonged to the Algonquian language family, which included among others the Abenaki, Penobscot, Passamaquoddy. Mi'kmaq, Mohican, Miami, and Lenape.

According to Shawnee tradition, the creator Meteelemelakwe created the ancestors of the Shawnee in the Upper World, where great spiritual power and sacred harmony existed. Then the creator lowered these first people down to earth in a basket, and they were instructed to journey to the Shawnee River, which was in the center of the Earth Island. According to tribal lore, those first people had many challenges that included crossing oceans, rivers and inhospitable terrain, and in the voyage, they had to fight underworld monsters as well as hostile humans and non-humans. During the journey, they gradually formed a powerful confederacy, which helped them reach their destination at the center of Island Earth.

According to tribal tradition, Meteelemelakwe, the creator, visited them and declared that they should be called Shāūwonoa. Actually, the name comes from the Algonquian term "Shawan" (south), or "Shawunogi" (southerner). The French called them "Chaouanons," and the Iroquois, with whom the Shawnee carried on a hostile relationship, referred to them by the derogatory name *Ontwaganha*, meaning "those who utter unintelligible speech."[2] Since most American Indians, including the Shawnee, did not have a written language, the spelling of their words depended on the listener and his ability to accurately transcribe them. As a result, there are over 150 different spellings referring to the Shawnee on maps, in journals, and in other accounts. That's also the case with the five septs or divisions of the Shawnee. They have been spelled in a variety of different ways, depending on the source cited. They were as follows, with some of the usual alternative spellings, but certainly not all of them:

Chalahgawatha (Chalaakathas, Chillicothe, Chalaka, Chalakatha)
Hathawekela (Asswikales, Sweickleys, Thawikila)
Kispokotha (Kispoko, Kispogogi, Kishpokotha)
Mequachake (Mekoche, Maccachee, Maguck, Mackachack)
Pekuwe (Piqua, Pekowi, Pickaway, Picks, Peckowitha)

Membership in a particular sept was inherited from the father, and each sept had a principal village that was usually named after that sept. For example, for a town to be named Chillicothe simply meant that the village was a principal village of a group of Chalahgawatha Shawnee. There were several Chillicothes, which was confusing to whites who encountered several towns with the same name.

Since Europeans first encountered the Shawnee Indians in the 1670s, not much is known about them prior to that time; but in the ensuing years, they appear to have been among the most traveled of American Indians. Colonists encountered Shawnee from Albany to the Atlantic coast, to Carolina and the lower Mississippi. In 1754, Edmond Atkin, a British trader and future superintendent of Indian affairs, described the Shawnee as "Stout, Bold, Cunning, and the greatest Travelers in America."[3] Their nomadic diaspora was most likely the result of a fiercely independent people's attempt to cope with the cultural upheavals brought about by the influx of Europeans into North America.

In the 18th century, the Shawnee's five septs or divisions, as listed above, were more than clans. Their dialects had minor differences across the septs, and although their culture was similar, the septs tended to live in separate communities even when they were in close proximity to each other. The Shawnee society was structured around clans called *m'shoma* within the various septs, and the clan system was generally patrilineal, meaning a person always belonged to his or her father's clan. Each sept was divided into six clans according to kinship, and each clan represented a spiritual facet of the Shawnee nation. The six clans and their spiritual representations were the Turkey, or Pellewomhsoomi Clan; Turtle, or Kkahkileewomhsoomi Clan; Rounded Feet, or Petakineeθiiwomhsoomi Clan; Horse, or Mseewiwomhsoomi Clan; Racoon, or θepatiiwohmsoomi Clan; and Rabbit, or Petakineeθiiwomhsoomi Clan.

Each person believed his clan was descended from a mythical ancestor who gave the clan its name, powers and potency in a specific field of life. For example, the Turkey Clan represented bird life, the Turtle Clan represented aquatic life, the Rounded Feet Clan represented carnivore animals with rounded feet or paws, the Horse Clan represented herbivorous animals, the Raccoon Clan represented clawed animals that could rip and tear, and the Rabbit Clan represented a peaceful and gentle nature. Shawnee society, like that of many other Native American groups, was exogamous, meaning that a person could only marry someone from a different clan.

In addition, each clan was a political as well as spiritual unit, having its own leadership. A clan had a *hokima*, or male social chief, who led the clan in times of peace. The clan also had a *neenawtooma*, or male war chief, whose duty was to lead the clan in times of war. There was also a corresponding Peace Woman and War Woman, who were known as *hokima wiikwes*.[4] They were influential in the chiefs' decision-making processes and oversaw the agricultural and domestic aspects of the village both in times of peace and war.

The Iroquois assault against the Erie Nation during the 17th century Beaver Wars extended as far as the Shawnee villages in southern Ohio. The Shawnee had few if any firearms and were no match for the Iroquois, who had been supplied with guns and ammunition by their Dutch trading partners. One Shawnee man reflected years later: "Upon our return from hunting, we found our town surprised and our women and children taken prisoner."[5] The violence that reached their villages caused the Shawnee to flee in search of "a Countrey at Peace."[6] The Shawnee fled west toward the Mississippi, south across the Ohio into the Carolinas, and east into present Pennsylvania, Maryland, West Virginia, and Virginia. By about 1680, the Shawnee homeland, along with the rest of Ohio, was almost completely uninhabited.

Unfortunately, the Shawnee were unable to find a "Countrey at Peace." The Indians in the west were hostile, and in the south, they encountered Europeans engaged in an Indian slave trade. So the Shawnee began to gravitate toward the middle Atlantic colonies, and by about 1710, most of the Shawnee were located along the upper Potomac and lower Susquehanna Rivers. Through all their journeys, the Shawnees still found themselves vulnerable to powerful neighbors, including the European colonists along the coast and the Iroquois to the north. The Iroquois in particular sought to dominate and control the independent-minded Shawnee, and in an attempt to gain a measure of security, the Shawnee tried to forge relationships with the European colonists. The problem was that the Shawnee viewed the relationships as agreements between equal partners, while the Europeans considered the relationships to be hierarchal, with the Europeans being the superior entity. They believed the Shawnee should be totally obedient and subservient in return for permission to reside on lands claimed by the Crown, and even to trade with the colonists. Often, the English colonists didn't even consult the Shawnee in matters that concerned them. For example, in the Albany Treaty of 1722, the English colonies negotiated a treaty exclusively with the Iroquois that prohibited the Shawnee from entering the area south of the Potomac River and east of the Appalachian Mountains. The Shawnee first learned of the treaty when William Keith, the lieutenant-governor of the colonies of Pennsylvania and Delaware, sent messengers to warn the Shawnee that any Indian who did not comply with the treaty would be put to death or sold into slavery.

The treaty frustrated the Shawnee, and they responded as they had many times before: by packing up and moving west in the direction of their ancestral homelands along the Ohio River, which they had left some seventy years prior. Moving meant more to the Shawnees than simply relocating. Their villages were centered around agricultural areas that had been painstakingly cleared, tilled and planted, so leaving a community for a new location generally resulted in an extended period of hunger until new fields could be cleared and crops grown. Their biggest disappointment was the threat of their loss of autonomy and independence. Europeans at best viewed the Indians as feudal vassals, and often they were considered as little more than wild animals roaming the forests.

Along with the Europeans, the Iroquois persisted in their attempt to expand their dominance over their neighboring tribes, and in collusion with the English colonial authorities, the Iroquois sent representative half-kings to supervise the tribes in the trans-Allegheny region. The British approved of the Iroquois' exertion of authority over the Ohio tribes, and in fact, it was the English who coined the term "half-king" for the Iroquois representatives who were sent as supervisors. In addition, the English made it a practice to deal only with the appropriate half-king on matters pertaining to the tribes in western Pennsylvania and Ohio. The Oneida chief Scarouady, also known in some sources as Monacatootha, was appointed by the Iroquois Council at Onondaga to oversee the Shawnee, but he quickly learned that his appointment as half-king over the Shawnee was challenging indeed.

The independent-minded Shawnee resented the imposition of a controlling English-Iroquois hierarchy, but initially they were not strong enough to fight it. Instead, they began to move farther west to distance themselves from the Pennsylvania authorities and the Iroquois. By 1728, most of the Shawnee lived in western Pennsylvania, western Maryland, and present West Virginia, but by the 1730s they had pushed into Ohio, establishing villages in their old homeland along the Ohio River, which they referred to a Kis-ke-pi-la-se-pe or "Eagle River." However, it was the Iroquois name "o-Y-o," meaning "Great River," that stuck. When they moved back into the Ohio River Valley, the Shawnee not only regained their homeland, but they also reclaimed their independence. Both the Pennsylvania authorities and the Iroquois were concerned when the Shawnee moved beyond their immediate control, because they were justifiably worried that the Shawnee would gravitate toward the French. In 1732, Patrick Gordon, the deputy governor of Pennsylvania, ordered the Shawnee to return; but the Shawnee didn't respond until 1738, and their message simply said, "The Tract of Land you have Reserved for us does nott sute us at Present."[7] The Shawnee were beginning to regain their spirited independence.

The years of forced travels after the Beaver Wars had scattered the Shawnee geographically, but now in Ohio, they were once again coalescing into a unified confederacy. More importantly, they began to reacquire their strength and confidence as a nation. Now that they were in their homeland, they considered themselves to be the masters of their own destiny. When the Iroquois half-king Scarouady ordered the Shawnee to return to Pennsylvania, they studiously rejected the concept of any outsider supervising them, and they insultingly ignored him. The perplexed Scarouady wasn't certain how to handle the recalcitrant Shawnee, so he did nothing other than remain at the Forks of the Ohio and kept up the pretext of being a half-king.

The Grand Iroquois Council at Onondaga was also irked by the Shawnee snub, so they sent a formal delegation, led by the Seneca chief Sagohandechty, to demand that the Shawnee return to Pennsylvania. Instead, the Shawnee were so angered by the arrogance of Sagohandechty "that they took a great dislike to him"[8] and killed him. The Iroquois uncharacteristically failed to respond, because they were unsure of the outcome against the aggressively defiant and militant Shawnee, who seemed inclined to fight rather than run or acquiesce as they had in the past. So instead of taking punitive action, the Iroquois merely complained to the Pennsylvania authorities about the murder of Sagohandechty. The Iroquois' tepid response reverberated among the other Ohio Indians, who began to reevaluate whether the Iroquois were still a dominant force in Ohio.

FOUR

The Lenape (Delaware) Migration into Ohio

The Lenape Are Pushed West Across Pennsylvania into Ohio

Although they are most commonly referred to as "Delaware," the name itself is a European designation based on their homeland along the Delaware River valley, which extended north to the lower Hudson River. Their name for themselves was Lenni Lenape, or simply Lenape. In their language, "Lenni" means "original, real, and pure," while "Lenape" simply means "man, men, or people," but the Delaware interpret it idiomatically as "original people," or "men among men."[1] Their homeland was called "Lenapehoking," which means "land of the people." Most historical references use the name Delaware and Lenape interchangeably.

The Lenape were associated with the Algonquin language group that was composed of other central and eastern woodland nations including the Cree, Chippewa, Potawatomi, Sauk-Fox, Shawnee, Miami, Mi'kmaq, Abenaki, Passamaquoddy, Narragansett, Mohegan, Mahican, Nanticoke, and Powhatan. The other main language group in the northeastern woodlands was the Iroquoian language family, which included the Five Nations of the Iroquois, the Erie, Huron, Susquehannock, Tuscarora, Neutral, Wenro, and Cherokee.

The Lenape Nation was composed of three subdivisions, referred to in sources as phratries,[2] which were based on a group's geographical location. The Lenape phratries were:

Muncee (Minsi, or Muncy), which means "people of the stony country."
Unami, "people down the river."
Unalachtigo, "people who live near the ocean."[3]

Those geographical areas likely pertained to the various sections of the Delaware basin. The Munsee lived in the hilly country around present Easton, Pennsylvania. The Unami lived in the area of the Schuylkill River and Brandywine Creek near present Philadelphia. And finally, the Unalachtigo lived in villages in the vicinity of Delaware Bay and present southern and eastern New Jersey.[4] The three divisions were each represented by animal totems or symbols, from which that unit "claimed a mythical descent."[5] The Unami were represented by the turtle, the Muncee or Minisi by the wolf, and the Unalachtigo by the turkey. The Unami were conceded to be the superior branch and its members were accorded precedence, because their ancestor the turtle was related to the great tortoise, which, according to Lenape legend, was the first of living beings, and supported the world on its back.

When the first European settlers arrived in North America in the early 17th century, it's estimated there were between 8,000 and 12,000 Lenape.[6] They had no large central villages, no capital, and no centralized governing structure like the Iroquois at Onondaga. For the most part, the Lenape villages were not organized into close-knit groups. Instead, the people were dispersed among separate smaller villages that were independent from their neighbors, and each had its own chief or sachem as the village authority. The villages were often located along smaller freshwater streams that fed into larger rivers or bodies of water, which gave them better protection from the elements than on the banks of a large river or bay. Occasionally, a few villages would be located in close proximity to one another, and for the overall good, the communities would loosely band together and look to the most influential chief in the area as their nominal leader.

They were essentially a hospitable, unaggressive, and peace-loving people who tried to avoid conflict, and did not present a threat to their neighbors. Unfortunately, that characteristic resulted in their being victimized first by the aggressive Susquehannock, and later by the more powerful Iroquois, who subjugated the Lenape and made them tributary. Many sources state that between 1700 and 1725, the extreme domination by the Iroquois resulted in the relegation of the Lenape to the status of women, and as such, they were devoid of both military and political power. In addition, the Lenape were required to accept the Iroquois as their masters, and could not wage war or negotiate treaties. The Lenape and the Iroquois have differing explanations of what the situation actually was.

The Moravian missionary George Henry Loskiel (1740–1814) wrote that according to the Lenape, the Iroquois, in an attempt to prevent further destructive wars between the Indian nations, convinced the Lenape to act as honorable, noncombatant peacemakers. As such, they would not engage in combat, and as a neutral party, they could effectively mediate and negotiate peace between warring factions. The references to the Lenape as having the status of women are best understood in the context of the matriarchal society of the tribes, and the position accorded to the "tribal matrons with regard to social policies. In effect, the tribal matrons could intervene with impunity, and propose a cessation of hostilities."[7] When the matrons decided to intervene, it effectively stopped the bloodshed, and more importantly, it spared the warriors the disgrace of having to sue for peace.

According to the Lenape, they regretted accepting the role of mediators, saying that in doing so, they sacrificed their independence and autonomy. However, since they pledged their sacred word of honor, they were unable to withdraw from the agreement. The Iroquois, on the other hand, scoffed at the Lenape explanation, and claimed that they had defeated the Lenape in battle, "and as a penalty, had reduced them to the disgraceful position of women."[8] An event that supports the Iroquois version of the story was an admonition to the Lenape by the Iroquois chief Canassatego in 1742. "We conquered you, we made women of you; you know you are women; we charge you to remove instantly; we don't give you liberty to think about it." This directive was given the Lenape by the Iroquois at the request of Pennsylvanians who claimed a large tract of Lenape homeland near the forks of the Delaware River above present Easton, Pennsylvania.

Not only were the Lenape victimized by their more powerful neighboring tribes, but after the death of William Penn in in 1718, they were also preyed upon by ruthless Pennsylvania land grabbers. In 1682, William Penn took possession of his land grant, which included a large portion of the Lenape homeland along the Delaware River. Unlike many of the other colonies, which were meant to be profitable enterprises, Pennsylvania, or "Penn's Woods," offered peace, justice, and religious tolerance, not only to Quakers like Penn, but also to members of other religious denominations, who were welcomed into the colony. Penn was adamant that the Indians living in the colony were children of God, entitled to love and respect, and should be treated equally and fairly.[9] He preached, "Don't abuse them, but let them have Justice and you win them."[10] Penn told the Indians that he was aware of the past behavior of whites, and he promised them peace, fair treatment, and an opportunity to redress grievances.[11] In support of his policy, Penn directed both the colonists and colony officials, "All Indians were to be entitled to the same liberty as the white settlers to improve the ground and to provide sustenance for their families. Goods traded to the Indians must be of the same quality as that sold in the marketplace, with no attempt to deceive the natives. If anyone by word or deed affronted or wronged an Indian, he would be subject to the same penalty under the law as if he had offended a white settler."[12]

William Penn's "holy experiment," as he called it, was certainly a new concept in dealing with the Indians, and not everyone found it palatable. Many Europeans considered the Indians as having no more recourse to the law or right to ownership of land than "the birds flitting in the trees, or wild animals roaming the forests."[13] As long as William Penn was in charge, the Indians in Pennsylvania were protected and had recourse to the law, but that changed after Penn died.

Before the death of Penn, Philadelphia grew rapidly, and it was on its way to becoming the largest city in the British American colonies. The growth of the city of Philadelphia had two distinct effects on the Lenape. First, the need for added land to expand the city limits and provide adjacent farmlands to feed the city's population resulted in the purchase of adjacent Lenape lands. Secondly, the increased hunting and trapping began to exhaust the game in the area, and the Indians had to travel farther to obtain food as well as furs to trade. Many of the Lenape relocated their villages farther west and northwest to be closer to the new hunting grounds, and white settlers filled the void in the vacated areas. The biggest change, however, was the shift in Indian policy by the new leaders of the colony. With William Penn's death, his second wife Hannah Callowhill initially managed Penn's affairs, and her three sons became the joint proprietors of the colony.

The new proprietors did not have the same ethical philosophy regarding the Indians as their father did, and they were more than willing to appropriate Lenape lands in whatever fashion was most expedient. One of their first measures was to designate a head chief or "king" of all the Lenape, even though the concept of one central authority was incongruous with the Lenape culture, which had always consisted of autonomous and independent communities. The brothers selected a village chief called Sassoonan to be their puppet, and they bestowed on him the lofty title of "king." The Penns calculated it would be less costly and more expedient to deal with one pliable person whom they could manipulate, rather than having to negotiate with and shower expensive gifts and merchandise on a host of village chiefs.

At the same time, the Lenape were also under the control of the Iroquois, and the council at Onondaga sent an Oneida chief named Shikellamy ("he causes it to be daylight for himself") to act as a resident supervisor or half-king over the Indians living in the conquered lands of Pennsylvania. Another strategy of the Penn brothers was to maintain a close relationship with the Iroquois to win their support in disputes with the Pennsylvania tribes, which included the Lenape. To facilitate the bond between the Pennsylvania authorities and the now Six Nations,[14] Conrad Weiser, who had lived with the Mohawk for several years and could speak many different Indian dialects, was the primary representative of Pennsylvania in dealings with the Iroquois. In his role as Pennsylvania ambassador to the Six Nations,

Weiser interacted closely with Shikellamy, and was able to promote extraordinarily good relations between Pennsylvania and the Iroquois League. Occasionally these terms were at the expense of other Indian tribes, most notably the Lenape.

One example in 1736 occurred when the Pennsylvanians wanted a large swath of the Lenape land in an area drained by the Susquehanna River that abutted the border with Maryland. Rather than negotiate the purchase with the Lenape, the Pennsylvanians approached the Iroquois through Conrad Weiser and Shikellamy, and they persuaded the Iroquois to sell the land to Pennsylvania. The dubious part of the deal was that the Lenape lived there, and the Iroquois had never laid claim to the land until they sold it to the Pennsylvanians. Though the Lenape protested, they were not strong enough to defy either the Pennsylvanians or the Iroquois, so they were forced to cede their land and move westward.

The following year, almost the same thing happened when Conrad Weiser and Shikellamy pressured the Lenape to accept the infamous "walking purchase." The Lenape homeland stretched more than 100 miles along the Delaware River north of Philadelphia. However, in 1737, James Logan, the Penns' land agent, along with William Penn's sons, produced an old unsigned draft of a 1686 deed that claimed the Lenape had agreed to sell William Penn the territory as far as a man could walk north from Wrightstown. The draft was unsigned because William Penn failed to supply the agreed-upon amount of trade goods, so the deal was never consummated. Logan and the Penn brothers met with the Lenape representatives and insisted that the agreement was still in effect. To soften the blow, they produced a map that indicated a man could walk at the most about 18 miles through the rugged forested wilderness, and they assured the Lenape that none of them would be displaced. The Lenape were in a quandary. Both Conrad Weiser and Shikellamy indicated that the Iroquois would support Pennsylvania's claim that the agreement was valid, and the Lenape were honor-bound to respect the earlier sale arrangement with the Penns. The Lenape grudgingly agreed to accept the terms of the Walking Purchase.

Without the knowledge of the Lenape, Logan and the Penn brothers had already reconnoitered the route and had sent teams to clear and grade a pathway. To further hedge their bets, Logan hired the three fastest long-distance runners in the colony, and the sale boundary would be determined by the runner who covered the most distance. The runners started off at a rapid pace on September 19, 1737, and after a day and a half, one of the men covered about 70 miles, to near present Jim Thorpe, Pennsylvania. Surveyors tacked on even more land by running their line northeast to the confluence of the Delaware and Lackawaxen Rivers. All in all, the Pennsylvanians claimed over 1.2 million acres, or approximately 1,875 square miles of land. As expected, the Lenape protested, but Weiser and Shikellamy had already convinced the Iroquois to support the Pennsylvanians. The Lenape had no alternative but to move farther west, and some Lenape relocated for a time in the already overcrowded Wyoming Valley near present Wilkes-Barre, Pennsylvania.

As the Lenape people were forced to abandon their traditional homelands, the geographic differences between the three phratries, or tribal divisions, became somewhat meaningless. The dialectal differences between the Unami and the Munsee came to differentiate those two branches of the Lenape in a political sense, but the Unalachtigo, "people who live near the ocean," merged for the most part with the Unami, whose language dialect was closer in pronunciation to their own. In time, the term Unalachtigo was no longer used to designate a Lenape phratry. From then on, the branches of the Lenape were either the Unami or Muncee.

The exodus to the Susquehanna River unexpectedly began to unify the Lenape. In the past, the Lenape lived in widely scattered autonomous villages stretching from southern Delaware to the Hudson River without any central authority, but now in close proximity to one another, they began to interact more as a nation. Sassoonan, who had been made "King of the Lenape" by the Pennsylvanians, was almost totally ignored by the Indians, even though the governor of Pennsylvania regularly furnished Sassoonan with presents, including "quantities of matchcoats, powder, lead, hats, stockings, shoes, red pigment for use as face paint, and strings of wampum.... Sassoonan was given a horse, saddle, and bridle, because who could expect a king to walk to Philadelphia."[15] Of course, Sassoonan "did his best to oblige his benefactors by doing their bidding, realizing that an uncooperative attitude would result in shutting off the supply of presents."[16]

At the same time, other Indian nations were also on the move, having been forced from their homelands. These included the Shawnee, who were being displaced from areas in southern Pennsylvania, western Maryland, and Virginia. The Shawnee belonged to the same Algonquin language family as the Lenape, so they considered the Lenape to be relatives and referred to them as "grandfathers." However, unlike the peaceful and placid Lenape, the Shawnee were restless, aggressive and truculent.

A band of Shawnee, without informing the Pennsylvania governor or the Iroquois half-king Shikellamy, crossed the Alleghenies and settled on the Upper Ohio or Allegheny River, where they found the fish and game were plentiful, and there were very few other Indian villages. Soon after, a group of young, adventuresome Lenape followed the Shawnee across the mountains and established a village on the Allegheny they called "Kittanning" (place on the big river), which would grow into the largest Indian town in western Pennsylvania.

Over time, a large number of the Lenape nation settled on the Ohio and Allegheny Rivers, where they were known as the "Western Lenape" or "Delaware." They established several towns in the area, including Logstown or Chininqué (often Shenango),[17] a large village at present Ambridge, Pennsylvania, about eighteen miles downstream from the Forks of the Ohio. Logstown was unique in that it was a cosmopolitan village composed of Lenape, Shawnee, and other expatriates who migrated to the area. Other Lenape villages soon appeared, including Shingas's Town near present McKees Rocks; Shanopin's Town just north of the Forks; Custalogas Village, also called Venango, at present Franklin, Pennsylvania; and Kichinipallin's town, called Loyalhanning, near present Ligonier, Pennsylvania. While the Lenape were establishing their villages, the restless Shawnee wanted yet more distance between themselves and the English colonies and the Iroquois, so they continued to move southwest along the Ohio River into southern Ohio.

For a while, the Lenape in western Pennsylvania had a good existence, but it wasn't long before the Iroquois once again exerted their dominance in the form of new half-kings who were sent by the Grand Council at Onondaga to maintain Iroquois superiority and supervise the Indians living in western Pennsylvania and Ohio. Tanacharison was sent as the principal half-king to supervise the Lenape. As far as can be determined, Tanacharison was born a Catawba, and he and his mother were captured by the Seneca and brought north from the Carolinas and adopted by the Seneca. Tanacharison was very intelligent and capable, and early on showed great promise as a leader. Sometime before 1747, he was recognized by the Iroquois Grand Council as their leading representative or half-king in western Pennsylvania and Ohio. In addition to the Lenape, he also supervised the Wyandot (Huron) and Mingo, or expatriate Iroquois, in the Ohio region. The Mingos were mostly western Seneca with a smattering of Indians from all the Six Nations. They were recognized by the

Grand Council at Onondaga as Iroquois relatives, and were considered "hunters," who had no authority to hold formal councils or speak for the Iroquois League.

Although the Iroquois claimed dominion over the tribes that moved into Ohio, the French claimed ownership of the territory west of the Allegheny Mountains. Their claim was based on the discoveries of the French explorers Cartier, Champlain, Charlevoix, Joliet, de Vrennes, de la Vérendrye, Marquette, Nicollet, and Radisson. The French claim had been affirmed by the British and reinforced in three separate treaties, including Ryswick in 1697, Utrecht in 1713, and Aix-la-Chapelle in 1748. However, as a result of the very competitive fur trade, English traders had blatantly and regularly penetrated the trans-Allegheny region, much to the consternation of the French, who considered the English to be trespassers. Notwithstanding the treaties that they had signed recognizing French ownership of the area called New France, the British now claimed the territory by right of Iroquois conquest during the Beaver Wars. The tenuous British claim was reinforced by the assertion that the British had sponsored John Cabot,[18] who was the first European to reach the Atlantic Coast of North America. Even more interesting was the fact that the British also used the Treaty of Utrecht to claim possession of the trans-Allegheny region, which was the same treaty that recognized French ownership. One provision of the treaty was recognition of British dominion over the Iroquois, and the British argued that since the Iroquois had conquered the Erie, English jurisdiction logically extended into those lands by right of conquest. Of course, the French were having none of that, and it would take a major war to determine who would ultimately take control of the area.

The western Lenape had only been settled on the banks of the Allegheny and Ohio Rivers for about two decades when, in 1749, they were startled by a large French military expedition commanded by Captain Pierre Joseph Céloron de Blainville that marched into their villages. Céloron had been ordered by the governor-general of New France, Roland-Michel Barrin de La Galissonièr, to reaffirm France's ownership of the territory by planting lead plates and posting the French royal coat of arms at principal rivers and streams around the area. (The burying of lead plates and posting notices to mark ownership of territory is similar to today's markings that define national boundaries, or even postings of "private property.")

In addition, Céloron was directed to awe the Indians into maintaining loyalty to the French and expel any English traders who were trespassing in New France. Céloron's expedition traveled down the Allegheny and Ohio Rivers, skirting the eastern and southern borders of present Ohio, and then marched up the Miami River to the Miami Indian village of Pickawillany near present Piqua, Ohio. From there they journeyed to Fort des Miamis at present Fort Wayne, then on to Fort Détroit, and along the southern shore of Lake Erie on the way back to the St. Lawrence River and Québec.

For many of the Lenape, the surprising arrival of Céloron's armed troops was disconcerting, but four years later in 1753, the arrival of a massive French army who began to build forts along the Allegheny River alarmed the Lenape even more. While Céloron's march was meant to reinforce French claims to the Ohio territory, the new governor-general, Michel-Ange Duquesne de Menneville, decided to do what should have been done years before, and militarily seal the border between New France and the English colonies. To do so, he ordered crusty 61-year-old Captain Paul Marin de las Malgue to lead a force of over 2,000 that included 300 soldiers, 1,700 militia, and about 200 Indians to establish themselves "on la Belle Rivière, which we are on the verge of losing if I do not make this hasty but indispensable effort."[19]

When Marin's troops began their march south from Presque Isle, at present Erie, Pennsylvania, the force alarmed and awed the Indians with its unprecedented and overwhelming size and power. It was ten times larger and better armed than Céloron's expedition, and one Indian reported that "the earth was trembling from the multitude of French who were at Rivière au Bœuf, and besides that … [t]hey are holding hands from Presquisle to La Chine."[20]

Just as disconcerting to the Indians in western Pennsylvania was the arrival in January 1753 of a party of Virginia militia under the command of Captain William Trent, who began to build a fort at the at the confluence of the Allegheny, Monongahela and Ohio Rivers, which was known as the Forks of the Ohio. The fort was officially named Fort Prince George in honor of the future King George III, but it was simply referred to as "Trent's Fort." The fort was rather insignificant, but it lay in the path of the French juggernaut that was approaching from the north, and it was apparent to the Indians that monumental changes were about to occur.

The war between the French and the English began in a hail of musketry in a remote forested glen at the top of Chestnut Ridge in Pennsylvania in the early morning of May 28, 1754, when 22-year-old Lieutenant-Colonel George Washington and about 40 militia troops and 20 Indians ambushed a French force of about 32 troops under the command of Ensign Joseph Coulon de Villiers de Jumonville. That incident was a preamble to the Seven Years' War (1756–1763), or as it was known in North America, the French and Indian War. British historian Horatio "Horace" Walpole, 4th Earl of Oxford, wrote, "The volley fired by a young Virginian in the backwoods of America set the world on fire."

With the start of the French and Indian War, most of the Indians in western Pennsylvania, particularly the Lenape, sided with the French. They saw this as an opportunity to escape Iroquois domination and also avenge themselves on the Pennsylvanians. After generations of being docile and peace-loving, the Lenape had been pushed to the point that they were transformed into a warrior nation and figuratively shed the petticoats that made them vassals of the Iroquois.

During the first years of the French and Indian War, the Lenape in western Pennsylvania supported the French by conducting attacks against the white Pennsylvania settlements. The Lenape village of Kittanning on the Allegheny River in particular served as the staging point for many of the raids. In 1758, Lieutenant Colonel John Armstrong led the "Kittanning Expedition," which penetrated deep into western Pennsylvania to attempt to put an end to the Indian depredations. Kittanning and a few other Lenape villages were destroyed, and the expedition was hailed as a success. While Armstrong was lauded as a hero, the raid did not achieve its objective of stopping the Indian attacks. Most of the Indians escaped, taking their white prisoners with them, and Armstrong's attackers suffered more casualties than they inflicted.

One of the villages that had been destroyed was the town of the Lenape chief Shingas, near present McKees Rocks, Pennsylvania. When the French and Indian War began, Shingas believed it was in the best interests of the Lenape to side with the French in order to free the tribe from the domineering Iroquois. He was a gifted orator and leader, as well as an accomplished warrior, and during the war he was often referred to as "Shingas the Terrible." Despite the belligerent-sounding name, Shingas was rather mild-mannered, and was never known to treat prisoners with cruelty. He adopted several young white captives as his children, who claimed that they were accorded equal treatment with Shingas's own offspring.[21]

After the destruction of Shingas's village, he and his brother Tamaqua (Beaver), moved west and established their village on the west bank of the Tuscarawas River at present Bolivar, Ohio. Tamaqua shared in the leadership of the village with Shingas, and was sometimes referred to as "King Beaver," although the term "king" was an English designation and was not generally used by the Indians. The town they established was known by several names, including Shingas's Town, King Beaver's Town, and the Tuscarawas, but most referred to it as "Beaver's Town."

By early 1758, it was evident to those Lenape remaining in the vicinity of the Forks of the Ohio that the ability of the French to successfully defend Fort Duquesne was very questionable. Rather than wait for the fort's capitulation to the British, the majority of the remaining Lenape moved westward into Ohio to place themselves beyond the range of the British army. Among those moving into Ohio at that time was Netawatwees,[22] or "skilled advisor" (c. 1686–1776) who became one of the leading spokesmen of the Lenape nation. He was a member of the Turtle phratry (Unami), and since the nation had more or less coalesced, the Lenape tended to look to the chief of the Turtle Clan for leadership, or in effect, a chief who was "first among equals."[23]

The village that Netawatwees established in Ohio was called "Cuyahoga Town," and it was located on the north side of the Cuyahoga River at present Cuyahoga Falls, Ohio. Around 1762, Netawatwees was recognized as the leading chief of the Ohio Lenape, and his village the site of the Delaware's main council fire. Prior to Netawatwees's move from Pennsylvania, Tamaqua and his brother Shingas were regarded as the Delaware leaders, but the mantle of authority shifted to Netawatwees when Shingas and Tamaqua began to lose influence. Shingas died in 1764, presumably from smallpox, and Tamaqua did not have sufficient backing to challenge Netawatwees for the leadership position.

FIVE

The Mingo
Migration into Ohio

Expatriate Iroquois Move into Ohio

Another group of American Indians who migrated into Ohio during the 18th century was called Mingo. The name was a corruption of the Lenape word "Mingwe," which translated as "stealthy" or "treacherous," and was applied to expatriate Iroquois who began to take up residence in western Pennsylvania and Ohio. They were mainly made up of Senecas and Cayugas, which is understandable, since those two Iroquois divisions were the westernmost of the Iroquois Confederacy. In fact, the prevalent Mingo dialect in Ohio during the 18th century was most similar to the Seneca language. However, there were also several Onondaga, Oneida, Mohawk, and Tuscarora Indians who migrated into Ohio, and were often considered part of the Mingo sub-group.

The migration of some Iroquois to the Allegheny and Ohio River valleys was a result of the interminable competition and regularly occurring wars between the French and English for control of the Great Lakes fur trade. Around 1715, the Senecas, who were the nearest of the Iroquois Confederacy to Niagara Falls, granted the French access to the Niagara portage, and in 1720, they also allowed the French to construct Fort Niagara at present Youngstown, New York. The French post benefited the Iroquois fur trade, but it caused the British to build Fort Oswego at present Oswego, New York, to counter the French post at Fort Niagara and establish a British colonial enclave in the Iroquois heartland. The presence of Forts Niagara and Oswego made many of the Iroquois feel hemmed in by the two major European powers, and that feeling was exacerbated by the depletion of game and the influx of unscrupulous traders who brought liquor and European diseases. As a result, some Iroquois, primarily Seneca, opted to leave the Iroquois homeland altogether and migrate into the lush, unspoiled forests of Ohio.

Some historians suggest that many of the early expatriate Iroquois who became the Ohio Mingo may have been Erie Indians or descendants of Eries who had been taken as children or young adults during the Beaver Wars, and never fully assimilated into the Iroquois culture. They would "have harbored not only memories of home but also an intimate knowledge of the region that eased the migration of them and their children."[1] Those early Mingos moved into Ohio by crossing the Genesee Valley to the headwaters of the Allegheny River and traveling down its length. Some of their first towns outside the Iroquois homeland were constructed in the 1740s at Conewango at present Warren, Pennsylvania; Buckaloons at present Irvine, Pennsylvania; and Kuskuski at present New Castle, Pennsylvania.

The first established Mingo town in Ohio was Mingo Bottom or Mingo Town, a few miles south of present Steubenville, Ohio.

Like the other tribes who entered Ohio, the expatriate Iroquois or Mingos continued to move westward into the state. By 1750 the greatest concentration of Indians was the 2,400 or so living in the Cuyahoga River Valley. They had likely been attracted by French traders like François Saguin, who had a post near present Valley View, Ohio, and the Pennsylvanian George Croghan, who established his trading post at the mouth of the Cuyahoga River at present Cleveland. Most of the natives in the Cuyahoga Valley were from each of the Six Nations, and more than half of those were Seneca.

The Mingo did not exist as an individual tribe or nation prior to the 18th century, and only coalesced as a separate entity around 1750. The Iroquois Council at Onondaga recognized them as Iroquois relatives, but rather than accept them as a separate division or nation, they were accorded the unique status of "hunters," who had temporarily left the Iroquois homeland, and as travelers had no authority to hold formal councils or speak for the Iroquois League. Around the time of the French and Indian War, the Mingo became a distinctive people who developed a cultural personality in tune with their geographic location and their neighbors, even to the extent that they were often at odds with the policies and diktats of the main Iroquois Council at Onondaga.[2] In fact, they were independent-minded enough to be placed under the supervision of Tanacharison, the half-king representative of the Iroquois Council.

The independent nature of the Mingos began to irk the Iroquois Grand Council. In 1750, when Virginia lieutenant-governor Robert Dinwiddie was unable to attend a council at Albany, Conrad Weiser suggested that he send presents to the Ohio Iroquois or Mingo, who were the nearest Iroquois to the Virginia Colony. Weiser's reasoning was that the Ohio Indians "were one and the same with the Six Nations and of their own blood."[3] The Grand Council at Onondaga was quick to set Weiser straight by stating emphatically that the Mingos "were but hunters, and not counsellors or chief men; and they had no right to receive presents that was due to the Six Nations."[4] The Iroquois Council further stated that if the Mingo were to receive a present, they "must receive [it] from the Six Nations' chief under whom they belong."[5] In that case it would have been half-king Tanacharison.

During the French and Indian War, the Six Nations sided with the English, but many of the Ohio area Mingo joined the Lenape and Shawnee in supporting the French. This caused consternation at the Iroquois Grand Council, because the Six Nations had taken great pains to present an artfully fashioned façade of unity among the member nations. They were concerned that Mingo detachment would negatively impact Iroquois standing as a cohesive and formidable power. Quite simply, the Grand Council at Onondaga did not want the increasingly independent-minded Mingo to taint Iroquois relations with the British, so they publicly disparaged the Mingo as "a mongrel population, a mixture of all the Iroquoian stock on the outskirts of the territory of the Seneca. This mongrel population of the Ohio and Allegheny valleys was known as 'Mingoes,' and was really beyond the jurisdiction of the Six Nations."[6]

Some historians depict the Mingo as having a bad reputation, portraying them as warlike and hostile to whites. That impression may have been a result of a band of Mingo warriors who were associated with the notorious Scots-Irish frontiersman Simon Girty. Girty served as liaison between the British and their Indian allies during the Revolutionary War, and was active in partisan operations against the Americans in Ohio and Western Pennsylvania. When Girty and his brothers were children in Pennsylvania, they were taken captive by the Seneca and adopted into the tribe. Girty lived with the Seneca for over seven years, and was fully assimilated into Seneca society. After he was repatriated and returned to his white family, he preferred the Seneca culture and maintained a profound affinity with the Indians. Since Girty dressed and indeed acted like an Indian, the Americans portrayed him as a villain and called him the "White Savage." Moravian missionary John Heckewelder wrote about his own near-lethal encounters with Girty and Girty's Mingo warriors, and because of their misdeeds, people on the frontier often referred to them as "Blue Mingo" or "Black Mingo."

The Mingo, though fiercely independent, were as a native culture no more warlike, violent or cruel than any other Indian society. Like other Iroquois, they were quick to respond to threats or actions against them, and possibly they did so more precipitously and violently than other cultures. However, not only did they produce fierce and implacable warriors, they also had eloquent spokesmen and proponents of peace. Logan, who was perhaps their most famous chief, was both a warrior and a statesman.

Whites referred to him as Logan (1740–1780) or John Logan, but his native name was Tah-gah-jute, meaning "His eyelashes stick out or above as if looking through or over something."[7] He was the son of Shikellamy or Swatana, an Oneida, and his mother was Neanoma, a Cayuga, although some unsubstantiated sources indicate he was the son of a white Frenchman who was captured by the Indians. Tah-gah-jute took the name Logan from his friend James Logan, who was at one time secretary to the acting governor of Pennsylvania. Tah-gah-jute or Logan was recognized as chief by the band of Mingo who eventually settled on the Scioto River in central Ohio.

Logan was initially very friendly with the white settlers until April 30, 1774, when a group of Virginians led by Jacob and Daniel Greathouse massacred about a dozen Indian men, women, and children. The senseless killing took place near the mouth of Yellow Creek on the upper Ohio River east of present Hammondsville, Ohio. Among the slain were Logan's wife Mellana, his brother Taylaynee, and his sister Koonay. Taylaynee's son Molnah was also killed. Koonay, who was pregnant at the time, was the wife of John Gibson, a prominent trader in the area. After the killing, the bodies of the Indians were mutilated, and Jacob Greathouse even ripped open Koonay's abdomen so he could scalp her unborn infant son. The atrocity was one of the events that sparked Lord Dunmore's War, and turned the formerly peaceful Logan into an implacable enemy of the whites in Ohio.

At the end of Dunmore's War in October 1774, Logan refused to attend the treaty negotiations. He instead stood under a great elm tree known as "Logan's Elm"[8] and offered an impassioned lament. His oration was printed in colonial newspapers, and also in Thomas Jefferson's book *Notes on the State of Virginia*. As a result of his speech, Logan is most remembered as "Logan the Orator." It should be noted that in his lament, Logan erroneously blamed Michael Cresap for the massacre of his kinfolk.

I appeal to any white man to say, if ever he entered Logan's cabin hungry, and he gave him not meat; if ever he came cold and naked, and he clothed him not. During the course of the last long and bloody war, Logan remained idle in his cabin, an advocate for peace. Such was my love for the whites, that my countrymen pointed as they passed, and said, Logan is the friend of the white men. I have even thought to live with you but for the injuries of one man. Col. Cresap, the last spring, in cold blood, and unprovoked, murdered all the relations of Logan, not sparing even my women and children. There runs not a drop of my blood in the veins of any living creature. This has called on me for revenge. I have sought it: I have killed many: I have fully glutted my vengeance. For my country, I rejoice at the beams of peace. But do not harbor a thought that mine is the joy of fear. Logan never felt fear. He will not turn on his heel to save his life. Who is there to mourn for Logan? Not one.[9]

Logan remarried a Shawnee woman, but as with his first wife, they also had no children. When the American Revolutionary War began, Logan sided with the British in hopes that a British victory would expel the whites from the Ohio area and preserve it as an Indian homeland. In 1780, after a return from Detroit, Logan was killed by his nephew, supposedly during an argument.

Initially, those western expatriate Iroquois who became known as Mingo were unsure of their own identity. As previously mentioned, a large concentration settled along the Cuyahoga River, while another group took up residence along the Ohio River below the Forks of the Ohio. The Ohio River Iroquois had been the first to move into the Ohio region, while the Cuyahoga River Iroquois had only recently arrived, so in effect, there were two Ohio Iroquois spheres of influence, with the Cuyahoga River Iroquois taking a more active role in the anti–French movement. The Ohio River Iroquois (Mingo) had not yet been drawn into the conflict between the French and English in the Ohio region, but that was about to change.

In April 1747, the Ohio River Iroquois were petitioned by the Miami Indians at Pickawillany to help them form an alliance between the Miami, the Iroquois, and the colony of Pennsylvania. The Miamis were in effect seeking protection from the French, who began to increase pressure on the breakaway Pickawillany Indians to cease trade with the English and return to the French fold. Less than a month later, after the Miamis joined Orontony's Rebellion against the French, they sent another request for an alliance with the Iroquois and the English colonies, along with an urgent plea for gunpowder with which to fight the French. In addition, they included the scalp of a French trader who had been killed by the Miamis. Like it or not, the Ohio River Iroquois were being drawn into the conflict.

Whatever initial hostility the Ohio Iroquois had toward the French was likely a result of the traditional antipathy of the Iroquois on the whole toward the French. The Iroquois had regularly sided with the English against the French ever since the summer of 1609, when Samuel Champlain, along with two French soldiers and about 60 Huron warriors, encountered an Iroquois war party of over 200 braves near the southern end of Lake Champlain. The Iroquois anticipated an easy victory over the Huron, but then Champlain fired his matchlock musket called an arquebus and killed two of the three Iroquois chiefs. Another of the French soldiers shot and killed the third chief. The unexpected gunfire and the loss of their leaders unnerved the Iroquois, and they ignominiously fled the scene. The Iroquois, however, had long memories, and they never forgot that event, nor did they ever forgive the French. That small skirmish in 1609 affected French and Iroquois relations for well over a century. There were other instances that reinforced the animosity between the French and the Iroquois, and the most notable was French military support of the Huron during the Beaver Wars. With that long history of acrimony between them, it wasn't surprising that the Ohio Iroquois initially exhibited anti–French sentiment.

However, it wasn't long before they, like the other Ohio Indians, began to question which faction it would be in their best interests to support. While British-manufactured trade goods were significantly better, less expensive, and more plentiful than French merchandise, that advantage was offset by the Englishmen's insatiable craving for land, which denuded the forests of game and timber and caused the Indians to be displaced. For the Lenape, Shawnee, and Mingo, it was the reason they were in Ohio in the first place. The French, on the other hand, didn't seem to be interested in creating European-like farms, villages, and cities in the wilderness, but were more interested in maintaining a monopolistic trade relationship with the Ohio Indians. The natives were quickly learning that they had to choose one side over the other, and even the Ohio Iroquois had to reevaluate their animosity toward the French.

By about 1749–1750, the distinction between the Cuyahoga River and Ohio River Iroquois had blurred to the point where they were grouped under the generic term "Mingo," and the terms "Iroquois," "Western Iroquois," "Ohio Iroquois," or "Six Nations" were rarely used in reference to them. Even more importantly, they began to consider themselves their own people, rather than members of the Six Nations. As such, they became more pragmatic with regard to what benefited them, as opposed to the desires of the Grand Council at Onondaga.

The Iroquois Confederacy believed the French were upsetting both "the tranquility and the security of the Ohio country."[10] Until then, they had been able to walk a fine line of neutrality between the French and the English, but now the Iroquois were concerned that the French were causing the Ohio Indians to distance themselves from the Iroquois, which was certainly true in the case of the Lenape and the Shawnee. Feeling somewhat out of touch with the main Iroquois Council, the Ohio Iroquois decided to "lay their old people aside" and look after their own affairs.[11] This was an acknowledgment that the interests of the Ohio Iroquois and the Grand Council at Onondaga were diverging, and it wasn't long before the Ohio Iroquois considered themselves Mingo, who were their own people with their own council fire.

Six

The Ohio Thoroughfares

"We will be known forever by the tracks we leave."

The first humans who entered Ohio found trails crisscrossing the forest floor that were made by animals who traveled between the watersheds, fording places, and salt licks. The Indians simply used those trails, knowing that animals generally followed the easiest and most direct routes through the wilderness. In his book *Ohio Indian Trails*,[1] Frank Wilcox described the Indian trails in detail, and his book remains a valuable resource today even though many of Wilcox's 1934 highway route numbers, town names and other landmarks have changed, been replaced, or simply disappeared. However, a revised edition of his book was published by the Kent State University Press in 2015 with updated information. Even so, most of the old traces of Indian trails that may have been evident in Frank Wilcox's youth, and were still discernable to some extent during our own personal explorations in the 1950s, have now for the most part been buried or covered by expanding developments, highways, shopping malls, schools, and other symbols of 21st-century "progress." Fortunately, it's still possible in some areas of rural Ohio to walk ancient forest pathways and have a sense of what the Ohio wilderness once was like.

To help identify the locations of trails, villages and posts, we've included maps for cross reference, which will give the reader a better sense of directions and distances. In most cases we've used the modern contemporary names for rivers and waterways, but where necessary in the text, we tried to reconcile the new with the old. For example, the Walhonding River was also known as "White Woman's Creek," and in fact, it was listed on several early maps and journals as such. In addition, some old sources did not differentiate between the Tuscarawas and the Muskingum Rivers, since the Tuscarawas was the upper tributary of the Muskingum. It's fairly common for different sources to disagree on a tributary name, particularly between British and French maps. The most notable example is the Allegheny River in western Pennsylvania. While the British considered the Allegheny to be a separate tributary of the Ohio River, the French considered the Allegheny the upriver section of la Belle Rivière (the Beautiful River), which the British called the Ohio.

The trails shown in the previous map were based on several sources, including *Ohio Indian Trails* by Frank Wilcox; the *Archeological Atlas of Ohio*, by William C. Mills; *Historic American Indian Tribes of Ohio*,[2] by the Ohio Historical Society; and other sources cited in this work. It should be remembered that the Indians didn't name the trails as the Europeans did, and the names that survive generally reflect a destination, a route, or a trail between two points. In addition, not all sources agree on a specific route or even a name, and they often slightly differ from one source to another. As previously mentioned, the course of

Ohio counties for reference.

a trail generally followed the least arduous route, and a reference to topographical charts would help pinpoint the course of a trail with some precision. It should be remembered that the trails in the present state of Ohio did not necessarily begin or end at the modern state line. Most of the major trails in Ohio were continuations of trails that extended into today's neighboring states. For a more detailed description of the majority of Ohio's Indian trails, we recommend the third edition of Frank Wilcox's *Ohio Indian Trails*.[3]

A. *The Lake Trail or the Shore Trail*

The Lake Trail followed the southern shore of Lake Erie from the Niagara River at present Buffalo, New York, past present Erie, Pennsylvania, and followed the southern Lake

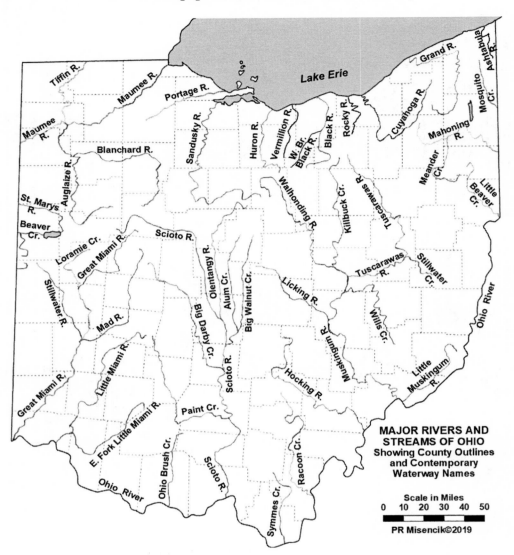

Major rivers and streams of Ohio showing county outlines.

Erie shoreline through present Cleveland, Ohio, to the Sandusky River southwest of Sandusky Bay. At that point, it joined the Great Trail and continued around the western edge of Lake Erie to Fort Detroit (present Detroit, Michigan).

More specifically, the eastern terminus of the Lake Trail was about a mile above or south of Niagara Falls, where in 1753 the French constructed Fort du Portage, which, along with Fort Niagara (1726) on Lake Ontario, protected the Niagara portage around the falls. The Lake Trail continued to the west along the Lake Erie shore and passed Presque Ile, present Erie, Pennsylvania, where in 1753 the French constructed Fort Presque Isle, officially named Fort de la Presqu'île, the first of their proposed chain of forts along the Allegheny River.

The trail continued east along the course of present U.S. Rt. 20 through present Conneaut, Ashtabula, Geneva, Perry, Painesville, Mentor, and the eastern Cleveland lakeshore suburbs to Cleveland, Ohio, where it crossed the Cuyahoga River. It was in present Cleve-

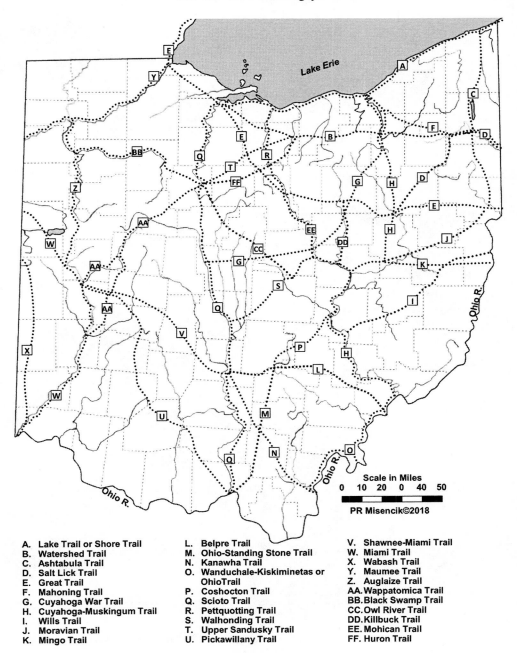

Major Ohio Indian trails in the 18th century.

A. Lake Trail or Shore Trail	L. Belpre Trail	V. Shawnee-Miami Trail
B. Watershed Trail	M. Ohio-Standing Stone Trail	W. Miami Trail
C. Ashtabula Trail	N. Kanawha Trail	X. Wabash Trail
D. Salt Lick Trail	O. Wanduchale-Kiskiminetas or	Y. Maumee Trail
E. Great Trail	OhioTrail	Z. Auglaize Trail
F. Mahoning Trail	P. Coshocton Trail	AA. Wappatomica Trail
G. Cuyahoga War Trail	Q. Scioto Trail	BB. Black Swamp Trail
H. Cuyahoga-Muskingum Trail	R. Pettquotting Trail	CC. Owl River Trail
I. Wills Trail	S. Walhonding Trail	DD. Killbuck Trail
J. Moravian Trail	T. Upper Sandusky Trail	EE. Mohican Trail
K. Mingo Trail	U. Pickawillany Trail	FF. Huron Trail

land, at the mouth of the Cuyahoga River, where around 1743 George Croghan, the "King of the Pennsylvania traders," established his trading post. From Cleveland, the trail continued west to present Rocky River, and from there it generally followed the course of present U.S. Rt. 6 to present Sandusky, Ohio, where the British established Fort Sandusky in 1761.

A few miles to the west of Sandusky near the site of the old Wyandot village of Anioton (present Crystal Rock, Ohio), the Lake Trail merged with the Great Trail, which crossed

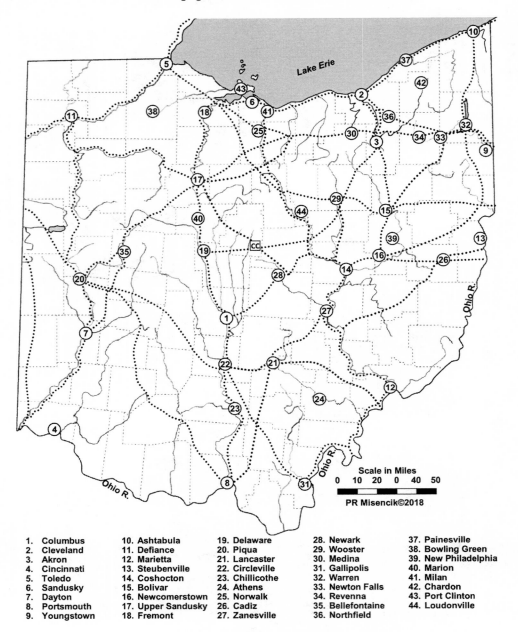

1. Columbus	10. Ashtabula	19. Delaware	28. Newark	37. Painesville
2. Cleveland	11. Defiance	20. Piqua	29. Wooster	38. Bowling Green
3. Akron	12. Marietta	21. Lancaster	30. Medina	39. New Philadelphia
4. Cincinnati	13. Steubenville	22. Circleville	31. Gallipolis	40. Marion
5. Toledo	14. Coshocton	23. Chillicothe	32. Warren	41. Milan
6. Sandusky	15. Bolivar	24. Athens	33. Newton Falls	42. Chardon
7. Dayton	16. Newcomerstown	25. Norwalk	34. Revenna	43. Port Clinton
8. Portsmouth	17. Upper Sandusky	26. Cadiz	35. Bellefontaine	44. Loudonville
9. Youngstown	18. Fremont	27. Zanesville	36. Northfield	

Indian trails in relationship to modern Ohio towns and cities.

Ohio diagonally from the Forks of the Ohio (present Pittsburgh, Pennsylvania). The merged Lake and Great Trail followed the western shoreline of Lake Erie to Fort Detroit.

B. The Watershed Trail

The Watershed Trail ran from its juncture with the Mahoning Trail in eastern Ohio near present Newton Falls on the Mahoning River. From there it followed the West Branch of the Mahoning and continued past the present towns of Ravenna and Kent, where the trail crossed the Cuyahoga River and followed the north bank of the river past Monroe Falls, Silver Lake, and Cuyahoga Falls. There it re-crossed the Cuyahoga River at the Lenape village of Cuyahoga Town. The Watershed Trail roughly followed Ohio Route 18 west through Medina, then paralleled Route 18 passing south of Wellington before turning northwest to present Milan, Ohio, where it crossed the Huron River and the Pequotting Trail a short distance south of the Moravian Indian town of New Salem or Pequotting on the Huron River. From there, the trail paralleled the present Ohio Turnpike and passed south of Sandusky to join the Great Trail and the Lake Trail near the site of the Wyandot village of Anioton west of the present city of Sandusky, Ohio.

C. Ashtabula Trail

The Ashtabula Trail began in the north at the junction where the Lake Trail crossed the mouth of the Ashtabula River in present Ashtabula, Ohio. It followed the west bank of the Ashtabula River south to the point where the river veers east, but the trail continued south, generally paralleling present Ohio Route 11 to Youngstown, Ohio. There it crossed both the Mahoning River and the Salt Lick and Mahoning Trails. From there the trail continued south along the course of present Ohio Route 7, to present Rogers, Ohio, where it had a junction with the Great Trail and the Moravian Trail.

D. The Salt Lick Trail or the Old Mahoning Trail

The Salt Lick Trail, sometimes referred to as the Old Mahoning Trail, overlapped the Mahoning Trail and the Great Trail for part of its length west of the Forks of the Ohio. It was primarily used by salt gatherers who used the salt spring at present Niles, Ohio. The Mahoning Trail, the Salt Lick Trail and the Great Trail overlapped from the Forks of the Ohio, and along the north bank of the Ohio River to the Beaver River, and up the Beaver River to near present Beaver Falls, Pennsylvania, where the Great Trail turned west toward present Negely, Ohio. The Mahoning and Salt Lick Trails continued up the east bank of the Beaver River to its confluence with the Mahoning River at present Willow Grove, Pennsylvania. From there, the Mahoning and Salt Lick Trails followed the Mahoning and entered Ohio at present Lowellville, Ohio, and continued along the course of the Mahoning River to the salt lick at present Niles, Ohio, for which the trail was named, and where the Lenape village of Salt Lick Town was located. From there the trails followed the north bank of the Mahoning River to present Newton Falls, Ohio, where the Watershed Trail continued west, and the Mahoning Trail continued northwest. The Salt Lick Trail, however, turned and followed the Mahoning River south to present Alliance, Ohio, then southwest to the Tuscarawas River, where Beaver's Town or Shingas's Town was located at present Bolivar, Ohio. Bolivar was also where General Lachlan McIntosh ordered Fort Laurens to be built in 1778, which was the only fort built in Ohio during the Revolutionary War.

E. The Great Trail

The Great Trail was so named, because it was the primary east-west route between Fort Duquesne at the Forks of the Ohio and Fort Detroit. However, the Great Trail did not begin at the Forks of the Ohio, but was an extension of the main thoroughfare that ran across Pennsylvania from the Lenape homelands around Delaware River and Chesapeake Bay.

From the Forks of the Ohio, the Great Trail, along with the Salt Lick Trail and Mahoning Trail, followed the Ohio River past Logstown at present Ambridge, Pennsylvania, to the Beaver River, where the Salt Lick and Mahoning Trails turned north and followed the Beaver River. The Great Trail, however, crossed the Beaver River just above its confluence with the Ohio, and proceeded northwest toward present Negely, Ohio. In 1764, Colonel Henry Bouquet's expedition against the Ohio Indians followed the Great Trail from Fort Pitt to the Tuscarawas River. He described crossing the Beaver River in his orderly book: "[We] crossed the Big Beaver Creek [River], which is twenty perches wide[4] [110 yards], the ford stony and pretty deep. It runs through a rich vale, with a pretty strong current, its banks high, the upland adjoining it very good timber."[5]

From present Negley, the Great Trail led west to north of present Lisbon, Ohio, then dipped southwest to present Dungannon, which was the site of a Lenape or Mingo village called Painted Post. From Painted Post, the trail veered northwest toward present Hanoverton, Ohio, then west along the north side of Sandy Creek through present Bayard, Ohio, southwest through present Minerva, Malvern, Waynesburg, and Magnolia, Ohio. From Magnolia, the Great Trail followed the route of present Ohio 183 and Cross Roads Road to Sandyville, and from there to Beaver's Town at present Bolivar, Ohio.

The Great Trail then led west along the course of present Ohio 212 to Beach City, and along present U.S. 250 south of Wooster, Ohio, and along the route of West Old Lincoln Way and County Road 30A to Jeromesville, Ohio. Then it followed the course of present County Highway 1775 to Ashland, and Ohio 96 to Olivesburg, then northwest along Ohio 603 to present Plymouth, Ohio. From there it veered more northerly toward present Monroeville and Castalia, Ohio, where it turned in a more westerly direction to merge with the Lake and Watershed Trails in the vicinity of western Sandusky Bay. From there the Great Trail followed the western shoreline of Lake Erie to Lake St. Clair, and on to Fort Detroit.

F. The Mahoning Trail

The Mahoning Trail overlapped the Great Trail and the Salt Lick Trail from the Forks of the Ohio along the north bank of the Ohio River to the Beaver River, and up the Beaver River to its confluence with the Mahoning River at present Willow Grove, Pennsylvania. From there, the trail followed the Mahoning River and entered Ohio at present Lowellville, then continued along the south side of the Mahoning River to present Newton Falls, Ohio, where it crossed the Mahoning and continued westerly to the south of present Ravenna, Ohio, roughly following Summit Road to Kent, Ohio. It crossed the Cuyahoga in the southern portion of Kent, and from there the trail passed Silver Lake and veered northwest, then passed through the present town of Northfield and joined the Cuyahoga War Trail and the Cuyahoga-Muskingum Trail at present Valleyview, Ohio, near the mouth of Tinker's Creek.

G. The Cuyahoga War Trail

The Cuyahoga War Trail had its northern terminus at the mouth of the Cuyahoga River at present Cleveland, Ohio, and its southwestern terminus at present Delaware, Ohio.

It followed both banks of the Cuyahoga River south past the sites of Ottawa Town, the Moravian village of Pilgerruh, and François Saguin's Post near Tinker's Creek, then continued to the Lenape village of Cuyahoga Town at present Cuyahoga Falls, Ohio, where the trail crossed the Cuyahoga River. The trail continued southwest along the portage path and joined the Tuscarawas River at present Barberton, Ohio, then continued southwest to present Wooster, Ohio, and then west to Jeromesville, where it veered southwest past present Loudonville to the Lenape village of Hell Town at the confluence of the Clear Fork and the Black Fork of the Mohican River. From there the trail continued southwest to pass southeast of present Butler, Ohio, and intercepted the East Branch of the Kokosing River, which it followed to present Fredericktown, Ohio. From Fredericktown, the trail proceeded westward to present Ashley, Ohio, and then followed the course of present U.S. 42 to its terminus at Delaware, Ohio.

H. The Cuyahoga-Muskingum Trail

The Cuyahoga-Muskingum Trail was a major north-south thoroughfare in present eastern Ohio. It stretched from the mouth of the Cuyahoga River at present Cleveland, Ohio, to the mouth of the Muskingum River at present Marietta, Ohio. Initially the trail overlapped the Cuyahoga War Trail south along both banks of the Cuyahoga River, to the Lenape village of Cuyahoga Town at present Cuyahoga Falls, Ohio. From there it crossed the river and followed the portage path past Summit Lake and present Nimisilla Reservoir to northwestern Massillon, where it joined the Tuscarawas River and followed the eastern bank to present Navarre, Ohio, where it turned southeast and crossed the Tuscarawas River north of present Bolivar, Ohio. It continued to Bolivar, where it crossed the Great Trail and passed the locations of Beaver's Town and Fort Laurens. From Bolivar, the trail led south, following the west bank of the Tuscarawas River past the Moravian mission villages of New Schoenbrunn, Goshen and Gnadenhütten to a point north of present Port Washington, where the trail turned southwest and followed Spoon Creek and the east bank of Mill Creek to present Coshocton. There the trail crossed the Walhonding River at the present Roscoe Village Historic Area, followed Ohio 16 to Dresden, Ohio, and continued along the Muskingum River to Zanesville. From Zanesville, the trail continued past Duncan Falls and followed the river to the bend southeast of present Stockport, then turned east directly toward a point opposite present Lowell, Ohio. From there the trail followed the Muskingum River to Marietta.

I. The Wills Trail

The Wills Trail extended southeast from Mingo Town on the Ohio River at present Mingo Junction, Ohio, to Will's Town on the Muskingum River at present Duncan Falls. The trail led west-southwest to present Cadiz, Ohio, and then turned southwest to pass south of Piedmont, Ohio, west of Salesville, Ohio, along the north side of Senecaville Lake, then south of Senecaville, Ohio, south of Pleasant City, Ohio, north of Cumberland, Ohio, and then west to present Duncan Falls, Ohio, where it met the Cuyahoga-Muskingum Trail.

J. The Moravian Trail

The Moravian Trail was an offshoot of the Great Trail that connected the Forks of the Ohio with the Moravian mission villages on the Tuscarawas. The trail entered the present state of Ohio at Negely, and continued westerly to Painted Post at present Dungannon (Columbiana County), Ohio. From there the trail turned southwest to present Carrollton, Ohio, and then followed the Indian Fork to its confluence with Connotton Creek, from which it turned south to Little Stillwater Creek. The trail followed the creek between present Uhrichsville and Dennison and terminated at the junction of the Cuyahoga-Muskingum Trail and the Mingo Trail on the Tuscarawas River about two miles northeast of Gnadenhütten.

K. The Mingo Trail

The Mingo Trail entered Ohio at Mingo Town (present Mingo Junction) on the Ohio River a short distance south of present Steubenville and terminated at Gnadenhütten. The trail followed Cross Creek west to present Township Road 212, which it followed to present U.S. 22, and passed north of present Cadiz, where it joined the Standingstone Fork of the Little Stillwater northwest of Cadiz. The trail followed the Standingstone Fork to the vicinity of the present Tappan Airpark, where the trail proceeded to present Deersville, Ohio. From Deersville, the trail continued westerly to Weaver Run, which it paralleled it to its confluence with Stillwater Creek. The trail crossed at the confluence and proceeded almost directly to Gnadenhütten.

L. The Belpre Trail

The Belpre Trail entered Ohio at present Belpre, Ohio, across the Ohio River from Parkersburg, West Virginia, and ran northwest to connect with the Scioto Trail at the village of Maguck near present Circleville, Ohio. It was one of the primary trails that connected the Lenape and Shawnee villages on the Scioto Trail with the Indian settlements along the Little Kanawha River in present West Virginia. From where the trail crossed into Ohio at Belpre, it led northwest through the present towns of Vincent and Chesterhill and followed the course of present Ohio 555 to Ringgold, Ohio, where the trail turned west to pass Wildcat Hollow north of Burr Oak Lake to present Corning, Ohio. From Corning, the trail followed present Ohio 155 through Shawnee, Ohio, and then about a mile on Ohio 93 to Monday Creek, from where the trail turned west and passed north of present Logan, Ohio, to Rockbridge on the Hocking River. The trail continued west into present Circleville, where it terminated at the Scioto Trail near the village of Maguck.

M. The Ohio–Standing Stone Trail

The Ohio–Standing Stone Trail ran from Lower Shawnee Town at the mouth of the Scioto River at present Portsmouth, Ohio, to the villages at Standing Stone, present Lancaster, Ohio.

From the mouth of the Scioto River, the trail followed the Ohio River to Sciotoville, where it turned northeast and roughly paralleled the Little Scioto River and the course of Ohio Route 139 to Jackson, Ohio. The trail crossed over Little Salt Lick Creek at its junction with Buckeye Creek northwest of Jackson, and followed along the east bank of Little Salt Lick Creek to west of Buffalo, Ohio. From there the trail followed the ridgelines to present Byer in Jackson County, Ohio, where it crossed Pigeon Creek, and followed the weaving ridgeline to the Rock House area, about six and a half miles east of Laurelville, Ohio. From there the trail led almost due north and joined the Hocking River, which it followed north to Standing Stone.

N. The Kanawha Trail

The Kanawha Trail was one of the most important trails between Ohio and the Virginia country, which now includes West Virginia. The trail entered Ohio across the Ohio River from the mouth of the Kanawha River, and followed the east side of Chickamauga Creek north to present Ohio 588, which it followed to Rio Grande, Ohio. From Rio Grande, it followed the course of U.S. 35 to Jackson, Ohio, and then turned northerly to present Londonderry. The trail then led northwest to Walnut Creek and then Little Walnut Creek, which the trail followed before it veered northwest and continued to present Kingston, Ohio. From Kingston, the trail followed the north bank of Congo Creek past Logan's Elm, then turned north to cross Scippo Creek at Cornstalk's Town and Grenadier Squaw's Town, then proceeded north to the village of Maguck.

O. The Wanduchale-Kiskiminetas Trail

The Wanduchale-Kiskiminetas Trail followed the Ohio River and connected the Belpre Trail and the Kanawha Trail at the points where they entered the present state of Ohio. The Lenape town of Wanduchale in the northeastern corner of Troy Township in Athens County, and the Lenape village of Kiskiminetas' Town (also Kishkeminetas' Old Town) at present Cheshire, Ohio, were two towns near either end of the trail for which the trail was named.

The eastern end of the trail was at present Belpre, Ohio, across the Ohio River from the mouth of the Little Kanawha River in West Virginia. From there the trail led southwest following the route of present Ohio 7, U.S. 50, and Ohio 833, General Hartinger Parkway, and Powell Street, and rejoined Ohio 7 to its terminus across the Ohio River from the mouth of the Kanawha River near present Gallipolis, Ohio.

P. The Coshocton Trail

The Coshocton Trail was a relatively short thoroughfare that connected the Lenape towns on the Muskingum, Walhonding and Tuscarawas Rivers with the major trails in southern Ohio. From the Forks of the Muskingum, the trail headed southwest to the Shawnee village of Wakatomika, at present Wakotimika, Ohio. From there the trail veered southerly to pass east of present Frazeyburg, and about a mile east of Gratiot, and then swung southwest to pass east of Buckeye Lake through Thornville. From Thornville the trail followed the course of Ohio 188 through Pleasantville, Lancaster, Amanda, and Circleville, before terminating at the village of Maguck

Q. *The Scioto Trail or the Warriors' Path*

The Scioto Trail was perhaps the most important of the north-south trails that crossed present Ohio. It was an extension of the Warriors' Path from the Deep South, and it entered Ohio at the mouth of the Scioto River at Lower Shawnee Town at present Portsmouth. Along its course it connected with fifteen of the major Indian trails that crossed present Ohio. The trail follows present U.S. 23 for most of its route from Portsmouth to Upper Sandusky.

From Portsmouth, the Scioto Trail followed U.S. 23 past the present towns of Lucasville, Wakefield, and Piketon. At Piketon, the trail left the course of U.S. 23, and followed the present CSX railroad line along the east side of the Scioto River to where the trail rejoined U.S. 23 at the railroad crossing north of present Chillicothe, Ohio. From Chillicothe, the trail continued along the course of U.S. 23 to Maguck at present Circleville.

Then from Maguck the Scioto Trail followed the course of present U.S. 23 to Columbus, Ohio, where the trail left the Scioto River and continued north following the Olentangy River via North High Street (U.S. 23). At present Stratford, Ohio, the trail shifted to the west bank of the Olentangy River, proceeded north through present Delaware, Ohio, and continued north to present Waldo, Ohio, where the trail diverged to the northwest and followed the present Marion-Waldo Road to Marion, Ohio.

From there it continued northwest along the route of present Ohio 423 and U.S. 23 to the present town of Little Sandusky, and followed the Sandusky River to Upper Sandusky. From Upper Sandusky, the Scioto Trail continued north to the Lenape town of Tymochtee, and continued north-northeast along the west side of the Sandusky River to present Tiffin, Ohio. From Tiffin, the trail led due north, and then followed the Sandusky River north to the Wyandot town of Junquindundeh or Lower Sandusky at present Fremont, Ohio. The trail then continued along both banks of the Sandusky River to join the Lake Trail, Great Trail and Watershed Trail, near the western end of Sandusky Bay.

R. *The Petquotting Trail*

The Petquotting Trail was a north-south trail that connected the Lenape village of Hell Town on the Clear Fork of the Mohican River west of present Loudonville, Ohio, with the Lake Trail where it crossed the Huron River near present Milan, Ohio. The Moravian mission settlement of New Salem was located on the Huron River just north of present Milan. The Ohio Indians called the Huron River the Petquotting, after the Lenape name "pay-ka-tunk," or "high round hill," and the Moravian mission settlement was also sometime referred to as Petquotting.

The trail began in the north at the Lake Trail near the mouth of the Huron River, and proceeded south through present Huron, Ohio, then past the site of the Moravian mission village of New Salem on the east bank of the river, and passed north and west of present Milan, Ohio, to the confluence of the East and West Branches of the Huron River. The trail paralleled the East Branch of the Huron River west of present Norwalk, Ohio, and continued in a southeasterly direction to present North Fairfield, then veered easterly to join the

Vermillion River at present Fitchville, Ohio. From there the trail followed the Vermillion River to southeast of present Savannah, Ohio, and joined Lehigh Mill Creek and paralleled it south to its confluence with the Jerome Fork. The trail followed the Jerome Fork east of present Ashland, passed present Jeromesville and joined the Mohican River, which it followed to present Loudonville, Ohio. The trail then led west through Loudonville to the Black Fork of the Mohican River, and followed the Black Fork southwest to its confluence with the Clear Fork, where Hell Town was located.

S. *The Walhonding Trail*

The Walhonding Trail provided a direct route between the Lenape villages in the Muskingum-Tuscarawas-Walhonding Rivers area with the Great Trail, the Petquotting Trail, the Owl River Trail, and the Scioto Trail.

From the forks of the Muskingum, the trail followed the Walhonding River past the confluence with Killbuck Creek to about a mile past present Warsaw, where it crossed to the north side of the Walhonding River. It continued across the Mohican River and followed the north bank of the Walhonding River and joined the course of present U.S. 36, following it westerly to present Howard, where the Lenape village of Coasoskis was located. From there it followed the north bank of the Kokosing River to present Mount Vernon, Ohio, where it crossed the river, and continued southwest to present Centerburg. From there, the trail followed present U.S. 36 to Perfect Creek, which the trail followed to Big Walnut Creek and Galena, Ohio, and then southwest to join the Scioto Trail at the confluence of the Olentangy and Scioto Rivers in present Columbus, Ohio.

T. *The Upper Sandusky Trail*

The Upper Sandusky Trail was mentioned by captive James Smith in his journal about his captivity.[6] According to Smith, the trail's southwestern terminus was at Upper Sandusky, from which it led east-northeast to present Osceola, Ohio, and then followed the north bank of Broken Sword Creek south of New Washington, Ohio, to present Plymouth, Ohio, where it crossed the Great Trail. From there it continued northeast to present Fitchville, Ohio, where it connected with the Watershed Trail.

U. *The Pickawillany Trail*

The Pickawillany Trail connected the Scioto Trail and Warriors' Path at Lower Shawnee Town at the mouth of the Scioto River with the Miami town of Pickawillany on the Great Miami River north of present Piqua, Ohio.

The trail's southern terminus was about one and three-quarter miles southwest of the mouth of the Scioto River, from which it followed Careys Run north and continued along the ridgeline northwest through present Cynthiana, Ohio, and northwest along the route of present Barrett Mill Road to Rainsboro, Ohio. From there the trail led northwest through Highland, Ohio, to Port William, crossed Caesar Creek, and continued to Cedarville. From Cedarville, the trail veered northwest and crossed over the Little Miami River at its confluence with Yellow Springs Creek. Then it continued northwest and crossed the Mad River between present Dayton and Springfield, Ohio, and then veered north to present Saint Paris, Ohio. From there the trail led west-northwest to Pickawillany.

V. The Shawnee-Miami Trail

The Shawnee-Miami Trail connected the Scioto Trail near Maguck with the Miami village of Pickawillany. From Maguck the trail led northwest along present Ohio 56 to London, Ohio. From London, the trail continued northwest to pass about three miles south of present Urbana to cross the Mad River at its confluence with Nettle Creek, where Ohio 55 crosses the Mad River. From there it followed Nettle Creek to where it met present U.S. 36, and then followed the course of U.S. 36 to Pickawillany.

W. The Miami Trail

The Miami Trail entered Ohio from the south at present Cincinnati, and followed present U.S. 42 north-northeast to Lebanon, Ohio. From there the trail continued north between the Great Miami and Little Miami Rivers, and passed southwest of Centerville, Ohio. The trail then veered northeast to pass east of present Dayton and turned northwest to present Troy, Ohio, where the trail crossed the Great Miami, and followed the Great Miami River north to Pickawillany. From Pickawillany, the trail continued northwest following present Ohio 66 through Houston, Fort Loramie, and Montezuma, and across the present Ohio state line to present Fort Wayne, Indiana.

X. The Wabash Trail

The Wabash Trail's southern terminus was at the Mouth of the Great Miami River west of present Cincinnati. It followed the right bank of the Great Miami River to present Hamilton, Ohio, where it crossed to the west bank and continued north along the river to Seven Mile Creek. It followed Seven Mile Creek to present Eaton, and then followed the course of present U.S. 127 to Greenville. From Greenville, the trail followed Ohio 49 to present Fort Recovery, where it joined the Wabash River and followed it for about a mile before proceeding directly to present Fort Wayne, Indiana.

Y. The Maumee Trail

The Maumee Trail began at the point where the Great Trail crossed the Maumee River at present Toledo, Ohio. It followed the north bank of the Maumee River southwest along present Ohio 295 through Maumee and Waterville and crossed to the south bank of the river at present Grand Rapids. It continued on the south bank along the present Miami Valley Scenic Byway, Ohio 110, to Napoleon, where it recrossed the river to the north side. The trail followed the river past Girty Island and continued along the river through Florida, Independence, and present Defiance, where the trail again crossed the river to the south side, then crossed the Auglaize River, and continued along the south shore of the Maumee River to present Fort Wayne, Indiana.

Z. *The Auglaize Trail*

The Auglaize Trail connected the Miami Trail from Fort Loramie with the Black Swamp Trail and the Maumee Trail at present Defiance, Ohio. The trail led north from Fort Loramie through present Minster and New Bremen, Saint Marys, and northeast of Spencerville, where the trail joined the Auglaize River and paralleled it through present Delphos, Fort Jennings, and Cloverdale. Just north of Cloverdale, the trail joined the Auglaize River and followed the west bank north to present Defiance, Ohio.

AA. *The Wappatomica Trail*

The Wappatomica Trail was a forked trail with its northern terminus at Upper Sandusky. It had one southwestern terminus at Pickawillany and another at the Forks of the Miami River and Mad River. From Upper Sandusky, the trail led southwest along the route of present Ohio 67 to present Marseilles, where it crossed Tymochtee Creek and continued along the course of present County Road 265 and Ohio 274 to Rushsylvania, Ohio. At Rushsylvania, the trail split, with the western fork heading southwest to join the Great Miami River at present Port Jefferson, Ohio, from which it followed the river to Pickawillany. From Rushsylvania, the easterly trail proceeded south to join the Mad River, which it followed south past present Zanesville in Logan County, Ohio, to the Shawnee village of Wappatomica, on the west bank of the river, about 2.25 miles south of Zanesville. From Wappatomica, the trail continued along the Mad River to its confluence with the Great Miami River at present Dayton, Ohio.

BB. *The Black Swamp Trail*

The Black Swamp Trail connected the Indian towns at the confluence of the Maumee and Auglaize Rivers at present Defiance, Ohio, with the Wyandot towns at Upper Sandusky. From Defiance, the trail led southeast along the course of the present Ayersville-Pleasant Bend Road through Ayersville to Pleasant Bend. From there the trail continued southeast through Leipsic, Ohio, and southeast to the Blanchard River, which it followed to present Findlay, Ohio. From Findlay, the trail followed a fairly direct route to present Carey, Ohio, and from there continued along Spring Run and Tymochtee Creek, to present Tymochtee, Ohio. From there the trail continued south along the Sandusky River, through Indian Mill to Upper Sandusky.

CC. *The Owl River Trail*

The Owl River Trail connected the Kokosing River with the Sandusky River at Upper Sandusky. The Kokosing and Mohican Rivers come together west of present Walhonding,

Ohio, to form the Walhonding River. Kokosing derives from the Lenape word *gokhos* (owl), and Kokosing means "where there are owls," or "place of owls," so it was natural to refer to the Kokosing as "Owl River." The Owl River trail connected with the Walhonding Trail at the Lenape village of Coashokis, at the mouth of Jelloway Creek on the Kokoshing River about a third of a mile east of present Howard, Ohio. The trail continued through present Mount Vernon, Ohio, then veered northwest to present Lucerne, Ohio, and then followed Ohio 95 to Mount Gilead, Ohio. From Mount Gilead, the trail continued northwest through present Wyandot, Ohio, where the trail veered west to Little Sandusky. The trail then followed the Little Sandusky River north to join the Sandusky River to Upper Sandusky.

DD. *The Killbuck Trail*

The Killbuck Trail was a short connector between the Walhonding Trail at the mouth of Killbuck Creek, where White Woman's Town was located, and its north terminus at the intersection of the Great Trail and the Cuyahoga War Trail at present Wooster, Ohio. The trail generally followed Killbuck Creek north on the east bank through the present towns of Killbuck and Millersburg, then passed west of Holmesville to present Wooster, Ohio, where it met the Cuyahoga War Trail and the Great Trail.

EE. *The Mohican Trail*

The Mohican Trail was a subsidiary or connecting trail that connected the Walhonding Trail with the Cuyahoga War Trail and the Petquotting Trail to the north. Its southern terminus was where the Walhonding and Mohican Rivers join at present Nellie, Ohio. From there it followed the heights along the Mohican River north to the confluence with the Lake Fork of the Mohican River southeast of present Loudonville, Ohio. The trail followed the Lake Fork of the Mohican River to west of Lakeville, Ohio, and continued north to the Jerome Fork, which it followed to present Jeromesville, Ohio, where it met the Cuyahoga War Trail.

FF. *The Huron Trail*

The Huron Trail ran from Upper Sandusky to present Fitchville, essentially paralleling the Upper Sandusky Trail to the north. The more southerly course of the Huron Trail provided a shorter route to the northeast for the Wyandot and Lenape villages to the south of Upper Sandusky, and also for the towns to the south along the Petquotting Trail.

From Upper Sandusky, the trail generally followed the old Lincoln Highway east to present Oceola, Ohio. From there the trail veered to the northeast and proceeded to New Washington, where it followed the course of the present railroad to Plymouth, Ohio. From Plymouth, the trail proceeded northeastward to near present Fitchville, Ohio, where it met the Watershed Trail.

PART II

Towns, Villages and
Posts of 18th-Century Ohio

Seven

The Moravian Mission Communities of Ohio

"The Great Spirit is everywhere; He hears whatever is in our minds and our hearts, and it is not necessary to speak to Him in a loud voice."—Black Elk

There were scores of Native American villages in present Ohio during the 18th century, and among them were the Moravian mission communities that were first established in 1772 and existed until 1823. They were an important aspect of Ohio's Native American history, and it's appropriate they are included here. The nine mission villages are grouped together, followed by the other Indian villages established in Ohio. In effect, the Moravian communities were a parallel facet of Ohio's 18th-century Native American history and discussing them separately provides a better understanding of their existence. The non–Christian Indian towns and villages in Ohio follow this section.

The Moravian Mission Communities

The accomplishments of the Moravian missionaries and their establishment of Moravian Christian mission communities among the Indians are an important part of 18th-century Ohio history, and a brief overview provides a better perspective of their activities. The Moravian Church, formally named *Unitas Fratrum* (Unity of the Brethren), dates back to the Bohemian Reformation of the 15th century, which makes it one of the oldest Protestant denominations. It began in 1457 in the Bohemian crown lands of Moravia, which are now located in the Czech Republic. From 1526 until 1918, Moravia was under Hapsburg rule as part of the Austro-Hungarian Empire, and German was the predominant language in that area.

The Moravian Church emphasized missionary work, and their emissaries traveled world-wide to spread their faith. They first traveled to Saint Thomas in the West Indies in 1732 to work among black slaves, and then on to four continents. In 1735, they established their first North America center of operations in Savannah, Georgia, but when that community failed in 1741, they moved their headquarters to Bethlehem, Pennsylvania. In 1744, the Brethren, as they referred to themselves, began their first Indian language school, and David Zeisberger (1721–1808) was among the students who learned the Lenape language. The following year, 1745, Zeisberger accompanied Christian Frederick Post (1718–1785) to the Mohawk River in New York, where they learned the Mohawk language in a village whose chief was Theyanoquin, also known as King Hendrick (c. 1691–1755).[1] King George's War (1740–1748) was raging along the New York frontier, and both Post and Zeisberger came under suspicion by the British authorities, who arrested and accused them of being French spies. They were imprisoned for fifty-one days before the charges were dropped, and when they were released, they remained with the Mohawks to continue mastering their language. Next, Zeisberger and Augustus Gottlieb Spangenberg (1704–1792) moved to an Onondaga village near present Syracuse, New York, to also learn the Onondaga language.

In 1746, Zeisberger and missionary John Martin Mack (1715–1784) established a mission named Gnadenhütten,[2] "huts of grace," on Mahoning Creek, near present Lehighton, Pennsylvania. Thirty years later, in 1776, Zeisberger would establish another mission village named Gnadenhütten in Ohio, which we will describe in detail. After Gnadenhütten on Mahoning Creek, Mack established a mission at Shamokin, at present Sunbury, Pennsylvania. In 1749, twenty-seven-year-old Zeisberger was ordained a full deacon and authorized to carry on full-fledged missionary work. At the same time, he was placed in charge of the Shamokin mission.

In 1755, at the start of the French and Indian War, the Gnadenhütten mission on Mahoning Creek was destroyed by Indians allied with the French, and ten white mission workers were killed in the attack. Zeisberger escaped almost certain death, because he arrived mere hours after the attackers had departed. The survivors of Gnadenhütten, along with the Shamokin community, abandoned the villages and established new towns called Nain and Wechquanach, closer to Bethlehem. However, in 1763, during Pontiac's Rebellion, Nain and Wechquanach were both destroyed by hostile Indians, and Zeisberger led the 125 Indian converts who survived the attack to Philadelphia, where they were placed in protective custody.

For some reason, most likely a reluctance on the part of the Iroquois to accept missionaries, the Moravian Brethren ended their efforts among the Six Nations. They began instead to direct their energies toward the Lenape, who provided a more hospitable welcome. Henceforth, most of the Moravian missionary work was among the Lenape in western Pennsylvania and Ohio.

In 1765, Zeisberger and ninety Indian converts established Friedenhütten, "huts of peace," a mission community on the Susquehanna River at present Wyasuling, Pennsylvania. In 1768, Zeisberger expanded his mission efforts by establishing a mission village called Goschgoschunk, "union of waters," near the headwaters of the Allegheny River at present Tionesta, Pennsylvania. The following year, 1769, he established another mission called Lawunakhannek, "northerly stream place," which was located about seven and a half miles up the Allegheny near present East Hickory, Pennsylvania. Two years later, in 1770, Zeisberger moved to the Beaver River area and founded Friedenstadt, "Town of Peace" across the Allegheny River from present West Pittsburg in Lawrence County, Pennsylvania.[3]

In 1771, the year after Zeisberger established Friedenstadt, the Grand Lenape Council at Gekelemukpechunk, "the place near the river bend,"[4] or New Comers Town on the Tuscarawas River in Ohio, sent messengers with a beaded belt[5] to Friedenstadt, inviting the Moravians to establish a mission village on the Tuscarawas River in Ohio. It appears the Lenape were more interested in whatever magic the Moravians might possess than in Christianity. The previous year, a smallpox epidemic ravaged the Lenape communities in Ohio, and the tribal elders at Gekelemukpechunk declared that the epidemic was caused by witchcraft. The elders also said the Lenape needed a more powerful magic than that of the witches to counter the contagion, and they hoped that having Christians with their formidable magic nearby would be beneficial. In addition to promising the missionaries their choice of land on which to build their village, Netawatwees, the principal Lenape chief, guaranteed that the Christian community would be able to live in peace and safety.[6]

In response to the wampum belt invitation, David Zeisberger visited Gekelemuk-pechunk in March 1771 and stayed in the home of Netawatwees. Zeisberger agreed to es-

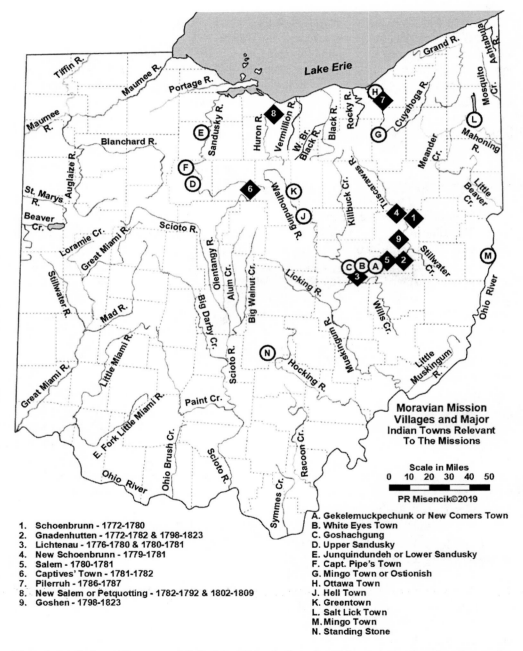

1. Schoenbrunn - 1772-1780
2. Gnadenhutten - 1772-1782 & 1798-1823
3. Lichtenau - 1776-1780 & 1780-1781
4. New Schoenbrunn - 1779-1781
5. Salem - 1780-1781
6. Captives' Town - 1781-1782
7. Pilerruh - 1786-1787
8. New Salem or Petquotting - 1782-1792 & 1802-1809
9. Goshen - 1798-1823

A. Gekelemuckpechunk or New Comers Town
B. White Eyes Town
C. Goshachgung
D. Upper Sandusky
E. Junquindundeh or Lower Sandusky
F. Capt. Pipe's Town
G. Mingo Town or Ostionish
H. Ottawa Town
J. Hell Town
K. Greentown
L. Salt Lick Town
M. Mingo Town
N. Standing Stone

Moravian mission villages established in Ohio during the 18th century, also showing major Indian towns that were relevant to the Moravian villages.

tablish a mission community in the area, but while at Gekelemukpechunk, he preached a sermon about the "corruptness of human nature, and the efficacy of Christ's atonement."[7] Unfortunately, he also disparaged the Lenape cultural beliefs in witchcraft, as well as their belief that sin could only be purged from a person by vomiting. Predictably, his lack of tact offended the Lenape shamans and healers, and no sooner did Zeisberger depart for Friedenstadt than the affronted medicine men campaigned to besmirch and condemn him. They denounced him as a "notorious deceiver"[8] and warned the community of the direst consequences if Zeisberger and his Christians were permitted to settle in the area. Fortunately, Glickhican (c. 1730–1782), a respected warrior and tribal spokesman at Gekelemukpechunk, was able to counteract much of the negativism toward Zeisberger and the Moravians. Besides being an esteemed leader, Glickhican was a Christian. Two years earlier, in 1769, he had visited Lawunakhannek with the purpose of driving the Moravians from the area, but first he listened to Zeisberger preach. He was so impressed that he converted to Christianity and was one of the leaders at Gekelemukpechunk who, in 1770, invited Zeisberger to the Tuscarawas River.

At a conference with Moravian church authorities and Indian converts, Zeisberger proposed to relocate the Pennsylvania missions to the Tuscarawas River in Ohio. His request was approved, and in the spring of 1772, Zeisberger informed Netawatwees of their planned move. That year Zeisberger led the first group of converts into Ohio, which was the beginning of the Moravian mission experience there. Zeisberger's first mission settlement in Ohio would be called Schönbrunn [Schoenbrunn] or "beautiful spring."

For purposes of historical continuity, we've listed the Ohio Moravian missions chronologically as they were established.

Schoenbrunn (*Schönbrunn*),[9] "Beautiful Spring" (1772–1777).
Now: New Philadelphia, Tuscarawas County
(40°27'51.86"N–81°25'7.06"W)

On March 10, 1772, en route to the principal Lenape village of Gekelemukpechunk, Zeisberger and his party, which included eleven converts, several Indian helpers and some children, passed through an area of rich bottom land with a large spring and an adjacent plateau. The site was on the east side of the Tuscarawas River[10] about fifteen miles northeast of Gekelemukpechunk, and Zeisberger recognized it as an excellent location for a town. While Zeisberger wanted to be near the Lenape villages, he didn't want to be too near, because he was concerned the non–Christian Indians would have a negative influence on his converts. Zeisberger differentiated by calling the non–Christian Indians "natives" or "wild Indians," and he referred to the baptized Indians as "Christian Indians" or "converts." By the same token, the non–Christian Indians and many of the whites often referred to the Christian Indians as "praying Indians."

Netawatwees agreed to allow the Moravians to build their mission on the parcel of land they selected, and in April, Zeisberger returned to Pennsylvania to bring an additional five Indian families to Ohio. On May 4, 1772, the Christian community began to clear land, plant crops, and erect temporary shelters. Rev. Edmund De Schweinitz (1825–1887), author of the *Life and Times of Zeisberger*, visited the area in the early 1860s and described the topography: "On both sides of the river, were bottom lands interspersed with small lakes, reaching on the western bank, to the foot of a precipitous bluff, on the eastern, to a declivity not quite so high. Near the base of the latter, the spring gushed in a copious stream from beneath the roots of a cluster of lindens and elms, and fed a lake nearly a mile long, united by an outlet with the Tuscarawas. Both lake and outlet were navigable so that canoes could be paddled from the river to the very foot of the declivity."[11]

Work on the village continued uninterrupted, and by June 9, the mission house was completed. Normally, the traditional Moravian missionary style village was laid out in the form of a cross, with the main street oriented east and west, and the church located in the center. However, the topography at the site on the Tuscarawas only allowed a layout in the shape of a "T" with the church opposite the intersection facing north. The 36 × 40-foot church was constructed of squared timbers, with a shingled roof, a cupola and bell, and it was dedicated on September 19, 1772. The church was also the meeting house, with space to seat about 300 people, and it had four glass windows.[12] Zeisberger's house was next to the church on the east side, and on the west side of the church was the home of missionary Johann Jungmann (1720–1808). Jungmann was born in Hochenheim in the Palatinate, and in 1731, at the age of eleven, he emigrated with his father to North America. He joined the Moravians, which greatly disappointed his family, and in 1772 he went to Schoenbrunn as a missionary, where he served as assistant pastor under Zeisberger.

The schoolhouse was built on the northeast corner of the intersection, opposite Zeisberger's home, and the dwellings of the rest of the community lined both sides of the two streets. When it came time to name the village, four names were proposed: Bethel, Goshen, Schoenbrunn, and Enon. The name Schoenbrunn was simply chosen by lot. As the population increased, another east-west street was added. In 1772, missionary Johann Ettwein (1721–1802) described the village as having 40 residence lots that were "three rods wide and six rods deep," or 49'6" × 99' (4,900.5 square feet).[13]

Netawatwees met with the missionaries several times during the construction of Schoenbrunn, and during one meeting he generously granted the Christian community an additional large parcel of land that stretched southward from the mouth of Stillwater Creek to within two miles of Gekelemukpechunk.[14]

On August 23, 1773, a year after Schoenbrunn was established, the population of the community consisted of 241 souls, of whom 204 were Indian converts and the remaining thirty-seven were missionaries and their families. These included missionaries John Heckewelder and Johann Ettwein. With the village comfortably established, Zeisberger, Heckewelder and Ettwein prepared rules for the community to live by. The rules were the first written civil legislation in present Ohio, and they listed the obligations for residing in the

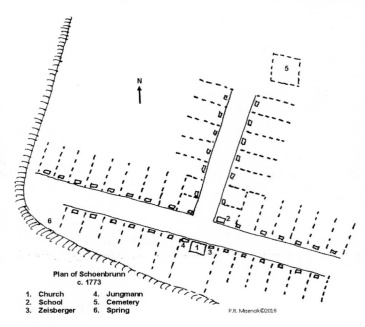

Plan of Schoenbrunn
c. 1773

1. Church   4. Jungmann
2. School   5. Cemetery
3. Zeisberger 6. Spring

P.R. Misencik ©2018

Plan of Schoenbrunn, c. 1773.

village. To live in the community, each person had to promise to conform to the rules, and if a person violated a rule, he or she would be admonished, and if they broke a rule the second time, they were expelled.

I. We will know no other God, but the one only true God, who made us and all creatures, and came into this world in order to save sinners; to Him alone we will pray

II. We will rest from work on the Lord's Day, and attend public service.

III. We will honor father and mother, and when they grow old and needy we will do for them what we can.

IV. No person shall get leave to dwell with us until our teachers have given their consent, and the helpers (native assistants) have examined him.

V. We will have nothing to do with thieves, murderers, whoremongers, adulterers, or drunkards.

VI. We will not take part in dances, sacrifices, heathenish festivals, or games.

VII. We will use no Tschappish or witchcraft when hunting.

VIII. We renounce and abhor all tricks, lies and deceits of Satan.

IX. We will be obedient to our teachers and to the helpers who are appointed to order in our meetings in the town and fields.

X. We will not be idle nor scold, nor beat one another, nor tell lies.

XI. Whoever injures the property of his neighbor shall make restitution.

XII. A man shall have but one wife—shall love her and provide for her and his children. A woman shall have but one husband, be obedient to him, care for her children, and be cleanly in all things.

XIII. We shall not admit rum, or any other intoxicating liquor into our towns. If strangers or traders bring intoxicating liquors, the helpers shall take it from them and not restore it until the owners are ready to leave the place.

XIV. No one shall contract debts with traders, or receive goods to sell for traders, unless the helpers give their consent.

XV. Whoever goes hunting, or on a journey, shall inform the minister or stewards.

XVI. Young persons shall not marry without the consent of their parents, and minister.

XVII. Whenever the stewards or helpers appoint a time to make fences or perform other work for the public good, we will assist and do as we are bid.

XVIII. Whenever corn is needed to entertain strangers, or sugar for love-feasts, we will freely contribute from our stores.[15]

XIX. We will not go to war, and will not buy anything of warriors taken in war.[16]

Other rules were later added that were applicable to daily meetings, administration of schools, and protocol for visitors to the community, as well as providing aid to the sick, needy, and troubled, and requiring that the poorest members of the community be provided the same food and clothing as the wealthiest members.

Schoenbrunn thrived, and based on the number of additional dwellings built each year, there appears to have been a steady increase in Indian converts. Records indicate that in 1772, thirty-nine Indian cabins were built; in 1773, ten more were constructed, followed by ten in 1774, twelve in 1775, and twelve in 1776, for a total of 83 Indian cabins. For sustenance, there was a thirty-acre fenced communal cornfield, as well as individual garden plots by each home.

The Indian men trapped and traded, while the women tended the cornfields, orchards, and livestock. All of the converts were given education, whereby they learned to read and write in German, English and Lenape. The school held as many as 100 children and adults at its peak. In 1775, there were 263 residents living in Schoenbrunn.

In 1772, a Lenape assistant to Zeisberger named Joshua arrived at Schoenbrunn with a party of Mohicans. On September 18, 1772, he began to lay out a second village on the west side of the Tuscarawas about four miles upriver near present Dover, Ohio. Joshua referred to the new village as "Upper Town." However, Netawatwees intervened and insisted that the new village should be located closer to Gekelemukpechunk, so the Upper Town site was abandoned. On October 9, Joshua began to lay out another mission town on the east side of the Tuscarawas, about seven and a half miles south of Schoenbrunn and eight and a half miles northeast of Gekelemukpechunk. The name chosen for the new town was Gnaden-hütten, or "huts of grace." Work progressed rapidly, and Zeisberger, who was in overall charge of the Ohio missions, conducted the first service at Gnadenhütten on October 17. By April 1773, Friedenstadt, the last remaining mission village in Pennsylvania was closed down, and its remaining residents transferred to Schoenbrunn and Gnadenhütten.

Lord Dunmore's War in 1774 resulted from the escalating violence between British colonists in present Kentucky, including the young frontiersman Daniel Boone, who clashed violently with the Shawnee and Mingo Indians who held treaty rights to hunt in the area south of the Ohio River. The Indians attacked the Kentuckians, and Kentucky frontiersmen struck back. The fighting escalated to the point that John Murray, the 4th Earl of Dunmore, declared war and raised an elite militia force to pacify the Indians.

The Moravian mission villages on the Tuscarawas were involved, because many Shaw-nee and Mingo war parties assembled in the vicinity of the upper Muskingum River west of the Moravian missions, and the Moravians were concerned that their Christian Indians were suspected of taking part in the raids. When it appeared that Lord Dunmore's force was marching toward the Forks of the Muskingum, it was feared that Dunmore intended to attack the neutral Lenape as well as the warlike Shawnee and Mingo. The Lenape were concerned even though the Grand Lenape Council and the new principal Lenape chief White Eyes had publicly declared their neutrality. To complicate matters, there were some young Lenape warriors who wanted to join the fight against the English colonists, especially when the Shawnee taunted the Christian Indians as being cowardly. The taunts caused many of the young, hot-headed Lenape warriors to declare they would never become Christians, and worse, they "flocked to Schoenbrunn; treated the municipal regulations of that orderly village with contempt, and behaved in a most insolent and insulting manner."[17] Fortunately for the Christian Indians and the Moravian villages, Dunmore's force did not reach the upper Muskingum or Tuscarawas Rivers, and the war ended with the defeat of the Indians at the Battle of Point Pleasant on October 10, 1774.

Partly as a result of Dunmore's War, White Eyes convinced the Grand Lenape Council to relocate the main Lenape village westward to the Muskingum. The area would better consolidate all the Lenape, who until then tended to live in smaller independent villages. As a result, the old New Comer's Town or Gekelemukpechunk was abandoned, and in 1775, a new village was established at the Forks of the Muskingum in present Coshocton, Ohio. With the move of the Lenape principal village, old Netawatwees, who still had considerable stature, along with his grandson Killbuck, granted Zeisberger a tract of land on the Muskingum on which to establish yet another mission village.

The American Revolutionary War, which began six months later in April 1775, had more of an impact on the Moravian mission towns in Ohio than Dunmore's War. While the missionaries and the Christian residents at Schoenbrunn and Gnadenhütten attempted to remain neutral and aloof from the hostilities, the non–Christian Lenape, for the most part, sided with the British. The Lenape believed it was a chance to escape the domination of the Iroquois and exact a measure of revenge against the Pennsylvanians for taking their homeland. They also believed the British afforded them the best chance of maintaining a homeland in Ohio. It wasn't long before the non–Christian Lenape who were allied with the British visited the mission towns to persuade the Christian Indians to join the British side. Those visits did not escape the notice of the Americans, who began to view the Christian Indians with suspicion. Ironically, the refusal of the Christian Indians to join the British cause led the British to suspect they were sympathetic to the Americans. In effect, they were regarded with suspicion by both factions.

Once again, the Moravians and their Christian Indians found it difficult to convince either of the combatants that they desired to remain neutral and left in peace. The British and their Indian allies questioned the neutrality of the Moravian and Indian residents at Schoenbrunn and Gnadenhütten, and the American faction also doubted the loyalty of the mission inhabitants.

In an effort to distance themselves from the warring factions, Zeisberger decided to accept Netawatwees' parcel of land on the Muskingum River and create a new village named Lichtenau, or "pasture of light." The residents of Schoenbrunn began the gradual relocation to Lichtenau in 1776, and by 1777 Schoenbrunn was completely abandoned, never to be repopulated. To prevent non–Christians from using the Schoenbrunn church, Zeisberger burned it to the ground on April 19, 1777.

Gnadenhütten, "Huts of Grace" (1772–1782 and 1798–1823).
Now: Gnadenhutten, Tuscarawas County (40°21'15.68"N, 81°26'5.47"W)

Shortly after the Moravian mission village of Schoenbrunn was established in 1772, Joshua, a Lenape assistant of David Zeisberger, laid out the new town of Gnadenhütten, or "huts of grace," on the east side of the Tuscarawas River at present Gnadenhutten, Ohio, about 7.7 miles south of Schoenbrunn. Zeisberger held the first service at Gnadenhütten on October 17, 1772. As mentioned previously, Zeisberger was not inclined to locate the Christian Indians too near to the non–Christian towns for fear his converts would be enticed back to their heathen ways. As a result, he established Gnadenhütten about 8.5 miles northeast of Gekelemukpechunk, which apparently satisfied Netawatwees.

By April of 1773, the remainder of the Christian Indians from the Moravian mission settlements in Pennsylvania were relocated to either Schoenbrunn or Gnadenhütten, and both villages had a complement of missionaries. The missionaries at Gnadenhütten were John Jacob Schmick and John Roth, who were accompanied by their wives. David Zeisberger, John Heckewelder, and Johann Jungmann, along with Jungmann's wife, were based at Schoenbrunn. Zeisberger was single at the time and would wed the former Suzanna Lecron in 1781. John Heckewelder was also single and married the former Sarah Ohneberg in 1780.

Most Indians who visited the missions were surprised to see the Christian Indians happily tending fields and living peacefully, but not all the Lenape were happy with their Christian neighbors. At first the introduction of Christianity merely created some confusion among the non–Christian Lenape, but when one of their esteemed leaders named

Echpalawahund left Gekelemukpechunk and joined the Christian community, many of the non–Christians became agitated and vocal in demanding that the missionaries "be banished from the country, as disturbers of the peace and hostile to their customs and sacrifices."[18] Fortunately for the success of the missions, the attitudes of the more tolerant Lenape prevailed.

Because of the increased friction between Indians and whites, Lord Dunmore's War in 1774 caused additional consternation among the residents of Gnadenhütten. The Shawnee and Mingo hunting grounds south of the Ohio River, which had been guaranteed to the Indians by treaty, were being encroached on by white settlements, and each side began to attack the other. It soon escalated into a full-blown war. While the Christian Lenape and Moravian missionaries publicly declared their neutrality, the practice of the hostile Indians forming war parties in the vicinity of the Tuscarawas missions worried the Moravians that the Christian Indians would be viewed as complicit. Even worse, many of the hostile Shawnee and Mingo, and even some of the non–Christian Lenape, taunted the Christian Indians as cowards. Dunmore's War ended after five months, but the American Revolutionary War created additional concerns for the inhabitants of the Christian villages.

In 1774, just prior to the Revolution, White Eyes was selected as principal chief of the Lenape, replacing the ninety-four-year-old Netawatwees, and in 1775, he successfully convinced the Grand Council to relocate the principal village from Gekelemukpechunk, or New Comers Town, to a new location at the Forks of the Muskingum in present Coshocton, Ohio. The new village was called Goschachgunk (black bear town), which was likely based on Conshaké, the old abandoned Wyandot town that was located nearby.

With the move to Goschachgunk, old Netawatwees, who still had stature among the Lenape, asked the Moravians to relocate closer to the Lenapes' new principal village. The concerns of Zeisberger regarding the Revolutionary War caused him to accept Netawatwees's offer to relocate, which put some additional distance between the Moravian villages and the war in the east. The village of Lichtenau ("pasture of light") was established on April 12, 1776, and was located about two and a half miles south of Goschachgunk. It took over a year to relocate all of the residents from Schoenbrunn and Gnadenhütten to Lichtenau. Even though Schoenbrunn ceased to exist as a mission town, Gnadenhütten remained active until 1778, when the last residents moved to Lichtenau. Schoenbrunn was never reoccupied by the Christians, but the Moravian missionaries and Christian Indians moved back to Gnadenhütten about a year after they left the town.

Unfortunately, the move to Lichtenau did not alleviate the mistrust of the British and Americans toward the Moravian Christian community, and the increasing hostility of both factions convinced the mission leaders to once again pull up stakes and search for a more suitable location. Thinking it best to return to the Tuscarawas River, a contingent of Moravians and Indians, under the leadership of William Edwards, left Lichtenau in April 1779 and reoccupied Gnadenhütten. In December of 1779, David Zeisberger led another contingent from Lichtenau up the Tuscarawas to about a mile south of present New Philadelphia, where they laid out a village called New Schoenbrunn. The village was on the west bank of the Tuscarawas about a mile west-northwest of original Schoenbrunn village. In the spring of 1780, John Heckewelder led the remainder of the Lichtenau villagers to establish yet another new mission town called Salem on the west bank of the Tuscarawas near present Port Washington, Ohio.

By the middle of 1781, the British and their Indian allies, were increasingly suspicious of the residents at the Tuscarawas River settlements,[19] so they decided to forcibly relocate them to the Sandusky River area, where they could be supervised and kept from mischief. In August of 1781, Loyalist Captain Matthew Elliott (1739–1814), with a force of about 300 warriors, mostly Lenape and Wyandot braves with some Shawnee, Ojibwe, and Ottawas, arrived at the mission settlements to take the Moravians and their Christian community west to the Sandusky River. Zeisberger argued for several days against leaving, and the Indians lost patience. Tired of Zeisberger's reluctance to move, a group of Wyandots took John Heckewelder and Gottlob Sensemann prisoner, stripped them and threatened to torture and burn them to death. At the same time, another group of Indians swarmed the missionary homes and plundered them. It was apparent to Zeisberger that resistance was futile and potentially fatal, so he informed Elliott they would peacefully relocate to the Sandusky River. Heckewelder and Sensemann were released, and the Indians returned some of the plunder, including the missionaries' clothing.

They departed the Tuscarawas missions on September 11, 1781, and arrived at the Sandusky River on October 1, where they were told to establish their village in the area of the mouth of Broken Sword Creek, on the Sandusky River about six and a half miles southeast of Upper Sandusky. The group took temporary shelter in the huts of an abandoned Wyandot village while they constructed more permanent shelters at a site about a mile farther upstream on the Sandusky River where good timber was available. By October 12, they had most of their "small and slightly built"[20] shelters under roof, and because they had been involuntarily relocated, the missionaries named their new community "Captives' Town."

It was too late in the year to plant crops, and though they were able to purchase some corn at exorbitant prices from traders, most of the Indians were reduced to roaming the woods in search of edible roots and wild potatoes. By January of 1782, the Indians were starving, so about 150 decided to return to Gnadenhütten and the other Tuscarawas mission villages to look for food and anything else they could bring back to Captives' Town. About a hundred Indians went to Gnadenhütten, and the rest went to search the other mission villages.

Unfortunately, when the Indians reached Gnadenhütten, they encountered a force of about 160 heavily armed Pennsylvania militia, under the command of Lieutenant Colonel David Williamson, who were on an expedition against hostile Indians in Ohio. The Pennsylvanians accused the Indians of taking part in the raids against American settlements and took them prisoner. The Indians, of course, denied the charges, but the militia locked the Indians in two buildings at Gnadenhütten while they voted on what to do with them. Most voted to kill the Indians, but sixteen of the militia were opposed, and didn't take part in the murders. Obadiah Holmes, Jr., one of the militia members, later implied that Williamson was opposed to the killing, but apparently did not try to stop it from happening.

When the captives were told they would be put to death the following morning, they asked for sufficient time to prepare by praying and singing hymns. On the morning of March 8, 1782, the Indians were taken to two buildings, which were designated "killing houses"; the men were placed in one and the women and children in the other. The prisoners were bound, hit on the heads with mallets and tomahawks, and then scalped. Twenty-eight men, twenty-nine women, and thirty-nine children were murdered, but two young boys, one of whom was scalped, somehow survived to tell what happened. Among those killed was Welepachtschiechen, or Captain Johnny, who was the chief of the Turkey phratry. The militia next looted the town, and their booty of furs, pewter, tea, clothing, and personal effects required eighty pack horses to carry away. Next the militia piled the bodies in the mission buildings and burned the village to the ground.

Obadiah Holmes, Jr., who did not take part in the killings, later wrote in his biography: "Obadiah Holmes Jr. on that fatal ground voted with the sixteen against the massacre and rescued at the risk of personal danger to himself from the high passions aroused in others and took home with him and reared and cared for him ten years an Indian boy of seven years of age."[21] Obadiah also wrote that at least one of the murderers suffered remorse. "One Nathan Rollins & brother had had a father & uncle killed, took the lead in murdering the Indians & Williamson was opposed to it; & Nathan Rollins had tomahawked nineteen of the poor Moravians, & after it was over he sat down & cried & said it was no satisfaction for the loss of his father & uncle after all."[22]

On March 23, 1782, Zeisberger at Captives' Town wrote in his diary, "To-day we have the first trustworthy news of the horrible murder of our Indian brethren at Gnadenhütten and Salem, March 7 and 8."[23] After the massacre, George Washington told American soldiers to avoid being captured alive, because he feared the hostile Lenape would savagely retaliate against captured Americans. That same year, 1782, Colonel William Crawford, a close friend of Washington, was captured by the Lenape near Upper Sandusky, and even though Crawford had not been present at Gnadenhütten, he was horribly tortured to death in retaliation for the massacre. On August 11, 1810, twenty-eight years after the Gnadenhütten massacre, the Shawnee chief Tecumseh told then Indiana territorial governor William Henry Harrison, "You recall the time when the Jesus Indians of the Delawares lived near the Americans, and had confidence in their promises of friendship, and thought they were secure, yet the Americans murdered all the men, women, and children, even as they prayed to Jesus."[24]

In 1783, although 4,000 acres surrounding Gnadenhütten had been reserved for the Indians as an act of indemnity, Congress opened the area to white settlement. In 1798, Zeisberger and many of the Christian Indians returned to the Tuscarawas from Canada, where they had moved in 1791 to escape the Ohio Indian Wars. Zeisberger reestablished Gnadenhütten, while he built the new village of Goshen about seven miles north.

Very few new Indian converts joined the Moravian mission communities, and the number of Christian Indians diminished due to deaths, forced removals, or simply because they decided to return to the wild. John Heckewelder had previously retired from missionary work in 1786, and with the deaths of missionaries William Edwards in 1801 and David Zeisberger in 1808, the Ohio mission communities were left without any effective leadership. In 1823, the remaining residents at Gnadenhütten gave up their title to the old mission village, but the Society retained some land including the graveyard on the Gnadenhütten tract and some private homes in the villages.

Lichtenau, "Pasture of Light" (1776–1780), later Indaochaic (1780–c. 1781).
Now: Coshocton, Coshocton County (40°14'23.86"N–81°52'16.76"W)

In 1774, the Grand Lenape Council appointed the young chief White Eyes to replace the ninety-four-year-old Netawatwees as principal chief of the Lenape, and in 1775, the Grand Lenape Council decided to consolidate the Lenape Indians around a new principal village. In 1776, they abandoned Gekelemukpechunk at present Newcomerstown, and established their new main village called Goschachgunk (black bear town) at the Forks of the Muskingum in present Cochocton, Ohio.[25]

Even though he was replaced as the head chief, Netawatwees still retained considerable power and status among the Lenape, and although he never became a Christian, he liked and respected the Moravian missionaries. When the Lenape established Goschachgunk, Netawatwees and his nephew Killbuck granted David Zeisberger a nearby tract of land upon which to establish another Christian Indian village. Zeisberger initially thought it would be good to relocate, because the British and their Indian allies as well as the Americans questioned the neutrality of the Moravian and Indian residents at Schoenbrunn and Gnadenhütten. One of the reasons for American distrust was that hostile Indians allied with the British often gathered in the vicinity of Schoenbrunn and Gnadenhütten on their way to conduct raids on American settlements on the Pennsylvania frontier. In the eyes of the Americans, that made the Christian Indians guilty by association. At the same time, the British and their Indian allies believed that the residents of the Moravian settlements were passing military intelligence on to the Americans. As a result of the growing friction, David Zeisberger decided to relocate the Christian settlements farther west to the Muskingum River in an effort to distance themselves from the warring factions. Zeisberger named his new village Lichtenau, or "pasture of light," and it was located about two and a half miles south of the Lenape village of Goschachgunk.

Zeisberger deliberately distanced Lichtenau from Goschachgunk, because he wanted sufficient separation between his Christian community and the non–Christian Indians. Lichtenau was established on Friday, April 12, 1776, with eight families that totaled thirty-five people, including Zeisberger and fellow missionary John Heckewelder. The first Christian service was held there the following day on Saturday, April 13. The village was laid out in the traditional Moravian mission village style in the form of a cross, with the main street oriented east and west and the chapel located in the center where the roads intersected. By Saturday, May 18, 1776, the chapel had been erected in Lichtenau, and the first "sacrament of the Lord's Supper"[26] was celebrated, followed by the baptism of "converts from heathenism."[27] Reverend William Edwards (1724–1801) joined Zeisberger in November 1776. Unlike the German Moravians, Edwards was an Englishman who joined the Moravian sect in 1749, and became a distinguished Moravian missionary among the Indians. The gradual relocation from Schoenbrunn and Gnadenhütten to Lichtenau took more than a year.

Of note, Lichtenau is where the first spelling book was introduced and used in what is now Ohio. The book was written and compiled by David Zeisberger, who had it published in Philadelphia in 1776, and it included lessons written in the Lenape language. Zeisberger's spelling book was published seven years before Noah Webster issued his spelling book in Hartford, Connecticut. Also of interest is that Zeisberger, who was a prolific writer, was forced to write in private and hide his correspondence and journals, because the Indians had been taken advantage of in several treaties, and they were extremely suspicious that "the white man's writing meant the taking of land."[28]

Unfortunately, the move of the Moravians and their Christian Indians to Lichtenau did not alleviate the mistrust of the British and Americans, especially when hostile Mingo and Wyandot warriors from the Sandusky River area used the nearby trails for their warpath against the American settlements. Pursuit of the hostile warriors by American troops led back to the area of the Lichtenau mission village, which circumstantially implicated the peaceful Christian Lenape. Another concern was that Lichtenau lost much of its good relationship with Americans following the deaths of Netawatwees in 1776 and White Eyes in 1778. "Goschachgunk, close by, was now almost constantly infested with painted braves who sought to molest their peace-loving neighbors by robberies, drunkenness in their village, and other outrages."[29]

The hostility of the British and American factions, and the presence of the nearby non–Christian Indians, persuaded the missionary leaders to once again pull up stakes and move to a more stable location. In April 1779, a contingent of Moravians and Indians under the leadership of William Edwards left Lichtenau and reoccupied Gnadenhütten, which had been abandoned the previous year. In December of 1779, David Zeisberger departed Lichtenau with another contingent of Christian Indians and missionaries and traveled up the Tuscarawas to a point about a mile south of the center of present New Philadelphia, where they began to lay out a new town called New Schoenbrunn. The remainder of the Lichtenau villagers departed the Muskingum in the spring of 1780 when John Heckewelder began the new mission town of Salem on the west bank of the Tuscarawas near present Port Washington, Ohio. On March 3, 1780, before leaving Lichtenau, a last service was held in the chapel, and then the chapel was destroyed to prevent it from being used for "heathenish purposes."[30]

After the departure of the last of the Moravian Indians from Lichtenau in 1780, the abandoned village was occupied by non–Christian Lenape, who renamed the town Indaochaic. They were suspected of conducting raids on American settlements in Pennsylvania, and as a result, Lichtenau/Indaochaic and the nearby village of Goschachgunk were destroyed by Colonel Daniel Brodhead's Pennsylvania troops during his Coshocton Expedition of April 1781.

There is some conjecture about the precise location of Lichtenau, but clues to its location can be ascertained from extant documents. Zeisberger described the site of the town as "a broad level of many acres stretched to the foot of the hills, with an almost imperceptible ascent, the river bank swelling out gently toward the stream in the form of an arc."[31] Rev. Edmund De Schweinitz, author of the *Life and Times of Zeisberger*, visited the site of Lichtenau in 1863, and was able to identify the site from relics and written observations of Mr. Samuel Moore, who along with his neighbor Mr. Samuel Forker, owned the farms on which Lichtenau was situated. Schweinitz believed he identified the site of the village with a good degree of certainty and claimed that "the town began near the residence of Mr. Moore, and the church probably stood in his yard, reaching across the lane to the land of Mr. Forker."[32]

An 1872 plat of Tuscarawas Township shows the residence of Samuel Moore at the present water pollution control plant about a quarter mile north of the intersection of Ohio Route 83 and County Road 271 on the east side of the Muskingum River. The 1872 plat does not show property belonging to Samuel Forker, but immediately south of Samuel Moore's property is property identified as belonging to the "Heirs of E. Tingel." That's relevant, because another source indicates that Lichtenau "was situated on the east side of the Muskingum river (on the farms now in the possession of Samuel Moore and the Tingle heirs)."[33] Based on those documents, we can assume the coordinates for Lichtenau were near 40°14'23.86"N–81°52'16.76"W.

New Schoenbrunn (New Schönbrunn) (1779–1781), also Tapacon, Tuppakin.
Now: New Philadelphia, Tuscarawas County
(40°28'6.96"N–81°26'25.83"W)

In 1776, David Zeisberger and the other Moravian missionaries relocated the Tuscarawas mission settlements of Schoenbrunn and Gnadenhütten to Lichtenau on the Muskingum River in an attempt to distance themselves as much as possible from the conflict of the Revolutionary War. However, the move did not appear to convince the British and American factions of their neutrality, because by the autumn of 1779, the non–Christian Lenape at Goschachgunk were becoming increasingly involved in the fighting on one side or the other. To add to the Moravians' angst, other warriors allied with the British, like the Wyandot and Mingo, regularly rendezvoused in the vicinity of Lichtenau before launching raids against American settlements across the Ohio. Those factors made the allegiance of the Christian settlements suspect in the eyes of the Americans. At the same time, the British factions were suspicious that the Christian settlements were using their proximity to the British-allied tribes as a means of gathering intelligence for the Americans.

Zeisberger concluded that remaining at Lichtenau was untenable, so in December of 1779, he led a contingent of Indians and missionaries up the Tuscarawas River to establish the village of "New Schoenbrunn." The new village was only about 1.25 miles west-northwest of the original Schoenbrunn, which had been abandoned two years earlier in 1777 and subsequently destroyed in the war.[34] New Schoenbrunn was located on the west side of the Tuscarawas River in the "south side" section of present New Philadelphia, which is divided from the main city of New Philadelphia by the Tuscarawas River. The village site was on the west side of the river, near the present intersection of Goshen Hill Rd. SE and Goshen Ave. SE, west of where U.S. 800 crosses the Tuscarawas River.

Another contingent of Christian Indians under William Edwards left Lichtenau in April 1779 and reoccupied Gnadenhütten. The remainder of the Lichtenau inhabitants departed in the spring of 1780 to establish yet another new town called "Salem" on the west bank of the Tuscarawas near present Port Washington, Ohio.

David Zeisberger was the overall superintendent of the Moravian mission settlements in Ohio, but Zeisberger and Johann Jungmann managed New Schoenbrunn, while Gottlob Sensemen and William Edwards administered to the Indians at Gnadenhütten. The leaders at the Salem mission were John Heckewelder and Michael Young (1743–1826). In the summer of 1780, Adam Grube traveled from Bethlehem, Pennsylvania, to visit the Ohio missions. He brought along his wife and a Miss Sara Ohneberg. Grube spent six weeks at the missions, during which Heckewelder and Sara Ohneberg fell in love. Grube married the two at New Schoenbrunn, which was the first marriage ceremony of a white couple in present Ohio.

Unfortunately, the move to New Schoenbrunn, Salem, and Gnadenhütten did not serve Zeisberger's purpose of distancing the Christian settlements from the war. By the middle of 1781, the British and their Indian allies still suspected them of passing military information to the Americans, and apparently there was some merit to their suspicions. For example, in the early months of 1781, John Heckewelder learned, probably from the Lenape Chief Killbuck, that pro–British factions of Lenape were organizing a war party to attack Fort Pitt. Heckewelder passed that information on to American Colonel Daniel Brodhead at Fort Pitt, who launched a pre-emptive strike against the Lenape at the Forks of the Muskingum.[35] At the same time, Killbuck passed information on to David Zeisberger regarding a Wyandot threat that any Lenape who did not join the fight against the Americans "would be killed with the Virginians."[36]

The Lenape chief Captain Pipe complained to Major William DePeyster, commander at Fort Detroit, that the Moravian missionaries and their "praying Indians" were not as neutral as they professed to be. Consequently, DePeyster issued orders to relocate the Moravians and their Christian Indians west toward the Sandusky River to limit their contact with the Americans.

In August 1781, Loyalist Captain Matthew Elliott (1739–1814), with a force of about 300 Lenape, Wyandot, Shawnee, Ojibwe, and Ottawa warriors, arrived at the Tuscarawas River mission settlements to relocate the Moravians and their Christian Indians west to the

Sandusky River. Zeisberger argued against leaving, which caused the non–Christian Indians to quickly lose patience, so they threatened to torture John Heckewelder and Gottlob Sensemann and burn them at the stake. Zeisberger realized that resistance was futile, and grudgingly agreed to peacefully relocate to the Sandusky River. Heckewelder and Sensemann were released, and the communities prepared to travel west.

They departed the Tuscarawas area on September 11, 1781, and arrived at the Sandusky River on October 1, where the missionaries were told to establish their village near the mouth of Broken Sword Creek on the Sandusky River about six and a half miles southeast of Upper Sandusky. The group first took temporary shelter in the huts of an abandoned Wyandot village while they constructed more permanent shelters at a site about a mile farther upstream on the Sandusky River. By October 12, they had most of their "small and slightly built"[37] shelters under roof, and because they had been involuntarily relocated, the missionaries named their new community "Captives' Town." That in essence marked the end of the Moravian Christian settlements of New Schoenbrunn, Salem, and Gnadenhütten.

New Schoenbrunn and Gnadenhütten were destroyed the following year, 1782, by David Willamson's militia during the expedition that resulted in the infamous Gnadenhütten Massacre.[38]

Salem (1780–1781).
Now: Port Washington, Tuscarawas County
(40°18'40.19"N–81°31'45.47"W)

In 1779, David Zeisberger decided that the village of Lichtenau, near the confluence of the Muskingum, Tuscarawas, and Walhonding Rivers, was untenable, because of its proximity to the various combatants in the American Revolutionary War. In December of that year, he established a village called "New Schoenbrunn" about 1.25 miles west-northwest of the original Schoenbrunn, which had been abandoned in 1777 and subsequently destroyed in the war.[39] At the same time, William Edwards led another contingent and reoccupied Gnadenhütten. The remainder of the Lichenau inhabitants departed in the spring of 1780 to establish Salem, a new village on the west bank of the Tuscarawas near present Port Washington, Ohio. The specific site of the town was "about a mile-and-a-half southwest of Port Washington, Ohio, on a beautiful plain, just opposite three bold hill-tops, and between the present track of the railroad and the Tuscarawas River."[40]

While Zeisberger was the overall superintendent of the Moravian mission settlements in Ohio, the leaders at the Salem mission were John Heckeweelder and Michael Young (1743–1826). With the assistance of workers from Gnadenhütten and New Schoenbrunn, a chapel of hewn log timbers was built at Salem that was 36 × 40 feet, and dedicated on May 22, 1780.[41]

In the spring of 1781, Colonel Daniel Brodhead (1736–1809), who was the American commander of the Western Department, led about 300 troops on an expedition against the hostile Ohio Indians. On April 15, 1781, Brodhead attacked Goschachgunk and killed fifteen warriors, while capturing twenty. Five Lenape from Salem were among the captured Indians. The soldiers killed all of the captives except the five Christian Indians, who were released. But on the Indians' return to Salem, they were fired on by a group of Brodhead's soldiers, and one was wounded.

Brodhead's men camped near Salem, and the colonel sent a message requesting that Heckewelder visit Brodhead's camp, and he also asked the Moravians to furnish Brodhead's troops with provisions. Heckewelder complied, and in return Brodhead said his troops would not molest the Moravians or the Christian Indians, "as these Indians had conducted themselves from the commencement of the war in a manner that did them honor."[42] However, while Brodhead was speaking with Heckewelder, one of his officers rushed in and told the colonel that some militia "were preparing to break off, for the purpose of destroying the Moravian settlements up the river."[43] Fortunately, Brodhead, with the assistance of Colonel Davis Shepherd, was able to restrain the men. Even so, Brodhead was concerned for the safety of the Moravian communities and proposed that the village residents accompany his troops to Fort Pitt for protection. The Moravian missionaries and the Christian Indians refused his invitation, but the Lenape Chief Gelelemend or Killbuck and his band at Goschachgunk accepted a similar offer by Brodhead and placed themselves under the protection of the Americans.

As a result of Brodhead's expedition, Captain Pipe and the warlike Indians left the Muskingum River area and relocated to the Sandusky River. Now, with the exception of the three Moravian mission villages, there were no Indian towns along the Tuscarawas and upper Muskingum Rivers. The mission towns' inhabitants had little more than a year before they would be forced to leave their communities on the Tuscarawas River.

On August 10, 1781, Loyalist Captain Matthew Elliott (1739–1814), with a force of about 300 Lenape, Wyandot, Shawnee, Ojibwe, and Ottawa warriors, arrived at Salem and informed the inhabitants that they, along with the residents of New Schoenbrunn and Gnadenhütten, were required to immediately relocate west to the Sandusky River. The British-allied Indians were suspicious that "the Praying Indians" were in league with the Americans and were passing military intelligence to them. The Moravians and their Christian Indians responded that they would not be able to leave at that time: "You see yourselves that we cannot rise immediately and go with you, for we are too heavy [have too much immovable property and crops ungathered], and time is required to prepare for it."[44] They added that after gathering their harvest and spending the winter, they would decide whether they would relocate to the Sandusky River. The British agent Matthew Elliot did not want to wait until the new year to relocate the Moravians, but Captain Pipe's Indians were inclined to wait. They knew the villagers' crops were ripening, and to move the Indians before the crops were harvested would cause them unnecessary hardship and possible starvation. Several councils were held, during which the Moravians argued against leaving. Tired of Zeisberger's reluctance to move, Elliot threatened to have John Heckewelder and Gottlob Sensemann burned to death at the stake. At the same time, a group of Indians plundered the missionary homes. That caused Zeisberger to capitulate, and he informed Elliott that they would peacefully move to the Sandusky River.

They departed the Tuscarawas mission villages on September 11, 1781, and arrived at the Sandusky River on October 1. That marked the end of Salem village's short existence. The missionaries were directed to establish their village in the area of the mouth of Broken Sword Creek, on the Sandusky River about six and a half miles southeast of Upper Sandusky, and the missionaries named their new community "Captives' Town."

Captives' Town (1781–1782).
Now: Nevada, Wyandot County (40°46'17.25"N–83°9'44.49"W)

Captives' Town was situated on the right bank (north bank) of the Sandusky River about a mile upstream from the mouth of Broken Sword Creek in present Antrim township in Wyandot County.

By the middle of 1781, the British and their Indian allies were of the opinion that the Moravians and their Christian Indians in the mission settlements along the Tuscarawas River[45] were passing military information to the Americans that was harmful to the British cause. David Zeisberger and the residents of his communities outwardly maintained a strict neutrality, and appeared to be neutral in the conflict. However, in researching Zeisberger's correspondence, it is fairly evident that his loyalties lay more with the American cause. Part of the reason may have been that the Moravian mission headquarters in North America was in Bethlehem, Pennsylvania, which was firmly under the control of the Americans.

As the Revolutionary War dragged on, several Indian chiefs, including the influential Lenape chief Captain Pipe and the Wyandot half-king Pomoacon, grew increasingly suspicious that the Moravian missionaries and their "praying Indians" were not as neutral as they professed to be. Consequently, they complained to Major William DePeyster, the commander at Fort Detroit, about the supposed perfidy of the Moravian mission settlements. In the summer of 1781, after receiving several complaints about the Moravians, DePeyster ordered his Indian allies to relocate the Moravians and their Christian Indians west toward the Sandusky River, which would limit their contact with the Americans.

In August of 1781, Loyalist Captain Matthew Elliott, with a force of about 300 warriors composed mostly of Lenape and Wyandot braves along with some Shawnee, Ojibwe, and Ottawa, arrived at the Tuscarawas River mission settlements to escort the Moravians and their Christian community west to the Sandusky River. Pomoacon informed Zeisberger that the missionaries and their Indian congregation were required to peacefully return with them to the Sandusky River, and they would be under his protection during the journey.

After some futile reluctance on the part of the Moravians, they departed the Tuscarawas area on September 11, 1781, and arrived at the Sandusky River on October 1. Pomoacon and Captain Pipe told the missionaries to establish their village in the area of the mouth of Broken Sword Creek on the Sandusky River about six and a half miles southeast of Upper Sandusky. The group first took temporary shelter in the huts of an abandoned Wyandot camp while they constructed more permanent shelters at a site about a mile farther upstream on the Sandusky River where there was good timber. By October 12, they had most of their "small and slightly built"[46] shelters under roof, and because they had involuntarily relocated, the missionaries named their community "Captives' Town."

They were hardly established when they were informed that all of the missionaries and their families were required to travel to Fort Detroit to be questioned by the fort's commander. Since the trip would be arduous, Zeisberger received permission from Captain Pipe and the minor chief Wingenund (well beloved) to allow two of the missionaries, Johann Jungmann and Michael Jung, along with all of the women and children, to remain at Captives' Town.

Leaving most of the community at Captives' Town, David Zeisberger, John Heckewelder and William Edwards made the journey to Fort Detroit, where they were joined six days later by Captain Pipe and Wingenund. At Fort Detroit, the Moravian missionaries were questioned by DePeyster, and when Captain Pipe arrived, they were interrogated again. However, the Moravians were surprised when Pipe said to DePeyster, "They are here before thine eyes, thou canst now speak good words to them, and I say to thee, speak kindly to them, for they are our friends, and I hold them dear and should not like to see harm befall them."[47]

As surprised as Zeisberger was at Captain Pipe's statement, it was nothing compared to what DePeyster felt. He had been subjected to Captain Pipe's complaints about the Moravians and "their praying Indians"[48] for the previous few years. DePeyster asked Captain Pipe point blank, "Did they correspond with the rebels?" Pipe answered, "There might be some truth about that thing, for he could not say it was all lies, but it would not happen again since they were away from there."[49] That didn't satisfy DePeyster, as it appeared that Pipe was admitting that the Moravians had indeed corresponded with the Americans. The British major argued the point with Captain Pipe for some time before he gave up in exasperation and acquitted the missionaries, allowing them to return to Captives' Town.

When Zeisberger returned to Captives' Town on November 22, 1781, he found that the villagers faced starvation, and they desperately needed a supply of food before winter set in. They obtained some corn from traders at Upper Sandusky, but even so, many of the Indians were reduced to roaming the forest in search of edible roots and wild potatoes to supplement their meager diets. Providentially, they obtained food from a nearby Shawnee village, whose inhabitants remembered that the Moravians had helped them survive the winter some thirty years earlier in the Wyoming Valley of Pennsylvania. As a last resort, the Moravians bought corn from traders, who charged the exorbitant price of eight dollars a bushel.

At the same time, Zeisberger put the Indians to work constructing additional buildings, including a chapel. By December 4, the roof was on the chapel, and the congregation held their first religious service. The chapel was built in the fashion of a "pole barn," with upright poles sunk in the ground, and the framework attached to the poles. The roof was shingled, and moss was packed in the joints between the wood siding.

The food supply was still critical, and some of the Indians decided to return to the Tuscarawas to search for food that was left behind in the abandoned missionary towns. In January of 1782, there were about two hundred souls living at Captives' Town, and about one hundred and fifty of the Indians returned to the old Moravian villages on the Tuscarawas to look for food. Zeisberger wrote in his journal, "We were now quite alone at the village."[50]

The departure of that many Indians from Captives' Town caused Captain Pipe and Pomoacon to once again complain to DePeyster, and on March 1, 1782, Zeisberger and Heckewelder were summoned to Fort Detroit to face DePeyster's questioning. This time, DePeyster demanded that all the Moravians, including their wives and families, make the trip. The Christian Indians, however, were to remain at Captives's Town, but it was obvious that Ziesberger and the other Moravian missionaries would not be returning. On March 14, just before they departed for Fort Detroit, one of the Indians returned from the Tuscarawas with news of the Gnadenhütten massacre tragedy that befell the Lenape Indians who went to the Tuscarawas in search of food.

Some had been captured and taken to Fort Pitt, but almost a hundred had been slaughtered at Gnadenhütten by 160 Pennsylvania militia under the command of Lieutenant Colonel David Williamson. After killing and scalping 28 men, 29 women, and 39 children, the militia piled the bodies in the mission building and burned the village down. The troops then looted the village, taking about 80 horses loaded with the Indians' furs, ornaments, household goods, and even their clothing. Zeisberger wrote in his diary on March 23, 1782, "To-day we have the first trustworthy news of the horrible murder of our Indian brethren at Gnadenhütten and Salem, March 7 and 8."[51]

Zeisberger's party arrived at Fort Detroit on April 20, 1782, and a short time after their arrival, they learned of another American expedition against the Christian Indians, this time to be aimed at Captives' Town. A large group of about 500 Pennsylvania militia under the command of Colonel William Crawford, a veteran Indian fighter and close friend of

George Washington, moved against the Indian towns along the Sandusky with the goal of completing the extermination that was begun at Gnadenhütten. Coincidentally, David Williamson, who had led the Gnadenhütten massacre, was second in command, having lost the election for command by four votes. The troops were so certain of success and of accumulating valuable plunder from the noncombatant Indians that they brought coils of rope with which to secure the Indians' horses and other possessions.

However, instead of finding a peaceful village of docile Indians, they were met by hundreds of well-armed and organized warriors under Captain Pipe, along with 100 British rangers. The battle took place on June 12, 1782, and after a day of fighting, the Americans found themselves surrounded. They attempted to break out at night, but the retreat turned into a rout. Most of the Americans managed to make their way back to Fort Pitt, but about seventy Americans were killed and several were captured. The Indian and British casualties were minimal, with about six killed and eleven wounded. Colonel Crawford was among the captured, and in retaliation for the Gnadenhütten massacre, Crawford and most of the prisoners were brutally tortured to death. Ironically, David Williamson, who was responsible for the Gnadenhütten massacre, managed to escape to safety.

After Zeisberger and the other Moravian missionaries departed for Fort Detroit, the Christian Indians remained at Captives' Town for some time longer. But in departure of the Moravians in March 1782 essentially ended the village's function as a missionary town. Zeisberger and his community were given a parcel of land in present Clinton Township, Macomb County, Michigan, which DePeyster obtained from the Ojibwe. There the Moravians established a settlement they called "New Gnadenhütten." Captives' Town was virtually abandoned when most of the Indians joined Zeisberger at New Gnadenhütten in Michigan, and others merely melted back into the wilderness.

By 1785 it was feasible for the Moravians and their Christian Indians to return to their beloved Tuscarawas valley. They departed New Gnadenhütten in the spring of 1786, but were delayed on the Cuyahoga River, because hostile Indians were reported in the Muskingum River area. The Moravian missionaries were also uncertain about the U.S. government's changing policy regarding the Indian settlements. The missionaries decided to wait until they received further clarification, so they established Pilgerruh, or "pilgrims' rest," a temporary village on the Cuyahoga River, where they would wait until it was safe and practical to continue.

Pilgerruh, "Pilgrim's Rest" (1786–1787).
Now: Valley View, Cuyahoga County (41°22'39.09"N–81°36'36.47"W)

Pilgerruh or "Pilgrim's Rest" was, as the name implies, a temporary village established by the Moravian missionaries David Zeisberger, John Heckewelder, and William Edwards. It was never meant to be a permanent settlement, but rather a place to provide food and shelter on the way back to the Tuscarawas after their five-year exile. Since 1781, they had been at Captives' Town on the upper Sandusky River, and in 1782, they founded a new mission settlement called New Gnadenhütten in present Clinton Township, Macomb County, Michigan. They were on their long-awaited return journey to their old mission settlements along the Tuscarawas River when they stopped on the Cuyahoga River and established the temporary town of Pilgerruh.

Of all the missions established by the Moravians in North America, Pilgerruh was the smallest and the most short-lived. The village consisted of twenty-eight buildings and contained about one hundred souls, and was only in existence for about ten months from June 18, 1786, until the last of the inhabitants departed on May 1, 1787.[52]

Pilgerruh has another distinction, in that of all of the mission communities founded by the Moravian missionaries, it is the least mentioned in the diaries and journals of David Zeisberger and John Heckewelder. The two generally provided written comments on all aspects of their various communities, but that was not the case with Pilgerruh. That factor makes it difficult to determine the exact location of the town. Surprisingly, there were at least two people who lived as late as 1850 who had been to Pilgerruh, but apparently no one bothered to document any specific information they had regarding the community.[53] Perhaps, since Pilgerruh was never meant to be a permanent settlement, it was not considered worth memorializing. In fact, the Indians referred to the town as "the night lodge on the Cuyahoga," which was how they referred to a temporary stopover.[54]

After their forced exile, the Moravian missionaries received word in 1785 that the American Congress had reserved the lands around the old mission towns on the Tuscarawas River for their use, but it wasn't until 1786 that Zeisberger and the other missionaries were able to move their congregation back to the Tuscarawas River area.

New Gnadenhütten, the community in Michigan they were leaving, was a well-planned and well-constructed town, and a group of speculative Frenchmen, thinking it would be abandoned by the Moravians and their flock, were waiting to take it over. However, in an act of kindness, John Askin, who was in a trading partnership with the celebrated Robert Rogers, along with Major Ancrum, the British commandant at Fort Detroit, purchased the town from the Moravians for four hundred dollars. In addition, Askin sent two of his trading sloops, the *Beaver* and the *Mackinaw*, to convey the Moravian missionaries and the Christian Indians as far as the mouth of the Cuyahoga River, from where they would journey to the Tuscarawas.[55]

The two vessels departed on April 28, 1786, but instead of the normal two- or three-day trip, adverse winds delayed the small convoy around the Bass Islands near Sandusky for about four weeks. Mr. Askin was forced to recall the sloop *Beaver* for his mercantile business, and most of the missionaries and Indians were put ashore west of Sandusky Bay, from where they journeyed by foot and canoe to the Cuyahoga. The sloop *Mackinaw* stayed with the group, and under the direction of William Edwards, carried the household goods and equipment, along with those pilgrims who were too old or infirm to journey overland.[56]

The entire congregation rendezvoused at the mouth of the Cuyahoga on June 8, 1786, but because of the long delays, it was too late in the year to travel all the way to the Tuscarawas and still have time to plant corn and crops to sustain them through the coming winter. Even in June, their precious food supply was running dangerously low, and Zeisberger wrote in his diary, "Hunger begins to fall sharply upon us! May the Savior soon help us out of our need."[57]

Another reason for stopping on the Cuyahoga was the news of hostile Indians in the Muskingum and Tuscarawas River areas. In addition, there were rumors that the American Congress was contemplating a change in the Indian policy that might rescind the rights to their reserved mission land. As a result, Zeisberger decided they should select a temporary place on the Cuyahoga River to plant crops, construct shelter, and await news of further developments that would allow them to continue to the Tuscarawas.

They trekked south, upstream along the Cuyahoga River, and about ten or twelve miles from the mouth of the river, they found the remains of an old Ottawa town. Near the abandoned town were old cleared garden fields that were overgrown with weeds but could still be made suitable to plant corn and other crops. On June 18, 1786, they pitched camp on the east side of the Cuyahoga River, and immediately worked to prepare the fields for planting. In a hurry to get crops in the ground, they planted corn, potatoes, beans, and pumpkins, and also a large quantity of turnips, because they were the least likely to fail.[58] Zeisberger recorded the planting in his diary: "We resolved, therefore to stay here this summer when our matters would become clearer, for at the present we are confused and know not rightly how things are with us. We laid out our camp upon the east side of the creek upon a height and the day after, Monday 19, we sowed the land on the west side where we wished to plant, and found good and in part quite clear land for this purpose, only it was very wild, the weeds standing as high as a man, which we had to cut down, thus having much trouble and labor."[59]

Once the crops were in the ground, the pilgrims constructed more permanent shelters. The Moravians and some of the Indians built substantial log cabins, but given the stated temporary nature of the community, many of the Indians were content to erect Indian-style huts that were merely a thin framework covered with bark mats. All in all, the village consisted of twenty-seven dwellings and a chapel, but unlike the previous Moravian mission villages that were neatly aligned, Pilgerruh was not laid out on a regular plan. Instead, the homes were scattered haphazardly around the chapel.[60]

In October 1786, Sarah Ohneberg Heckewelder, the wife of missionary John Heckewelder, became severely ill. John, Sarah, and their daughter Anna Salome had to return to Bethlehem, where Sarah could receive the appropriate medical care. Although he revisited the Muskingum and Tuscarawas missions, Heckewelder never again returned to a permanent missionary post. David Zeisberger and his wife Susanna Lecron Zeisberger, whom he married in 1781 at Litiz, Pennsylvania, remained at Pilgerruh, along with missionary William Edwards. Zeisberger was sixty-five years old at the time, and Edwards was sixty-two, and both men were becoming somewhat frail.

During the winter months, Zeisberger occupied his time by mastering the Lenape language and compiling a vocabulary. It was his intention to leave something of God's Word printed in the Indian language. Coincidentally, while at Pilgerruh, Zeisberger received a letter from the American Superintendent of Indian Affairs stating that George Washington requested vocabularies of the different Indian languages from people who were living among the Indians. Zeisberger forwarded a copy of his Lenape dictionary to Washington. While the request was made in Washington's name, it had actually originated from Catherine the Great of Russia, who was interested in compiling a universal dictionary.[61]

In spite of hurriedly planting crops upon their arrival at Pilgerruh, the congregation found itself faced not only with a critical food supply, but also a shortage of other necessities. If it weren't for the friendship of a trader and frontiersman named William Wilson, many of the community might not have survived the winter. Wilson was a partner in a Pittsburgh store called Duncan and Wilson, which carried on a brisk trade between Fort Pitt and Fort Detroit. The main route for the store's pack trains was along the trails that ran alongside the Cuyahoga River, which took them past Pilgerruh. After visiting Pilgerruh, Wilson, who was educated, intelligent, and spoke several Indian dialects, became friendly with the small mission community. When he saw their needy state, he obligingly supplied the congregation with much- needed food, clothing, cooking utensils, and even cattle, all of which he provided for "cash or credit."[62]

James Hillman was a drover for the Duncan and Wilson pack trains, and on one trip, he stopped at Pilgerruh, where he delivered four kegs of flour. Hillman noted on the invoice that he visited the "Moravian Town" on "October ye 24th 1786." He also wrote in his journal, "We took the Indian trail for Sandusky, until we arrived at the 'Standing Stone' [Kent, Ohio], on the Cuyahoga, a little below the mouth of Break-neck creek, where the village of Franklin is now.[63] There we left the Sandusky trail and took one direct to the mouth of Tinker's creek, where was a little town built by HECKEWELDER and ZEISBERGER, with a number of Moravian Indians."[64]

A fairly precise location of Pilgerruh was determined during the archeological study conducted by David Sanders Clark in 1936. Based on extant documents along with Clark's own archeological excavations, he determined the village site was on a slight rise on the south side of the present intersection of Hathaway Road and Canal Road in Valley View, Ohio. During his excavations in 1936, Clark located several post holes, stone fireplaces, and other artifacts that indicated a white-influenced habitation. While road building and the canal construction certainly altered the terrain, it's likely that the town stood on the slight hill rise at coordinates 41°22'39.09"N–81°36'36.47"W, just south of the present Valley View Police and Fire Department building.

During the winter of 1786–1787, Zeisberger received news from General Richard Butler, the commander at Fort Pitt, that the Indians in the vicinity of the Tuscarawas were still hostile, and the Moravians and their Christian Indians would be in great danger if they returned to that area. Butler recommended that the Moravians give up the idea. In March 1787, Zeisberger yielded to Butler's advice, and abandoned his plan to continue to the Tuscarawas. In April 1787, the Zeisbergers and William Edwards, along with the greater part of their Christian Indian congregation, moved to the Petquotting River, which is now called the Huron River, where they founded another community called New Salem. A few families delayed leaving Pilgerruh, but by May 1, 1787, the village of Pilgerruh was completely abandoned.

New Salem (1787–1809; 1802–1809),
also Petquotting, Pequottink, Pettquotting.
NOW: MILAN, ERIE COUNTY (41°19'50.98"N–82°34'47.81"W)

New Salem, or Petquotting, as it was often called, was located on the east bank of the Huron River about three miles north of present Milan, Ohio, in Erie County. The Huron River was also known as Petquotting, or in Lenape, pay-ka-tunk ("high round hill"). On maps and in journals, the river was known by several other names, and "Huron River" first appeared on a 1778 map by Thomas Hutchins. Sources also show it as Bald Eagle Creek, Naudowessi Sipi, Riviére aux Hurons, and Guahadahuri. James Smith, who was a captive of the Caughnawaga Indians, referred to the river as Canesadooharie.[65]

In 1787, the name Pequotting or Petquotting for the river was apparently still commonly used, and even though the Moravian missionary David Zeisberger named his Christian Indian mission New Salem, he most often referred to the village in his journals as Petquotting. As a result, many sources refer to the mission as Pequotting or Petquotting on the Huron River.

The mission was founded in April of 1787, when the Moravian missionary David Zeisberger led a contingent of Moravian missionaries and Indians from their temporary settlement of Pilgerruh[66] on the Cuyahoga River to establish a new Christian settlement in the Sandusky area. The Moravians had previously founded the Christian Indian towns of Schoenbrunn, Gnadenhütten, Lichtenau, New Schoenbrunn, and Salem in the Tuscarawas

River area, and for a time, they were held at Captives' Town on the Sandusky, and New Gnadenhütten in present Michigan.

Zeisberger and his group departed Pilgerruh on April 1, 1787, but entries in Zeisberger's diary hint that some members of his flock may have made the journey the previous year to prepare for the group's arrival. For example, Zeisberger wrote that on April 11, "Anna Johanna came from Pettquotting. They were almost shipwrecked on the rocks in a storm. These, especially Anna Paulina, when, the next morning, they were at early service, could do nothing but weep, at again hearing the word of God, of which they had heard nothing the whole winter."[67] Another entry, dated April 27, 1787, states, "Another canoe went to Pettquotting to get corn, a good day's journey from here."[68]

The same day that Zeisberger dispatched a canoe to Petquotting, an Indian named Titawachkam met the group with a message from three Lenape chiefs, Pipe, Welandawecken, and Pomoacan, who were in the Sandusky River area. The message was a request that Zeisberger establish his mission community on the Sandusky River "between Lower Wyandot Town [present Fremont] and Monsey [Muncee] Town."[69] Muncee Town was a Lenape village on the east side of the Sandusky River about three miles downstream from present Fremont, near where the Ohio Turnpike crosses the Sandusky River. Zeisberger refused Captain Pipe's invitation to come to the Sandusky, and instead he continued to his original destination on the Petquotting or Huron River.

The mission group arrived at the Huron River on May 8, 1787, and they immediately began to construct living shelters consisting of bark-covered huts. Zeisberger discovered that a French trader resided about a mile from the lake[70] near the present town of Huron, Ohio. During the construction of the mission's living quarters at New Salem, Zeisberger and his wife lived with the Frenchman.[71]

Zeisberger worked to create an Eden in the wilderness, which was a unique blend of white and Indian cultures. On June 6, 1787, the missionaries consecrated their house of worship, and they soon built a schoolhouse and instituted regular class hours. The community worked hard to clear and cultivate their fields, erect fences, and plant orchards, crops of corn, beans, squash and pumpkins. In addition, each family had its own vegetable garden.

However, the small community could hardly have been established at a riskier time. The Ohio Indian Wars were raging, and though the inhabitants of New Salem assiduously refrained from involvement in the war and refused to support either side, they were consequently distrusted by both the white and Indian warring factions. Indians who remained detached from the war flocked to the small mission settlement not so much to hear the word of God, but mostly to find a measure of safety from the fighting. After the first full year on the Huron River, which was also the height of the mission's success, there were 212 converts living at New Salem.[72]

As nonmilitant pacifists, the Christian community at New Salem remained somewhat aloof from the war through the end of 1790, but that period of detachment ended abruptly. On January 4, 1791, Zeisberger wrote in his diary, "We heard very bad and dangerous news on the part of the ill-disposed Indians, of their wicked designs against us."[73] On January 8, Zeisberger sent messengers to the Lenape Captain Pipe to ascertain the validity of the Indian threat to New Salem, and they returned four days later with a troubling message. Captain Pipe advised the Christian community to leave New Salem in the spring, and he also admitted that he was probably going to move farther west of the Sandusky River.[74]

Later that month, the trader Mathew Elliot, who was also the British representative for Indian Affairs, visited New Salem. He told Zeisberger that if they relocated to Fort Detroit, he would arrange for transportation, and he guaranteed the support and assistance of Alexander McKee (c. 1735–1799), who was an agent of the British Indian Department.

On February 15, 1791, Zeisberger received a message from a council of Indian chiefs at the town of Gigeyunk[75] with an even more alarming message. Zeisberger referred to the Indian council as "the Assembly of Hell."[76] Their message, in spite of its somewhat friendly greeting, was very ominous: "My friends, we hereby make you aware and certain that ye can no longer abide in Pettquotting. Make yourselves ready for departure, and in two months' time something will be told you; then ye will hear exactly, but if you refuse to arise ye will see and suffer the same as upon the Muskingum."[77] That was a not-so-veiled reference to the massacre of 96 Christian Indians at Gnadenhütten on March 8, 1782.

Zeisberger decided to accept Matthew Elliot's offer of assistance and the protection of the British, so on March 12, he sent his fellow missionary William Edwards to Fort Detroit with a request for help in relocating the mission community. Edwards returned on March 25, with the disquieting news that although Elliot and McKee promised support, they would first have to consult with the governor in Québec. Since that could take several months, Elliot advised Zeisberger to remain at New Salem, where they could plant their crops in the spring and move the following autumn. Elliot added that if Zeisberger was forced to move earlier, the New Salem refugees could find temporary sanctuary on Elliot and McKee's adjoining farms on the Detroit River.

However, the situation was becoming increasingly distressing, and Zeisberger felt he could not delay the move much longer. While Edwards was still en route to and from Fort Detroit, Zeisberger learned that several Indians, including whole families, had been killed by American militia, and it wouldn't be long before they attacked the Indians at New Salem. On March 28, three days after Edwards arrived back at New Salem, Zeisberger sent him back to Fort Detroit to advise Elliot and McKee that they would accept their offers of temporary sanctuary on their farms. Edwards was also directed to ask the British if they would send a ship to assist in transporting the refugees' belongings and supplies. If necessary, Edwards was told to hire a boat from a Mr. Askin. Since Zeisberger anticipated the move would be necessary, he had had his congregation build more than fifty canoes during the previous month and a half. Even so, the move was daunting, and it took thirty-five days to accomplish. Fortunately, Mr. Askin's ship *Sagina* met them at Sandusky Bay, where all of the heavy gear, along with the community's food supplies, were put on board for the trip to the Detroit River. Most of the refugees and their cattle traveled by foot, skirting the southern shore of Sandusky Bay and across the Maumee River, where they turned north toward the mouth of the Detroit River. Zeisberger and his party were the last to leave New Salem on April 14, and they arrived at the Detroit River on May 4, 1791.

The move to the Detroit River was advantageous for the Moravians and their Christian Indians, because it provided them with a measure of safety that they did not have on the Huron River. It was also profitable for Elliot and McKee, because it provided them with cheap labor. The refugees remained at their new mission on the Detroit River for nearly a year. Zeisberger called the village "Die Warte," or "The Watchtower," because it overlooked both the Detroit River and Lake Erie from the Canadian side of the river near present Amherstburg, Ontario.

During the previous year and a half, the Ohio Indians won major victories over the Americans, defeating General Harmar at Gigeyunk in October 1790, and General St. Clair at the Battle of the Wabash in November 1791. As a result, the confidence and belligerence of the Indians increased to the extent that Zeisberger was concerned that his small community on the Detroit River was at risk. During the first month of 1792, Zeisberger concluded that it would be prudent to move his flock even farther out of harm's way. In April 1792, they relocated up the La Tranchée River, which is now called the Thames River, and established "Fairfield," which they hoped would be their permanent home. The community was located on the north bank of the Thames River between present Thamesville and Bothwell, Ontario.

In 1798, after spending almost six years at Fairfield, Zeisberger was drawn back to his original missionary area along the Muskingum and Tuscarawas Rivers, where he established a new mission on a site near the old Schoenbrunn mission. He named the new community Goshen, and it was where David Zeisberger died at the age of 87. He is buried in the Goshen-Indian Cemetery in Goshen, Ohio.

In 1802, some eleven years after David Zeisberger left the Huron River, the Moravian elders at Bethlehem, Pennsylvania, decided to reestablish the old New Salem mission. They determined that most of personnel who would rebuild New Salem would come from the Fairfield mission, along with residents of Goshen. Gottfried Oppelt was named the head missionary, and he was assisted by Johann Benjamin Haven. It took about two years to prepare for the move, during which time Haven received training from Zeisberger at Goshen. Finally, they were ready to restart the mission, and on June 9, 1804, Oppelt arrived at the site of New Salem with 36 Indians, eight canoes, nineteen cows, and eight horses.[78] Haven had arrived a short time earlier with a small contingent from Goshen. They immediately began work to rebuild the community and make it self-sustaining, but only thirteen months after they arrived, Oppelt and Haven learned that their little mission community was again in jeopardy. This time, the threat wasn't from hostile Indians or warlike white troops, but rather from land-hungry settlers and speculators.

On July 4, 1805, Indian representatives and agents of the U.S. government signed the Fort Industry Treaty, which finalized the sale of a huge area of land that stretched from the Cuyahoga and Tuscarawas Rivers to a point 120 miles west of the Pennsylvania state line. The western boundary of the Fort Industry Treaty purchase extended south from present Port Clinton, Ohio, to just south of present Mount Gilead, Ohio. Unfortunately for the missionaries at New Salem, the Huron River and New Salem mission community were well within the land designated for white settlement. Even worse was the realization that there were no government grants or other protections for the land on which the New Salem mission stood. The Fort Industry Treaty signaled the end of the New Salem mission. In 1809, the mission area was taken over by white settlers, and the Moravian missionary community of New Salem ceased to exist.

Goshen (1798–1823).
Now: Goshen, Tuscarawas County (40°26'34.72"N–81°24'33.93"W)

Goshen was the last of the Christian Indian villages founded by the Moravians in Ohio during the 18th century. It was established in 1798 by David Zeisberger, who returned to the Tuscarawas Valley from Fairfield on the La Tranchéee River (now called the Thames) in present Ontario, Canada. The Moravians and their Christian Indians had moved to the safety of Canada in 1791 because of the renewed Indian Wars in Ohio. After spending almost seven years in Canada, Zeisberger was drawn back to his original missionary area along the Muskingum and Tuscarawas Rivers.

In 1797, in preparation for his return to the Tuscarawas River, Zeisberger received a grant from the federal government of 4,000 acres for the old mission villages of Schoenbrunn, Gnadenhütten, and Salem. A survey was conducted of the old sites, and Zeisberger found that Gnadenhütten was now covered with a "dense wilderness of bushes and trees, and infested with rattlesnakes. Here and there the ruins of a chimney projected from the midst of a blackberry or sumac thicket."[79] The party burned away most of the underbrush and found the ground was covered with human bones, the remains of the Christian Indians massacred by Pennsylvania militia in March 1782. The bones of the Indian martyrs were interred, and Zeisberger and several Indian families took up residence at Gnadenhütten, while he worked to establish the new community of Goshen.

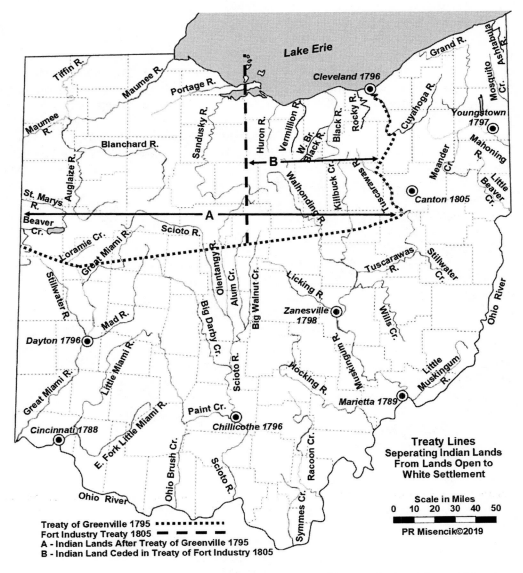

Map showing Indian lands as a result of the treaty of Fort Industry, July 4, 1805.

In 1798, Zeisberger laid out the village site of Goshen on the west side of the Tuscarawas River opposite an island about seven miles northeast of Gnadenhütten. Although there is not an island in the Tuscarawas River adjacent to the present town of Goshen, there may have been one in 1798. The closest island is about .7 miles upstream, or northwest of the present town; however, more evidence indicates that the actual site of the Goshen mission village was indeed where the present town of Goshen is located. Local historians have determined that Zeisberger's mission house was located at present 2317 Goshen Valley Drive, SE. A portion of the home that now occupies the site is made of logs that locals claim are remnants of the old mission house, which was completed on November 13, 1798. The first church was completed a month later in December 1798. The cemetery where David Zeisberger is buried is located about 150 yards west of the mission house site.

Not long after the establishment of Goshen, white settlers began to arrive in the area, and they provided the Indians with liquor, which had a negative effect on the community. The Moravian missionaries petitioned Governor St. Clair to allow them to prevent the sale or barter of intoxicants within the settlement, and the Territorial Legislature passed a measure that allowed the missionaries to seize alcohol that was brought into the settlement. However, "not only passing traders, but the town's neighbors tempted the Indians in every possible way."[80] Zeisberger complained that "a regular gang of thieves and desperados infested the vicinity of Goshen, who worked Incalculable damage to the missions."[81] Zeisberger tried to stop the bad influence on the Indians, and the Indians promised to reform, but "during the Holy Passion week (1805), most of the converts were intoxicated."[82] Worse yet, the traders complained to the Territorial Legislature that the prohibition of alcohol at Goshen was "an infringement on the rights and liberties of a free people,"[83] and the law was repealed.

Few new Indian converts joined the Goshen community, and the number of Christian Indians diminished due to deaths and forced removals, or because they simply returned to the wild. William Edwards died at Goshen on October 8, 1801, at the age of seventy-eight, and David Zeisberger died there on November 7, 1808, at the age of eighty-seven. With Zeisberger's death, the Moravian mission villages were left without effective guidance, and the Goshen community declined. The deteriorating situation forced the Moravian elders in Bethlehem to reevaluate the viability of the Ohio missions. From once self-sufficient communities, they had become an unbearable drain on church finances. As a result, the Brethren opened negotiations with the U.S. government to divest themselves of the properties, and an agreement was reached on August 4, 1823, to relinquish title to the Ohio mission properties for $6,654, plus an annuity payment of $400 to the Indian residents in lieu of a reservation. The Society retained some land, including the graveyard on the Gnadenhütten tract, some private homes in the villages, and the missionary house and graveyard at Goshen, where David Zeisberger, William Edwards, and Gelelemend, also known as Killbuck, were buried along with several other members of their old community.

The Indian Villages of 18th-Century Ohio

Legend of Map Showing Indian Towns

No.	Town Name	Alternate Names	Nation	County
1	Agushawas		Ottawa	Putnam
2	Anioton	Aniauton, Contontia	Wyandot	Erie

No.	Town Name	Alternate Names	Nation	County
3	Standing Stone	Shawnee Town	Shawnee	Fairfield
3	French Margaret's Town	Margaret's Town	Lenape	Fairfield
3	Beaver's NewTown	Assinink, Hockhocking	Lenape	Fairfiled
3	Tarhe Town	Crane's Town	Wyandot	Fairfield

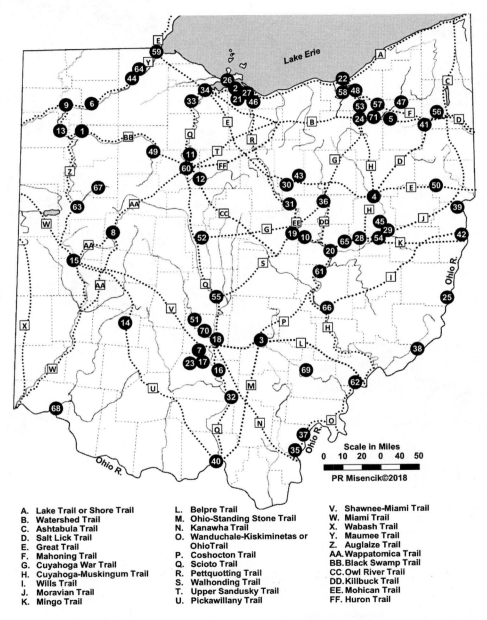

A. Lake Trail or Shore Trail
B. Watershed Trail
C. Ashtabula Trail
D. Salt Lick Trail
E. Great Trail
F. Mahoning Trail
G. Cuyahoga War Trail
H. Cuyahoga-Muskingum Trail
I. Wills Trail
J. Moravian Trail
K. Mingo Trail

L. Belpre Trail
M. Ohio-Standing Stone Trail
N. Kanawha Trail
O. Wanduchale-Kiskiminetas or
　　OhioTrail
P. Coshocton Trail
Q. Scioto Trail
R. Pettquotting Trail
S. Walhonding Trail
T. Upper Sandusky Trail
U. Pickawillany Trail

V. Shawnee-Miami Trail
W. Miami Trail
X. Wabash Trail
Y. Maumee Trail
Z. Auglaize Trail
AA. Wappatomica Trail
BB. Black Swamp Trail
CC. Owl River Trail
DD. Killbuck Trail
EE. Mohican Trail
FF. Huron Trail

Approximate position of Indian towns and villages relative to trails and rivers. Because of the map's scale, a circled number may represent more than one village if they are in fairly close proximity to one another.

No.	Town Name	Alternate Names	Nation	County
4	Beaver's Town	King Beaver's Town, Shingas's Town, The Tuscarawas	Lenape	Tuscarawas
5	Big Son's Town	Bigson's Town, Big Sun's Town	Mingo	Portage
6	Black Snake's Town	Snake's Town	Shawnee	Henry
7	Blue Jacket's Town #1		Shawnee	Pickaway
7	Pecowick	Pickoweekee, Pickoweeke	Shawnee	Pickaway
8	Blue Jacket's Town #2		Shawnee	Logan
8	Buckonghelas Town #1		Lenape	Logan
8	Wakatomika #2	Wapatomica, Waketomika, Waketamwki	Shawnee	Logan
9	The Glaize		Multi-national	Defiance
9	Blue Jacket's Town #3		Shawnee	Defiance
9	Big Cat and Buckonghelas Town		Lenape	Defiance
9	Captain Johnny's Town	Kekewepelethy's Town	Shawnee	Defiance
9	Tetapachksit's Town		Lenape	Defiance
9	Little Turtle's Town		Miami	Defiance
9	Traders' Town		European	Defiance
10	Tullihas	Walhonding Town, Owl Town, Mohiccons Town	Mingo	Coshocton
10	Hundy	Old Hundy	Lenape	Coshocton
10	New Hundy	Hundy	Lenape	Coshocton
10	Mohawk		?	Coshocton
10	Captain Pipe's Town #2		Lenape	Coshocton
10	White Woman's Town		Lenape	Coshocton
11	Captain Pipe's Town #3	Old Pipe's Town	Lenape	Wyandot
12	Captives' Town		Moravian Lenape	Wyandot
12	Pipe's Town	Pipetown, Captain Pipe's Town #4	Lenape	Wyandot
13	Charloe		Ottawa	Paulding
14	Chillicothe	Old Chillicothe, Old Town	Shawnee	Greene
15	Pickawillany	Tawixtwi Town, Pick Town	Miami	Miami
15	Chillicothe	Pickawillany	Shawnee	Miami
16	Chillicothe		Shawnee	Ross
17	Chillicothe	Upper Chillicothe, Old Chillicothe, Lower Shawnee Town	Shawnee	Ross
18	Chillicothe	Kispoko	Shawnee	Ross
18	Cornstalk's Town		Shawnee	Pickaway
18	Grenadier Squaw's Town	Nonhalema's Town	Shawnee	Pickaway

No.	Town Name	Alternate Names	Nation	County
18	Kispoko	Kispoko Town, Lower Shawnee Town	Shawnee	Pickaway
18	Maguck	Magueck, Magung, Maqueechaick	Lenape	Pickaway
19	Coashoskis		Lenape	Knox
20	Conshaké	Wyandot Old Town, Muskingum, Fugitive's Town	Wyandot	Coshocton
20	Goschachgunk	Coashoking, Coshocton, Muskingum	Lenape	Coshocton
20	Lichtenau	"Pasture of Light"	Moravian Lenape	Coshocton
21	Contuntuth	Wyandot Town, Canoutout, Chanondet Cantontia	Wyandot	Erie
22	Croghan's Trading Post	George Croghan's Post	European	Cuyahoga
23	Crooked Nose's Town	Wockchaalli, Waccachalla	Shawnee	Ross
24	Cuyahoga Town		Lenape	Summit
24	Mingo Town	Ostionish, Logan's Town	Mingo	Summit
24	Gwahago		Mingo	Summit
25	Delaware Town		Lenape	Belmont
26	Fort Sandoské	Fort Sandoski	French Wyandot	Ottawa
27	Fort Sandusky		British	Erie
27	Ogantz	Ogontz	Ottawa	Erie
28	Gekelemukpechunk	Kacalamúkpechink, New Comer's Town, Netawatwees's Town, Kekalemapehoong, Neghkuunque, Red Bank, Kighalapegha	Lenape	Tuscarawas
29	Gnadenhütten	"Huts of Grace"	Moravian Lenape	Tuscarawas
29	Goshen		Moravian Lenape	Tuscarawas
29	Three Legs Town	Three Ledges, The Ledges	?	Tuscarawas
30	Greentown	Green Town, Lenape Town	Lenape	Ashland
31	Hell Town	Clear Town, Clear Water Town	Lenape	Ashland
32	Hurricane Tom's Town	Harriskintom, Salt Lick Town	Shawnee	Ross
33	Junqueindundeh	Lower Sandusky, Wyandot Town, Junquindundeh, Dunkeindundeh	Wyandot	Sandusky
34	Junundat	Junandot, Ayonontout, Sunyeneand	Wyandot	Sandusky
35	Kanauga		Likely Shawnee	Gallia

No.	Town Name	Alternate Names	Nation	County
36	Killbuck Town		Lenape	Holmes
37	Kiskiminetas	Kiskiminetas Old Town	Lenape	Gallia
38	Koshkoshkung		possibly Lenape	Washington
39	Logan's Town	Yellow Creek	Mingo	Jefferson
40	Lower Shawnee Town	Chillicothe, Sonuonto, Sinhioto, Chalahgawatha, St. Yotoc, Scioto Town	Shawnee	Scioto
41	Mahoning Town	Old Mahoning Town, Mahoning Old Town	Lenape	Trumbull
42	Mingo Town	Mingo Bottoms, Crow's Town	Mingo	Jefferson
43	Mohican John's Town	Mohickon John's Town, Johnstown, Mohican John's Old Town, Old Town	Mingo	Ashland
44	Nawash's Town	Naiwash, Naiwasha, Neywash, (Maumee River Ottawa Villages)	Ottawa	Wood
44	Tontoganee	Tontaganee, Tontogany, Tonedog-o-ney, (Maumee River Ottawa Villages)	Ottawa	Wood
44	Petonquet's Town	Anapatonjowin, Kinjoino's Town, (Maumee River Ottawa Villages)	Ottawa	Wood
45	Schoenbrunn	"Beautiful Spring"	Moravian Lenape	Tuscarawas
45	New Schoenbrunn	Tapacon, Tuppakin	Moravian Lenape	Tuscarawas
46	New Salem	Petquotting, Pettquotting, Pequottink	Moravian Lenape	Erie
47	Onandaga Town		Mingo	Portage
48	Saguin's Post	French House	French	Cuyahoga
48	Ottawa Town	Tawas	Ottawa	Cuyahoga
48	Pilgerruh	"Pilgrims' Rest"	Moravian Lenape	Cuyahoga
49	Ottawa Village		Ottawa	Hancock
50	Painted Post		Lenape or Mingo	Columbiana
51	Puckshenose's Town		Shawnee	Pickaway
52	Pluggy's Town	Mingo Town	Mingo	Delaware
53	Ponty's Camp	Pontiac's Camp	Ottawa	Summit
54	Salem		Moravian Lenape	Tuscarawas
55	Salt Lick Towns	Big Salt Licks, Mingo Town	Mingo	Franklin

No.	Town Name	Alternate Names	Nation	County
56	Salt Lick Towns	Sickeunk, Kseekheoong, Captain Pipe's Town #1	Lenape	Trumbull
57	Seneca Town		Mingo	Summit
58	Shattar's Post	Joseph Shattar's Trading Post	French	Cuyahoga
59	Tushquegan		Ottawa	Lucas
60	Upper Sandusky	Wyandot Old Town, Old Town, Half-King's Town, Dunquat's Town	Wyandot	Wyandot
61	Wakatomika #1	Waketomika, Wapetomica, Waketameki, Wankatammikee	Shawnee	Muskingum
62	Wanduchale's Town	Wyandachale, Wandochale, Winaughala, Wanduxales	Lenape	Washington
63	Wapogkonetta	Wapaghkanetta, Wapahkanetta, Wapakonákunge, Wapoghoognata, Wappaukenata, Warpicanata, Wauphauthawonaukee	Shawnee	Auglaize
64	Waugau	(Maumee River Ottawa Villages)	Ottawa	Wood
65	White Eyes Town		Lenape	Coshocton
66	Will's Town	Wils Town, Sekeyunck, Saug-eha-ungh, The Salt Licks	Lenape	Muskingum
67	Shawnee Town	Shawneetown	Shawnee	Allen
68	Le Baril		Miami	Hamilton
69	Shawnee Town	Shawneetown	Shawnee	Athens
70	Shawnee Town		Shawnee	Pickaway
71	Silver Lake		Mingo	Summit

It's not surprising that Indian villages in Ohio were situated along trails and waterways, and larger Indian towns or multiple villages were located near junctions where trails and rivers intersected. They were the highways of the 18th century, and as such were the primary routes of communication and travel across the area for trade or war. They were also a means of exchanging cultural and diplomatic concepts between the disparate nations.

In many instances, the first creatures to make a trail were the forest animals, who found the easiest and most expeditious route for migration or visiting salt licks, springs and water courses. When the Indians arrived, they simply followed the animal tracks, which became the Indians' trails, and later the white men widened them with pack trains and wagons. Since the trails were generally the easiest and most direct routes, it's not surprising that many of today's roads and highways follow the course of the old Indian trails.

Not many villages were permanent in the sense that they remained in one specific location for more than a few years. While the Indians hoped for permanence, the area may have become over-hunted, over-fished, or over-trapped. In addition, wars, incursions by European settlers, or other factors forced Indians to pull up stakes and relocate, so permanence in this context is a relative term, and it must be remembered that 18th-century Ohio was very fluid and dynamic with regard to the forces acting on the Ohio Indians. While some towns existed in one location for several years, others were transient and temporary, serving as hunting camps or stopovers. Not every Ohio county had an Indian village where Indians resided for extended periods of time, but we've endeavored to include the temporary camps or villages that were noteworthy.

To simplify things, we've divided the map of Ohio into four quadrants, and listed the communities within each section of the state. With a few exceptions, the communities are

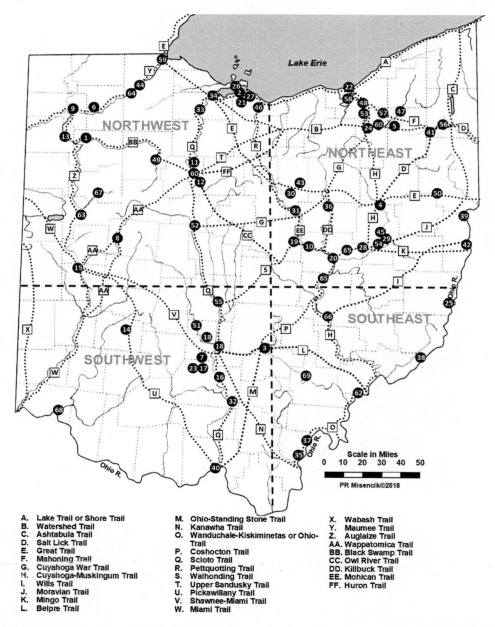

A. Lake Trail or Shore Trail	M. Ohio-Standing Stone Trail	X. Wabash Trail
B. Watershed Trail	N. Kanawha Trail	Y. Maumee Trail
C. Ashtabula Trail	O. Wanduchale-Kiskiminetas or Ohio-	Z. Auglaize Trail
D. Salt Lick Trail	Trail	AA. Wappatomica Trail
E. Great Trail	P. Coshocton Trail	BB. Black Swamp Trail
F. Mahoning Trail	Q. Scioto Trail	CC. Owl River Trail
G. Cuyahoga War Trail	R. Pettquotting Trail	DD. Killbuck Trail
H. Cuyahoga-Muskingum Trail	S. Walhonding Trail	EE. Mohican Trail
I. Wills Trail	T. Upper Sandusky Trail	FF. Huron Trail
J. Moravian Trail	U. Pickawillany Trail	
K. Mingo Trail	V. Shawnee-Miami Trail	
L. Belpre Trail	W. Miami Trail	

Quadrants used in the following four chapters. Numbers may represent more than one community in fairly close proximity.

listed alphabetically by the town's most common name. The towns named after a chief or headman have a number to Indicate the chronological order the towns were established; for example, Blue Jacket's Town #1. In the case of the Shawnee towns named Chillicothe, which simply means "principal village of the Chalahgawatha," there were occasionally more than one Chillicothe in existence at the same time. The name of the county and nearest modern town will help identify the specific Chillicothe being discussed.

Our descriptions of Indian villages are based on contemporary journals, 18th-century mapmakers, and the efforts of other historians, whom we credit as sources. We've also added GPS coordinates to help pinpoint the site of a town, but without credible archeological evidence, the specific location is often an educated guess. There is as much description as possible regarding the location of an Indian community, along with any other names it may have been called, the time period of its existence, and where the community may have subsequently relocated.

EIGHT

Towns and Posts
of Northeast Ohio

"Only to the white man was nature a wilderness, and only to him was the land infested with wild animals and savage people. To us it was tame, Earth was bountiful, and we were surrounded with the blessings of the Great Mystery."—Black Elk

4. Beaver's Town (c. 1756–c. 1764),
also King Beaver's Town, Shingas's Town, the Tuscarawas.
NOW: BOLIVAR, TUSCARAWAS COUNTY (40°38′59.49″N–81°27′16.26″W)

At the start of the French and Indian War, the Lenape Indians in western Pennsylvania were allied with the French and conducted attacks on the English colonial border settlements in the Province of Pennsylvania. The village of Kittanning on the Allegheny River served as the staging point for many of the raids. In 1758, an expedition led by Lieutenant Colonel John Armstrong's mission was to penetrate deep into western Pennsylvania to put an end to the Indian depredations. The operation was called the "Kittanning Expedition" and began with the destruction of the Lenape village of Kittanning, which gave Armstrong's attack its name. Despite the destruction of Kittanning and a few other Lenape villages, the assault did not achieve its objective of stopping the Indian attacks. While it was hailed as a success, and Armstrong was lauded as the "Hero of Kittanning," most of the Indians escaped with their prisoners, and Armstrong's attackers suffered more casualties than they inflicted.

One of the villages destroyed in the Kittanning Expedition was the town of the Lenape chief Shingas, which was near present McKees Rocks, Pennsylvania. Shingas believed it was in the best interests of the Lenape Indians to side with the French in order to free the tribe from the domineering Iroquois. He was a gifted orator and leader, as well as an accomplished warrior, and during the war he was often referred to as "Shingas the Terrible." Despite his frightening name, Shingas was rather mild-mannered and was never known to treat prisoners cruelly. As a matter of fact, he adopted several young white captives as his children, who claimed they were accorded equal treatment with his own offspring.[1]

After the destruction of Shingas's village during the Kittanning Expedition, Shingas and his brother Tamaqua ("Beaver") moved west and established their village on the west bank of the Tuscarawas River at present Bolivar, Ohio. The town was located near the junction of the Great Trail, the Cuyahoga-Muskingum Trail, and the Salt Lick Trail.

Tamaqua shared in the leadership of the village with Shingas, and was sometimes referred to as "King Beaver," although the term "king" was an English appellation and was not generally used by the Indians. The town they established was known variously as Shingas's Town, Beaver's Town, King Beaver's Town, and "The Tuscarawas," but most referred to it as "Beaver's Town."

David Zeisberger and John Heckewelder, two Moravian missionaries who preached among the Ohio Indians, visited the site of Beaver's Town in the spring of 1762. Heckewelder described the area: "[O]n the 11th of April [1762], we arrived at Tuscarawas [Beaver's Town] on the Muskingum [Tuscarawas River], after a pilgrimage of thirty-three days. We entered our cabin singing a hymn. The cabin which [Christian] Post had built before [a mile and a half above the Indian town

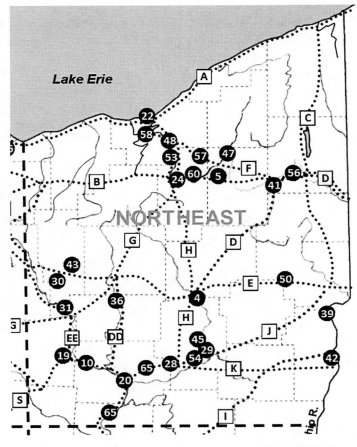

Numbers may represent more than one community in fairly close proximity.

of Tuscarawas, which was just above the present site of Bolivar], about four rods [792 feet] from the stream. No one lived near us on the same side of the river; but on the other, a mile down the stream, resided a trader, named Thomas Calhoon, a moral and religious man. Farther south was situated the Indian town called Tuscarawas; consisting of about forty wigwams."[2]

Forty dwellings would have been a fairly substantial village and would indicate the town had somewhere between 200 and 300 villagers. At the time, most Lenape settlements were rather small, consisting of between 30 and 75 people. In 1755, the Welsh surveyor and geographer Lewis Evans[3] produced the most accurate map of the Ohio country to that time. Evans's map depicted the site of the Indian town "Tuscarawas" [Beaver's Town] as "between the forks of the Tuscarawas River and the Big Sandy Creek."[4] If Evans was correct in siting the town between the forks of the two streams, it would have placed the Indian town on the east side of the Tuscarawas, which is contrary to other accounts. For example, Thomas Hutchins, the geographer with Henry Bouquet's expedition in 1764, remarked, "The Indian village was called 'King Beaver's Town at Tuscarawas,' and it was then occupied by Lenape Indians, who had removed from the vicinity of Fort Duquesne before the time of the evacuation by the French in 1758. King Beaver's Town stood on the west bank of the Tuscarawas, nearly opposite the mouth of Big Sandy Creek."[5]

While Heckewelder was at Beaver's Town in the summer of 1762, he attended the funeral of Shingas's wife. In his journal he mentions describes "the warrior who had terrorized hundreds of white settlers, his cheeks now wet with tears, his head bowed in grief as his wife's body was laid in the earth."[6]

Several other noteworthy white men visited Beaver's Town, including the famous ranger leader Major Robert Rogers. Rogers wrote:

> The 13th [January 1761], traveled six miles, and came to the Delawares' Town, called Beaver Town. This Indian town stands on good land on the west side of the Maskongam River, and opposite to the town on the east side, is a fine river [Sandy Creek] which discharges itself into it. The latter is about thirty yards wide, and the Maskongam about forty; so that when they both join they make a very fine stream, with a swift current running to the southwest. There are about 3,000 acres of cleared ground round this place. The number of warriors in this town is about 180. All the way from the Lake Sandusky I found level land and a good country. No pine trees of any sort; the timber is white, black, and yellow oak, black and white walnut, Cyprus, chestnut, and locust trees. At this town I staid till the 16th, in the morning, to refresh my party, and procured some corn of the Indians to boil with our venison.[7]

After Pontiac's Rebellion in 1763, which most of the Lenape supported, the tribe abandoned their village site on the Tuscarawas and moved to "Beaver's New Town," or Hockhocking, at the head of the Hocking River at Standing Stone, near present Lancaster, Ohio. However, Shingas did not move with them, because the chief died during the winter of 1763–64, presumably of smallpox.[8]

5. Big Son's Town (Bigson's Town, Big Sun's Town) (c. 1790s–1806). NOW: STREETSBORO, PORTAGE COUNTY (41°14'14.89"N–81°19'44.60"W)

Big Son's Town is mentioned by Frank Wilcox in his book *Ohio Indian Trails*, but he does not show it on his map. Nevertheless, there are some anecdotal accounts regarding an Indian variously named Big Son, Bigson, or Big Sun, who supposedly had a village in the area of present Streetsboro, Ohio.

Wilcox lists the town as being on a local branch trail that he calls the Chagrin Trail, which ran from the mouth of the Chagrin River at present Eastlake, Ohio, to join the junction of trails that converged near present Bolivar, Ohio. Wilcox's description of the trail reads: "From Onondaga Town [at Aurora] the Chagrin Trail continued over the pond-studded, rolling land of the watershed, south of Big Son's Seneca [Mingo] Town at Streetsboro and so on to the lakes around Kent."[9]

Most accounts indicate that Big Son was a Seneca or Mingo, but there is little information regarding him or his village. Several sources claim that Big Son was the son of Stigwanish, who supposedly had his village on the Cuyahoga River at Mingo Town or Ostionish. There is some speculation that early accounts often confuse Stigwanish with Big Son. In fact, there is no definitive proof of the relationship between the two Indians. As mentioned, some accounts claim Stigwanish was the father of Big Son, yet other accounts list them as brothers. To further muddy the waters, an event concerning one of the Indians was often ascribed to the other, leading some researchers to question whether two Indians may have been known as Stigwanish.

Big Son likely had his village near present Streetsboro, but where or when is not certain. Some historical references mention Big Son's involvement in the murder of an Ojibwe medicine man in 1798, and also implicate him in the death of Daniel Diver in 1806. For the latter deed, Big Son was reputedly imprisoned at present Warren, Ohio.

10. *Captain Pipe's Town (c. 1779–1780).*
Now: NELLIE, COSHOCTON COUNTY (40°20'9.62"N–82° 3'51.89"W)

Captain Pipe or Konieschquanoheel, "maker of daylight," who was also called Hopocan, "tobacco pipe" (c. 1725–1794), was the nephew of Custaloga, a hereditary sachem of the Muncee Lenape. At the beginning of the French and Indian War in 1754, he lived at various times at Venango at present Franklin, Pennsylvania, at Custaloga's Town at the confluence of French Creek and North Deer Creek, and also at Cussewago at present Meadville, Pennsylvania. Around 1775, Captain Pipe succeeded Custaloga as a chief of the Muncee or Wolf phratry, and around 1760, he established his own village, Sickeunk or Salt Lick Town, on the Mahoning River at present Niles, Ohio.

When the Revolutionary War began in 1775, Captain Pipe and his village remained neutral; however, in February 1778, American General Edward Hand (1744–1802) led a force of 500 militia on an expedition against the British-allied Mingo in Ohio. To the Pennsylvania militia, one Indian was no different from another, and when they discovered the peaceful village of Captain Pipe's Salt Lick Town, they immediately attacked. Captain Pipe and most of the warriors were away hunting, so there were only a handful of women, children and old people in the town. In the attack, Captain Pipe's mother, brother, and several children of Pipe's extended family were among those killed. In spite of the murder of his peaceful villagers, Captain Pipe remained neutral and did not seek revenge. In 1780, he moved his village more than eighty miles southwest to join the Lenape at Goschachgunk, at present Coshocton, Ohio.

The principal Lenape chief at the time was White Eyes, who had succeeded the aging Netawatwees. White Eyes favored accommodation with the Americans and hoped that Congress would support making Ohio an Indian state as part of the United States. However, in November of 1778, White Eyes was murdered by the Americans at Fort Pitt, and the leadership of the Lenape was thrown into turmoil. The two contenders for principal chief were Killbuck, or Gelelemend, who was the grandson of Netawatwees, and Captain Pipe, who was backed by his uncle Custaloga.

The Lenape were divided as to what course of action should be taken in the Revolutionary War. Killbuck wanted to side with the Americans, and Captain Pipe now favored joining the British, because he believed the Americans would eventually destroy the Indians to seize their land for settlement. There was also a large faction of Lenape who wished to remain neutral.

That resulted in a schism that divided the nation between pro–American and pro–British factions, and those who favored neutrality. The neutral faction was primarily the Christian Lenape at the Moravian mission villages. The differences in opinion prompted Captain Pipe to leave Goschachgunk, and establish a new village about fifteen miles up the Walhonding River, which became known as Captain Pipe's Town. The town was near the junction of the Walhonding and Killbuck Trails.

Captain Pipe's Town on the Walhonding River was in existence until late 1780, when Pipe considered the Lenape villages on the Tuscarawas, Muskingum and Walhonding Rivers too vulnerable to American attack. Convinced that it was only a matter of time before the Americans struck, Pipe abandoned his town. After spending some time near Pluggy's Town in present Delaware, Ohio, he relocated to the Sandusky River area, where he established a town on Tymochtee Creek near present Crawford, Ohio. It was fortuitous that he moved when he did, because in April 1781, a strong force of Virginians under Colonel Daniel Brodhead marched to the Muskingum area and laid waste to the Lenape towns, including the principal village of Goschachgunk.

19. Coashoskis (c. 1774–c. 1780s).
NOW: HOWARD, KNOX COUNTY (40°24'21.30"N–82°19'15.81"W)

In 1775, after stopping at the villages of New Comer's Town, White Eye's Town, Co-a-shocking, Old Hundy and New Hundy, Nicholas Cresswell visited the Lenape town of Coashoskis. He wrote the following in his journal:

Wednesday, August 30th, 1775. My bedfellow [the sister of an Indian at Old Hundy] very fond of me this morning wants to go with me. Find I must often meet with such encounters as these if I do not take a Squaw to myself. She is young and sprightly, tolerably handsome, and can speak a little English. Agreed to take her. She saddled her horse and went with us to New Hundy about 3 miles off, where she had several relations who made me very welcome to such as they had. From there to Coashoskis, where we lodged in my Squaw's Brother's, made me a compliment of a young wolf but I could not take it with me. *Thursday, August 31, 1775.* At Coashoskis. Mr. Anderson could not find his horse. Sold all my goods for Furs. In the afternoon rambled about the Town, smoking Tobacco with the Indians and did everything in my power to make myself agreeable to them. Went to see the King [chief]. He lives in a poor house, and he is as poor in dress as any of them, no emblem of Royalty or Majesty about him. He is an old man. Treated me very kindly, called me his good friend, and hoped I would be kind to my Squaw. Gave me a small string of Wampum as a token of friendship. My Squaw uneasy to see me write so much. *Friday, September 1st, 1775.* At Coashoskin Mr. Anderson found his horse. Saw an Indian Dance in which I bore a part. Painted by my Squaw in the most elegent manner. Divested of all my clothes, except my Calico short breech-clout, leggings, and Mockesons. A fire was made which we danced round with little order, whooping and hallooing in the most frightful manner. I was but a novice at the diversion and by endeavoring to act as they did made them a great deal of sport and ingratiated me much in their esteem. This is the most violent exercise to the adepts in the art I ever saw. No regular figure, but violent distortion of features, writhing and twisting the body in the most uncouth and antic postures imaginable. Their music is an old Keg with one head knocked out and covered with a skin and beat with sticks which regulates their times. The men have strings of Deer's hoofs tied round their ankles and knees, with gourds with shot or pebblestones in them in their hands which they continually rattle. The women have Morris bells or Thimbles with holes in the bottom and strung upon a leather thong tied round their ankles, knees and waists. The jingling of these Bells and Thimbles, the rattling of the Deer's hoofs and gourds, beating of the drum and kettle, with the horrid yells of the Indians, render it the most unharmonious concert, that human idea can possibly conceive. It is a favourite diversion, in which I am informed they spend a great part of their time in Winter. Saw an Indian Conjuror dressed in a Coat of Bearskin with a visor mask made of wood, frightful enough to scare the Devil. The Indians believe in conjuration and Witchcraft. Left the Town, went about two miles. Camped by the side of a run. A young Indian boy, son of Baubee, a Frenchman, came after us and insists on going with us to Fort Pitt. Find myself very unwell this evening, pains in my head and back. Nancy seems very uneasy about my welfare. Afraid of the Ague.[10]

Apparently young Cresswell called his Indian woman companion Nancy, and a few days later Nancy summoned an old woman healer to treat Cresswell. He rapidly recovered but was uncertain if it resulted from the Indian woman's treatment. Cresswell's party, including Cresswell, Anderson, their lady companions, and apparently the young boy, traveled to Fort Pitt, where the two Englishmen left their Indian companions. Cresswell's last entry concerning "Nancy" was dated "*Wednesday, September 20th, 1775.* N. [Nancy] uneasy at parting with me. Obliged to promise her to return in two moons."[11]

Cresswell didn't return to his Indian squaw Nancy. Instead he traveled through Virginia and up to New York, writing in his journal about the Revolutionary War. In July 1777, he sailed back to England, and on Saturday, April 21, 1781, thirty-one-year-old Nicholas Cresswell married Mary Mellor at Wirksworth in Derbyshire. Cresswell died in 1804 at the age of fifty-four.

Based on Cresswell's account, we know there was an Indian village named Coashoskis, and that it was no more than a day's ride from New Hundy. Frank Wilcox, in his book *Ohio Indian Trails*, places Coashoskis at the mouth of Jelloway Creek on the Kokosing River at present Howard, Ohio, which is reasonable for lack of any other documentary evidence. The distance from the assumed location of New Hundy, west of present Warsaw, Ohio, to Howard, Ohio, is about seventeen miles along the Walhonding Trail, which approximates present Ohio 715 and U.S. 36. Unfortunately, there are no other contemporary accounts that provide a description of Coashoskis. The town was in existence prior to Nicholas Cresswell's visit in 1775, and likely would not have existed much beyond the mid–1780s.

20. *Conchaké (1748–c. 1752),*
also Wyandot Old Town, Muskingum, Fugitive's Town.
Now: Coshocton, Coshocton County (40°17'13.90"N–81°50'41.86"W)

Conchaké was established in 1748 by Wyandot Indians under Nicholas Orontony; they had previously occupied villages along the south shore of Sandusky Bay. See the Junundat and Anioton sections in this book for a more detailed explanation of Orontony and the Wyandots. The purpose of Orontony's move to Sandusky Bay was to escape the French trade monopoly and expand the Wyandot fur trade to include trade with the English, whose merchandise was cheaper, more plentiful, and of superior quality. The French viewed Orontony's action as a defection that, if allowed to spread to other tribes, could threaten French sovereignty in New France.

The French tried to coerce the Wyandots to return to the fold, and when that didn't work, they increased the pressure. Rather than submit, the Wyandots fought back, and tensions escalated to the point that in 1747 open rebellion broke out between Orontony's Wyandots and the French. Even more alarming to the French was that Orontony's breakaway from the French spread to the Miami Indians under Memeskia at Pickawillany, who also joined in the rebellion. The tension with the French increased to the point that a combined force of Wyandots and Miamis burned the French Fort des Miamis at present Fort Wayne Indiana.

The French could not allow the rebellion to continue to spread, and in September of 1747 a convoy of French regular troops arrived at Fort Detroit to crush Orontony's rebellion before it attracted more Indian allies. The overwhelming force that would soon be arrayed against him convinced Orontony that his people would be engaged in a savage, bloody, and likely unwinnable war. As a result, in early 1748, Orontony burned his palisaded village on Sandusky Bay, and set off with most of his Wyandots across Ohio. By December, Orontony and his people had traveled about 105 miles southeast, where they established a town known as Conchaké. The town was located on both sides of the Tuscarawas, with the main part of the town on the north side of the river about 1.7 miles northeast of the junction of the

Tuscarawas, Walhonding, and Muskingum Rivers, and about .6 miles south of the present intersection of Airport Road and County Road 621 in Canal Lewisville, Ohio. The town was situated on the Mingo Trail, the Walhonding Trail, and the Cuyahoga-Muskingum Trail.

Orontony's town consisted of about 100 families, including about 150 warriors. The Pennsylvania trader George Croghan established a trading post at Conchaké,[12] complete with a residence and a storehouse called "The King's House." Around 1753–1754, Croghan's trading house was seized by the French and his goods were confiscated.[13] In 1756, Croghan itemized his losses; the list included the notation, "one store-house at Muskingum, £150."[14]

Around 1750, a smallpox epidemic struck the area and decimated the population of Conchaké, and one of the victims was the redoubtable Nicholas Orontony. With the loss of their leader, some Wyandots remained at Conchaké, others returned to the Sandusky Bay area, and some traveled northeast to Kuskusky near present New Castle, Pennsylvania. By 1754 only a few Indians remained at Conchaké, and by the following year the town was deserted. In November 1764, Colonel Henry Bouquet and his force of 1,500 men camped on the site of the abandoned Conchaké, and it was there that the Ohio Indians delivered up their white captives to Bouquet.

Historian Russell H. Booth was able to pinpoint the location of Conchaké by using data from various historical accounts. One source was frontiersman Christopher Gist, who described his visit to the Wyandot town from December 14, 1750, to January 15, 1751. Gist referred to the town as "Muskingum." His entry dated December 14, 1750, described the village: "The Town of Muskingum consists of about one hundred Families. When We came within site of the Town, We perceived English Colours hoisted on the King's House, and at George Croghan's."[15] The "King's House" refers to Croghan's storehouse and trading post, and the other was Croghan's residence.

Of interest, on December 26, 1750, Gist witnessed the killing of a woman prisoner who attempted to escape. Some historians erroneously state this happened at White Woman's Town, but it actually occurred at Conchaké. Gist wrote in his journal:

> This Day a Woman, who had been a long Time a Prisoner, and had deserted, & been retaken, and brought into the Town on Christmas Eve, was put to Death in the following manner: They carried her without the Town & let her loose, and when she attempted to run away, the Persons appointed for that purpose pursued her, & struck Her on the Ear, on the right Side of her Head, which they beat her flat on her Face on the Ground; they then stuck her several Times, thro the Back with a Dart, to the Heart, scalped Her, & threw the Scalp in the air, and another cut off her Head: There the dismal Spectacle lay till the Evening, & then Barny Curran Desired Leave to bury Her, which He, and his Men, and some of the Indians did just at Dark.[16]

On January 15, 1751, Gist departed Conchaké. His entry for that date was: "We left Muskingum, and went W 5 M, to the White Woman's Creek, on which is a small town; this White Woman[17] was taken away from New England, when she was not above ten years old, by the French Indians; she is now upwards of fifty, and has an Indian Husband and several Children. Her name is Mary Harris."[18]

Gist's journal indicates that Conchaké was about five miles from White Woman's Town, and that it was on the Muskingum River. Croghan apparently considered the White Woman's Creek (Walhonding River) to be an extension of the Muskingum. The entry also refers to George Croghan's residence and storehouse (King's House), which would have been of substantial construction.

William Trent (1715–1787) passed through the town in 1752. Apparently, there were inhabitants there at the time, but Trent does not mention the size of the town in the body of his journals. However, Trent added notes to his journal that expanded on his description of the town. Like Gist, Trent refers to Conchaké as Muskingum. Trent arrived at Conchaké on June 29, 1752, and it was there he learned of the destruction of Pickawillany on June 21. "We got to Muskingum, 150 miles from the Logstown, where we met some white men from Hockhocken, who told us the town [Pickawillany] was taken and all the white men killed."[19] Trent's notes referring to Conchaké state, "A Mingo town on the north bank of the Tuscarawas, five miles east of the mouth of White Woman's Creek in what is now Coshocton County. In 1751 it contained about one hundred families. Bouquet was there in 1764, and Colonel Brodhead led an expedition against it in 1780. The distance from Logstown to Muskingum by Indian trail was 122 miles."[20] While Trent's estimate of the population may be accurate, his description of Conchaké as a Mingo town may need an explanation. Trent's notes were added at a later date, sometime after 1780, and the town had changed hands several times since it was originally established by the Wyandot Chief Orontony. Trent's estimate of the distance from the town to the mouth of White Woman's Creek also needs some analysis. The Walhonding River was often called White Woman's Creek, and in fact it was depicted that way on many maps. The mouth of the Walhonding is only about 1.7 miles southwest of Conchaké. White Woman's Town was located at the confluence of Killbuck Creek and the Walhonding River, about 5.5 miles northwest of the Wyandot Town. It's conceivable that Trent erroneously referred to Killbuck Creek, where White Woman's Town was located, as White Woman's Creek.

In 1754, French military engineer Lieutenant Gaspard-Joseph Chaussegros deLéry was en route from Fort Detroit to Fort Duquesne when he passed through Conchaké on Easter Sunday, March 30, 1754. DeLéry's route took him down the Walhonding, which he refers to as the Rivière Couchaké, and almost to the Forks of the Muskingum, which deLéry calls Rivière Naguerréconnan (Beaver). Just shy of the forks, deLéry turned east to Conchaké, and arrived at the site of the Wyandot town in the late afternoon. DeLéry's observation of the town was: "Couchaké [*sic*] is a place where the Hurons took refuge during the war [Orontony's Rebellion, 1747–48]; 120 died during the summer. One can still see the graves and the remains of the village which was there at the time. Only two of the cabins are left."[21] Once again, the two remaining buildings were likely the remains of Croghan's post at Conchaké, since the trader would certainly have constructed stout structures as a residence and a storehouse. DeLéry also mentions the smallpox epidemic that claimed Nicholas Orontony as one of its victims.

Charles Stuart, who was captured by Indians in 1755, passed through the site of Conchaké on the way to Sandusky. Stuart said that on November 23, 1755, "We Continued Travelling near the river for ab^t 10 miles thro' Land Cover'd with the ground Oaks of Barrend But yet the Soil Seem^d pretty good—the s^d barrens seem^d ab^t 1½ Miles bro^d at the Broadest part and ended at the House where an Eng: Indian Trader had Formerly Lived and where was an Indian House of Both wch were deserted, S^d Two Houses stood Close on the Bank of Muskingom where was 2 small Springs Under s^d Bank Containing Exceeding Good Water."[22]

By 1755, when Stuart passed through Conchaké, the town was empty of inhabitants, but the remains of George Crogan's two buildings were still standing. Stuart's contribution to identifying the location of the town was his mention of the "2 small Springs" at the riverbank. A survey of the Tuscarawas River in 1797 mentions two springs on the south bank of the Tuscarawas, where there were once two small islands. That location is about 1.75 miles east-northeast of the Forks of the Muskingum and agrees with Russell Booth's deduction regarding the position of Orontony's town.

22. Croghan's Post (c. 1743–1748), also English Trading Post.
NOW: CLEVELAND, CUYAHOGA COUNTY (41°29'59.69"N–81°42'15.51"W)

George Croghan (1718–1782) emigrated to Pennsylvania from Ireland in 1741, and within a few years he was regarded as "King of the Pennsylvania fur traders." He was quick to learn the Indians' languages and customs, and was particularly fluent in Iroquois and Lenape dialects. He was generally held in high regard by the Indians, as much for his fair dealing as for his intimate knowledge of their language, habits and customs. As a result, he was very effective in spreading English influence in the French-controlled Ohio territory.

The French, however, considered the trans-Allegheny region as part of "New France," and their claim had been validated in several treaties between France and England. Yet, in spite of those treaties, English fur traders regularly crossed the Allegheny Mountains to trade with the Indians. The French considered the English fur traders as illegal trespassers who threatened their sovereignty, and they began to implement interdiction measures to prevent English colonists from entering New France. As previously mentioned, the Indians preferred British trade merchandise, because it was more plentiful, less expensive, and considered to be of superior quality in comparison with French trade goods. Additionally, the British naval blockade of French ports during King George's War (1740–1748) caused French trade goods to slow to a trickle, and prices soared on whatever merchandise managed to slip through the British blockade

To counter the growing number of fur traders from the English colonies, and also to maximize their own presence in Ohio, the French decided to establish a trading post on the Cuyahoga River. In 1742, François Saguin, a French-Canadian, was sent by Robert Navarre, the intendent at Fort Detroit, to establish a post in Ohio. Saguin's orders were to promote good will and loyalty to France among the Indians, and also to provide intelligence regarding English influence among the natives. However, Saguin's foremost responsibility was to generate a profit and maintain a steady flow of valuable furs to Fort Detroit. Saguin established his trading post on the west side of the Cuyahoga River near its confluence with Tinker's Creek. His post sat astride the Cuyahoga–Muskingum Trail and the Cuyahoga War Trail, and was only a short distance from the Lake Trail.

With a good location on a busy Indian thoroughfare, Saguin was well placed to conduct a lucrative trade in furs. However, around 1743 or 1744, a year or two after Saguin built his post, George Croghan established a trading post at the mouth of the Cuyahoga, at present Cleveland, Ohio, about eleven miles north of Saguin's post.

While transient English traders presented a challenge to Saguin, the competition from Croghan was devastating. Saguin couldn't compete with the Irishman either in terms of quantity, quality, or price, and Indians, like shoppers everywhere, were quick to ascertain where they would get the best deal. Saguin begged the intendent at Fort Detroit to send greater amounts of trade merchandise, including gunpowder and lead, so he could win over the Indian trade, but his pleas fell on deaf ears. The French authorities at Fort Detroit considered Saguin's venture a losing proposition, which they didn't care to support any further. In 1745, Saguin was ordered to abandon his trading post and return to Fort Detroit, where he could concentrate his trade among the northern Indians. So, in the short period of a year or two, Croghan had in effect run Saguin out of business.

Crogan's post was very successful. However, in 1747, friction between the Sandusky Bay Wyandots under Nicolas Orontony and the French at Fort Detroit flared into a war that affected trade in the region as far east as the Cuyahoga River. To make matters worse, the French believed that Croghan was complicit in fomenting the Wyandot rebellion. An official French report declared that the English traders on the Cuyahoga River had been responsible for the Indian rebellion, and though it didn't mention Croghan by name, it was clear who they considered the guilty party. The French went so far as to place a bounty on Croghan's head. The claim of Croghan's involvement in the Indian uprising may have been valid, because the English trader John Patten stated, "Croghan … had at all times persuaded the Indians to destroy the French and had so far prevailed on them, by the presents he had made them, that five French had been killed by said Indians, in the upper part of the country; that self-interest was his sole motive in everything he did, that his views were to engross the whole trade, and to scare the French from dealing with the Indians."[23] It appears from Patten's derogatory comments that, along with that of the French, his own fur trade may have been negatively impacted by Croghan.

The French hostility toward Croghan was serious enough, but a decline in the northern Ohio fur trade convinced Croghan to abandon his Cuyahoga River trading post. In 1748, he shifted his operation to the west, first at Pickawillany, and then as far as the Falls of the Ohio at present Louisville, Kentucky. That ended Croghan's trading venture on the Cuyahoga. Other traders from the English colonies used the site as temporary posts from time to time. An early history of Cleveland notes:

> After the British took possession in 1760, French and English traders continued together to traffic with the Indians on the waters of Lake Erie. No doubt a post was kept up at some point or points on the river during the large part of the Eighteenth Century, but such establishments are so slight and temporary that they are seldom noticed in history. A trading house is a very transient affair. A small log cabin covered with bark constituted all of what is designated as an establishment. If the Indian customers remove, the trader follows them, abandons his cabin, and constructs another at a more convenient place. Within a year the deserted hut is burned to the ground, and all that remains is a vacancy of an acre or two in the forest covered with grass, weeds, briers and bushes.[24]

24. Cuyahoga Town (c. 1757–1764).
Now: Cuyahoga Falls, Summit County (41°7'28.62"N–81°29'48.97"W)

Cuyahoga Town was established by the Lenape chief Netawatwee[25] ("Skilled Advisor") around 1757, at present Cuyahoga Falls, Ohio, near the junction of the Watershed Trail and the Cuyahoga Muskingum Trail. It was also at the northern terminus of the Cuyahoga–Tuscarawas portage.

The Lenape had originally been driven from their homeland along the Delaware River by unscrupulous Pennsylvanians who took their land through fraudulent schemes and blatant theft. In most cases the land grabs were abetted by the Iroquois. The Iroquois dominated the Lenape, and not only sold their land out from under them, but publicly referred to Lenape warriors as women. By the 1740s, most of the Lenape had been forced across Pennsylvania, and established their villages along the Allegheny and upper Ohio Rivers.

When the French and Indian War began in 1754, most of the Lenape sided with the French, primarily to escape Iroquois domination, and to retaliate against the Pennsylvanians. At first the war went well for the French, especially after Braddock's defeat on the Monongahela in July 1755, and Lenape warriors supported the French by raiding homesteads along the Pennsylvania frontier. In September 1756, the Kittanning Expedition, composed of 300 Pennsylvania provincial troops under Colonel John Armstrong, raided the Lenape villages along the Allegheny, with the main assault directed at the large village of

Kittanning, which was a staging point for many of the Lenape raids into Pennsylvania. Although Armstrong's attack was not a clear-cut success, since the Pennsylvanians suffered more casualties than the Indians, the raid made the Lenape aware of their vulnerability to future attacks.

Several of the Lenape leaders moved farther west to distance themselves from the Pennsylvanians, and Netawatwees relocated his village to the north bank of the Cuyahoga River at present Cuyahoga Falls, Ohio. They first took refuge in the Cuyahoga Gorge at Big Falls, which was a series of falls on the Cuyahoga River at the present site of the Ohio Edison Gorge Dam.[26] There are several caves and deep overhangs in that area of the gorge, which provided shelter to the Lenape during the early months of 1757. The most famous cave is called the "Mary Campbell Cave" or "Old Maid's Kitchen." It's reputed to have been used as a temporary shelter by Mary Campbell, who had been captured by the Lenape at the age of ten or eleven; she remained with the Lenape from 1758 until she was repatriated in 1764.

In the spring of 1758, Netawatwees relocated his village a few hundred feet north to a site above the gorge, where he established a permanent village near the present intersection of Francis Avenue and Campbell Street. The village was called Cuyahoga Town.

At the time, the principal chiefs or spokespersons of the Lenape were Shingas ("wet, marshy ground") and his brother Tamaqua ("beaver"), but around 1762, the mantle of authority shifted toward Netawatwees at Cuyahoga Town. One reason was that Netawatwees was a member of the Turtle phratry or kinship group, while Shingas and Tamaqua were of the Turkey phratry. Even though the three Lenape groups, Turtle, Turkey, and Wolf, were theoretically equal, the Lenape generally looked to the chief of the Turtle phratry

Sally Misencik in front of Mary Campbell Cave (author photograph).

for leadership. However, the most significant reason for the shift in authority toward Netawatwees was that Tamaqua and Shingas were inclined to accommodate the British, while Netawatwees urged a more militant stand against them. As a result, both Shingas and Tamaqua lost influence among the Lenape in favor of Netawatwees. In spite of the popular movement, it took some time for all of the Ohio Lenape or "Western Delaware" to recognize Netawatwees as their leading chief and recognize Cuyahoga Town as the site of the Lenape's main council fire.

In 1763, after the French and Indian War ended, the Ottawa chief Pontiac formed a confederation of Great Lakes tribes to drive the victorious British out of the region. That war was known as "Pontiac's War," or "Pontiac's Conspiracy." The war was brutal and bloody, and though the most significant battles were fought in 1763, the conflict continued in one form or another until about 1766. In 1764, Colonel Henry Bouquet led a force of 1,500 militia and British regular soldiers to the Forks of the Muskingum to subdue and pacify those Indians still engaged in the uprising.

During Bouquet's march, Netawatwees abandoned Cuyahoga Town and established a new village called Gekelemukpechunk ("the place near a river bend") on the north bank of the Tuscarawas River. Gekelemukpechunk became the new chief village and the location of the Great Council Fire of the Lenape Nation. For some reason, the British began to refer to Netawatwees as "New Comer," and his town as New Comers Town. There is a fictional story that the name "New Comer" resulted when a white captive named Mary Harris jealously murdered her Indian husband and cast blame on the "new comer" woman who won his affection. See White Woman's Town for more information.

Henry Bouquet campsite, Winfield, Tuscarawas County, Ohio (author photograph).

28. *Gekelemukpechunk (c. 1764–c. 1776), also Kecalamúkpechink, New Comer's Town, Netwawatwees's Town, Kekalemapehoong, Neghkuunque, Red Bank, Kighalapegha.*
Now: Newcomerstown, Tuscarawas County (40°16′32.90″N–81°35′20.52″W)

Gekelemukpechunk ("the place near a river bend")[27] was a Lenape village established by Netawatwees ("Skilled Advisor") on the north side of the Tuscarawas River east of present Newcomerstown, Ohio. Around 1762, Netawatwees began to be recognized as the leading chief of the Ohio Lenape, or, as they were sometimes called, the "Western Delaware," and consequently his village was considered the site of the Lenape's main council fire. Prior to Netawatwees's move from Pennsylvania, Tamaqua and his brother Shingas of the Turkey clan were regarded as the Lenape leaders, but the mantle of authority shifted to Netawatwees. That was because Tamaqua and Shingas were considered too willing to accommodate the British, while Netawatwees urged a more militant stand against them. Notwithstanding the popular movement, it took some time for Netawatwees to be recognized as the leading chief by all the Lenape. For some reason yet unknown, the British began to refer to Netawatwees as "New Comer."[28]

In 1763, after the end of the French and Indian War, the Ottawa chief Pontiac formed a confederation of Great Lakes tribes who had been allied with the French. Their goal was to drive the victorious British out of the region. That war was known as "Pontiac's War," or "Pontiac's Conspiracy." The war was brutal and bloody, and though the most significant battles were fought in 1763, the conflict continued in one form or another until about 1766. In 1764, Colonel Henry Bouquet, the commander at Fort Pitt, led 1,500 militia and British regular soldiers to the Forks of the Muskingum in an attempt to subdue and pacify those Indians who were still engaged in Pontiac's uprising. It was during that time that Netawatwees relocated from Cuyahoga Town to Gekelemukpechunk on the north bank of the Tuscarawas River, which became principal village and site of the Great Council Fire of the Lenape Nation.

In the meantime, Shingas died in 1764, presumably from smallpox, and Tamaqua lost additional stature to Netawatwees during Bouquet's expedition into the Ohio country. Most of the Lenape Indians were settled in the area of the Forks of the Muskingum, and when Bouquet's force approached in October of 1764, he was met by representatives of the Indian tribes. By this time much of the impetus had gone out of Pontiac's War, and the chiefs were reluctant to engage Bouquet's force in battle. On October 14, several Lenape chiefs met with Bouquet and offered belts of peace symbolizing a chain of friendship, but Bouquet refused the friendship belts and the Indians' peace overtures. Instead, he demanded that before any peace talks could commence, all of the white captives taken by the Indians had to be returned for repatriation. Bouquet scheduled a meeting on November 10 and made it clear that he expected all of the chiefs to attend.

The Lenape were divided on whether to accede to Bouquet's demands, and they were more at a loss on how to respond to the return of the white captives. Certainly, some of the captives were eager to return to their homes in the colonies, but many of them had lived with the Indians for years and were fully assimilated into the Indian community. Some had been taken captive at so young an age that the Indian life was all they knew. Most were part of Indian families, with spouses and children, and they did not want to be separated from them. In short, a large percentage of the former white captives did not want to be repatriated.

In addition, most of the Lenape were angered at Bouquet's haughty rejection of their peace overtures and his imperious demands, and when some chiefs like Tamaqua and Custaloga decided to accept Bouquet's condition, they encountered backlash. The Lenape began to call Custaloga an "old woman"[29] for agreeing to Bouquet's terms, and Tamaqua's influence and authority among the Lenape diminished even more as a result of his meek acceptance of Bouquet's orders.

Netawatwees, on the other hand, refused to attend the meeting with Bouquet, which heartened the Lenape, but angered Bouquet. As a result, Bouquet took the unusual and unrealistic approach of attempting to strip Netawatwees of his chieftainship. On November 11, 1764, Bouquet announced that "from this Moment he is no more a Chief,"[30] and he ordered the Lenape to select a "more cooperative 'king.'"[31] The Lenape went through the motions and named Tatpiskahong as the replacement for Netawatwees, but his chieftainship was more cosmetic than real. The Ohio Lenape tacitly ignored Bouquet in that regard and continued to accept Netawatwees as their principal chief.

In spite of Netawatwees's refusal to meet with Bouquet, the chief was reluctant to risk a war over the return of the white captives, and he considered it more prudent to acquiesce on that issue. About 260 English, French, and former slaves who had been captured by the Lenape and Shawnee were brought to Bouquet's camp to be repatriated.[32] Many of the captives had to be forced to accompany Bouquet on his return to Fort Pitt, but many escaped and returned to Ohio during the march, and they continued to do so for several years, even after they had been reunited with their white families.

Netawatwees's village was called Gekelemukpechunk, but because of the British penchant for naming a village after the resident chief, it was often referred to as "New Comer's Town." As the chief village of the Ohio Lenape, it was large with well-constructed dwellings. In fact, like several villages in the area, New Comer's Town had houses that were almost identical to homes in the white colonial settlements. In 1765, a Lenape chief sent a message to Bouquet at Fort Pitt requesting a handsaw, 300 shingle nails, and a draw knife.[33] A 1772 description of New Comer's Town described the houses as "some of logs and the others the bark of trees, fastened by elm bark to poles stuck in the ground and bent over at the top,"[34] in the traditional style of Eastern Woodland Indians' wigwams.

Along with the bark houses, there were also well-built log houses, with "stone chimneys, chambers and sellers [*sic*]" that were "well shingled with nails."[35] Not only did some Indians live in colonial-style houses, but one account describes meals that were served on "ceramic plates at stone fireplaces."[36] In addition, the traditional standard meals of the Ohio Indians, consisting of corn, beans, squash, fish, and venison, were enhanced with new menu items that previously had been found only in white households. The Indians now served cabbage, turnips, and cucumbers, and occasionally "'good veal,' biscuits, traditional hominy, and 'Indian-cake, baked in the ashes,' washed down with milk and topped off with chocolate or a kettle of tea."[37]

The exact location of Gekelemukpechunk has not been determined, but from written descriptions and early maps, it appears to have been on the north side of the Tuscarawas River east of present Newcomerstown. There are two possible sites about one and a half miles apart. A survey map dated 1797[38] compared with a current topographical chart appears to show New Comer's Town about .75 miles from the center of present Newcomerstown, and just east of the Pilling Street bridge. In addition, vestiges of the town were located at this site during the 1797 survey. The other possible site is about three miles east of Newcomerstown,

Sally Misencik in door of bark-covered wigwam at Fort Roberdeau, Altoona, Pennsylvania. Note adjustable smoke-hole flap at top. Blockhouse-style log houses with shingle roofs in background (author photograph).

near the point where U.S. 77 crosses the Tuscarawas River. A 1781 French map based on Hutchins's 1764 map shows New Comer's Town near the confluence of the Tuscarawas River and present Dunlap Creek, about where the I-77 bridge crosses the Tuscarawas River.

The Moravian missionary David Zeisberger wrote the most complete description of New Comer's Town from his visit on March 5, 1775:

> Gekelemukpechunk, which is situated on the Muskingum River, is rather a large Indian town and is said to consist of 100 houses which I think is quite likely. Most of them are block houses. The chief's house is a studded house with a floor and stairs of cut wood. It has a brick chimney, a shingle roof and is the biggest one in the town. A few other houses have shingle roofs too. The countryside is beautiful and consists of a vast plain. The land on both sides of the river is good. The river 'here' is about as wide as the Delaware near Easton, but 6 miles further down a tributary flows into it which is just as wide.... Most of the Indians here were Unami and belong to the Turtle Clan. There are a few Munsee, part of them come here only a year ago, namely from Goschgoschunk [a mission town at present Tionesta, Pennsylvania] where they several times attended our services and were very friendly to us.[39]

Netawatwees himself was on congenial terms with the Christian missionaries, particularly the Moravians David Zeisberger and John Heckewelder, whom he provided the land on which to establish their Christian settlements of Schönbrunn and Gnadenhütten. Netawatwees also didn't seem to mind that many of the Lenape Indians converted to Christianity, but the old chief never converted. One of the things that troubled Netawatwees was the discernable friction and lack of unity between the various denominations of Christian

Section of a 1781 French map based on Capt. Thomas Hutchins's map of 1764 (Library of Congress, Geography and Map Division-2001695748).

missionaries. He mentioned that "he could not understand why there were so many different denominations." He even considered traveling to England to ask the king about that, saying the matter "was disturbing to his heart."[40]

In 1774, a breach occurred among the Lenape, many of whom considered the old Netawatwees "unfit for the charge & desire that the neighboring Indians will take notice, etc."[41] They began to look to the young chief White Eyes, and the Lenape Council selected him as their new leader. White Eyes pressed for a consolidation of all Lenape at a new location at the junction of the Muskingum, Tuscarawas, and Walhonding Rivers, which was agreed to by the Grand Lenape Council. Around 1775–1776, soon after the start of the Revolutionary War, the Lenape, including Newtawatwees, relocated. The new Lenape village was called Goschachgunk (Black Bear Town), and the name was likely based on the Wyandot name Conshaké. With the move, Goschachgunk became the new Lenape capital. The town was located in the present city of Coshocton between Third Street and the river.

20. Goschachgunk (c. 1775–1781), also Coashoking, Coshocton, Muskingum.
Now: Coshocton, Coshocton County (40°16′26.90″N–81°52′8.29″W)

In 1774, Koquethagechton or White Eyes had been chosen to replace ninety-six-year-old Netawatwees as the principal chief of the Lenape,[42] and in 1775, White Eyes proposed to relocate the principal town of the Lenape from Gekelemuckpechunk or New Comer's Town to the Forks of the Muskingum. The Lenape traditionally lived in smaller scattered villages, and White Eyes thought it best to consolidate the Ohio Lenape communities. There was not much initial support for the move, but after much debate in the council, White Eyes made an eloquent speech about strengthening the common defense of the Lenape through closer communities, and the council approved the plan. The move was made around 1775–1776, and the location chosen was on the southeast side of the Forks of the Mukingum. The town was called Goschachgunk or "Black Bear Town," and the name was likely based on the old Wyandot name Conshaké.

With the move, Goschachgunk became the new Lenape capital, and the site of the Lenapes' Grand Council Fire. John Heckewelder, who called the village "Goshochking," described the town: "The dwellings were built in the cabin and not the usual wigwam style."[43] The village extended from the river to Third Street, and the principal avenue in the town corresponded with present Second street, with the cabins standing close together in two long rows on each side of the avenue. "The remains of fire-places, which are said to have been at the north end of each of the cabins, could be easily discerned by the first white settlers of the place."[44]

Netawawatees, who was no longer the principal chief, apparently still had stature and prestige among the Lenape, and although he never became a Christian, he liked and respected the Moravian missionaries. When the Lenape established Goschachgunk, Netawatwees and his grandson Killbuck granted David Zeisberger a tract of land nearby upon which to establish another Christian Indian village, which the Moravians named Lichtenau. In October 1776, Netawatwees attended a council at Fort Pitt, where he died before the council was concluded. He was about ninety-eight years old.

White Eyes was the principal chief, and Killbuck and Captain Pipe were influential leaders. In September 1778, they signed a treaty with the United States at Fort Pitt. One of the provisions of the treaty was that Ohio would become an Indian state and admitted to the Union as the 14th State. In addition, White Eyes was commissioned a lieutenant-colonel in the American Army to lead the Lenape in support of American military operations against British forces at Detroit and Indiana.

Unfortunately, the treaty to create an Indian state in Ohio was never presented to Congress for ratification. The primary reason was that with the surrender of Burgoyne at Saratoga in 1777, and the resultant Franco-American alliance, the Americans no longer were urgent about maintaining the Ohio Indians as allies. White Eyes continued to press for ratification of the treaty, but to no avail, and in the autumn of 1778, he died at age forty-eight. The Army under General Lachlan McIntosh reported: "November 20th, 1778. Heard that the advance party of the army came to Tuscarawi night before last: likewise that Col. White Eye died not far from Pittsburg from an old illness plus smallpox."[45] Moravian missionary David Zeisberger mentioned the death of White Eyes in his diary: "[November] The 20th. We received news in a letter from Colonel Gibson that the first troops from the army had arrived at Tuscarawi yesterday evening, and also that Colonel White Eye had died not far from Pittsburgh 15 days ago today. He had an old illness and then got small pox in addition to that."[46] Several years later, George Morgan, the Indian agent and former friend of White Eyes, claimed that White Eyes was murdered or "treacherously put to death" by an American militia officer on November 5, 1778.

After the death of White Eyes, Captain Pipe became leery of American promises, especially since his mother, brother and brother's children had been killed by American troops in 1778. Pipe no longer believed in American willingness to protect the Lenape, and he began to consider joining the British as allies. A short time later, Captain Pipe left the

Goschachgunk area, leaving Killbuck as the principal leader. Captain Pipe initially moved his village farther up the Walhonding River, and eventually relocated to Tymochtee Creek in the Upper Sandusky River area. In 1780, Gelelemend, or Killbuck,[47] with about thirty Lenape who supported the American cause, left Goschachgunk and returned to Gekelemukpechunk or New Comer's Town, which was Netawatwees's old village.

It was fortunate they did, because in early April 1781, believing that the Lenape were going to join the British, a strong force of 300 Virginians under Colonel Daniel Brodhead marched to the Forks of the Muskingum. On April 19, Brodhead's troops destroyed Goschachgunk, surprising a number of Indians who remained in the town. They killed fifteen warriors and captured twenty, five of whom were Christian Indians. The Christian Indians were released, but the rest of the prisoners were killed by Brodhead's troops.[48] After Brodhead's troops destroyed Goschachgunk, they also burned the abandoned mission village of Lichtenau to the ground.

30. *Greentown (Green Town) (c. 1783–c. 1815), also Lenape Town.*
Now: Perrysville, Ashland County (40°41'38.83"N–82°19'33.44"W)

Greentown, in Ashland County, Ohio, was established in 1782 by Lenape Indians who left Hell Town at the confluence of the Clear Fork and Black Fork of the Mohican River. Hell Town was abandoned in 1782 as a result of encounters with American troops and the alarming 1782 massacre of Christian Indians at Gnadenhütten by Pennsylvania militia. Paxomet, the Lenape chief at Hell Town who was also known as Captain Thomas Armstrong[49] (c. 1745–c. 1816), led most of his villagers about eight miles northwest up the Black Fork of the Mohican River, where they established a new village called Greentown. It's believed Paxomet was either half-white or a white person whose family name was Steen or Steene, and was reputedly captured as a youth and raised by the Lenape. Greentown was about 2.7 miles north-northwest of present Perrysville, Ohio, and supposedly was named for British Loyalist Thomas Green. It was situated on the north side of the river, about 0.7 miles west of the intersection of present Ohio Routes 39 and 511.

Not all of the Lenape followed Paxomet to Greentown. Some fled to the Indian settlements on the Sandusky River, while others fought for the British under the leadership of Thomas Green. Thomas Green is and was a fairly common name, so it's difficult to detail his life with accuracy. However, according to popular legend, Green enlisted in the American Army on February 18, 1776, but apparently had a change of heart. He enlisted in Captain Rudolph Bunner's Company of the 2nd Pennsylvania Battalion under Colonels Arthur St. Clair and Joseph Wood but deserted the very same day. Green then joined John Butler's Company of Butler's Rangers, a partisan Loyalist group that fought on the side of the British. Butler's Rangers mostly operated in western New York and northern Pennsylvania and had a reputation for brutal and violent warfare. Records indicate that a Private Thomas Green began service with Butler's Rangers on Christmas Day 1777 and served with the group until October 24, 1778.

Thomas Green reputedly was buried at Greentown, and for some unknown reason the Indian village bore his name. Interestingly, in 1813, ten years after Ohio became a state, the township in which Greentown was located was supposedly named after Thomas Green. If that is true, it's ironic that a township was named in honor of a deserter from the American Army who subsequently fought for the British against the Americans.

Greentown was a substantial village with between "150 and 200 families who lived in

Greentown historical markers (author photographs).

pole cabins. In the center of the town was a council house built of logs."[50] The cabins were primarily situated on a plateau-like hill in the vicinity of the council house, and a burial ground was located on the knoll to the west of the village.[51]

Although Greentown was principally a Lenape village, sources indicate there may have been some Mingos living there. Jonathan Chapman (1774–1845), better known as "Johnny Appleseed," often visited Greentown, where he had a friendly rapport with the inhabitants. The Moravian missionary John Heckewelder wrote that he visited Greentown in 1808. Heckewelder commented that the Lenape originally called Europeans *Wapsid Lenape* (white people). However, members of the Virginia militia often carried swords, and the Lenape gave Virginians the name *Mechanschican* (long knives) to distinguish them from other white people. In New England, the Lenape endeavored to imitate the sound of the national name of the English, which they pronounced *Yengees*."[52] The Lenape liked and respected the Quakers from their dealings with William Penn, and "they call them *Quakœls*, not having in their language the sound expressed by the letter R. They say they have always found the Quakers to be good, honest, affable and peaceable men, and never have had reason to complain of them."[53] As Heckewelder once rode by a cabin at Greentown, he said he heard an Indian comment in his language, "See! What a number of people are coming along! What! And among all these not one *long knife*! All *Yengees!*" Then the Indian spotted Heckewelder, and corrected himself, "No! One *Quœkel*."[54]

About 1809, white settlers began to move into the Greentown area, although a French-Canadian fur trader named Jean Baptiste Jerome had been living in the area of present Jeromesville, Ohio, prior to that time. When the War of 1812 began, the white settlers were concerned that the local Indians might support the hostile Indians, who were allied with the British. That concern was exacerbated after American Major General William Hull surrendered Fort Detroit on August 16, 1812, to a lesser force of British troops commanded by Major General Isaac Brock and Shawnee warriors under Tecumseh. Fearing that the local Indians would join forces with the British and Tecumseh, the local white population decided to remove the Indians from that area.

In late August 1812, American militia troops under a Captain Douglas arrived at Greentown to oust the Indians. The removal was not without incident. Paxomet, who was still chief of the village, strongly objected to the forced removal. There were about eighty warriors in the village,[55] which caused Douglas some anxiety in case the Indians resisted. Paxomet tried to reason with Douglas, and even offered to surrender all of the Indians' guns and warlike weapons, in addition to having a roll call each day to guarantee that no Indians were supporting the British.[56] Douglas was unmoved, and in desperation Paxomet asked a local settler named Peter Kinney to intercede on the Indians' behalf. Kinney argued so heatedly in favor of the Indians, and railed against the injustice, that Douglas drew his sword and threatened Kinney. Douglas then asked another settler named James Copus to help him convince the Indians to leave peacefully. Copus, who settled in the area in 1809, was well-respected by the Indians, and he argued so vehemently against the Indians' forced removal that Douglas threatened to arrest him as a traitor.

The stalemate was broken when Douglas personally guaranteed the safety of the Indians and assured them their property would not be molested if they agreed to leave. Reluctantly, Copus persuaded the Indians to abandon Greentown based on Douglas's personal guarantee that "their property would remain safe until peace, and that no violence would be offered his Indians on their way to Urbana, the point to which they were to be removed."[57] Before the Indians departed, James Kinney and a James Cunningham assisted the Indians with a detailed inventory of all of their property. James Copus's sons Henry, James and Wesley were with their father at the time, and witnessed the Indians' departure. Years later, Wesley, who was nine years old when the Indians left Greentown, recalled the event. He said that when the Indians departed under escort of Douglas's troops, eight or ten soldiers remained in the village. When the Indians were barely out of sight, "to the surprise and horror of Mr. Copus and his three sons, [the soldiers] deliberately set fire to the village, and nearly everything in it was consumed in their presence."[58] The departing Indians saw the smoke from their burning village and believed they had been duped by Copus, who assured them their property and possessions would be safe. The Greentown Indians were marched across the Black Fork to present Lucas, Ohio, and then to Mansfield and eventually Urbana, where they were placed under the jurisdiction of John Johnson, the federal agent in Piqua.

Around September 10, 1812, the Zimmer (Zeimer or Seymour) family was killed and scalped by Indians. The local people believed that some of the departing Lenape from Greentown murdered the Zimmers in retaliation for the destruction of their village. Following the death of the Zimmers, James Copus asked for protection for his family, and they temporarily took residence in a nearby blockhouse. By September 14, Copus considered it safe enough to return home, and he and his family were escorted back by nine soldiers. The following day, September 15, seven of the soldiers were washing at a nearby spring when they were attacked by Indians. One wounded soldier ran to the Copus cabin, and when James Copus opened the door, he was killed by a musket ball in the chest. The remaining soldiers and Copus family members eventually drove the Indians off. Three soldiers along with James Copus were killed in the fight, and several were wounded, including young Nancy Copus, who was shot in the knee.

Even Jean Baptiste Jerome, who was described as a man of positive character, generous, and devoted to friendships, was suspected of aiding the British and hostile Indians. He was arrested and imprisoned in Wooster, while his wife and young daughter accompanied the Indians to Urbana. Jerome was released several weeks later through the intercession of his neighbors, but he never saw his wife and daughter again. They both died of exposure shortly after their removal.

Paxomet never returned to Greentown, and instead settled along the Sandusky River. After the war, his sons often returned to visit their old friends, including the Copus children. Though Indians camped on the site of Greentown from time to time, the Lenape village was not reestablished after its destruction in 1812.

24. Gwahago (c. 1750s–c. 1809), likely a reference to Mingo Town or Ostionish.
NOW: VALLEY VIEW OR AKRON, CUYAHOGA OR SUMMIT COUNTY

A 1755 map by Le Sieur Robert de Vaugondy (1688–1766) depicts an Iroquois village called Gwahago on the east bank of the Cuyahoga River, upstream or south of the mouth of a tributary that is most likely Tinker's Creek. Vaugondy refers to the Sandusky River as Rivière Blanche (White River), which he apparently copied from a 1746 map by Jean Baptiste Bourguinon d'Anville (1697–1782) who labeled the Sandusky River "Rivière des Femmes Blanch" (River of White Women). D'Anville must have assumed the Sandusky to be an extension of the Walhonding River, which was referred to as White Woman's Creek.

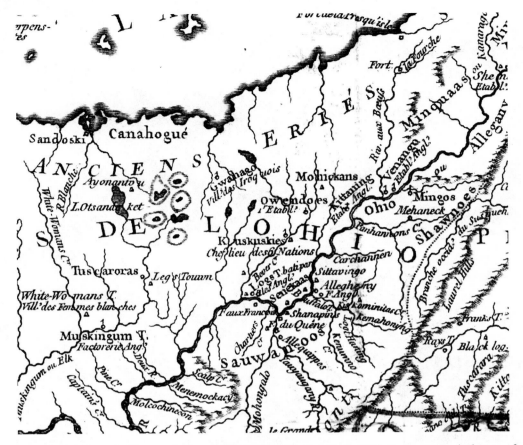

Section of Robert de Vaugondy map of 1755 showing Gwahago Vill' des Iroquois (Library of Congress, Geography and Map Division-74693316).

It's important to know that cartographers often copied older maps, which gives the illusion of accuracy by indicating agreement among different mapmakers. Apparently, the English cartographer Dr. John Mitchell (1711–1768) also used French maps as a basis for his 1755 map, because he likewise referred to the Sandusky River as "R. Blanc" (White River).

Regarding the Indian village of Gwahago, Mitchell placed the site of the Iroquois town at the same location as shown on Vaugondy's 1755 map. Mitchell shows the site on the east side of the Cuyahoga, also upstream or south of the mouth of Tinker's Creek. Mitchell also referred to the Cuyahoga River as the "Gwahago River," and the Indian village Gwahago is likely a corruption of the word Cuyahoga that Mitchell used as a name for the town, as in the case of the Lenape Chief Netawatwees's "Cuyahoga Town."

The scale on the Vaugondy and Mitchell maps makes it difficult to determine the precise site of Gwahago, and the distances depicted on Mitchell's map are not very accurate. For example, the distance is shown as 40 miles between the mouth of the Cuyahoga and Fort Sandusky, but it is actually closer to 63 miles. Mitchell places Gwahago about 30 miles from the mouth of the Cuyahoga, which would place the Indian town somewhere between present Peninsula, Ohio, and Akron, Ohio, depending on how close the distance followed the twists and turns of the Cuyahoga River. Mitchell's distance estimate would place Gwahago near the location of Ostionish or Mingo Town, which was likely located near the conflu-

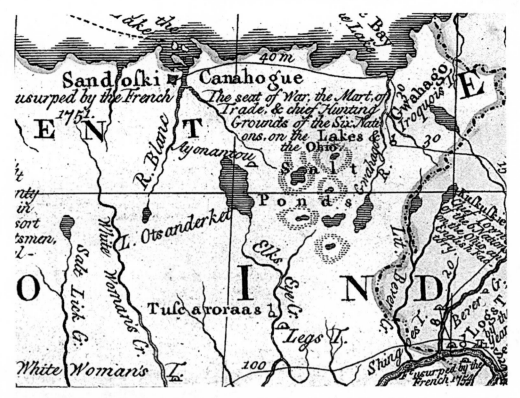

Section of John Mitchell map (1755) showing Gwahago Iroquois T. and Gwahago [Cuyahoga] River (Library of Congress, Geography and Map Division-74693187).

ence of the Cuyahoga and Little Cuyahoga Rivers between Cuyahoga Falls and Akron. It's probable that Gwahago was not a separate Iroquois or Mingo town, but merely a reference to Ostionish or Mingo Town.

Both Vaugondy and Mitchell place a significant amount of importance on the Cuyahoga River. They both label the area between the Cuyahoga and Sandusky Rivers as "Canhogué," which appears to be a reference to the Cuyahoga River. Mitchell expands on the designation Canhogué by defining the region as "the seat of war, the mart of trade, and the chief hunting grounds of the Six Nations on the Lake and the Ohio."[59]

Evans's map of 1755 shows a Mingo town on the west side of the Cuyahoga upstream (south) of François Saguin's trading post that he labeled as "French House." This reinforces the concept that Gwahago, Mingo Town, and Iroquois Town all refer to the same Mingo village on the Cuyahoga River.

Incidentally, according to popular belief, the name Cuyahoga comes from the Mohawk word "Cayagaga," meaning "crooked river," which seems logical since the river follows a very serpentine course and has an overall "U" shape. Another source indicates the river was named "Cuyohaga," which in the Seneca language means "place of the jawbone." An examination of Mohawk language books shows that the Mohawk word for "crooked" is *te-yots-hà-k-tonh*, and the word for "river" is *ka-hyón-ha*. According to the *Handbook of the Seneca Language*, the Seneca word for "jaw" is *kyo-há-keh*, which seems phonetically closer to the word Cuyahoga. So perhaps Cuyahoga does not mean "crooked river" after all, but rather has a connotation to the word "jaw."

Section of Evans's 1755 map (Library of Congress, Geography and Map Division-74693076).

31. *Hell Town (c. 1770–1782), also Clear Town, Clear Water Town.*
Now: LOUDONVILLE, ASHLAND COUNTY (40°36'18.73"N–82°15'19.83"W)

Lenape Indians under chief Paxomet (c. 1745–c. 1816), established Hell Town either in 1770[60] or 1775-76.[61] The location of the village was 2.25 miles southwest of present Loudonville, Ohio, on a 260-foot hill immediately southwest and overlooking the confluence of the Clear Fork and Black Fork of the Mohican River. It was the site of a previous Mingo encampment from about 1755. Paxomet was also known as Captain Thomas Armstrong,[62] and was believed to be either half-white or a white person whose family name was Steen or Steene, and who was captured as a young boy and raised by the Lenape.

Despite its unusual name, there was nothing sinister or satanic about Hell Town. It was originally called "Town of the Clear Water" or "Clear Town," because it was situated on the clear waters of Clear Fork; however, to the visiting German-speaking Moravian missionaries, the word for "clear" was "hell," and the village subsequently became known as "Hell Town."

The village was located adjacent to the Cuyahoga War Trail, which was a major Indian thoroughfare that ran from present Cleveland, south along the Cuyahoga River to the Tuscarawas River and then west-southwest to present Delaware, Ohio, where it joined the north-south Scioto Trail. In the vicinity of Hell Town, Ohio, Route 95 follows the course of the Cuyahoga War Trail, although a portion of the old trail lies under the man-made Pleasant Hill Lake.

The Lenape lived at Hell Town through most of the Revolutionary War until 1782. Many Lenape sided with the British during the war and carried out raids against the American frontier settlements. After the surrender of British General Cornwallis at Yorktown, Virginia, in October 1781, the Americans launched punitive attacks against the Ohio In-

Confluence of the Clear Fork and Black Fork of the Mohican River. Hell Town was located on the hill in the background (author photograph).

dians. The number of clashes with American units increased, and when word reached the Lenape of the Gnadenhütten massacre of Christian Indians by Pennsylvania militia, Paxomet felt it was prudent to remove his villagers to another location.

Paxomet led most of his villagers about eight miles northwest up the Black Fork of the Mohican River, where they established a new village called Greentown. However, not all of the villagers followed Paxomet. Some fled farther west to the Sandusky River area, and others joined British partisan units to continue the fight against the Americans. By the end of 1782, the Lenape village of Hell Town was abandoned.

10. Hundy (c. 1774–c. 1781), also Old Hundy.
Now: Warsaw, Coshocton County (40°20'7.37"N–82°0'8.86"W)

Most sources referring to Hundy locate the village on the north side of the Walhonding River, or White Woman's Creek, as it was often called in the 18th century. The specific location of the village is difficult to determine, because contemporary descriptions are rather vague. For example, one reference mentions "Old Hundy, a Munsie town on the north side of the Walhonding between the mouths of Killbuck and Mohican creeks."[63] In this reference to Mohican Creek, it's not clear whether the author meant the mouth of Mohawk Creek or the mouth of the Mohican River. At any rate, the straight-line distance from the mouth of Killbuck Creek to Mohawk Creek is more than six and a half miles, and from Killbuck

Creek to the mouth of the Mohican River is more than twelve miles. Unfortunately, there doesn't appear to be a more precise description of the town's location.

In 1775, Nicholas Cresswell (1750–1804), an English diarist, traveled through Ohio with a companion named John Anderson and visited Hundy on August 29. Young Cresswell described his unusual welcome, but his description of the town's location is not very detailed. He wrote:

> [On] August 29th 1775, Left White-Eye's town [north of present West Lafayette, Ohio]. Saw the bones of one Mr. Cammel, a White man, that had been killed by the Indians. Got to Co-a-shoking [Goschachgunk, present Coshocton] about noon. It is at the forks of the Muskingham. The Indians have removed from Newcomer Town to this place. King Newcomer [Netawatwees] lives here. Sold part of my goods here to good advantage. Crossed a branch of Muskingham and went to Old Hundy, this is a scattering Indian settlement. Lodged at a Mohawk Indian's house, who offered me his Sister and Mr. Anderson his Daughter to sleep with us, which we were obliged to accept.[64]

The next day, Cresswell continued, "Wednesday, August 30, 1775. My bedfellow very fond of me this morning and wants to go with me…. Agreed to take her."[65]

Cresswell returned to Goschachgunk [present Coshocton] fairly early the next day, and described activities in the afternoon. That would seem to indicate that Hundy was an easy half-day journey from Goschachgunk on foot or horseback. Cresswell indicated that his woman companion had a horse to ride, as did Cresswell and Anderson. He said that the chief's sister who left with him "saddled her horse and went with us to New Hundy about 3 miles off, where she had several relations who made me very welcome to as much as they had."[66]

Present Warsaw, Ohio, near the confluence of the Walhonding River and Beaver Run, is about eight and a quarter straight-line miles from present Coshocton, but Cresswell likely followed the slightly meandering Walhonding River, in which case the distance would be about ten miles between the two points. So it would seem that Hundy would be somewhere in the vicinity of present Warsaw, Ohio, which would place it between the sites of White Woman's Town at the mouth of Killbuck Creek and Captain Pipe's Town near the mouth of Mohawk Creek. Mohawk Creek instead of Mohican Creek is probably what the author meant in the source cited, since there is no Mohican Creek in the vicinity.

Ms. Siegrun Kaiser, Ph.D., wrote, "[N]ach 1774 ein deutlicher Nordwest-Trend der Munsee zu beobachten. Zwischen der Mündung des Killbuck Creek und des Mohican Creek in den Walhonding Creek gründeten sie ihre neue Siedlung *Old Hundy*."[67] Translated: "After 1774, a significant northwest trend of the Munsee can be observed. Between the mouth of Killbuck Creek and the Mohican Creek in the Walhonding Creek, they founded their new settlement of Old Hundy." Dr. Kaiser further states that in 1775, the Muncees also established the village of New Hundy three miles west of Old Hundy.[68] There is no indication of when the town of Old Hundy ceased to exist, but it's unlikely it survived Colonel Daniel Brodhead's 1781 expedition against the Indians who lived in the area of the Forks of the Muskingum.

36. Killbuck Town (c. 1760s–c. 1770s).
NOW: HOLMESVILLE, HOLMES COUNTY (40°39′1.77″N–81°56′58.61″W)

There are several references to a Lenape village called Killbuck Town, but there are also a number of challenges in determining its location and time period. Part of the problem is that there were two prominent Lenape chiefs named Killbuck, and it's sometimes difficult to determine, which Killbuck is being referenced.

The older Killbuck, or Killbuck Sr. (1710s–1780s), also named Bemino, was born around 1710. According to various sources, he was either the son or the brother of Netawatwees, the principal Lenape chief. The younger Killbuck, or Killbuck Jr. (c. 1737–1811), also named Gelelemend (Leader) was born about 1737, and it follows that he was either the grandson or nephew of Netawatwees. Most sources refer to Gelelemend or Killbuck Jr., as the grandson of Netawatwees, but the only reference to support that premise comes from a single statement in David Zeisberger's diary dated April 16, 1776: "John Killbock, Netawatwees' grandson (he is something of a headman at Goschachgunk) came with quite a number of Indians and they offered to help us in our work."[69] Killbuck Jr., is often referred to as John Killbuck and John Henry Killbuck, while his father, Killbuck Sr., is often called "Captain Killbuck."

As a counterpoint to Zeisberger's diary entry, there is considerably more evidence to indicate that Netawatwees and Killbuck Sr. were brothers, and Killbuck Jr. or Gelelemend was the nephew of Netawatwees. Zeisberger's diary entry for January 3–4, 1776, reads: "Killebock's son said to them: 'I am very glad that I came hither.... It is true that my uncle, the chief desires that I should take his place."[70] Zeisberger's February 2, 1776, diary entry reads: "Jo Peepe from chief Netawatwees in the company of two of the latter's councilors, one being the son of old Killebock. After the service, the latter informed our conference brethren that he had talked with his uncle, the chief, and had told him the following: 'My uncle: I will now tell you what I intend to do....' His uncle thereupon had replied to him: ...Thereupon John Killebock said to the chief...."[71] Zeisberger's diary dated April 21, 1776, states: "Gelelemend, or John Killbuck, who after Netawatwees has been destined to be the Chief asked Brother David among other things to what extent a believer or one who wished to accept the faith could busy himself with a Chief's affairs? ... He further said, that is Killbuck, that as early as last fall, he had a notion in his heart to move to us. He also said that some time ago before we had come here he had spoken with his uncle, the Chief about it, namely that he would like to move to Gnadenhütten. At that time he, the chief had had no objection."[72] A month later, on May 30, 1776, Zeisberger again wrote in his diary: "John Killbuck with his wife as visitors and they spent the night here.... His desire to live with us was becoming even greater. He said that only a few days ago he had spoken with his uncle Netawatwees about this and had revealed to him his desire to be with the Bretheren."[73] Another entry in Zeisberger's diary on June 17, 1776, reads: "John Kilbuck ... told us that his uncle Netawatwees had advised him to build a house in Goschachgunk even if he would decide to live with us."[74] Whether Gelelemend was the grandson or nephew of Netawatwees is only important in maintaining historical accuracy, but it doesn't have significant impact on our discussion of Killbuck Town.

To further confuse the issue, there may have been yet another Killbuck or Kill-buck who was active on the Virginia frontier during the French and Indian War, and many of his exploits were attributed to Bemino, or Killbuck Sr. Samuel Kercheval (1767–1845) wrote about a Shawnee Indian named Kill-Buck who was active in the upper Potomac River region of present West Virginia and western Maryland. Kercheval wrote: "Kill-buck was a Shawnee, a savage of strong mental powers, and well acquainted with all the families in the settlement before the war broke out."[75] If in fact the Kill-buck that Kercheval wrote about was Shawnee, he would have been no relation to either Bemino or Gelelemend who were members of the Turtle phratry of the Lenape nation.

Getting back to Killbuck Town in Ohio, *The Handbook of American Indians, Part 1,* states that Killbuck Town was a Lenape village on the east side of Killbuck Creek, about 10 miles south of Wooster, Ohio, in Wayne County. Further, it was occupied as early as 1764 by a chief named Killbuck, from whom it received the name.[76] If so, it must have been the residence of Bemino, the older Killbuck, since Gelelemend, the younger Killbuck, was not considered a chief until the death of Netawatwees in 1776. Gelelemend is mostly associated with the Lenape villages of Gekelemuckpechunk at present Newcomerstown and Goschachgunk at present Coshocton, Ohio.

By 1781, the Lenape nation was solidly divided between the pro–British and pro–American factions, with the Christian Indians trying to remain neutral. As more and more Lenape shifted to the pro–British faction, Gelelemend, who led the pro–American faction, was ousted as the principal Lenape chief, and sought refuge at Fort Pitt. From there he joined American Colonel Daniel Brodhead's expedition against his former Lenape villages on the Muskingum River. After the Revolutionary War, Gelelemend converted to Christianity, was baptized "William Henry," and was a member of the Moravian settlements in Ohio until his death in 1811. He was buried near David Zeisberger in the Goshen Cemetery.

As mentioned, Killbuck Town was likely the residence of Bemino, or Killbuck Sr. However, the entry in the *Handbook of American Indians* is somewhat questionable, because it indicates the town was on the east bank of Killbuck Creek. Thomas Hutchins, who accompanied Henry Bouquet's

Top and bottom: Grave of Gelelemend in the Goshen Cemetery (author photographs).

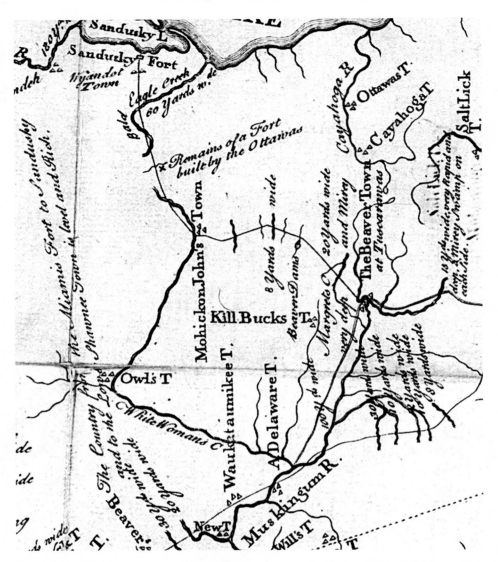

Section of Hutchins's 1764 map showing Kill Bucks T (Library of Congress, Geography and Map Division-2001695748).

1764 expedition into Ohio and visited the area, produced maps in 1764 and 1778, and both maps show Killbuck Town on the west bank of Killbuck Creek. Since Hutchins actually visited the site, we can assume his placement of the town on the west bank is more likely.

  The question remains, where on Killbuck Creek was the town actually located? The *Handbook* states that it was about ten miles south of present Wooster, Ohio, which would place the village north of present Holmesville, in Holmes County near the boundary between Holmes and Wayne Counties. Frank Wilcox lists Killbuck Town's location at present Big Prairie, Ohio, in Holmes County; however, his description in the text refers to the present town of Killbuck as the former site of the Indian village. Big Prairie is about seven miles west of Killbuck Creek, which excludes it as the site of Killbuck Town. Also, there

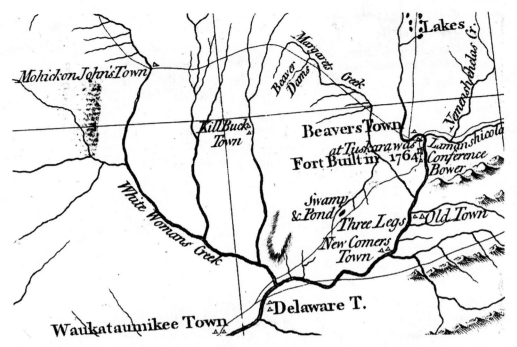

Section of 1778 Hutchins's map showing KillBuck Town (Library of Congress, Geography and Map Division-74696155).

is no documentation that would indicate that present Killbuck was the site of the Indian village Killbuck Town. The book *Ohio Place Names* gives the following description for the present town of Killbuck: "Holmes County. Settled in 1811. This village was named for a Native American known as Killbuck, who played a prominent role in events of the region. The place was first known as 'Shrimplin's Settlement,' after the earliest white settler, Abraham Shrimplin. A less likely version claims a settlement date of 1882 and theorizes that the village was named when an Indian hunter killed a buck and shouted, 'Kill 'em buck!'"[77] An account in *Our Hometown Holmesville, Ohio*, indicates that the Lenape village of Killbuck Town was "a short distance from the Crossing Place northwest of the Big Spring near today's Route 83 and the Holmes/Wayne County Line."[78] That would place the site of the Indian village near the confluence of Killbuck Creek and Tea Run, about two miles northwest of present Holmesville, Ohio, which agrees with the location in the *Handbook of American Indians*. However, there is an incongruity in *Our Hometown Holmesville, Ohio*. It states that at that location, "Chief Killbuck and his tribe of Delawares, about 1791, appeared to have a permanent town."[79] That date is difficult to reconcile with either of the Killbucks, since Bemino, or Killbuck Sr., reportedly died between April 28, 1779, and November 10, 1780. In addition, he apparently went blind some time before he died. On April 28, 1779, Zeisberger wrote that the older Killbuck was "quite blind," and on November 10, 1780, Zeisberger referred to him as the "late, blind chief."[80]

Based on that information, it would be quite impossible for Killbuck Sr., to have had a village on Killbuck Creek in 1791. It's difficult to place the younger Killbuck in a town on upper Killbuck Creek at any time during his adult life. Gelelemend is often mentioned as being at Gekelemukpechunk and Goschachgunk during the time they were in existence. Then from about 1781 until the end of the Revolutionary War, he was at Fort Pitt, and later he converted and took up residence in a succession of Moravian mission villages until his death at Goshen in 1811.

It's quite probable that it was Benimo, or Killbuck Sr., who had his residence on upper Killbuck Creek between the early 1760s and 1770s. He was somewhat active on the side of the British during the French and Indian War, because there is a record that in 1761, "Killbuck, a Delaware [Lenape] headman … led at least one pack train of horses carrying ammunition from Fort Pitt to Sandusky for a wage of one dollar per day."[81]

Based on all available information, we can best conclude that, between about 1760 and the 1770s, Benimo or Killbuck Sr. likely had a village called Killbuck Town on higher ground on the west bank of Killbuck Creek near its confluence with Tea Run, almost two miles northwest of present Holmesville, Ohio.

39. *Logan's Town (c. 1773–c. 1774), also Yellow Creek.*
Now: Yellow Creek, Jefferson County
(40°34'25.63"N–80°40'11.11"W)

The Mingo chief Logan had a village on the west bank of the Ohio River at the mouth of Yellow Creek. There is some question regarding Logan's Mingo name. He was the son of Shikellamy, who had two sons named Logan: Logan Elrod and Logan the Orator. Logan the Orator, whom we are discussing, was variously called Tahgahjute, Technechdorus, Soyechtowa, and Tocanioadorogon. Sometime around 1773, Logan moved from his village at the mouth of Beaver Creek, at present Glasgow, Pennsylvania, about fifteen miles up the Ohio River to present Yellow Creek, Ohio.

On April 30, 1774, a party of white men led by Daniel Greathouse enticed most of the town's residents across the Ohio River with the promise of liquor and sport. When the Indians crossed over, the white men attacked and brutally killed them. Logan was on a hunting trip and was absent when the event occurred, but his wife Mellana, his brother Taylaynee, Taylaynee's son Moinah, and Logan's sister Koonay were among those killed. After the killings, the bodies were mutilated, and Jacob Greathouse even sliced open Koonay's abdomen so he could scalp her unborn son. The only survivor was Koonay's two-year-old daughter, who was eventually returned to her father John Gibson, the husband of Logan's sister Koonay. The event became known as the "Yellow Creek Massacre," and it was one of the major incidents that led to Lord Dunmore's War of 1774.

Logan left his village at Yellow Creek after the death of his family and moved west toward the Scioto River, from where he launched retaliatory raids against white settlements on the frontier. During Lord Dunmore's War, he personally took thirty scalps,[82] and at the end of the war, he refused to attend the Camp Charlotte council. Instead, he gave an impassioned speech known as Logan's Lament under a huge tree at what is now Logan's Elm Pickaway County Park, about five and a half miles south of Circleville, Ohio. (See Chillicothe at Westfall for more on Logan's Lament and Logan Elm.)

During the American Revolutionary War, he sided with the British and continued his fight against the Americans. Logan became an alcoholic, and during the summer of 1780, while traveling between the Sandusky River and Fort Detroit, he became involved in an argument with a group of Indians, and was killed during the ensuing fight.

41. *Mahoning Town (c. 1755–c. 1778)*
also Old Mahoning Town, Mahoning Old Town.
NOW: NEWTON FALLS, TRUMBULL COUNTY (41°11'18.20"N–80°58'41.33"W)

Mahoning Town was a Lenape village on the Mahoning River, but the specific location is somewhat questionable. Historian Charles A. Hanna indicates the town was at or near present Newton Falls, Ohio, which is about ten miles west-northwest of Salt Lick Town at present Niles, Ohio. However, mapmaker Tomas Hutchins, who accompanied Henry Bouquet in 1764, and who actually visited the town, shows it on his map about two miles southeast of Salt Lick Town on the Mahoning River near present McDonald, Ohio. John McCullogh (1748–1823), who was captured by the Lenape in 1756 when he was eight years old, and repatriated by Bouquet in 1764, left a narrative that mentions both Salt Lick Town (Kseek-heoong) and Mahoning Town. McCullough wrote that about the time that General Forbes took Fort Duquesne in November 1758, the Indians who held McCullough left Shenango or Logstown at present Ambridge, Pennsylvania, and traveled to the Salt Licks on the west branch of the Beaver (Mahoning) River, where the Indians were establishing a new village called Kseek-heoong (place of salt) or Salt Licks Town. The following spring (1759), they traveled about fifteen miles upstream to a town called Mahoning. McCullough remained at Mahoning Town until after the Battle of Bushy Run in August 1763, and then was taken to "Cayahawge" or Cuyahoga Town at present Cuyahoga Falls, Ohio.[83]

McCullogh's description appears to support the hypothesis that Mahoning Town was indeed west of Salt Lick Town, and if the fifteen-mile journey upstream on the Mahoning River is fairly accurate, it would place Mahoning Town somewhere in the vicinity of present Newton Falls, Ohio.

The mapmaker Thomas Hutchins also mentioned the town in his journal of Bouquet's march. His details from Lake Erie to Mahoning Town are as follows. The annotations in brackets are by historian Charles A. Hanna. The distances have to be taken with a grain of salt, since they are at best estimates made by Hutchins. For example, Hutchins gives the distance from Lake Erie to Cuyahoga Town as 18 miles, but actually the straight-line distance is about 28.4 miles, and following the twists of the Cuyahoga, it would be somewhat farther. Although Hutchins's map places Mahoning Town east of Salt Lick Town, Charles Hanna's annotations—correctly, in my opinion—place the village in the vicinity of Newton Falls.

> From this Lake [Erie] to Cuyahoga Town is 18 miles, the path mostly Along the Creek, through level Timbered Land free from Swamps. At the Town the Creek [Cuyahoga River] is 17 yards wide.
> After crossing the Creek, the Path Leads [eastward] through level Timbered land, 11 miles, to a Branch of Cayahoga [the Main Branch] 10 yards wide, at which [probably at Kent] is A good Fording.
> Then through Swampy Land for 9 Miles, to a Swamp, two Miles over. This Swamp, the French, sometimes ago, Bridged, by laying Logs A Cross the Path; but it is now much out of Repair.
> After Crossing the Swamp, the Path leads [south of Ravenna] by A Savannah on the Left hand and continues for 5 Miles through Thickets, but not Mirey; then [through the present townships of Edinburg, Palmyra, and Paris, Portage County] Along level, Timbered Land, 15 Miles, to Mohoning Town on [the west side of Mahoning Branch of] Beaver Creek [probably at or above the site of present Newton Falls].[84]

Several other maps place Mahoning Town east of or downstream from Salt Lick Town, but in almost every case they indicate they are referring to Thomas Huchins's 1764 map.

As can be seen from some of the journals that are referred to, the Mahoning River was often called the Beaver, because it connected with the Beaver River in the vicinity of present

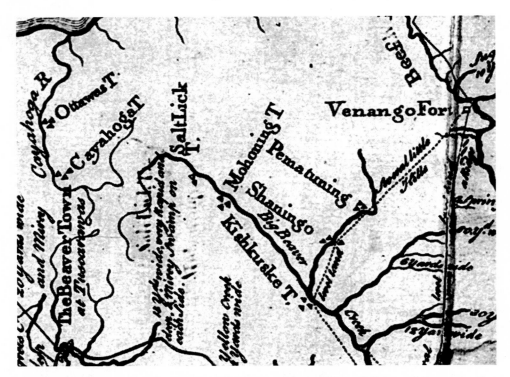

Section of Thomas Hutchins's 1764 map showing Mohoning Town (Library of Congress, Geography and Map Division-2001695748).

Legend of 1781 French map showing that much of its information was based on Thomas Hutchins's map (*Par Hutchins Capitaine Anglais*) (Library of Congress, Geography and Map Division-gm71002166).

New Castle, Pennsylvania, and many considered it an extension of the Beaver. Indians often referred to areas of the Mahoning as "Kuskusky," "Kuskuskiesw," and "Kushkuskin," which is probably a derivation of the Seneca term "koskohsh-ehtoh," meaning "by the falls" or "by the rapids." However, David Zeisberger surmised that the word comes from "quis-quis," which is an Onandaga word for hog. The French-Onondaga dictionary lists the word for hog as "kouich-kouisch."

Incidentally, while young John McCullough was at Mahoning Town, he witnessed the murder of a fur trader by the name of Thomas Green. According to McCullough, a Lenape named Mus-sough-whese, who was a nephew of Ket-tooh-ha-lend, McCullogh's adopted brother, stole Tom Green's horse, and Green pursued Mus-sough-whese to Mahoning Town. At Mahoning Town, Mus-sough-whese and Ket-tooh-ha-lend met Green and offered to return the horse. Mus-sough-whese had a pistol and knife concealed under his blanket, and Ket-tooh-ha-lend had a tomahawk. McCullogh says:

> I observed them coming out of a house, about two hundred yards from ours. Ket-tooh-ha-lend was foremost, Green in the middle. I took slight notice of them, until I heard the report of a pistol. I cast my eyes towards them and observed the smoke, and saw Green standing on the side of the path, with his hands across his breast. I thought it had been him that had shot. He stood a few moments, then fell on his face across the path. Ket-tooh-ha-lend sunk his pipe tomahawk into his skull. Mus-sough-whese stabbed him under his armpit with his scalping knife. He had shot him between the shoulders with his pistol. The squaws gathered about him and stripped him naked, trailed him down the bank, and plunged him in the creek. There was a fresh in the Creek at the time, which carried him off. Mus-sough-whese then came to me (where I was holding the horse; as I had not moved from the spot where I was when Green was shot), with the bloody knife in his hand. He told me that he was coming to kill me next. He reached out his hand and took hold of the bridle, telling me that that was his horse. I was glad to parlay with him on the terms, and delivered the horse to him. All the Indians in the Town immediately collected together, and started off to the Salt Licks, where the rest of the Traders were, and murdered the whole of them, and divided their goods amongst them, and likewise their horses.[85]

There is no definitive information regarding when Mahoning Town ceased to exist as a Lenape village, but its residents may have elected to distance themselves from the Pennsylvanians sometime during the American Revolutionary War. They likely moved to the Lenape settlements along the Muskingum and Tuscarawas Rivers, or farther west to join the Lenape, who sided with the British, as did Captain Pipe and Buckonghelas.

24. *Mingo Town (c. 1740–c. 1809),*
also Ostionish, Logan's Town, Gwahago.
Now: Akron, Summit County (41°7'6.85"N–81°31'40.64"W)

At the time that Netawatwees established Cuyahoga Town around 1757, there was a Mingo village located across the Cuyahoga River. A few sources refer to the Mingo village as "Logan's Town," but the Mingo chief Logan did not move into Ohio from Pennsylvania until about 1770, and he established his first village at present Wellsville, Ohio, on the Ohio River, about 57 miles southeast of Cuyahoga Town. Frank Wilcox, in his book *Ohio Indian Trails*, refers to Ostionish at the confluence of the Cuyahoga and the Little Cuyahoga Rivers, but he refers to it as an Ottawa town.[86] Interestingly, his reference is the only one I could find that used the name Ostionish.

The exact location of the Mingo village is not known, and even its name and village leader or chief is difficult to determine. In his 1854 book, Gen. Lucius Verus Bierce (1801–1876) refers to a Seneca village whose chief was Stygwanish [*sic*].[87] The village had an orchard planted by the Indians that Bierce claimed was still standing in his time. He described the location as being on the Cuyahoga River near the north line of Boston Township, Summit County, about a half-mile south of Ponty's Camp. That would place the village about ten miles in a straight line from the Falls of the Cuyahoga, and quite at odds with other descriptions that indicate the Mingo village was opposite or nearly opposite the Lenape village of Cuyahoga Town. Another anomaly is Bierce's description of Stigwanish: "Among the Tawas was a celebrated chief called Stigwanish by the Indians and Seneca by the whites."[88] Tawas was a reference to the Ottawa Indians, and it pertained to an Ottawa village on the Cuyahoga, and if Stigwanish was a Mingo or Seneca Indian, the Ottawas would not have had him as their chief. It's possible that Bierce mistakenly referred to the site of the old Ottawa village farther north on the east bank of the Cuyahoga River opposite François Saguin's post, which was shown on some maps as "Tawas."

The Ashatabula and Western Reserve Historical Societies mention Stigwanish as a Seneca (Mingo) chief who was also known variously as "Standing Stone," "Standing Rock," or simply as "Seneca." The *Encyclopedia of Cleveland History* describes Stigwanish as a Seneca (Mingo) chief who remained in Ohio after Mad Anthony Wayne's 1794 victory over the

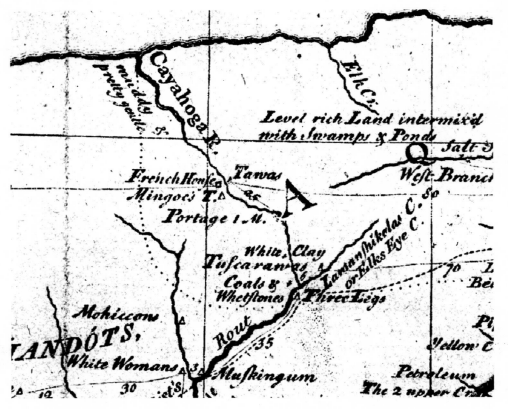

Section of Lewis Evans's 1755 map. Note: Cuyahoga Town had not yet been established when this map was made (Library of Congress, Geography and Map Division-75693767).

Indians at the Battle of Fallen Timbers, and in 1796 assisted Moses Cleaveland in his survey of northern Ohio.

While most sources agree that a Mingo village was on the southern or western side of the Cuyahoga, its location ranges from directly opposite Netawatwees's Cuyahoga Town to the site mentioned by General Bierce about ten miles north-northwest. Other sources show Mingo town near present Ira, Ohio, and also at Ghent, Ohio.

I believe the site of Mingo Town or Ostionish was likely at the location mentioned by Wilcox at the confluence of the Cuyahoga and the Little Cuyahoga Rivers. It's logical that it would have been established on the portage route between the Cuyahoga and Tuscarawas Rivers, and near the junction of the Watershed and Cuyahoga–Muskingum Trails. However, I believe Wilcox erroneously identified it as an Ottawa village. Whether Stigwanish was the chief is also subject to question. Ostionish may very well be a corruption of the name Stigwanish; however, it's unlikely Stigwanish was the chief of the village when it was established in the 1740s, because according to most documentation he was active as late as 1809, some sixty years later.

Stigwanish's name became a part of local lore through 18th-century accounts. A document titled *The Coppacaw Story, Indians of Ohio and the Western Reserve Area and Cuyahoga River*,[89] written in 1962, mentions Stigwanish as the Mingo (Seneca) chief of the village on the Cuyahoga, and claims Stigwanish constructed a large totem pole at the site and treated it as a god. However, totem pole construction was generally confined to the Indians of the Pacific Northwest Coast, and more specifically by the Tlingit, Haida, Bella Coola, Chinook, Tshimshian, and Coast Salish tribes. Even among those Indians, totem poles were not worshiped as gods, or objects of veneration, but rather were meant to inspire respect or tell a story.

The Case Western Reserve online *Encyclopedia of Cleveland History* provides the following information regarding Stigwanish, but without references or source information:

> **Stigwanish**, also known as Stigwandish, Stigonish, or Seneca, a prominent Indian chief in the early years of Cleveland's settlement whose name translates as Standing Stone, was chief of the Seneca Indians remaining in Ohio after "Mad" Anthony Wayne's 1794 victory at Fallen Timbers. He helped the first survey party of the Western Reserve in 1796, and remained in the settlement, helping Job Stiles and his wife Tabitha Cumi and others survive the winter of 1796–97. Edward Paine, Jr., whose family settled Painesville, wrote, "Seneca has the dignity of a Roman Senator, the honesty of Aristides, and the philanthropy of William Penn." Stigwanish continually traveled to Cleveland, Painesville, Ashtabula, and his wintering residence near the Cuyahoga River in Streetsboro Twp. Stigwanish moved to Seneca County (named after him) in 1809. Before the start of the War of 1812, most Indians in northeast Ohio left for Canada to aid the British and plan raids along Lake Erie's south shore. Stigwanish warned that the British were inciting the Indians. When the British finalized their plans, Stigwanish warned settlers, so that most women and children were evacuated from lakeshore settlements. However, spies alerted the British, who canceled their plans. Stigwanish died in 1816.[90]

Much of what was written about Stigwanish appears to be in the romantic genre that was common in the 19th century. That style had a tendency to glorify the "noble savage" and his way of life. Although Stigwanish actually may have lived in the area prior to the War of 1812, he wasn't necessarily a chief or village leader, and may not have resided at Mingo Town on the Cuyahoga River.

It's not known when Mingo Town on the Cuyahoga or Ostionish ceased to exist, but 1809, when Stigwanish supposedly moved to Seneca County, is taken as an arbitrary date.

42. Mingo Town (c. 1740s–c. 1785),
also Mingo Bottoms, Crow's Town.
Now: Mingo Junction, Jefferson County
(40°19′19.27″N–80°36′23.00″W)

Mingo Town was located at present Mingo Junction, in Jefferson County, Ohio, on the west side of the Ohio River immediately north of the mouth of Cross Creek. Cross Creek received its name because it is one of two creeks that empty into the Ohio River directly opposite each other. Incidentally, the creek on the West Virginia side of the Ohio River is also named Cross Creek.

Mingo Town was the Ohio terminus of the Mingo Trail that connected with the Tuscarawas River near the Moravian mission village of Gnadenhütten. Mingo Town was also referred to as "Crow's Town," and is mentioned in Lieutenant Thomas Hutchin's 1764 account of the water route from Fort Pitt to the Ohio Indian Towns. From "Yellow Creek,[91] on the Right. Then 25 Miles to the Crow's Town on the Right [now Mingo, Jefferson County, Ohio], at which A Creek empties into the Ohio, and another on the Left, almost opposite each other [the two Cross Creeks]."[92] The village is shown as "Crow's Town" on William C. Mill's 1914 map,[93] and also as Crow's Town in Frank Wilcox's *Ohio Indian Trails*. For some inexplicable reason, Wilcox shows the location of Crow's Town near present Mingo Junction on his map, but he states, "On this trail [the Mingo Trail] was a town called Crow's Town, probably in the vicinity of Cadiz [Ohio]."[94] The two locations are more than twenty-one miles apart.

Mingo Town was established by expatriate Iroquois, who moved into the Allegheny and upper Ohio River region during the mid-1740s.[95] They were predominantly Seneca, which is understandable, because the Seneca were the westernmost of the Iroquois Nations. However, there were representatives of all of the Six Nations among what became known as the Mingo group. Initially most of the tribes who migrated from the east settled along the Allegheny and upper Ohio Rivers, but by the late 1740s and 1750s, two factors caused many of them to move farther west into Ohio. One factor was the depletion of game from so many villages competing for the food supply,[96] but the bigger factor was the establishment of French and English military posts along the Allegheny River, which threatened the Indians' existence in that area.

It's not specifically known when Mingo Town was founded, but when the white captive Mary Jemison spent the summers of 1757–1758 there, the town was well established, and appeared to have been in existence for several years. She described the village as a small Indian town at the mouth of the Shenanjee River, which was the name the Mingos called Cross Creek on the western side of the Ohio River. According to Mary, another stream emptied into the Ohio River directly opposite Shenanjee. The town was pleasantly situated on the Ohio, and "the land produced good corn; the woods furnished a plenty of game, and the river abounded with fish."[97] Mary mentioned that while she was at Mingo Town, and during the time of the corn harvest, Fort Pitt was taken from the French by the English, which occurred on November 28, 1758. Mary said her Indian community established their summer residence at Mingo Town on the Ohio River, but spent their winters near "the mouth of the of the Sciota [Scioto] where they established their winter quarters." On the Scioto, the forests were "well stocked with elk, deer, and other large animals; and the marshes contained large numbers of beaver, muskrat, &c. which made excellent hunting for the Indians; who depended, for their meat, upon their success in taking elk and deer; and for the ammunition and clothing, upon the beaver, muskrat, and other furs that they could take in addition to their peltry."[98]

On April 14, 1765, according to George Croghan, "about eighty Seneca Indians came up from their town at the Two Creeks."[99] The following month, on May 17, 1765, Croghan returned the visit to Mingo Town. "We came to a place called Two Creeks, about fifteen miles from Yellow Creek, where we put to shore; here the Senecas have a village on a high bank, on the north side of the river."[100] The following year, on June 19, 1766, George Croghan paid yet another visit to Mingo Town, and he described its location by his reckoning to be 71 miles below Fort Pitt,[101] downstream on the Ohio River.

The 1768 Treaty of Fort Stanwix specified that the Ohio River was the demarcation boundary between white lands to the east and Indian lands to the west. Prior to that time, the Mingos had villages on both sides of the Ohio River, but after the treaty, the Indians on the east side were forced to give up their land and move west across the Ohio.

George Washington mentioned Mingo Town when he passed through on October 22, 1770, to examine land on the Kanawha River. He described the village as being situated on the west side of the Ohio River a little above Cross Creeks. He wrote that the town "contains about twenty cabins and seventy inhabitants of the Six Nations." At the time, the Mingos were apparently mustering a war party, because Washington wrote, "We found and left 60 odd warriors of the Six Nations going to the Cherokee Country, to proceed to war against the Cuttawbas."[102]

The Moravian missionary John Heckewelder passed through Mingo Town on April 19, 1773, and again on April 27, 1778. Interestingly, his diary entry for 1773 mentions the Indian village, but the 1778 entry does not. Normally, both Heckewelder and David Zeisberger commented on the Indian villages they visited; Heckewelder's silence in his 1778 entry may be a simple omission, or more likely the Indians had not yet returned to Mingo Town for the summer months. We can determine that the village was in existence at least during the summer months until 1782, because it was mentioned as the starting point in Ohio for the ill-fated 1782 Crawford expedition against the Ohio Indians. However, the village did not remain an Indian town very long after that time.

By 1784, white settlements reached the area, and white squatters disregarded the boundary stipulated in the Treaty of Fort Stanwix to cross the Ohio River and establish residences on Indian lands. One of the leaders was Joseph Ross, who, along with several other families, disregarded the prohibition on white settlement and settled in the area of Mingo Town. It was there that Ross fathered the first white child born in what is now Jefferson County, Ohio. Troops were sent from Fort McIntosh to dislodge the squatters, and after initially threatening to fight to stay on Indian land, the squatters gave in and recrossed the river to the east side. However, the following year they once again crossed back into Ohio.

During that time period, 1783–1784, it was clear to the Indians living at Mingo Town that their land would soon be appropriated by aggressive white settlements, and they abandoned their village forever. By 1786, the land around Mingo Bottoms sold for about a dollar an acre, and the U.S. Army even considered building a fort there. Instead, the fort was built in 1786 three miles north at present Steubenville, Ohio, and was named Fort Steuben.

10. *Mohawk (dates unknown).*
Now: Mohawk Village, Coshocton County
(40°19'11.27"N–82°4'46.67"W)

Mohawk is another Indian town that probably did not exist as a permanent village. Other than a supposition by Frank Wilcox in *Ohio Indian Trails* about a town in this location, there is no other documentation that indicates an Indian Village was located here. The vicinity of the Tuscarawas, Muskingum and Walhonding Rivers was one of the most visited areas in Ohio by white mapmakers, soldiers, frontiersmen, and missionaries, yet none of them left any indication of an Indian town near present Mohawk Village, Ohio. Even Wilcox's reference is very uncertain. He wrote: "A short distance south of the Walhonding, near where stood White Woman's Town at Warsaw, is the village of Mohawk, probably once an Indian village."[103]

The *History of Coshocton County* refers to present Mohawk Village, but makes no mention of an Indian town at that location. It reads in part: "Mohawk Village, lying in the little valley of Mohawk Run, from which it received its name, in the southwestern part of the township, was laid out in 1859 by William and James Thompson."[104] The description includes an account of the first dwellings and businesses in the town, and also a colorful story of how the town became known as "Jericho" because of a fight between an Irishman and a Scotsman over the way school was conducted. The Irishman, who apparently lost the fight, wrote an account of the many wrongs he had suffered, comparing his experience to the biblical traveler who was assaulted by thieves on the road from Jerusalem to Jericho. As a result, the town was unofficially referred to as Jericho.

While there is scant documentary evidence supporting the location of an Indian town at present Mohawk Village, it's quite possible that Indians may have camped temporarily there.

43. *Mohican John's Town (c. 1760–c. 1814),*
also Mohickon John's Town, Johnstown, Mohican John's
Old Town, Old Town.
Now: Jeromesville, Ashland County *(40°47'31.89"N–82°10'48.62"W)*

Around 1760, after leaving Tullihas at the confluence of the Kokosing and Mohican Rivers, Mohican John relocated his village to the confluence of Jerome Fork of the Mohican River and Oldtown Run, about a mile south of present Jeromesville, Ohio. The village stood on the east bank of Jerome's Fork opposite the mouth of Oldtown Run.[105] Because of its location on Oldtown Run, this village is often referred to in sources as "Old Town." We know the move occurred sometime around 1760, because George Croghan passed Mohican John's Town at the end of December 1760 or early January 1761.[106] In addition, "Mohickon John's Town" was shown in the approximate location of present Jeromesvile on Hutchins's 1765 map.

Mohican John's Town on Jerome's Fork was located near the junction of several trails including the Great Trail, which was a major thoroughfare that connected Fort Duquesne at present Pittsburgh with Fort Sandusky and Fort Detroit. Descriptions of nearby trails from cited sources follow: "Branched off at Mohican Johnstown passing through Plain town-

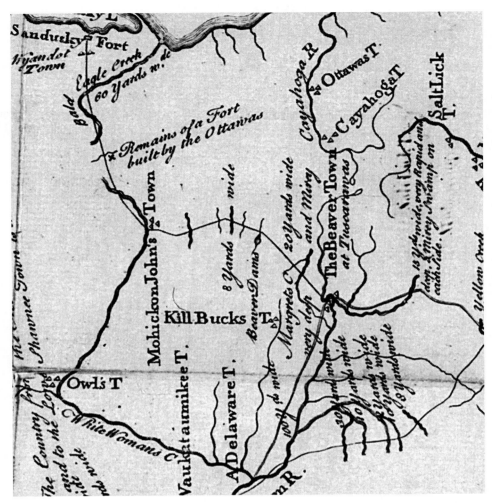

Section of Hutchins's 1764 map (Library of Congress, Geography and Map Division-2001695748).

ship[107] by the 'long meadow'[108] or perhaps a little south by Mohican John's Lake in Wayne County.[109] Thence across Killbuck some twelve miles south of Wooster, where [Robert] Rogers crossed that stream, and probably Col. Crawford also crossed and encamped near O'Dell's [sic] on his expedition to the Moravian settlement on Sandusky creek in Crawford county.[110] There was another trail from Mohican Johnstown running northwest to Greentown, by or near the site of Goudy's old mill,[111] to the Quaker springs in Vermillion township.... From Mohican Johnstown another trail ran up the Jerome Fork, a favorite route of the Mohicans on their hunting excursions on the Black River."[112]

There is no documented explanation regarding why Mohican John moved his village from Tullihas, but as previously discussed, moves were initiated for any number of reasons. These include relocating to an area where fish and game were more plentiful or to distance themselves from encroaching settlements or hostile environments.

In January 1761, the celebrated French and Indian War ranger Major Robert Rogers returned from Fort Detroit along the Great Trail and passed Mohican John's Town. Rogers wrote, "Our general course about southeast, traveled about six miles, and crossed Maskongam,[113] running south, about twenty yards from the Creek, on the east side, which is called Mingo Cabbins. There were but two or three Indians in the place, the rest were hunting. These Indians have plenty of cows, horses, hogs, etc. The 8th, halted at this town to mend our mogasons and kill deer, the provisions I brought from Detroit being entirely expended. I went a hunting with ten of the Rangers and by ten o'clock got more venison then we had occasion for."[114] Rogers referred to the town as "Mingo Cabbins," which indicates that some Mingos, or expatriate Iroquois, also resided in Mohican John's small community. Quite possibly Mohican John was an expatriate Mohawk of the Iroquois League, which would have made him a Mingo.

In 1764, Thomas Hutchins, the cartographer with Colonel Henry Bouquet, described the route from Fort Pitt to Sandusky and on to Fort Detroit, and he mentioned Mohican John's village. "From this place it is twenty-seven miles to the principal N.W. branch of the Muskingum [Mohican Fork], 25 yards wide at the ford, near which is situated Mohickon John's Town. It consisted only of a few houses. The path takes over good land the whole of the above distance, well timbered and watered at every two, three, and four miles, with rivulets from six to eight yards in width, easily crossed when not raised with freshes."[115] Hutchins added: "This Town is always inconsiderable, consisting only of a few houses."[116]

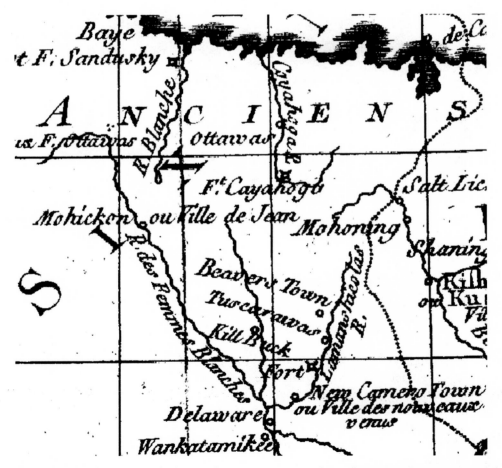

Section of La Tour's 1784 map (Library of Congress, Geography and Map Division-2015591094).

Mohican John was apparently on good terms with the white traders who entered the Ohio area, because on March 7, 1771, he warned the Pennsylvania trader George Croghan that the Iroquois (Mingos) were forming a confederation to attack the English.[117]

There is some indication that Mohican John temporarily moved from the Mohican River Oldtown Run site, and then returned. That is based on a short cryptic sentence in the *History of Wayne County Ohio* that reads, "He removed to the 'Old Town' home in 1795, and left about 1814."[118] If Mohican John did indeed leave the Old Town site, there is no other information regarding that temporary relocation. However, that notation may be the reason some sources allege another location for Mohican John's town. For example, one source claims, "Mohican John's town of the 1760s was located on the Black Fork of the Mohican River near present day Mifflin, Ohio." That claim appears to be based on Hutchins's 1765 map, which does not have sufficient scale or detail to definitively identify the location of the town.

One source indicates that Mohican John left his Old Town village about 1814. If indeed he was alive at that time, he may very well have been forced to move by the influx of white settlers who simply ignored the 1785 treaty of Fort McIntosh that guaranteed Indian lands in northwestern Ohio. His move may have been precipitated by the white homesteaders' concerns regarding the loyalty of their Indian neighbors during the War of 1812, similar to the forced removal of the Lenape Indians at Greentown, ten or so miles southwest of Mohican John's Town. There is no other information regarding Mohican John.

The last depiction of Mohican John's Town was on a 1784 map by the French cartographer Brion de la Tour, who placed it in the general location of the Old Town site. It's shown as "Mohickon ou Ville de Jean" (Mohickon or city of John) on the R, des Femmes Blanches (River of the White Women), which was an early name for the Walhonding River.

10. New Hundy (c. 1775–c. 1781), also Hundy.
NOW: NELLIE, COSHOCTON COUNTY (40°20'37.97"N–82°2'58.94"W)

While there is no reference to Old Hundy in Frank Wilcox's book *Ohio Indian Trails*, he mentions that New Hundy was located on the Kokosing River at the former village of Zuck, Ohio, in Knox County.[119] The Kokosing is a tributary of the Walhonding that begins at the confluence of the Walhonding and Mohican Rivers west of present Walhonding, Ohio. The Walhonding Trail traveling west to east, "traversed the flats south of Mount Vernon, and crossing the river at the foot of the main street, descended the north bank of the Kokosing over the Gambier Campus [Kenyon College], apparently to avoid the tangle in the flats to the south, and taking to the ridge reached Howard [U.S. 36], 'Coashoskis,' at the mouth of Jelloway Creek; thence it followed the present highway [U.S. 36] through Millwood to Zuck or 'New Hundy.'"[120]

Wilcox provides a wonderful description of the route of the Walhonding Trail, but it's difficult to reconcile his assertion that New Hundy was located at Zuck when evidence seems to indicate otherwise. For example, Weslager in his book *The Delaware Indians*, wrote, "Old Hundy, a Munsie town on the north side of the Walhonding between the mouths of Killbuck and Mohican creeks; New Hundy, built two or three miles west of Old Hundy, where in 1775 the chief Windaughala ("council door"). Father of Buckongahelas, had his residence."[121]

The young Englishman Nicholas Cresswell, who had the amorous evening in Old

Hundy with his Indian host's sister, left Old Hundy the following day and rode to New Hundy. Cresswell wrote, "Wednesday, August 30, 1775. My bedfellow very fond of me this morning and wants to go with me. Find I must often meet with such encounters as these if I do not take a squaw to myself. She is young and sprightly, tolerably handsome, and can speak a little English. Agreed to take her. She saddled her horse and went with us to New Hundy about 3 miles off, where she had several relations who made me very welcome to such as they had."[122]

In the case of Cresswell, who wrote of his visit to New Hundy in 1775, we can be fairly certain he measured his distance as he followed the trail along the meandering riverbank. But Weslager, who wrote that the distance between the two towns was two or three miles, is a modern writer who may very well have meant the shortest distance between two points. Either way, it's improbable that New Hundy was located at Zuck, because the distances wouldn't make sense. Zuck is about four and a quarter miles from the mouth of the Mohican River and almost thirteen miles from the likely location of Old Hundy at present Warsaw, Ohio.

Since contemporary descriptions place Old Hundy between the mouths of Killbuck Creek and either Mohawk Creek or the Mohican River, and New Hundy reputedly two or three miles farther west, it appears the most likely location of New Hundy would be in the area of the Walhonding River near the mouth of Darling Run, less than a mile east of present Nellie, Ohio. There is no indication of when New Hundy ceased to exist, but like Old Hundy, it's unlikely it survived Brodhead's 1781 campaign against the Lenape.

47. Onondaga Town (dates unknown).
Now: Aurora, Portage County (41°19'2.72"N–81°19'58.34"W)

A few sources indicate that an Onondaga town existed at present Aurora, Ohio, which would have placed that village only about two miles from the Onondaga village at Geauga Lake. While it's not unusual that two towns would have been located in such close proximity, it may also be a case of people referring to the same town. If one or the other town was indeed located in present Aurora, Ohio, it would likely have been sited near the Aurora Branch River at the eastern edge of Aurora.

47. Onondaga Town (dates unknown).
Now: Geauga Lake, Portage County (41°20'42.30"N–81°21'45.60"W)

Frank Wilcox in *Ohio Indian Trails*[123] states that an Onondaga Indian town was located on the Aurora Branch River southeast of Geauga Lake. That would place the location of the village north of present Treat Road, and in the vicinity of the abandoned Geauga Lake Amusement Park parking lot. I was unable to locate any other documentary evidence of an Indian village at this location other than some non-specific Onondaga references pertaining to the area. The book *Portage Heritage* indicates that there was a combined Onondaga and Oneida village a mile to the west of Palmyra, Ohio, and another in Aurora, Ohio.[124] I have not found any other information regarding an Onondaga or Oneida village in the vicinity of Palmyra, and since there is no other documentation, it may at best have been a transient camp or temporary hunting village. Coincidently, Geauga is an Onondaga word meaning "raccoon."

While there is scant documentary evidence regarding an Onondaga village in the vicinity of Geauga Lake, it's not impossible nor improbable that a group of expatriate Iroquois camped or even established a village in the area. The Onondaga were one of the original Five Nations of the Iroquois, and as the central nation geographically in the Iroquois Confederacy, their specific homeland was at present Syracuse, New York. After the Beaver Wars of the mid–17th century, Ohio was almost devoid of permanent Indian settlement until refugee tribes moved into the Ohio area in the 18th century. Along with the refugee Lenape, Shawnee, Wyandot, and Miami Indians, some expatriate Iroquois also moved into the area, and they became known generically as "Mingos." The word Mingo is Algonquin in origin and is akin to the Lenape word for the Iroquois, "Mingwe," meaning stealthy or treacherous. Most of the Mingos who relocated to Ohio were from the two westernmost of the Iroquois nations, the Seneca and the Cayuga, but it's certainly likely that some Onondaga as well as Oneida and Mohawks moved into Ohio as well.

The Moravian missionary David Zeisberger mentioned his encounters with Onondaga Indians who came to the Christian towns of Schoenbrunn and Gnadenhütten, so it's not inconceivable that Onondaga families established villages in Ohio. Unfortunately, specific information regarding the village has not been found.

48. *Ottawa Town (c. 1742–c. 1776), also Tawas Town, Tawas.*
Now: Valley View, Cuyahoga County (41°22′39.48″N–81°36′35.60″W)

There is considerable evidence regarding the existence of a village of Ottawa Indians on the east bank of the Cuyahoga River about ten miles south of the river's mouth at present Cleveland, Ohio. However, there is little documentary evidence regarding the time period the village was populated or even how large it may have been. We do know its location and that it existed prior to the Moravian village of Pilgerruh (1786–1787), because the pilgrims mentioned they took advantage of the relatively cleared garden plots of the old Ottawa village.

The Ottawa village was generally referred to as Ottawa Town and "Tawas," a corruption of "Ottawas," and on maps of the period it's represented both ways. Lewis Evans's 1755 and 1771 maps show the town as "Tawas" across the Cuyahoga River from "French House," the location of François Saguin's old trading post. It's believed that Ottawa Town was occupied during the time Saguin operated his post between 1742 and approximately 1745.[125]

Charles Whittlesey, in his book *Early History of Cleveland*,[126] places the abandoned Ottawa Town a short distance below (downstream, or north) of Tinker's Creek, at the site where Zeisberger and his congregation established Pilgerruh, but Whittlesey doesn't mention a time period when Ottawa Town was in existence. We can be fairly certain of the location of Ottawa Town, based on the establishment of Pilgerruh at the abandoned Ottawa village site. David Sanders Clark's archaeological study in 1936 located the precise site of Pilgerruh, which was on the site of Ottawa Town. (See Pilgerruh.) Also, Zeisberger's diary places the location of Pilgerruh, and by extension Ottawa Town, adjacent to the "Upper Fording Place" on the Cuyahoga, which was a shallow riffle area in the Cuyahoga River that facilitated easy crossings. The Upper Fording Place can still be seen as a shallow area next to the north side of the present Hillside Road Bridge.

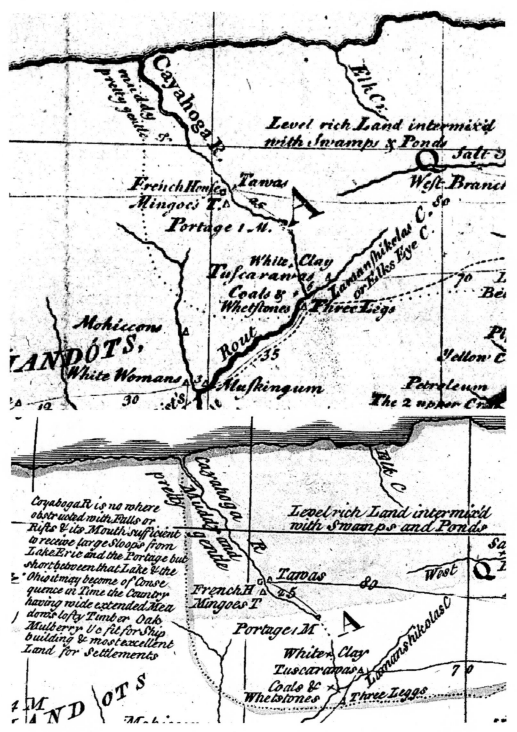

Top: Section of 1771 Lewis Evans map (Library of Congress, Geography and Map Division-74694156). *Bottom*: Section of 1755 Lewis Evans map (Library of Congress, Geography and Map Division-75693767).

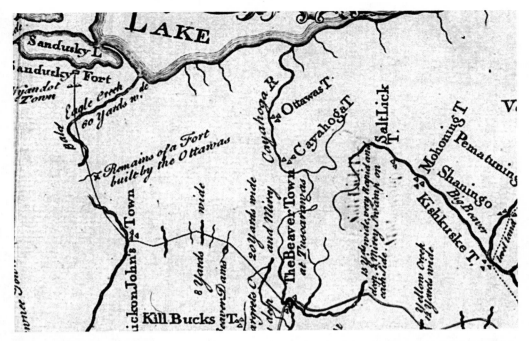

Section of Thomas Hutchins's 1764 map (Library of Congress, Geography and Map Division-2001695748).

Assuming that Ottawa Town on the Cuyahoga was populated during the period François Saguin operated his trading post, the question remains as to when it was abandoned by the Ottawa. Lewis Evans's map, dated 1750, clearly shows [Ot]tawa Town, but that is not conclusive since it also shows François Saguin's "French House," even though Saguin had ceased trading there about five years previously. A clue as to when Ottawa Town had been vacated may be found in David Zeisberger's description of the old Ottawa garden fields. He wrote that the old Ottawa garden plot "was very wild, the weeds standing as high as a man, which we had to cut down, thus having much trouble and labor."[127] That would indicate that perhaps several years had passed since the Ottawa left. The fields were untended long enough to allow the weeds to grow as high as a man, but not yet have new trees grow up as the forest reclaimed the land. It's estimated that it takes about ten years for shrubs and young trees to reach appreciable size on an untended farm field. Based on that rough estimate, we can assume that Ottawa Town was abandoned no earlier than sometime around the beginning of the American Revolutionary War.

50. *Painted Post (c. 1750–c. 1780).*
Now: Dungannon, Columbiana County
(40°44'4.58"N–80°52'52.83"W)

The Indian town of Painted Post was located near the junction of the Great Trail, the Ashtabula Trail, and the Moravian Trail at present Dungannon, Ohio. Wilcox wrote: "The little town of Dungannon, lying on a knoll in a basin formed by the intersection of several creeks, is now far from major highways. It was once called 'Painted Post,' from the peeled tree which bore 'war marks' at this junction with the Moravian Trail. It was once a spot of major importance, but now sleeps in its pleasant isolation."[128] William C. Mills agrees with the location but does not mention anything more about the town. He wrote that the Moravian Trail was a branch of the Great Trail that extended from Painted Post in Columbiana County to a juncture with the Cuyahoga–Muskingum Trail near Conchake.[129]

John Heckewelder provides some insight on the name "painted post," although it is not in conjunction with the Indian town in Ohio. In 1798, he visited the area around present Elmira, New York, which was then called Newton, and he made the following observation: "Eighteen miles from Newton we came to a small town called the Painted Post, so named because the Indians when going to war, used to assemble at a painted post. Which was fixed in this place, where they painted themselves in their usual frightful manner, were equipped, and arranged into companies, and regulated all their warlike enterprizes. Here also, after an encounter, they brought their prisoners, to kill or otherwise dispose of, according to their customs. In the Indian country there are many such painted posts."[130]

Painted Post in Ohio was near several streams, including Sandy Beaver Creek and Willard Run. Given its location on slightly higher ground, with an adequate water supply, and near the junction of major Indian thoroughfares, it would be a likely place for an Indian village. Unfortunately, neither Wilcox nor Mills provides any additional information regarding the town, its inhabitants or the time period of its existence. Also, a search of all available contemporary accounts and journals relevant to the area has not provided any other information about the village.

If there was an Indian town in that area, it would most likely have been either a Mingo or Lenape village. The Mingo chief Logan had his village at the mouth of Yellow Creek, about fifteen and a half miles southeast of Painted Post. That would make it the closest Indian village to Painted Post, but there were several Lenape villages within thirty miles.

If it was a Mingo town, it could have been established as early as the 1740s, but since the Mingos were generally hostile to the white Europeans, it would not likely have survived beyond the Revolutionary War. If it was a Lenape town, it would probably have been established sometime after the mid–1750s, and it could have survived as late as the 1780s.

53. Ponty's Camp (c. 1760), also Pontiac's Camp.
Now: Peninsula, Summit County (41°16'17.13"N–81°33'49.69"W)

Pontiac was reputedly born about 1720 near the confluence of the Auglaize and Maumee Rivers at present Defiance, Ohio. His father was an Ottawa, and it's believed his mother was Ojibwe (Chippewa). He was a natural leader, and in 1755, he led the Ottawa and Ojibwe warriors at Braddock's defeat on the Monongahela. In 1760, after the French defeat at Québec, the famous ranger Robert Rogers was sent to take possession of Fort Detroit for the British. Along the way, Rogers was met by Pontiac, who objected to the English invasion of their territory, but when Pontiac learned the French had been defeated in Canada, he allowed Rogers to continue on to Fort Detroit. The 1760 meeting between Rogers and Pontiac was reputedly at the mouth of the Cuyahoga River. Actually, the meeting between Rogers and Pontiac may not have taken place on the Cuyahoga River at all. Historian Howard Henry Peckham states that Rogers and his party met an Ottawa representative at the mouth of the Cuyahoga, but it was not Pontiac. In Rogers's journal, there was no mention of Pontiac at the meeting; however, in 1765, he published a revised and embellished account of the meeting in which Rogers said he was met by "Ponteack, who claimed he was the King and Lord of the country I was in."[131] Peckham adds that Rogers's "elaborate and incongruous" account of the meeting "has been accepted as truthful by many historical investigators from Lewis Cass[132] to the present." Peckham further states, "If Pontiac accosted Rogers at all during this journey, the meeting took place at the mouth of the Detroit River on November 27 in company with a number of other chiefs."[133]

Other than Rogers's claim that he encountered Pontiac on the Cuyahoga, there is very little documentary evidence other than rumor that Pontiac ever resided on the Cuyahoga. In fact, Roger's own account does not make that claim. There were indeed Ottawa camps and settlements along the river at various times, but there does not appear to be any evidence to support the premise that Pontiac resided at any of them.

General L.V. Bierce is probably the first to mention Ponty's Camp. Bierce was an interesting character who, in 1838, appointed himself commander-in-chief of the "Patriot Army" during the Canada Patriot War (1837–1839), which consisted of a series of losing battles to free Canada from British rule. After Bierce lost two battles, he went home. He wrote *Historical Reminiscences of Summit County* in 1854, which is a collection of tales based on popular, romanticized legend as well as a mix of factual data. For example, Bierce mentioned Ponty's Camp as being on the west side of the Cuyahoga River about half a mile northwest of an old Seneca village. He claimed, "It was a celebrated place in early times, and was one of the great land marks of the country."[134] Bierce claims the town was a "celebrated place for the collecting of war parties, previous to starting their expeditions. They had erected here, a wooden God—a kind of home-made Mars—to whom they made offerings and sacrifices, to propitiate his favor, before starting on a war-march. The offering generally consisted of tobacco—and, on leaving they usually hung two or three pounds around his neck, for his use during their absence."[135]

In 1921, Peter Cherry likely used Bierce's work as a source when he wrote, "Pontiac was called the tiger of the Northwest. In his early manhood he spent much of his time in a village of his people, on the Cuyahoga. 'Ponty's Camp,' was a well known land mark to the earliest adventurers across the Alleghenies. In Lewis Evan's map of the Middle British Colonies, London, 1755, the point is designated as 'Tawas.'"[136] Cherry further states, "Half a mile north of the Village of Boston, in the Cuyahoga Valley, was 'Ponty's Camp.' It was situated on the west side of the river. It was a noted place in the early times and its site was given on many early maps and was generally known throughout the entire Northwest."[137]

Frank Wilcox apparently used both Bierce and Cherry's works as supporting evidence. Wilcox wrote that Pontiac was rumored to have resided on bottom land, near a "fine spring" on the west side of the Cuyahoga River, about one-half mile north of Boston Mill.[138] Wilcox later refers to a branch trail that "continued down Brandywine Creek to Ponty's Camp, one half mile north of Boston Mills on the Cuyahoga."[139] Actually, the mouth of Brandywine Creek is about one and three-quarter miles from Boston Mills, but Wilcox likely meant the branch trail joined the Cuyahoga Trail, which then led south to Ponty's Camp.

Though it's unlikely that Pontiac actually lived for any length of time on the Cuyahoga River, other Ottawa Indians certainly did. Their villages are shown on 18th-century maps as "Tawas," "Ottawas T," or simply "Ottawas." It's likely that both Cherry and Wilcox made the extrapolation that Pontiac was associated with those sites. Lewis Evans's 1755 map depicts a settlement named "Tawas" (Ottawas) on the east side of the Cuyahoga River opposite "French House," or François Saguin's trading post. Hutchins's 1764 map shows the location as "Ottawas T" approximately at the same location, and a French map dated 1781 shows

"Ottawas" at that approximate site. Interestingly, both Cherry and Wilcox indicate that Pontiac's Camp was on the west side of the river, yet the maps they use as evidence depict the Ottawa towns on the east side of the river.

As mentioned, there were several Indian villages in the Cuyahoga River Valley during the 18th century, including Ottawa Town. However, there is little evidence that Pontiac actually lived in any of them.

48. *Saguin's Post (1742–1745), also French House.*
Now: Valley View, Cuyahoga County (41°21'56.31"N–81°36'50.33"W)

Through the treaties of Ryswick in 1697 and Utrecht in 1713, the British government acknowledged French ownership of the vast area west of the Allegheny Mountains known as "New France." And French ownership was once again reaffirmed in the Treaty of Aix-la-Chapelle in 1748. Even so, English traders continuously streamed across the Alleghenies into New France to take advantage of the lucrative Indian fur trade. The French, of course, regarded the English fur traders as illegal trespassers, but because of the limited number of French troops in the few posts like Fort Detroit and Fort des Miamis at present Fort Wayne, Indiana, the French were unable to effectively interdict incursions by English traders.

In an attempt to counter English incursions, the French decided to locate a trading post on the Cuyahoga River. In 1742, Robert Navarre, the intendant[140] at Fort Detroit, ordered the French-Canadian fur trader François Saguin to establish the post. Saguin's orders were to regain and maintain the French fur trade initiative in the northeastern area of New France, while promoting goodwill and loyalty between the French and the Indians. He was also directed to provide intelligence regarding English influence among the Indians, but his foremost responsibility was to generate a profit and maintain a steady flow of valuable furs to Fort Detroit.

Saguin arrived on the Cuyahoga reportedly with two canoe loads of merchandise, and he chose his location well. He built two sturdy log buildings to serve as his residence and warehouse on the west bank of the Cuyahoga River less than a quarter-mile north of the mouth of Tinker's Creek, which entered the Cuyahoga River from the east. He also cleared fields to plant corn and cultivate a garden next to the post, indicating that Saguin planned to remain in the area for the long term. His post was situated on two major north-south Indian trails, the Cuyahoga–Muskingum and the Cuyahoga War Trail, which provided access from both the northern Lake Trail and the Watershed and Great Trails to the south. An Ottawa Indian village was a short distance to the north on the opposite side of the river, while Mingo Town was located on the west bank of the Cuyahoga River to the south. From when it was established, Saguin's post became very popular with the Indians, and he attracted customers from many different nations, including the Mingo, Mohican, Ottawa, Ojibwe, Lenape, and even the distant Abenakis.[141] In fact, Saguin's business was remarkably robust, and by the end of his first season, he had acquired about 200 bales of valuable furs.

Saguin's trading post was so popular that for a time Indians and traders referred to the Cuyahoga River as Rivière au Saugin, or "Saguin's River." For example, in 1754, de Lery referred to the Cuyahoga as Rivière de Saguin, and in 1764, the British engineer Montressor depicted it as River de Saguin. However, the river was mostly called Cuyahoga or something fairly close in pronunciation. Most sources claim that the word Cuyahoga means "crooked," from the Mohawk Cayagaga, and indeed the course of the Cuyahoga, especially near its mouth at Cleveland, is very serpentine. However, the Seneca called it Cuyohaga, or "place of the jawbone," so its original meaning is subject to debate. The river was depicted differently on maps and in journals because of differences in pronunciation and difficulties in transcribing Indian words. For example, the Lenape name for the river was Diohaga, and on some maps and journals it was also written as Kayahoga. A map dated 1763 by Bowen and Gibson refers to the Cuyahoga as "Guahago," which is similar to Bowen and Gibson's 1763 map, which depicts the river as "Gwahago." That is likely the result of mapmakers copying other mapmaker's works. That may also be evidenced from the maps of Evans in 1758, Jeffries in 1758, Hutchins in 1764, and Andrews in 1783, who all spelled the river as "Cayahoga." However, in 1777, Hawkins inexplicably changed the spelling of the river to "Cauhogue." It's only fair to add that for a time, the Cuyahoga River was one of several rivers in northern Ohio that was referred to as "La Rivière Blanche" or the "White River."

While François Saguin's name was attached to the Cuyahoga for a short time, a nearby river still retains a connection to the French fur trader. During the time he was in Ohio, Saguin also traveled to surrounding areas, where he established temporary trading posts. One of the places he regularly visited was on what is now the Chagrin River near present Chagrin Falls, Ohio. That river also became known as "Saguin's River," and the name stuck, but because the Indians in the area only had the "sh" sound in their language, the name was corrupted to "Shaguin," and from there it was further corrupted in English to "Chagrin."

Unfortunately for Saguin, his business was so lucrative that about a year after he established his post on the Cuyahoga, George Croghan, the "king of the Pennsylvania traders," set up a competing post about eleven miles away at the mouth of the Cuyahoga River at present Cleveland, Ohio. Saguin couldn't compete with the Irishman either in terms of quantity, quality, or price, and the Indians, like shoppers everywhere, were quick to ascertain where they would get the best deal. The Indians especially wanted liquor, gunpowder and lead, items that Saguin had in short supply. He sent message after message to Navarre at Fort Detroit asking for greater amounts of trade merchandise, including liquor and especially gunpowder and lead, so he could win over the Indian trade, but his pleas fell on deaf ears. Navarre and the French authorities at Fort Detroit considered Saguin's venture a losing proposition, and they decided to cut their losses and not support it any further. In 1745, Saguin was ordered to abandon his trading post and return to Fort Detroit, where he could concentrate his trade with the northern Indians. Thus, in the short period of a year or two, Croghan and the English trade had run Saguin out of business.

After Saguin abandoned his enterprise on the Cuyahoga, his trading post was depicted on maps as late as 1755 as "French House." That was because mapmakers tended to rely on word-of-mouth information rather than personal on-site observation. No trace of François Saguin or his post remains, other than a corruption of his name that is attached to the beautiful little town of Chagrin Falls and the nearby Chagrin River.

56. *Salt Lick Town (c. 1758–c. 1786), also Sickeunk, Kseekheoong, Captain Pipe's Town.*
Now: Niles, Trumbull County (41°10′5.01″N–80°47′16.48″W)

A map by Lewis Evans dated 1755 shows "Salt Springs" on the waterway labeled "West Branch," which refers to the Mahoning River. Evans erroneously placed the salt spring to the north of the river, but he did not indicate an Indian town at the site of the salt spring on either his 1755 or 1771 map. There was indeed a town at the site, because John McCullough, who was a captive of the Lenape from 1756 to 1764, wrote: "We then moved to where they were settling a new town, called Kseek-he-oong, that is, a Place of Salt, a place now well known by the name of Salt Licks, on the West Branch of Beaver [Mahoning River in Weathersfield Township, Trumbull County, Ohio] where we lived about one year. We moved there about the time that General Forbes took Fort Duquesne from the French,"[142] which occurred in November 1758. The Irish fur trader George Croghan visited the town in 1760,[143] as did the Moravian missionary John Heckewelder on October 13, 1786.[144]

During the Revolutionary War, the Lenape village of Salt Spring Town or Sickeunk was one of the towns whose chief was Konieschquanoheel or Captain Pipe (c. 1725–c. 1818?), of the Wolf phratry. He was also known as Hopocan, "tobacco pipe." Around 1772, Captain Pipe succeeded his maternal uncle Custaloga as chief when he led his group of Lenape into Ohio during the French and Indian War. When the American Revolutionary War began, Captain Pipe initially remained neutral, refusing to take up arms against either the British or the Americans.

In February 1778, American General Edward Hand (1744–1802) led a force of 500 militia on an expedition against the British-allied Mingos in Ohio, and also to destroy a cache of British military equipment deposited at the mouth of the Cuyahoga (present Cleveland) for the Indians' use. During the expedition, the frontiersman Simon Girty (1741–1818) served as a guide and interpreter for the Americans.

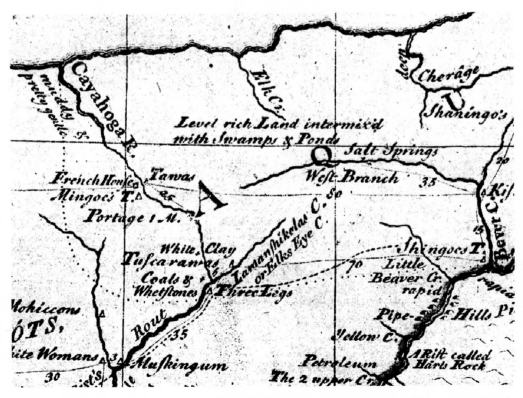

Section of Lewis Evans's 1755 map (Library of Congress, Geography and Map Division-75693767).

General Hand's "badly cloathed"[145] and ill-equipped militia marched from Fort Pitt to the Mahoning River without finding any Indians. The party was frustrated, cold, and tired, and after a fruitless search for hostile Indians, Hand ordered the expedition to return to Fort Pitt. On their return, they discovered footprints in the snow that led them to the small, peaceful Lenape village of Salt Lick Town. The village's warriors and many of the younger men were away hunting, so there were only a handful of women, children and some old men in the town, including Captain Pipe's mother and brother, and his brother's children. To General Hand's unruly militia, one Indian was no different from another, so they immediately attacked. Most of the villagers scattered and ran for the woods, but General Hand reported that the militia was "so Impetuous that I could not prevent their Killing the Man & one of the Women."[146] Hand was able to save another woman "with difficulty."[147] However, the woman, in an effort to save her life, told the troops about another Lenape camp about ten miles away.

Hand sent a detachment of militia to capture the Indians at the other camp and bring them back, but when the troops got there, they immediately attacked. Once again, the warriors were away, and the camp only contained four women and a boy. The militia killed and scalped the boy and three of the women. All of the dead had been shot repeatedly, and there was an argument about who should get credit for killing the young boy. Simon Girty was asked to arbitrate, and he announced that Captain Zachariah Connell[148] of the militia was credited with the killing.

General Hand blamed the "savage" killing of the peaceful noncombatant Lenape Indians on the undisciplined militia, while justifying the killing on the frustration of the troops at not having located Indian warriors to attack. He wrote; "Notwithstanding this Savage Conduct, I verily believe the Party would behave well if they had men to contend with."[149]

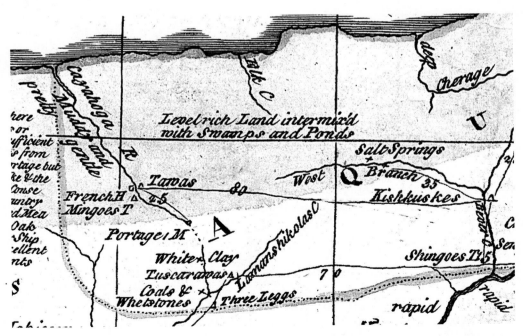

Section of Lewis Evans's 1771 map (Library of Congress, Geography and Map Division-74694156).

In spite of the death of his relatives at the hands of American troops, Captain Pipe initially remained neutral, and did not seek revenge.

When General Hand and his motley troops returned to Fort Pitt, they were ridiculed for the failure to locate and punish any hostile Indians and for returning with the scalps of one old man, four women, and a boy, all of whom were friendly to the Americans. The frontiersmen derisively referred to Hand's expedition as the "Squaw Campaign," an event that marred Hand's reputation. In a sense, the ill-fated expedition proved to have a positive effect in that it demonstrated that disciplined regular troops rather than untrained militia, were necessary to conduct a frontier campaign.

Later that year, 1778, American General Lachlan McIntosh ordered the construction of Fort Laurens at present Bolivar, Ohio, and he also demanded that the Ohio Lenape join the Americans in an attack on Fort Detroit. If the Lenape refused, McIntosh threatened to exterminate them. Instead, Captain Pipe along with other Lenape leaders decided to ally themselves with the British, and Pipe moved his community to Goschachgunk at present Coshocton, Ohio.

Some of Captain Pipe's villagers apparently remained at Salt Lick Town at least until after John Heckewelder's visit in 1786. Other Indians stopped to gather salt there until white settlements completely took over the area in the 1790s. While the salt spring served the needs of the Indians and frontiersmen, the salinity or concentration of salt in the water was insufficient for commercial use. There was an attempt by Samuel Holden Parsons to commercially produce salt around 1789, but Parsons died prior to finalizing the undertaking. Some sporadic interest in the salt spring continued until the early 1800s. The spring itself, including the site of Salt Lick Town, was covered by fill dirt during the construction of the B&O Railroad in 1902, but a small amount of salt water continued to bubble to the surface a short distance south of the original salt spring.

57. Seneca Town (c. 1740s–c. 1770s).
Now: Twinsburg, Summit County (41°18′42.75″N–81°26′26.96″W)

This is another Indian town that is difficult to prove existed, because other than a cursory mention in *Ohio Indian Trails*, there is no other documentary evidence. Wilcox wrote that, from the Onondaga town at Aurora, Ohio, "there must have been a branch trail running west over the marshes at the head of Tinker's Creek to a Seneca Town at Twinsburg, and continuing west to Macedonia and Northfield, and down to Willow Lake."[150]

The present town of Twinsburg is on higher ground adjacent to Tinker's Creek, which is a large stream that would easily qualify as a small river. The logical place for a town would have been near the Public Square in Twinsburg, which is at the intersections of Ohio Routes 82 and 91.

Apparently, there was some sort of school in Twinsburg that educated American Indians, because there is mention of a Potawatomi Indian named Simon Pokagon (1830–1899) who attended school there. An entry in *The Hutchins Family of Allegan County, Michigan*, states: "At about the time Harrison and David [Hutchins] arrived in Michigan, Simon Pokagon, who was about Harrison's age returned from an Indian school at Twinsburg, Ohio, where he had learned much of the White Man's culture."[151] Another entry expands on the biography of Simon Pokagon: "On reaching his fourteenth year, [he] was sent to school at Notre Dame, Ind. for three years; then, encouraged by his mother in his desire for education, he attended Oberlin College, Ohio, for a year, and next went to Twinsburg, Ohio, where he remained two years. It is said that he was educated for the priesthood, spoke four or five languages, and bore the reputation of being the best educated full-blooded Indian of his time."[152]

If indeed the town was inhabited by Seneca, as the name implies, it would fall into the category of being a Mingo village since the Mingos were expatriate Iroquois. There is no information regarding its date of establishment or when it ceased to exist, but the expatriate Iroquois began to enter present eastern Ohio around the mid–1740s. So a Seneca settlement at present Twinsburg may very well have been established in the late 1740s to the beginning of the French and Indian War in 1754. The Mingos were, for the most part, hostile to the English colonists who later became Americans, and as a result, it's unlikely that the Mingos, who allied with the British during the American Revolutionary War, would have maintained a village in a vulnerable location like present Twinsburg. Rather, it's likely that at the beginning of the Revolutionary War, they abandoned their village, and moved west where they joined forces with Pluggy at present Delaware, Ohio.

58. *Shattar's Post (c. 1786–c. 1800),*
also Joseph Shattar's Trading Post.
Now: Cleveland, Cuyahoga County (41°27′3.83″N–81°41′4.15″W)

Joseph du Shattar,[153] a young Frenchman and a longtime employee of the North West Company, conducted a lively fur trade along the northern section of Ohio, primarily between the Cuyahoga and Sandusky Rivers during and after the American Revolutionary War. The North West Company, headquartered in Montreal, was the offshoot of the French fur trade in New France dating back to the second half of the 17th century. The name "North West Company" can be found in some documents as early as 1770. However, the company was officially organized in 1779 by a group of Montreal traders who attempted to break the stranglehold of the Hudson's Bay Company on the North American fur trade.[154]

Around 1786, du Shattar decided to go into business for himself, and he established a trading post on the west bank of the Cuyahoga River. His trading post was about nine miles from the river's mouth in the vicinity of present Jennings Road and Dennison Avenue in the Old Brooklyn neighborhood of present Cleveland, Ohio. In conjunction with his business, du Shattar established a couple of satellite posts in the Sandusky and Huron River areas, and he employed fur traders to work the satellites and visit Indian villages. A Mr. Ebenezer Merry of Milan, Ohio, who in 1842 claimed to have known Joseph du Shattar, said that two of du Shattar's associates were John Baptiste Flemming and Joseph Burrall. Information regarding Burrall hasn't been located, but in Flemming's case, Merry was likely referring to John Baptiste Flammand, the Quèbec-born trapper, who operated du Shattar's satellite post on the Huron River.

In 1790, du Shattar married Mary Pornay at Detroit, and they had at least two children. It's not known where the first child was born, but sources indicate their second child was born at du Shattar's post on the Cuyahoga River in 1794. Information regarding the children, including their names and sex, has not yet been located.

At first, du Shattar was able to maintain the friendship and goodwill of his Indian customers, but apparently his employees did not have the same business sense. They were rough-hewn fur traders, who were not much more civilized than their temperamental Indian customers, and they often treated the Indians with a certain amount of arrogance and contempt. For example, in the Sandusky area, one of du Shattar's employees, a Frenchman by the name of Beaulieau (Beaulieu), "appropriated" the wife of an Indian, which incited the offended native to gather a war party and attack Beaulieau's post in order to rescue the woman. In the process, much of the trade merchandise at the post was seized by the Indians, but a tentative peace was established after Beaulieau appeased the Indians with a quantity of liquor.

While alcohol quelled the uprising at Sandusky, the continued supply of liquor to the Indians resulted in other serious quarrels. The traders customarily provided spirits to the Indians to make them more compliant and less aware of unfair or unscrupulous trades. However, liquor didn't always keep the Indians submissive. One fight broke out at the Cuyahoga post when the Indians accused the traders of cheating them in the trade of firearms, and a lethal battle took place when the Indians attempted to steal the firewater. During the fight, participants were killed on both sides.

By the late 1790s, an influx of white settlers into area drove the Indians farther west, and the fur trade era was essentially over along the Cuyahoga River. Du Shattar's trading post remained in existence to about 1796, when General Moses Cleaveland and the surveyors of the Connecticut Land Company laid out the plans for the City of Cleaveland.[155]

Joseph du Shattar apparently remained in the area even after his trading post ceased to exist, because in 1812, he reportedly helped capture an Ojibwe Indian named John O'Mic, who murdered the trappers Michael Gibbs and Daniel Buell at Pipe Creek in Sandusky, Ohio. O'Mic was tried in Cleaveland and publicly executed on Public Square. Apparently, the remains of de Shattar's trading post existed well into the 19th century, as evidenced by an account in the *Early History of Cleveland*: "He [du Shattar] had a post nine miles up the river, which is probably the one whose remains have been observed in Brooklyn, opposite Newberg."[156]

71. *Silver Lake (?–c. 1809).*
NOW: SILVER LAKE, SUMMIT COUNTY (41°9'1.09"N–81°27'23.42"W)

Silver Lake is a small spring-fed lake in Summit County, Ohio, where according to local legend, a Seneca or Mingo village stood until around the beginning of the War of 1812. I haven't been able to locate any historical documentation confirming the existence of the village, but it is such a beautiful site that it's likely Indians either camped or established a village there.

A historical marker indicates: "Silver Lake was previously known as Wetmore's Pond, named for Judge William Wetmore, an agent for the Connecticut Land Company. In 1808, Wetmore built a cabin overlooking the spring-fed lake, which was then a part of Portage County. Local lore records his friendship and conscientious dealings with the Native Americans, likely Seneca, who inhabited a populous village between the lake and the Cuyahoga River. The tribe left the area to join the British during the War of 1812, but later sided with the United States."

Local amateur historians have further expanded on the story of the Indian village located there, and most indicate the village contained about 500 Seneca Indians under a Chief Wabmong. A village of 500 would have been a very large village indeed, since contemporary accounts say most Indian villages contained fewer than 100 men, women and children.

Only a major village like Gekelemukpechunk (New Comer's Town) might have a population approximating 500. In 1775, David Zeisberger wrote, "Gekelemukpechunk, which is situated on the Muskingum River, is rather a large Indian town and is said to consist of 100 houses, which I think likely." A fairly substantial village might have 200 to 300 villagers, but most Indian settlements were rather small, consisting of between 30 and 75 people.

If the Indian village at Silver Lake had been one of the major or otherwise significant villages with a large population, it would certainly have been represented on contemporary maps or in contemporary journals. Thomas Hutchins's map of 1764 clearly shows Cuyahoga Town and Ottawa Town on the Cuyahoga, but there is no indication of a town in the vicinity of Silver Lake, even though other small Indian towns are represented on Hutchins's map. The same can be said of the 1771 Lewis Evans map, which shows small Indian communities like Mingoes Town on the west side of the Cuyahoga River, White Woman's Town on the Walhonding, as well as some of the more major Indian villages in the area, but there is no reference to a town in the vicinity of Silver Lake.

I was unable to locate any documentary information on a chief Wabmong, and unfortunately, the few references to the chief and his village in works by local writers do not list credible sources on which their information was based. In actuality, the beautiful site of Silver Lake would undoubtedly have attracted some Native Americans and enticed them to set up camp, or even establish a seasonal village that they visited at different times of the year. It wasn't unusual for Indians of the northeastern woodlands who lived in semi-permanent villages to rotate between two or three locations, and regularly move to where the crops grew better, the fish and game were more plentiful, or simply for a change of scene.

45. *Tapacon Town (1779–1781),*
also Tuppakin, New Schoenbrunn, New Schönbrunn.
Now: New Philadelphia, Tuscarawas County
(40°28'6.96"N–81°26'25.83"W)

Tapacon, as far as can be determined, is mentioned in only one contemporary source, a biographical account of John Leith (1755–1837), a trader who was adopted by the Lenape in 1774 at the beginning of Lord Dunmore's War. In *A Short Biography of John Leith*, the notes state, "Tapacon, or, more correctly, Tuppakin, was the Indian name for New Schönbrunn, the upper Moravian mission town upon the Tuscarawas, on the west side of that stream, one and a quarter miles south of the present site of New Philadelphia."[157] For more information, see "New Schoenbrunn" in the Moravian Mission Villages section.

10. *Tullihas (c. 1750–c. 1762),*
also Walhonding Town, Owl Town, Mohiccons Town.
Now: Walhonding, Coshocton County *(40°21'47.28"N–82°9'43.97"W)*

Tullihas was first mentioned by James Smith, a soldier with Braddock's ill-fated expedition who was captured by Caughnawaga Indians[158] prior to the battle on the Monongahela and was adopted and lived with them until he escaped in 1759. In 1755, he was taken to "the west branch of the Muskingum [Walhonding River], about twenty miles above the forks, and rested at a village called Tullihas, inhabited by Delawares [Lenape], Caughnewagas, and Mohicans."[159]

Not only is there a lack of information regarding an Indian named Mohican John, who had at least two villages in Ohio, but there is some controversy regarding where his towns were located. Mohican John was an actual person, because the Moravian missionary John Heckewelder wrote about meeting him. Heckewelder wrote, "This once great and renowned [Mohican] nation has almost entirely disappeared, as well as the numerous tribes who descended from them; they have been destroyed by wars, carried off by the small pox and other disorders. So early in the year 1762, a number of them had emigrated to the Ohio, where I became acquainted with their chief who was called by the whites 'Mohican John.'"[160] Unfortunately, Heckewelder doesn't give us any more information regarding the chief or his Indian name, which is unusual because Heckewelder's writings are usually replete with information.

The original homeland of the Mohicans, or more properly Mahican, was in the area of present northwestern Connecticut, western Massachusetts, southern Vermont, and along the northern Hudson River valley. They were of Algonquin stock, and were related and shared a kinship with their southern neighbors, the Lenape. Their name *Muh-he-ka-neew* came from their homeland along the Hudson River, and means "people of the continually flowing waters." Many Mahican settled in western Massachusetts near Stockbridge, and that branch became known as the Stockbridge Indians. They sided with the British during the French and Indian War, and were allied with the Americans during the Revolution.

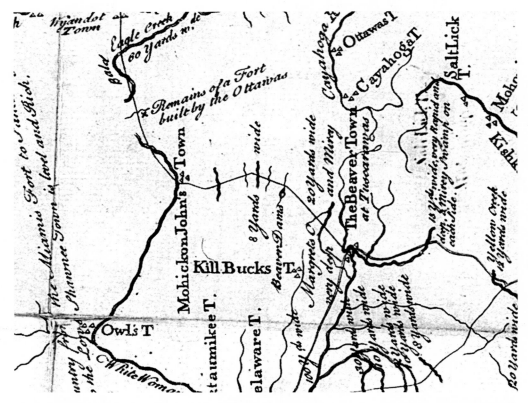

Section of Hutchins's 1764 map (Library of Congress, Geography and Map Division—2001695748).

Sources Indicate that Mohican John moved into the Ohio area sometime during the 1750–1755 period. B.F. Bowen states, "Mohican John, with his tribe was driven from Connecticut and Rhode Island. He came to Ohio in 1755 and first located at Tullihas, on the Big Mohican, where Owl Creek enters."[161] According to white captive James Smith, Tullihas was "an Indian village on the west branch of the Muskingum, about twenty miles above the forks."[162] The term "west branch of the Muskingum" referred to the present Walhonding River, and "twenty miles above the forks" would have placed Tullihas at the junction of the Kokosing and Mohican Rivers near the present hamlet of Walhonding, Ohio. Hutchins's map of 1764 refers to the Indian town as Owl Town, because it was situated in the fork where Owl Creek (Kokosing River) and Mohican Creek (River) joined to form the Walhonding River, or White Woman's Creek on Hutchins's map. "Owl Town seems to have been identical with Tullihas, to which James Smith was carried as a captive in 1755."[163] Evans's 1755 map shows a town called "Mohiccons" in the about the same location. Hutchins apparently made his 1764 map after Mohican John relocated to what became Mohican John's Town, since "Mohickon John's Town" is also depicted on Evans's map. The date of Mohican John's move from Tullihas to Mohican John's Town is difficult to determine, but it was likely around 1760, because the Pennsylvania trader George Croghan passed "Mohican John's Village" on the Great Trail between present Reedsburg and Jeromesville, Ohio, at the end of December 1760 or early January 1761.[164]

There were different Indian towns with the same apparent names, because chiefs periodically relocated their villages for several reasons. The different locations of the villages of Mohican John is a case in point, and to make matters worse, some sources indicate that he

Section of Evans's 1755 map (Library of Congress, Geography and Map Division-75693767).

had towns in improbable places. The most credible locations for Mohican John's villages are his first town at Tullihas at the confluence of the Kokosing, Mohican, and Walhonding Rivers from about 1752 to 1760. Next, he established his town about 1760 near the confluence of the Jerome Fork of the Mohican River and Oldtown Creek, about a mile south-southeast of present Jeromesville, Ohio. Any other village location ascribed to him cannot be verified by credible sources.

61. *Wakatomika #1 (1758–1774), also Waketomica, Waketomika, Wapetomica, Waketameki, Wankatammikee.*
NOW: DRESDEN, MUSKINGUM COUNTY (40°7′3.94″N–82°0′14.48″W)

Wakatomika was a Shawnee village located on the west bank of the Muskingum River at present Dresden, Ohio.

The town was established around 1758, when the Shawnee abandoned Lower Shawnee Town, which was their principal village at the mouth of the Scioto River. At that time, most of the Shawnee relocated up the Scioto to establish towns in the vicinity of present Chillicothe and Circleville, Ohio, which some Shawnee referred to as the "lower" towns or settlements. Others settled in the "upper" community of Wakatomika along the Muskingum River. The British cartographer Thomas Hutchins recorded Wakatomika as "Wankatammikee" on his 1764 map of the Ohio and Muskingum River areas.

Site of Wakatomika on the Muskingum River (author photograph).

The principal civil chief or "Hokima" at Wakatomika was the Mekoche chief Kisinoutha ("big wolf"), sometimes referred to as "Hardman." Like most Mekoche chiefs, Kisinoutha was a proponent of peace and diplomacy with the whites. Although the Shawnee customarily grouped together according to their sept or division, by the early 1760s, some Shawnee drifted away from their traditional septs and banded together under a popular or charismatic leader. Not only did the Shawnee begin to break away from their traditional sept communities, but those who moved to the Muskingum were more ambiguous about being part of an established Shawnee nationalistic agenda. They maintained strong cultural ties with the western Shawnee, but adamantly insisted on their independence to decide what was best for their specific community. For example, the Wakatomika Shawnee dealt

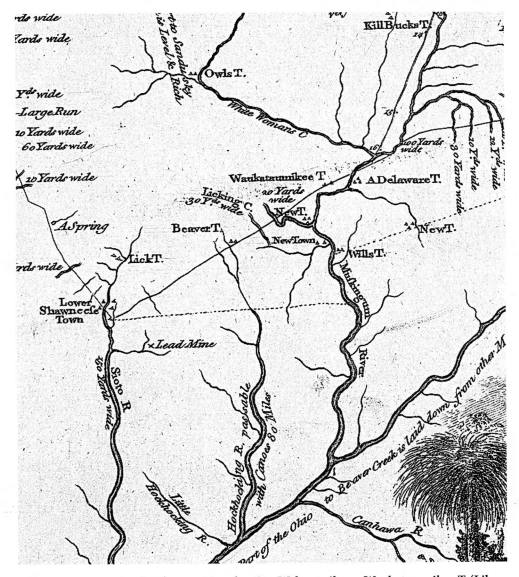

Section of Thomas Hutchins's 1764 Map showing Wakatomika as Wankatammikee T (Library of Congress, Geography and Map Division 2001695748).

with the British independently of the Western Shawnee during peace talks in 1762 and 1764. Even though the Wakatomika Shawnee claimed they were separate from the Western Shawnee, Kisinoutha maintained a close relationship with the Shawnee villages along the Scioto, and kept a residence at Blue Jacket's Town, which he frequently visited.

Although the Mekoche chief Kisinoutha attempted to maintain a peaceful coexistence with the English, events in 1774 resulted in the Wakatomika Shawnee "taking up the hatchet" against their Virginia neighbors. In April, a party of Virginians murdered about fifteen Indians along the upper Ohio River. The slain Indians included some Mingos, Lenapes, and Wakatomika Shawnee. In somewhat of a role reversal, the Scioto Shawnee tried to peacefully mediate the tension between the English authorities and the Wakatomika Shawnee, but the Wakatomikans were having none of it. Instead they insisted on their customary right to retaliate, and along with their Mingo neighbors, they launched raids against the Virginia settlements. The whites and Indians continued to attack each other, and the raids degenerated into a full-scale conflict known as Lord Dunmore's War, which raged from May through October 1774.

In August 1774, 400 Virginia militia under the leadership of Colonel Angus McDonald (1727–1778) marched from Fort Pitt and up the Muskingum in what was referred to as the "Wakatomika Campaign." McDonald's troops destroyed Wakatomika along with four other smaller villages in the area. With the destruction of Wakatomika on the Muskingum, Kisinoutha led his community west, settling temporarily among the Shawnee along the Scioto River. From the Scioto, they continued west to the Mad River in present Logan County, Ohio, where they established a new town that was also named Wakatomika.

65. White Eyes Town (c. 1770–1776).
Now: West Lafayette, Coshocton County
(40°17′3.8″N–81°44′55.36″W)

Most sources place the location of the town on the north bank of the Tuscarawas River in the southeast quadrant of the intersection of U.S. 36 and Ohio 93, about one mile north of West Lafayette, Ohio. However, a 1782 map by Crèvecouer shows White Eyes's village on the south bank of the Tuscarawas River, and another source places the Village about 30 miles south at present Duncan's Falls, Ohio.[165]

The town was named for its chief Koquethagechton or Coquetakeghton[166] (c. 1730–1776), but because of his lighter complexion and his noticeably lighter-colored eyes than most Native Americans, he was popularly known as "White Eyes," "Captain White Eyes," "George White Eyes," and "Grey Eyes." White Eyes was born into the Turtle Clan of the Lenape Nation, while the tribe was migrating across Pennsylvania. He was first mentioned as taking part in treaty negotiations near the end of the French and Indian War.

After the end of the French and Indian War, the influx of European settlers from the English colonies into Western Pennsylvania forced the Indians along the upper Ohio and Allegheny Rivers to migrate farther west into what is now Ohio, and the Lenape band containing White Eyes moved into the Muskingum River valley. They originally became a part of Lenape chief Netawatwees's village Gekelemukpechunk on the eastern fringe of present Newcomerstown. Around 1770, White Eyes became a chief in his own right and established his town on the Tuscarawas River about 10 miles west of Gekelemukpechunk. Records indicate that a white girl named Rachel Doddridge became the wife of White Eyes and supposedly bore him one son who was named George Morgan Whites Eyes. It's questionable whether Rachel actually was the mother of George Morgan White Eyes, because of the difficulty in reconciling Rachel's age with motherhood. Rachel was supposedly taken captive after a Lenape raid on the Doddridge farm in the 1770s, and most sources indicate she was about five years old at the time of her capture. Genealogical records indicate that Rachel was born after 1767, because her father Phillip was married in that year. Also, Rachel was born before her sister Hannah, who was born in 1778, so based on the assumption that Rachel was born sometime after 1767, it would have been virtually impossible for Rachel to be the mother of George Morgan White Eyes, who was born in the early 1770s. While it's unlikely that Rachel bore White Eyes any children, it is not impossible that she became his wife as a teenager. The most likely explanation is that White Eyes had more than one wife, perhaps even simultaneously, as polygamy was not unusual among Indian cultures. George Morgan White Eyes graduated from the College of New Jersey (Princeton) in 1789.[167]

Many of the Lenape in the Muskingum valley embraced Christianity, since the area was the center of missionary activity by the Moravian missionaries led by Davis Zeisberger (1721–1808) and John Heckewelder (1743–1823). Zeisberger founded three Christian Indian villages in the area, Schoenbrunn, Gnadenhütten, and Lichtenau. The historical marker regarding White Eyes indicates that he embraced Christianity, but that is only partially accurate. While many of the Lenape Indians under White Eyes converted to Christianity, White Eyes remained a non–Christian, but he allowed the missionaries access to his community, and ensured that the Christian Lenape remained full members of the larger tribal community rather than becoming a splinter group.

By 1774, many of the Lenape considered ninety-six-year-old Netawatwees unfit to lead

White Eyes historical marker (author photograph).

the nation, and the younger White Eyes was selected as the principal chief. This created a minor breach that lasted until Netawatwees died in 1776, but White Eyes only survived Netawatwees by two years. In 1775, White Eyes petitioned the Grand Lenape Council to centralize the nation around a new town at the Forks of the Muskingum, and the town of Goschachgunk was established there in 1776. Goschachgunk became the new principal town of the Lenape in Ohio, and the site of the Grand Council Fire. At that point White Eyes Town was abandoned.

After Lord Dunmore's War ended in 1774, White Eyes petitioned Virginia Royal Governor Dunmore for a royal grant in the Ohio Country, which would be a permanent homeland for the Lenape Indians. The American Revolutionary War, which began in 1775, brought an end to those negotiations when Lord Dunmore was forced to leave Virginia and take refuge on a Royal Navy ship. Undaunted, White Eyes began to negotiate with the fledgling U.S. government, who were interested in securing the allegiance of the Indians on the frontier, if for no other reason than to keep them from joining with the British. In April 1776, as part of this initiative, White Eyes addressed the 2nd Continental Congress in Philadelphia, and in 1778 a treaty was signed at Fort Pitt that promised to establish a Lenape (Delaware) state with representation in Congress. In effect, the Indian state in Ohio would become the 14th of the United States. In addition, White Eyes was commissioned a lieutenant-colonel in the American Army, and he planned to lead the Lenape in support of American military operations against the British.

Unfortunately, the treaty to create an Indian state in Ohio was never presented to Congress for ratification. After the surrender of Burgoyne at Saratoga in 1777 and the resultant Franco-American alliance, the Americans felt no urgency to maintain the Ohio Indians as allies. White Eyes unsuccessfully pressed for ratification of the treaty, but in the autumn of 1778, he died under mysterious circumstances at the age of forty-eight. The Army under General Lachlan McIntosh reported: "November 20th, 1778. Heard that the advance party of the army came to Tuscarawi night before last: likewise that Col. White Eye died not far from Pittsburgh from an old illness plus smallpox."[168] Moravian missionary David Zeisberger mentioned the death of White Eyes in his diary: "[November] The 20th. We received news in a letter from Colonel Gibson that the first troops from the army had arrived at Tuscarawi yesterday evening, and also that Colonel White Eyes had died not far from Pittsburgh 15 days ago today. He had an old illness and then got small pox in addition to that."[169]

Several years later, George Morgan, the Indian agent and former friend of White Eyes, claimed that White Eyes was murdered or "killed by treachery."[170] Sources indicate that Rachel Dodderidge, the wife of White Eyes died in 1788, when she was about 21 years old. According to some accounts, she was murdered by white men.

10. White Womans Town (c. 1750–c. 1780).
NOW: WARSAW, COSHOCTON COUNTY (40°19′36.82″N–81°56′23.78″W)

The "white woman" for whom the town was named was Mary Harris, who was captured as a child on February 29, 1704, during an Indian attack on the Deerfield settlement in Massachusetts. At the time, France and England were engaged in Queen Anne's War (1702–1713), and the savage attack on the frontier settlement was typical of many that were carried out by both sides during the hostilities. The French force that attacked Deerfield consisted of about 48 tough Canadian rangers and about 250 Abenaki, Caughnawaga,[171]

Huron, and Pocumtuc Indians. They were commanded by John-Baptiste Hertel de Rouville (1668–1722), who was reviled by New Englanders because of his propensity for attacking isolated and poorly defended settlements.

The raiders swept into Deerfield before dawn and took the town by surprise. Some Deerfield residents successfully fought off the attackers from fortified homes, but seventeen of the forty-one houses in the town were destroyed, and many of the others were looted. Of the 291 residents, only 126 escaped death or capture; 56 townspeople were killed in the attack, including 22 men,[172] 9 women, and 25 children. Those captives who could not make the trek back to Canada were killed on the spot. They included men, women, children, injured or infirm who were too weak to keep up, and would slow down the war party's escape. The raiders took 109 captives back to Canada, including young Mary Harris, whom sources indicate was about nine years old at the time.

Mary was adopted by the Indians, but the details of her early life in an Indian community were not recorded. As she grew into womanhood, she became the wife of a Caughnawaga Indian and bore him several children, of whom at least two were sons. Most of Caughnawaga Indians were Iroquois expatriates from upstate New York, but several other tribes were also represented at the Jesuit-administered village. These would certainly include some Delaware or Lenape Indians, which would explain how Mary Harris became the wife of a Lenape.

Mary and her Indian family were still in Canada in 1744, because Joseph Kellogg of Suffield, Connecticut, who was also a captive, encountered her family at that time. Kellogg wrote, "Two young men, Mary Harrises children, have been with me twice, which have lodged at my house. One of them is a very inteligable man about thirty years of age, and from them indeavored to critically examine them about the affairs of Canada."[173] That must have been shortly before Mary and her family moved to Ohio, because a French map dated 1746 implies that Mary Harris was then living on the Walhonding River, since the map referred to the Walhonding River as "Rivière des Femmes Blanc" or the River of the White Women.

On January 15, 1751, frontiersman Christopher Gist encountered Mary Harris at her town in Ohio, and documented the meeting in his journal. "Tuesday [January] 15, [1751].[174] We left Muskingum, and went W. 5M., to the White Woman's Creek, on which is a small Town; this White Woman was taken away from New England, when she was not above ten Years old, by the French Indians; She is now upwards of fifty, and has an Indian Husband and several Children—Her name is Mary Harris: she still remembers they used to be very religious in New England, and wonders how the White Men can be so wicked as she has seen them in the Woods."[175]

On a British map dated 1750, Mary's village was depicted as "White Woman's Town" and a 1755 British map showed the Walhonding River as "White Woman's Creek." These were the first mentions of the phrase on British maps. Walhonding, or Woalheen, was the Indians' name for the stream, and in the Lenape language it means "to dig a hole."

According to Coshocton, Ohio, researcher Scott Butler, Mary and her family returned to Canada during the French and Indian War, likely around 1755, because in 1756, she is reported to have provided care and comfort to English prisoners in Canada. At that time, she "made herself known as Mary Harris to a Pennsylvania man captured in the Seven Years' War. She told him, too, that she had been 'taken Captive when a Child, from Deerfield, New England.' One of her sons, Peter, had by now become an important war leader."[176] It's not known what became of White Woman Mary Harris after that time.

In the 19th century, several romanticized legends sprang up about the White Woman of Coshocton County, and with each iteration, the tales became more lurid. The most persistent account states that Mary Harris's beauty captivated a chief named Eagle Feather, who took her for his wife. She often accompanied Eagle Feather on hunting expeditions, and when he went to war, Mary admonished him not to return without some good, long-haired scalps to adorn their "wigwam parlor." Apparently, Mary became very jealous when Eagle Feather captured another white woman and took her as his second wife. The new woman was referred to as the "new comer."

Mary wasn't happy with the arrangement, so one night Mary killed Eagle Feather with a tomahawk and blamed the murder on the newcomer. Predictably, as a result of Mary's screaming accusations, the newcomer fled the town in a panic. The Indians pursued and captured the newcomer at a neighboring town. She was brought back to White Woman's Town, where she was executed. The legend mistakenly refers to an entry in Christopher Gist's journal, regarding the execution of a recaptured white woman captive, claiming it pertained to the death of the newcomer. That wasn't the case, and it did not have anything to do with Mary Harris. The sad event took place almost a month earlier at Conchaké, which Gist referred to as Muskingum Town. See the Conchaké section of this book.

The legend ignores the fact that in Gist's account, the name of the town where the woman captive was murdered was Muskingum Town, and not White Woman's Town. The legend also claims that the town to which the "new comer" fled and was recaptured was henceforth known as "Newcomers Town." Newcomer's Town was not named after the unfortunate mythical woman who was executed for the murder of the equally mythical Eagle Feather, but it was named for Netawatwees (c. 1686–1776), meaning "skilled advisor," whom the British called "New Comer."

To complete the legend, the story claims that Mary Harris married again and had several more children. This, in spite of the fact that Gist accurately described her as being "upwards of fifty." If she was about age 9 to 11 when she was captured at Deerfield in 1704, she would have been at least fifty-six when Gist encountered her in 1751. It would have been unusual for any woman to have several more children after that age. There is no documentation of an Ohio Indian named Eagle Feather. According to Scott Butler, the earliest mention of Eagle Feather and Mary Harris was in 1876. Even though the legend of the conniving and murderous White Woman was debunked in a 1924 article by George Franklin Smythe,[177] the story continues to persist in many different venues, including some local "historical" publications. It's not known when Mary Harris died.

The book *History of Coshocton County, Ohio, Its Past and Present 1740–1881*, states that the prominent Lenape Wingenund was the chief at White Woman's Town around 1776 after he moved up from Standing Stone/Assinink. Around 1778, he and his pro–British followers relocated to the upper Sandusky River area. He was present at the burning of Colonel Crawford near Captain Pipe's Town in 1782.[178]

NINE

Towns and Posts
of Southeast Ohio

"In our every deliberation, we must consider the impact of our decisions on the next seven generations."—Iroquois Maxim

25. *Delaware Town (dates unknown).*
Now: Jacobsburg, Belmont, County (39°54'34.66"N–80°48'55.36"W)

Delaware Town is shown on William C. Mills's 1914 map on the west side of the Ohio River across from Moundsville, West Virginia, and also in southeastern Belmont County on the map in Frank Wilcox's *Ohio Indian Trails*. It is likely one of many Indian towns in local legend that never existed, or else were short-term, transient sites of Indians on the move. With the exception of those two books, I couldn't find any information regarding the town in books or journals, or on 18th-century maps. In fact, Wilcox's information regarding Delaware Town is contradictory, in that he places it near Bridgeport in Belmont County. However, on page 134, Wilcox states that Delaware Town is at present Delaware, Ohio, in Delaware County, but on his enclosed map, he correctly indicates that village as Mingo Town.

There is no other documentary evidence to support a town called "Delaware Town" in present Belmont County.

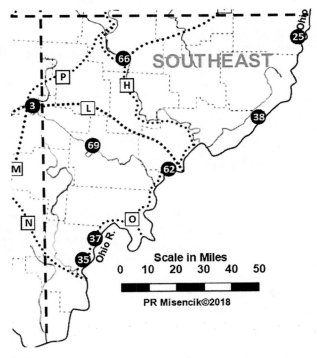

Numbers may represent more than one community in fairly close proximity.

35. *Kanauga (dates unknown).*
Now: Kanauga, Gallia County (38°50'28.36"N–82°8'55.54"W)

Kanauga, on the Ohio River opposite the mouth of the Kanawha River, seems like it would have been a logical location for an Indian village. It was at the junction of two well-traveled river thoroughfares and very near the junction of two major trails, the Kanawha Trail and the Wanduchale–Kiskiminetas Trail. However, other than a vague reference by Frank Wilcox in his 1934 book, there seems to be no documentary evidence of an Indian town located there.

Wilcox's assertion of the town is contained in his description of the Kanawha Trail. "The trail led from the Indian town of Kanauga, opposite the mouth of the Kanawha, across the flats to Gallipolis"[1] Other than Wanduchale's Town and Kiskiminetas, I could find no other evidence of an 18th-century Indian village on the north side of the Ohio River between present Marietta and Portsmouth, Ohio. One possible explanation is the number of floods that have consistently ravaged the area. For example, Gallipolis, Ohio, which is only about three and a half miles upstream (southwest) from present Kanauga, recorded the following floods: in 1834 the flood crested at 63 feet, in 1901 at 53 feet, and in 1913 at 62.8 feet. At 35 feet, most of the flats bordering the Ohio River were underwater, which included the present town of Kanauga. The National Weather Service indicates that a 60-foot flood would place most of the Ohio River basin under water for a distance of up to one mile from the river's shoreline. Floods were not unique to that area of the Ohio River. In 1753, a massive flood destroyed Lower Shawnee Town at present Portsmouth, Ohio, which forced the Shawnee to rebuild their city on higher ground.

If in fact a town was located there, it was likely a temporary village or a camp. In that particular area, the town would probably have been inhabited by Shawnee Indians, but I could find no Shawnee word that approximates "kanauga." It's possible that Frank Wilcox merely assumed a town existed in that location even though there was an absence of any supporting documentation.

37. *Kiskiminetas (c. 1756–c. 1770s), also Kiskeminetas Old Town.*
Now: Cheshire, Gallia County (38°56'23.01"N–82°7'23.98"W)

Kiskiminetas was a Lenape town near present Cheshire, Ohio. There was another village of that name located on the Kiskiminetas River near West Vandergrift, Pennsylvania. Sources do not agree on the location of Kiskiminetas, but perhaps the best indication comes from Bouquet's 1764 expedition against the Ohio Indians. In his "Fourth ROUT [*sic*] down the Ohio," he places Kiskiminetas 8 miles upstream from the mouth of the Big Canawha (Kanawha River),[2] which is at or near the present location of Cheshire, Ohio.

John Heckewelder, the Moravian missionary, says the name comes from "Gieshgumanito," meaning "make daylight," while the captive John McCullough, who was taken to the town in 1756, says that it comes from "Kee-ak-kshee-man-nit-toos," meaning "cut spirit." In the Lenape language, "Gisckhschummen" from "Gischapan" means "to cut with a knife," and "Gischachummen" means "to make light" or "to enlighten."[3] It's also been suggested that the name means "plenty of walnuts." It's not known exactly when the residents relocated to the Ohio River from Pennsylvania, but it must have been after McCullough was taken to the Pennsylvania town in 1756.

Section of 1755 Evans map showing Kishkeminetas old T. [Kiskiminitas] (Library of Congress, Geography and Map Division-75693767).

Other than some old maps, like the 1755 Evans map above, and some references to the town's location, no other documentary evidence has been found concerning Kiskiminetas on the Ohio River. In fact, while most sources indicate it to have been a Lenape village, a few sources list it as a Shawnee town. Also, there is no evidence regarding the years the town was in existence.

38. *Koshkoshkung (1770s?).*
Now: New Matamoras, Washington County
(39°31'22.09"N–81°3'56.30"W)

In *Ohio Indian Trails*, Frank Wilcox indicated an Indian village called Koshkoshkung located on the Ohio River at the present town of New Matamoras, Washington County, Ohio.[4] Unfortunately, although Wilcox shows the village on a map, he does not include any other information. The *Archeological Atlas of Ohio* by William C. Mills, published in 1914, also shows the town of Kosh-kosh-kung in Washington County, in the approximate location of New Matamoras, Ohio,[5] but like Wilcox's later work, it provides no supporting information. It's likely that Wilcox simply accepted Mills's assumption that there was a town called Koshkoshkung in that location.

Although there is no documentation that supports the existence of a town called Koshkoshkung in Washington County, Ohio, there were villages in Pennsylvania that Moravian missionary David Zeisberger referred to as Kaskaskunk. The first was located at the junction of the Shenango and Mahoning Rivers in present Lawrence County, Pennsylvania. That community later relocated to a site near present New Castle, Pennsylvania. The *History of Butler County, Pennsylvania* states that "Kosh-kosh-kung was on Beaver Creek, seven miles south of the site of New Castle, Lawrence County, about where Newport now stands."[6]

Each of those locations is more than one hundred miles north-northeast of where Mills and Wilcox sited Koshkoshkung on their maps in Ohio. If in fact the Lenape had a village there, it may have been a temporary or seasonal location used by the Kosh-kosk-kung Lenape in Pennsylvania.

69. Shawnee Town (Shawneetown) (dates unknown).
Now: Beaumont, Athens County (39°23'7.79"N–82°8'17.55"W)

A map in *The Archeological Atlas of Ohio* indicates the existence of a village called Shawnee Town in the vicinity of present Beaumont, Ohio, about four and a half miles north of Athens, Ohio, in Athens County. However, no supporting description or documentation can be found regarding a permanent Indian village in Athens County, with the possible exception of the Lenape chief Wanduchale's Town near the southeast corner of the county. A search of 18th-century maps does not indicate any Indian villages in Athens County other than Wanduchale's Town. These include the following maps: John Patten, 1753; Lewis Evans, 1755 and 1777; John Mitchell, 1755; Robert Vaugondy, 1755; Thomas Hutchins, 1764 and 1778; M. Hawkins 1777; French map of 1781; and Brion LaTour, 1784.

The local historical societies and associations state, "Athens proper wasn't home to any Native people when white people settled the area in the late 18th century." They add that there is no evidence of any permanent Indian settlements between the end of the Adena and Hopewell mound-builder eras (1,000 bc to 700 ad) and the beginning of white settlement in the area. The main reason was that the topography, which consisted of steep hills and narrow valleys, is less conducive to necessary agriculture than surrounding areas.

Therefore, it's likely there were no permanent Indian villages in Athens County, with the possible exception of Wanduchale's Town, which may not have been in Athens County, but rather was located in present Washington County. However, there is a possibility that references to a Shawnee village near Athens stemmed from a temporary war party or hunters' encampment.

62. Wanduchale's Town (c. 1739–c. 1766),
also Wyandachale, Wandochale, Windaughala, Wanduxales.
Now: Little Hocking, Washington County
(39°15'44.17"N–81°42'8.10"W)

Wanduchale's Town was a Lenape village on the north side of the Ohio River located between present Belpre, Ohio, and Apple Grove, Ohio. Christopher Gist wrote that the town consisted of about twenty families and was located on the SE side of Sciodoe [Scioto] Creek.[7] The chief was Wanduchale, the father of the prominent Lenape war chief Buckonghelas. In some sources, Wanduchale is referred to as Windaughala, Wandohela, and Wanduxales. His town was one of the towns for which the Wanduchale–Kiskiminetas Trail was named, and according to Gist, it was at the time the westernmost of the Lenape villages. Lewis Evans's map of 1755 shows the village, labeled as "Wanduxales old T.," situated opposite the mouth of the Little Kanawha at present Belpre, Ohio. Another town called Wyanduxales was shown on the east side of the Scioto River just above its mouth.

Apparently Wanduchale's Town was one of the earliest Lenape settlements in present Ohio, having been established around 1739. Frontiersman Christopher Gist wrote in his journal on January 27, 1751, that he visited a small village of Delawares [Lenape] and he

Section of Lewis Evans's 1755 map (Library of Congress, Geography and Map Division-75693767).

stayed "at the house of an Indian whose name was Windaughalah, a great man and a chief of this town, and much in the English interest."[8] John Jennings's journal, dated March 11, 1766, states, "At three o'clock in the afternoon passed by Little Kanawha, or Lifting Creek; at five passed the Wanduxales Creek; at half-past five encamped for the night." He further states that on the next day, "At six o'clock in the morning, left our camp: at seven passed the Hockhocking Creek [Hocking River]."[9] Based on the times in Jennings's journal, Wanduchale's town was initially located near the mouth of Little Hocking River near the present town of Little Hocking, Ohio. Apparently, the community later moved to the Scioto River, but there is no documentary evidence that indicates when that may have occurred. Then around 1775, Wanduchale left the southern Ohio area and established a town called Hundy or New Hundy on the Walhonding River between Killbuck Creek and the Mohican River.

66. *Will's Town (Wils Town) (?–1782),*
also Sekeyunck, Saug-eha-ungh, The Salt Licks.
Now: Duncan Falls, Muskingum, County
(39°52'22.59"N–81°54'32.31"W)

Will's Town was a Lenape village that most sources agree was located at present Duncan Falls, Ohio, in Muskingum County. However, one source places Will's Town at the mouth of

Will's Creek,[10] about twenty miles north of Duncan Falls. That placement likely arises from an erroneous assumption that Will's Town must have been located at or near Wills Creek. Based on Thomas Hutchins's journals, historian Charles Hanna wrote that Will's Town was located on the Muskingum River at Duncan Falls. His first entry states, "The path down the Muskingum … continues 3 miles to Will's Town, Se-key-unck, or the Salt Licks (now Duncan Falls), 50 miles from the Ohio. Will's Town has 35 Houses in it, and about 45 Warriors, & 80 Women & Children. The Houses are close together, and their Cornfields in sight of the town."[11] Another of his entries in reference to Will's Town states, "There is, about 100 yards below Will's Town, A Ledge of Rocks A Cross the River [Duncan's Falls] which Occasions the Water to Run very Rapid and shallow over them. 5 Miles above the Town there is much such another place."[12]

The town was shown on several 18th-century maps including the following two by Thomas Hutchins (1764) and Brion De La Tour (1784).

In 1766, Presbyterian minister Charles Beatty (c. 1715–1772) journeyed into the Tuscarawas and Muskingum valleys and visited Will's Town, which he referred to a Saug-eha-ungh and the Salt-Lick. He said the town contained about twenty houses and was populated by Indians who were receptive to his Christian preaching.[13]

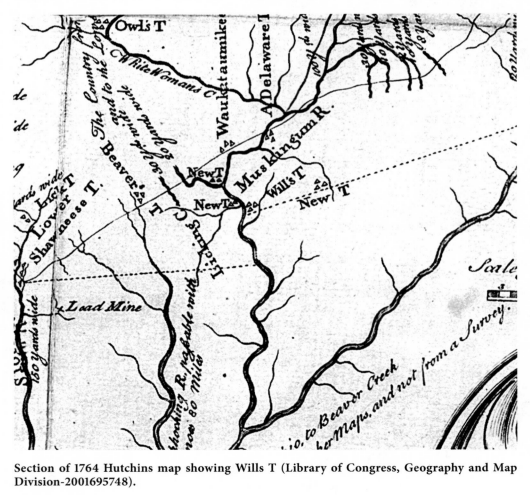

Section of 1764 Hutchins map showing Wills T (Library of Congress, Geography and Map Division-2001695748).

Thomas Hutchins also visited the town in the latter part of 1763, by traveling down the Muskingum from Wakatomika at present Dresden, Ohio, to Will's Town. His journal states, "After crossing the Creek, the Path leads through level land, 3 Miles, to a fording at Muskingum; for 2 Miles of the way the Path is Commanded on the Right by A very high, Steep Ridge. The Ford is 200 yards wide, with a good Bottom. The Path still Continues through level Land, free from underwood, 3 Miles to Will's Town, Se-key-unck, or the Salt Lick [now Duncan's Falls], 50 Miles from the Ohio. Will's Town has 35 houses in it and about 45 Warriors, & 80 Women & Children. The Houses are close together, and their Cornfields in sight of the Town. The Muskingum is not Fordable opposite the Town."[14]

The chief of the village was known as "Captain Will," who was one of the more notorious Lenape war chiefs allied with the French during the French and Indian War. Captain Will along with other Lenape war chiefs obtained supplies, arms and ammunition from the French at Fort Duquesne, and launched devastating raids on white settlers in Pennsylvania, Maryland, and Virginia.[15]

Not much other information is available regarding Captain Will or the residents of Will's Town. However, since he had been a combatant ally of the French during the French and Indian War, there is a good chance he was involved in Lord Dunmore's War of 1774.

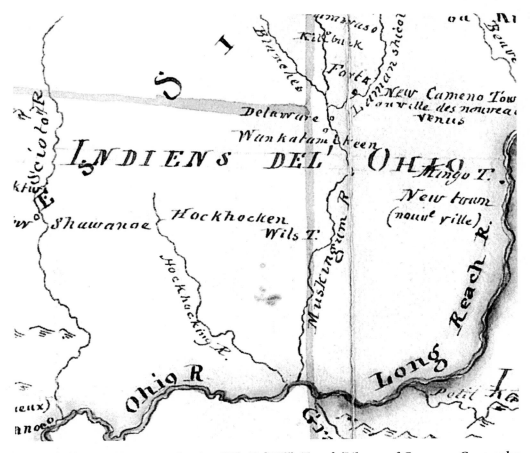

Section of 1784 LaTour map showing Wils T. [Will's Town] (Library of Congress, Geography and Map Division-2015591094).

He likely took part in the American Revolutionary War on the side of the British, because Will's Town was destroyed by American Colonel William Crawford's troops during their 1782 expedition against the Ohio Indians. Crawford's force of 500 militia destroyed a swath of Indian villages across Ohio, but were stopped by a combined force of Lenape, Mingo, Wyandot warriors and about 100 Butler's Rangers at what became known as "Battle Island," north of Upper Sandusky. The Americans retreated piecemeal, and Crawford was captured and later tortured and burned to death at Captain Pipe's Town on Tymochtee Creek, near present Crawford, Ohio.

It's not known what became of Captain Will or the inhabitants of Will's Town after the destruction of their town in 1782, but they likely joined one of the nearby Lenape communities under Captain Pipe, Buckongahelas, or another of the militant Lenape war chiefs.

TEN

Towns and Posts
of Northwest Ohio

"One thing to remember is to talk to the animals. If you do, they will talk back to you. But if you don't talk to the animals, they won't talk back to you, then you won't understand, and you will fear, and when you fear, you will destroy the animals, and if you destroy the animals, you will destroy yourself."—Chief Dan George, Tseil-Wauyuth Nation

2. Anioton (c. 1739–c. 1764), also Aniauton, Contontia.
NOW: CRYSTAL ROCK, ERIE COUNTY (41°26'30.55"N–82°50'35.81"W)

Referencing old journals and maps, the most likely location of Anioton was on the hilltop presently occupied by the Crystal Rock Campground about .4 miles south of Crystal Rock, Ohio, in Margaretta Township, Erie, County Ohio.

Anioton was established by Huron or Wyandot Indians associated with Nicolas Orontony who moved from the Fort Detroit area to distance themselves from the belligerent Ottawa, Potawatomie, and Ojibwe tribes. That antagonism stemmed from Orontony's reluctance to take part in their wars with the Indians to the south. Unfortunately, the warlike Ottawas and the other Three Fires Confederacy tribes were not inclined toward peace, and worse, they accused Orontony's Wyandots of plotting to join the southern tribes against them. The rift grew deeper until Orontony, along with another chief named Angouriot, moved to the southwestern shore of Sandusky Bay on the south shore of Lake Erie.[1]

The relocation also allowed Orontony's Wyandots to distance themselves from the aggressively monopolistic French trade policies and take advantage of the English fur trade, whose merchandise was for the most part superior in quality, more plentiful, and less expensive. That advantage was due to in large part to the advanced state of the industrial revolution in England compared to the rest of Europe, and also because England's supply routes were much shorter and less arduous. Also, to a large extent, the English trade distribution was more efficient and less corrupt.[2]

Some sources indicate that a third chief named Anioton joined Nicolas Orontony and Angouriot in the move to Sandusky Bay; however, other sources indicate that Anioton was merely a corruption of the tribal name "Wyandot." The location of the village of Anioton can best be determined by several extant references. On March 21, 1755, Gaspard-Joseph

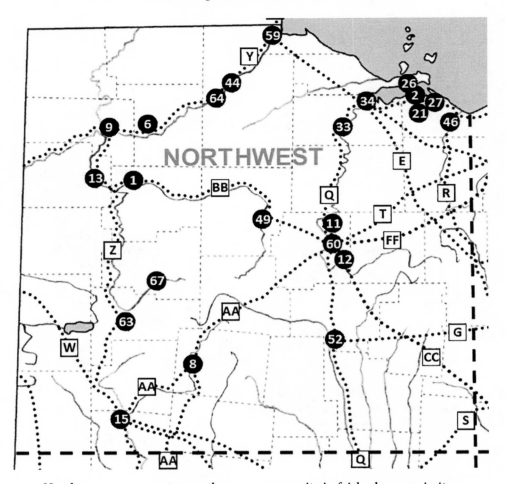

Numbers may represent more than one community in fairly close proximity.

Chaussegros de Léry attempted to canoe across Sandusky Bay from south of present Port Clinton: "March 21st Friday, at seven in the morning, we embarked to the foot of the swamp, east of Lake Dotsandoské. We made about a league[3] and a half, and then crossed the portage of the great lake, which we found full of ice. This made us retrace our steps to the portage of the Anioton village, which we did. At 5 o'clock, we arrived at this village where only three cabins and some palisades remained."[4]

The late historian Charles E. Frohman used deLéry's journal to determine the likely sites of many northern Ohio Indian villages including Anioton. Frohman determined that the southern terminus of the Anioton portage was approximately at Venice. Venice lies within the city limits of Sandusky in the area of the intersection of Venice Road and Fremont Avenue. Frohman concluded, "The distance from the Bay to the site of Anioton is given as one league;[5] this is the approximate distance from Venice to Crystal Rock on Wahl Road east of the Northwest Road in Erie County." He continues, "Crystal Rock is an ideal site for a village and fortification, with several small caves and flowing springs. A level-topped hill rises about thirty feet above the surrounding land. The fact that many Indian artifacts have been found at this site confirms its use."

We visited the site in 2016, and the hill site where Anioton was located was occupied by the Crystal Rock Campground on Crystal Rock Avenue, a quarter-mile north of Wahl Road, and about a half-mile south of the present town of Crystal Rock, Ohio. The town was just north of the Lake Trail and about a dozen or so miles east of the major intersection where the Lake Trail, the Great Trail, the Watershed Trail, and the Scioto Trail all came together. In 2016, it was evident that the location was well suited for a village. It had flowing streams, and was situated on high ground with steep terrain to the north, which made it very defensible.

In some sources Anioton is erroneously referred to as Junundat, Wyandot Town, and Sunyeneand. However, Junundat was sited about ten miles to the west, near the mouth of the Sandusky River,[6] and Sunyeneand or Junqueindundeh was a town situated about nine miles up the Sandusky River at present Fremont, Ohio.

When Orontony and his Wyandots moved away from the Fort Detroit area, the French perceived his move as a shift in allegiance toward the English. A couple of years later, the Miami chief Memeskia also left the sphere of French influence near Fort des Miamis at present Fort Wayne, Indiana, and relocated to western Ohio, where he established the village of Pickawillany. Having two major defections was more than the French were willing to accept. As a result, the French began to pressure and intimidate both chiefs to return to their respective folds. Both Memeskia and Orontony resisted, and in 1747,[7] Orontony began to attack French troops and French fur traders. During this rebellion, known as "Orontony's Conspiracy" or "Orontony's Rebellion," the Miami chief Memeskia joined the fight against the French, and Orontony incited the Miamis to burn and destroy Fort des Miamis.

To the French, the rebellious attitude of the Indians and their preference for English trade merchandise posed a distinct threat to their control of the Ohio territory, and the French responded with overwhelming force. In September of 1747, French reinforcements poured into Fort Detroit to prepare for punitive operations against the rebellious tribes.

Hill on which Anioton was located, looking south (author photograph).

Rather than face the French troops in what promised to be a savage war, Nicolas Orontony moved his Wyandots from Junundat and Anioton southeast across Ohio, and established the village of Conchaké at the confluence of the Muskingum,[8] Tuscarawas, and Walhonding Rivers at present Coshocton, Ohio. Orontony died in Conchaké around 1750, presumably from smallpox.

Apparently, when Orontony quit the Sandusky Bay area, some Wyandots chose to remain at Anioton, because in 1755, eight years after Orontony's rebellion, de Léry visited the town, which still consisted of three cabins and the remains of a palisade. However, during Henry Bouquet's 1764 expedition, the village, which Bouquet referred to as "Contontia," was uninhabited. Contontia could either be a confused reference to Anioton, or a mistaken reference to "Contuntuth," an Indian village located about three and a half miles southeast at present Castalia, Ohio.

8. Blue Jacket's Town #2 (c. 1777–1787).
Now: Bellefontaine, Ohio, Logan County
(40°21′30.29″N–83°45′43.02″W)

In 1777, Blue Jacket or Waweyapiersenwaw (c. 1743–1810) joined the militant Shawnee faction who allied themselves with the British, and he relocated his village from Deer Creek in present Ross County to present Blue Jacket Creek in Bellefontaine, Ohio.

At his new town, Blue Jacket came in contact with his father-in-law, Jacques Duprépont Baby, and the British commander at Fort Detroit, Henry Hamilton. Henry Hamilton appointed Blue Jacket a captain in the British Army and assigned him to be an interpreter. There are some indications that through Blue Jacket's association with white people, the Shawnee chief began to adopt a white lifestyle and introduced farming and trading to his villagers. He was reported to be a kind person who treated others with respect. Margaret Paulee, who was captured by the Shawnee in 1779 when she was twenty-six and adopted into the tribe to take the place of a deceased daughter, wrote: "There was an Indian chief named Blue Jacket, who had married a half-French woman of Detroit, they living in what was considered grand style, having curtained beds and silver spoons. I was fond of visiting this house; they always seemed kind and desirous of giving me tea &c."[9] Another woman named Mrs. Honn was captured by the Shawnee in 1780, and wrote that she was very fortunate to have been taken into the family of Blue Jacket. She said the chief treated her very well, and at the time she tended Blue Jacket's cattle, and churned butter for their family group.[10]

Not long after Blue Jacket moved to western Ohio, the Shawnee villages along the Little Miami, Great Miami, and Mad Rivers became the staging points for raids against the Americans who moved into present Kentucky. However, by 1777 and 1778, the Indians had mixed results due to the large numbers of tough, well-armed frontiersmen who made up the population of Kentucky. Perhaps the Shawnees' most successful raid during 1778 was when they captured Daniel Boone and several other Kentuckians, but even after a lengthy siege, they were unable to take Boonesborough. Worse yet, the vengeful Kentuckians launched a retaliatory raid against Chillicothe at Oldtown, during which the famous war chief Blackfish was mortally wounded. Blackfish's death elevated Blue Jacket to the position of the most influential war chief.

By the end of 1778, the Shawnees were reinforced by about 240 Lenape warriors under chiefs Wyondochella and Buckongahelas, who broke away from the neutral faction on the Muskingum and Walhonding Rivers. They established a town about three miles north of Blue Jacket's Town. Even with the addition of the Lenape, Blue Jacket did not have sufficient numbers to wage a prolonged war against the numerically superior and better armed Kentuckians. He attempted to recruit the Creek Indians to join his alliance but met with little success. However, in 1778 Henry Hamilton and British agent Alexander McKee led an expedition to recruit the tribes in Indiana, and Blue Jacket accompanied them. Their plan was not only to recruit Indians, but also recapture Vincennes, Kaskaskia, and Cahokia, which the Americans had recently taken. Hamilton's force captured Fort Sackville at Vincennes on December 17, 1778, but it was too late in the season to push on to Kaskaskia and Cahokia. While Hamilton and McKee strengthened Fort Sackville, Blue Jacket and British agent Matthew Elliott were sent to spread the word of the victory among the Shawnee and Mingo villages in Ohio in hopes of attracting additional warriors.

Returning along the Ohio River, Blue Jacket's scouts reported large numbers of Kentuckians between them and Great Miami River. Elliott was afraid of trying to get past the American frontiersmen, and he convinced most of the group to return with him to Vincennes. Blue Jacket refused to abandon his mission, and successfully continued alone. Back at Vincennes, Elliott covered his faintheartedness to Hamilton by falsely claiming that Blue Jacket ordered him to return.

The successful capture of Fort Sackville at Vincennes was short-lived, because the following year, George Rogers Clark not only recaptured the fort, but bagged Henry Hamilton in the process. Blue Jacket, however, learned a lot by observing British military operations, and in the process proved to be a talented leader and tactician, which were traits that would serve him well in the future.

In the following years a flood of settlers moved into Kentucky, and American raids against the Indian villages north of the Ohio River became more frequent. It was evident that more than two years of border warfare had not stemmed or even slowed the surge of land-hungry immigrants onto Indian lands. Even worse, many of Blue Jacket's allies were giving up the fight. Wyandots, Ottawas, Potawatomis, and Ojibwes stopped sending warriors to support Shawnee war parties, and some were negotiating separate peace terms with the Americans. Even a few Shawnee leaders were giving up the fight. In 1779, Shawnee chiefs Yellow Hawk and Black Stump left Ohio and relocated to the Tennessee River. Only the Mingos remained largely committed and resolute.

On October 5, 1779, the Shawnee captured a military supply flotilla on the Ohio, which provided them with much-needed provisions, ammunition, weapons, and a large amount of money. In early 1780, the British sent a unit of tough rangers to assist the Shawnee against the Americans, and two war parties of Cherokees journeyed north to join Blue Jacket. The influx of rangers and Cherokees prompted other Indians along the Wabash and Illinois Rivers to send support. In addition, Major Arent Schulyer DePeyster, the commander at Fort Detroit, promised that as soon as the ice cleared on the lakes and rivers, he would send a detachment of soldiers along with two fieldpieces to join the fight against the Kentuckians. It seemed that perhaps the fortunes of war were finally turning in favor of the Shawnee.

In the spring of 1780, Blue Jacket and about 700 Indian warriors took part in a massive raid led by Captain Henry Bird against the Kentucky settlements. In June, they captured Ruddell's Station (present Ruddell's Mills) on the South Fork of the Licking River in Kentucky. Two days later they captured Martin's Station near present Paris, Kentucky, followed by the capture of two smaller stations. In total, Bird's force captured over 400 men, women, and children, whom they marched back to Fort Detroit. Although the expedition was deemed a success, and previously would have decimated the population of Kentucky, there were now so many white settlers in the area that the raid only served to enrage the Kentuckians.

The Kentuckians struck back with retaliatory raids in 1780 and 1782. They not only destroyed several Shawnee towns, but also burned the precious crops and food supplies that were sustaining the Indians. Many of the Shawnee towns were forced to relocate farther north or west. Blue Jacket's Town was one of the few that escaped destruction, yet the American raids were so effective that the Shawnee were only able to mount one major attack in 1782. On August 19, 1782, the Indians along with British rangers crushed the Kentuckians at the Battle of Blue Licks, but then the Indians suffered a greater loss. Without warning, the British stopped fighting the Americans, because the Revolutionary War was winding down, and the British were engaged in peace talks with the Americans.

With the end of the war in 1783, Americans flooded into Kentucky and even north across the Ohio River. In May 1783, the Shawnee also began to engage in peace talks with the Americans, but they were in a weakened position. In the Treaty of Paris that ended the Revolutionary War, the British did not include any provisions on behalf of their Indian allies. The United States considered the Indians who fought on the side of the British as a subjugated people who had no valid claim to the territory ceded by the British. When they appealed for help, the British only advised them to hope the United States would deal honorably with them.

In August and September 1783, representatives of several Ohio Indian nations met at Upper Sandusky. At the urging of Thayendanegea or Joseph Brant (1743–1807) they formed an Indian confederacy committed to preserving Ohio as an Indian homeland. They agreed that no treaty or land sale would take place without the approval of the entire tribal confederacy, and Blue Jacket was one of the leaders who formulated the confederacy policy. Unfortunately, tribal resolve began to buckle when the might of the United States exerted pressure on individual nations. The first to cave were the mighty Iroquois, who ceded all claim to lands west of New York and Pennsylvania. Other nations followed suit as they were individually pressured to surrender huge areas of Ohio. The Shawnee felt particularly betrayed when the Wyandots and Lenape, who had hosted the Upper Sandusky conference in the first place, ceded the country occupied by the Shawnee, including Blue Jacket's Town and Buckongahelas's Town. The Shawnee had never felt more alone, but after only two years of peace, they were ready to once again fight for their homes and villages.

The Americans were equally resolute, and bluntly told the Shawnee that if they did not accept the new land boundaries, there would be war. The American position was that "it was not a question of the Indians ceding *their* lands—the United States already owned the Northwest, so it was theirs 'to *give* not to receive.'"[11] They told the Shawnee, "This country belongs to the United States—their blood hath defended it, and will forever protect it."[12] The American show of force intimidated many Shawnee, and though several walked out of the council in disgust, others meekly signed the Treaty of Fort Finney on January 31, 1786. That treaty forced the Indians to relinquish any claim to almost all of the Shawnee land in eastern and southern Ohio. Surprisingly, Blue Jacket's Mekoche half-brother Red Pole was one of the chiefs who signed the document.

Blue Jacket disavowed the treaty, as did the Lenape chief Buckongahelas. The two vowed to carry on the fight against the Americans, but in early October 1786, General Benjamin Logan struck the first blow of the Northwest Indian War. Acting on orders of George

Rogers Clark, Logan led a force of 800 Kentuckians up the Great Miami River and attacked several Shawnee towns, including Mackachack, the principal town of the Mekoches. Ironically, it was the Mekoche Shawnee at Mackachack who were more inclined to seek a peaceful compromise with the Americans, and their village even flew an American flag, which was ignored by the Kentuckians during the attack. About a dozen warriors were killed outright, and the old Mekoche chief Moluntha, and his wife Nonhelema, the Grenadier Squaw, were taken prisoner. Colonel Hugh McGary, who had been at the Battle of Blue Licks four years earlier, and who bore much of the blame for the defeat, asked the old chief if he had fought in the battle. Moluntha had not been there, but apparently misunderstood the question and just repeated the phrase, "Blue Licks," which McGary interpreted as an assent. With that, McGary drew his tomahawk and buried it in the ninety-four-year-old chief's head. As Moluntha tried to get up, McGary killed him with a second blow and then scalped him. After looting and destroying Macachack, the Kentuckians fell upon and destroyed several other towns, including Blue Jacket's Town.

Blue Jacket immediately struck back at the Kentuckians by attacking the small settlement of Drinnon's Lick. Only two men were in the village when the Indians attacked, and an Irishman named Jerry Hays fought the Indians at the gate before they overwhelmed him. The other white man was killed as he tried to run away. The Indians were inclined to kill Hays, but Blue Jacket was impressed with the Irishman's bravery and spared his life. Hays was taken back to Blue Jacket's village and was released the following year. Afterward, he consistently attested to Blue Jacket's kindness and humanity.

In 1787, Blue Jacket relocated his village about seventy-one miles northwest to a multi-nation Indian community called the Glaize at the junction of the Maumee and Auglaize Rivers at present Defiance, Ohio.

9. *Blue Jacket's Town #3 (see the entry for The Glaize later in this chapter).*

8. *Buckongahelas Town #1 (1778–1787).*
NOW: BELLEFONTAINE, LOGAN COUNTY (40°23′31.21″N–83°45′11.92″W)

Buckongahelas, also written as Pachgantshihilas (c. 1720–1805), "one whose movements are certain," was born in the present state of Delaware. As a result of the loss of their homeland in the Delaware River basin, the Lenape were forced to move west, and he and his family first settled near present Buckhannon, West Virginia. In the early to mid–1770s, they relocated to the Lenape villages around Goschachgunk at the Forks of the Muskingum at present Coshocton, Ohio.

Buckongahelas fought on the side of the French during the French and Indian War, and fought in Pontiac's Rebellion and Lord Dunmore's War. When the Revolutionary War began in 1775, Buckongahelas broke with the Lenape chiefs Netawatwees and White Eyes, who wished to remain neutral. He argued that the Indians would have to fight to keep their lands in Ohio, and an alliance with the British would be their best chance of stopping the flood of American settlers pouring across the Allegheny and Ohio Rivers. The Lenape were divided as a nation between remaining neutral, joining the war, or leaving Ohio altogether. For the most part, those who wanted to join the British relocated to western Ohio, but those who wished to remain neutral either left Ohio to distance themselves from the war, or stayed in their villages on the Muskingum, Walhonding and Tuscarawas Rivers. When the Shawnee war chief Blue Jacket relocated his village to western Ohio to join the British war effort, Buckongahelas joined him. Blue Jacket established his town on present Blue Jacket Creek in Bellefontaine, Ohio. In 1778, the Lenape chiefs Buckongahelas and Wyondochella left the Muskingum River with their followers, which included over 240 warriors, and established their town on present Buckongahelas Creek less than three miles north of Blue Jacket's Town in present Logan County, Ohio.

Buckongahelas and Blue Jacket became close allies during the Revolutionary War, and after the death of the Lenape chief White Eyes in November 1778, Buchongahelas, Captain Pipe, Machingwe Pushis ("Big Cat") and Gelelemened ("Killbuck") became the most influential Lenape chiefs. Of the four, Killbuck favored an alliance with the Americans, while the other three opted to side with the British.

In 1781, Buckongahelas led a war party through the Tuscarawas River area just after troops led by American Colonel Daniel Brodhead (1736–1809) swept through the area, destroying peaceful Lenape villages and crops. The Lenape referred to Brodhead as Machingua Keeshock, "the great moon." Near present Coshocton, Buckonghelas found the bodies of fifteen dead Lenape warriors who had been bound, tomahawked and scalped by members of Brodhead's force. It was even worse when Buckongahelas learned that Killbuck, whom the Americans called Colonel William Henry, had been part of Brodhead's force and had led an attack against a party of his own people.

Buckongehelas warned the Christian Lenape at Gnadenhütten that they were not safe, because the Americans would return and destroy them as the Conestogas in Pennsylvania had been murdered by the Paxton Boys in 1763. He offered to lead them west, "where the fields shall yield you abundant crops; and where your cattle shall find sufficient pasture; where there is plenty of game; where your women and children, together with yourselves, will live in peace and safety; where no long knife shall ever molest you! Nay I will live between you and them, and not even suffer them to frighten you!—There you can worship your God without fear."[13] Buckongahelas was telling the Christian Lenape that they did not have to join in the fight or forsake their Christianity, but he was still willing to protect them.

Unfortunately, the Christian Indians refused his offer, and replied that Buckongahelas and Captain Pipe had violated the Christian commandments by waging war. They added that they were happy where they were in their mission villages and did not wish to relocate. Buckongahelas told them that he respected their decision, but he believed they were making a very serious mistake by living unprotected within range of the Pennsylvanians. If the villagers had accepted Buckongahelas's offer, they would not have been forcibly removed to Captives' Town later that year, and the terrible massacre of ninety-six Christian Indians at Gnadenhütten in March 1782 would likely not have occurred.

When the Revolutionary War ended with a British defeat, it also ended British support for the militant Indians, who would now have to face the victorious Americans alone. The prospect of a savage and bloody war was daunting, and many of the leaders blamed each other for their predicament. Captain Pipe, the preeminent war chief of the Lenape, was blamed by many chiefs, including Buckongahelas, for the Lenapes' difficulties.

In September 1783, representatives of several Ohio Indian nations met at Upper Sandusky and at the urging of Thayendanegea or Joseph Brant (1743–1807) formed an Indian confederacy committed to preserving Ohio as an Indian homeland. Their confederacy was tested when the victorious Americans presented the Treaty of Fort MacIntosh in 1785 and the Treaty of Fort Finney on January 31, 1786, which drastically reduced the Indians' area.

The Americans bluntly informed the tribes that if they did not agree to the treaties and accept the new land boundaries, there would be war.

Buckongahelas and Blue Jacket refused to accept the American land-grab and vowed to carry on the fight. That was the start of what became known as the "Northwest Indian War" or the "Ohio Indian Wars." In early October 1786, General Benjamin Logan struck the first blow when he led a force of 800 Kentuckians up the Great Miami River and destroyed several Shawnee and Lenape villages, including the towns of Buckongahelas and Blue Jacket.

The warring Indians were forced to flee, and many decided to move west into present Indiana and Illinois, and some even relocated west of the Mississippi River. However, Buckongahelas and Blue Jacket continued to fight for their land in Ohio. With their villages destroyed, the two chiefs led their respective followers north to the junction of the Auglaize and Maumee Rivers where a new multi-national community known as the Glaize had been established. The Glaize was populated by members of several different Indian nations, who were committed to fight against the Americans.

After winning battles against Generals Arthur St. Clair and Josiah Harmar, the Indians were defeated in August 1795 by General Anthony Wayne at the Battle of Fallen Timbers. That battle ended the Northwest Indian Wars, and Buckongahelas was forced to acknowledge that their fight for Ohio was a lost cause. He signed the Treaty of Greenville, and later said, "All who know me, know me to be a man and a warrior, and I now declare that I will for the future be a true and steady friend of the United States as I have heretofore been an active enemy."[14] Buckongahelas never broke his promise.

11. Captain Pipe's Town #3 (c. 1780–c. 1787), also Old Pipe's Town.
Now: Crawford, Wyandot County (40°55′29.63″N–83°19′3.02″W)

Around 1780, Captain Pipe relocated his village from the Walhonding River to Tymochtee Creek. During the move, he temporarily resided at the Mingo chief Pluggy's town at present Delaware, Ohio. The best information regarding the location of Captain Pipe's Town at Tymochtee Creek comes from Rev. Parker B. Brown's extensive research on Crawford's 1782 Sandusky Expedition, determining the specific site where Crawford was executed. Rev. Brown places Captain Pipe's Town immediately northwest of the present intersection of Wyandot County Route 29 and Crawford Township Highway 106.

Captain Pipe's move to the Sandusky River area was to join the British war effort. At the same time, the Lenape Council at Goschachgunk, under the leadership of Killbuck, attempted to ingratiate themselves with the Americans by declaring war against the Mingos, who had allied with the British from the very beginning of the Revolutionary War. By early 1781, Captain Pipe and the other British-allied Lenape Indians carried out raids against American settlements along the Virginia, Maryland, and Pennsylvania frontiers, and the Americans were quick to retaliate. In March of 1781, Colonel Daniel Brodhead, in command of Continental troops and Pennsylvania militia, along with Lenape warriors under Killbuck, marched on the Lenape villages along the Tuscarawas and Muskingum Rivers. On April 20, they destroyed the former Moravian mission village of Lichtenau, and laid waste to Goschachgunk. Twenty Indians were killed in the attack, and sixteen warriors were captured, bound, and then slaughtered. Twenty noncombatant prisoners were led back to Fort Pitt.

In spite of Brodhead's attack on the Muskingum and Tuscarawas Lenape, the militant western Indians, primarily Captain Pipe and the Wyandot Chief Dunquat, believed the Christian Indians in the Moravian settlements were not neutral, and were in fact passing along military intelligence to the Americans. They convinced Major DePeyster at Fort Detroit to order the forced removal of the Christian Indians from their mission towns and relocate them to the Sandusky River, where they could be prevented from engaging in anti–British conduct.

In the summer of 1781, the Christian Lenape and the Moravian missionaries were escorted to the Sandusky River, where Captain Pipe ordered them to establish their village near the mouth of Broken Sword Creek on the Sandusky River. Because they were forcibly relocated, the Moravian missionaries named the village Captives' Town. Unfortunately, the Christian Indians were not allowed time to harvest their crops before they relocated, and during the winter, food was so scarce the people were starving. By late winter, the famine at Captives' Town was so severe that a hundred or so Lenape decided to return to the Moravian mission settlements on the Tuscarawas to gather whatever food they could find to bring back to Captives' Town. However, while they were there, a party of Pennsylvania militia arrived at Gnadenhütten, and on March 8, 1782, they systematically murdered ninety-six Lenape men, women, and children before looting and destroying the town in what became known as the

"Gnadenhütten Massacre." When he heard the news, Captain Pipe was enraged that the Americans would wantonly murder peaceful families that included women and children.

In 1782, Colonel William Crawford, a personal friend of George Washington, led an expedition against the Indians in the Sandusky River area. On June 4, 1782, Crawford and his force of about 500 militiamen marched about two and a half miles north from Upper Sandusky, where they encountered a strong force of between 350 and 600 Wyandot and Lenape Indians. During the fight, Captain Pipe's warriors outflanked the Americans and drove them into defensive positions in and around a grove of trees, which became known as "Battle Island."

Simon Girty asked the Americans to surrender, but Crawford believed his men had inflicted more casualties than they actually had, and thought the Indians were losing interest in the fight.

That belief was reinforced

Battle Island monument (40°51'42.98"N–83°16'2.56"W).

the next day, when the Indians only sniped at the Americans from long range. In fact, the Indians were waiting for British reinforcements that arrived that afternoon. British agent Alexander McKee brought 140 Shawnee under Chief Blacksnake, and the additional warriors were able to complete the encirclement of the American positions. That night the Americans attempted to withdraw under cover of darkness, but were discovered, and the retreat turned into a disorganized rout.

Colonel Crawford lost contact with the main body, and he and a small group followed the Sandusky River to the south and southeast. On June 7, Crawford and Dr. John Knight were discovered by Lenape Indians under Chief Wingenund. They were taken prisoner and marched to Captain Pipe's Town on Tyomochtee Creek. There a council of chiefs met to decide their fate, with Simon Girty acting as interpreter for the prisoners.

Captain Pipe, who led the council, was still incensed over the Gnadenhütten Massacre, and he angrily blamed Crawford for the slaughter of the Christian Indians. Crawford denied involvement and expressed his regret for the atrocity. Crawford then stated that he "very much favored the Indians at the Salt Licks of Mahoning," meaning that he tried to prevent the murder of Captain Pipe's mother, brother and other villagers during the 1778 attack on Salt Lick Town by General Edward Hand's troops.

At that moment, Captain Pipe's sister-in-law Micheykapeeci asked to speak. She had been at Salt Lick Town during Hand's attack. During the massacre, Crawford prevented Micheykapeeci from being killed by the militia troops, and he believed her testimony would save him. Instead, Micheykapeeci denounced him as one of the leaders of the men who murdered Pipe's mother and her husband, who was Pipe's brother. After his sister-in-law gave her grief-stricken testimony, Captain Pipe ordered Crawford's face to be painted black, and he declared Crawford to be "cut-ta-ho-tha," which meant that he was condemned to death by fire.

The Battle Island monument (40°51'42.98"N–83°16'2.56"W).

As he successfully had done with Simon Kenton in 1778, Simon Girty attempted to save Crawford's life by telling Captain Pipe that Crawford was an old friend. Pipe replied that "as commander of an invading army that was determined to kill Indians, he had to die painfully."[15] Girty next offered his beautiful horse and a stack of merchandise if Captain Pipe would spare Crawford, but Pipe refused, saying angrily that if Girty were to stand in his place it would not save Crawford. Crawford appealed to Wingenund, whom he once was on friendly terms with, but Wingenund told him, "If Williamson had been taken, you might have been saved, but as it is, no one would dare interfere on your behalf. The King of England, if he were to come in person, could not save you."[16]

The place of execution was a glade on Tymochtee Creek about three-quarters of a mile west of Captain Pipe's Town. The following is taken from the account of Dr. John Knight, who was a witness to the event.

When we went to the fire the Col. was stripped

naked, ordered to sit down by the fire and then they beat him with sticks and their fists. Presently, I was treated in the same manner. Then they tied a rope to the foot of a post about fifteen feet high, bound the Col's hands behind his back and fastened the rope to the ligature between his wrists. The rope was long enough for him to sit down or walk around the post once or twice and return the same way. The Col. Then called to Girty and asked if they intended to burn him?—Girty answered yes. The Col. Said he would take it all patiently. Upon this Captain Pipe, a Delaware chief, made a speech to the Indians viz.: about thirty or forty men, sixty or seventy squaws and boys.

> When the speech was finished, they all yelled a hideous and hearty assent to what had been said. The Indian men then took up their guns and shot powder into the Colonel's body, from his feet as far up as his neck. I think not less than seventy loads were discharged upon his naked body. They then crowded around him, and to the best of my observation, cut off his ears; when the throng had dispersed a little, I saw the blood running from both sides of his head in consequence thereof.
>
> The fire was about six or seven yards from the post to which the Colonel was tied; it was made of small hickory poles, burnt quite through the middle, each end of the poles running about six feet in length. Three or four Indians by turns would take up individually, one of these burning pieces of wood and apply it to his naked body, already burnt black with powder. These tormentors presented themselves on every side of him with the burning faggots and poles. Some of the squaws took broad boards, upon which they would carry a quantity of burning coals and hot embers and throw on him, so that in a short time he had nothing but coals of fire and hot ashes to walk upon.
>
> In the midst of these extreme tortures, he called to Simon Girty and begged him to shoot him; but Girty making no answer he called to him again. Girty then, by way of derision, told the Colonel he had no gun, at the same time turning to an Indian who was behind him, laughed heartily, and by all his gestures seemed delighted at the horrid scene. Col. Crawford at this period of his sufferings besought the Almighty to have mercy on his soul, spoke very low, and bore his torments with the most manly fortitude. He continued in all the extremities of pain for an hour and three-quarters or two hours longer, as near as I can judge, when at last being almost exhausted, he lay down on his belly; they then scalped him and repeatedly threw the scalp in my face, telling me "that was my great captain." An old squaw whose appearance every way answered the ideas people entertain of the Devil, got a board, took a parcel of coals and ashes and laid them on his back and head, after he had been scalped, he then raised himself upon his feet and began to walk around the post; they next put a burning stick to him, but he seemed more insensible of pain than before.
>
> The Indian fellow who had me in charge, now took me away to Capt. Pipe's house, about three-quarters of a mile from the place of the Colonel's execution. I was bound all night, and thus prevented from seeing the last of the horrid spectacle. Next morning, being June 12th, the Indian untied me, painted me black, and we set off for the Shawnese town, which he told me was somewhat less than forty miles from that place. We soon came to the spot where the Colonel had been burnt, as it was partly in our way; I saw his bones lying amongst the remains of the fire, almost burnt to ashes; I suppose after he was dead, they had laid his body on the fire.[17]

Reverend Parker B. Brown, who extensively researched Crawford's 1782 Sandusky Expedition, devoted quite a bit of his studies to determine the exact location of the site where Crawford was executed. Brown determined the burn site was about 600 feet south-southwest of the present Crawford Burn Site Monument, and almost a mile west of Captain Pipe's Town.[18]

In contrast to Dr. Knight's account, other accounts claim that Girty repeatedly tried to intercede for Crawford, but Captain Pipe silenced Girty and threatened him with death if he spoke another word on the matter. Girty's daughter later explained that when Crawford asked Girty to shoot him, Girty said that if anyone interfered, they would have been killed on the spot. Accounts also state that Girty shed tears for Crawford during the ordeal, "and ever after always spoke of Crawford in the tenderest terms."[19]

Dr. John Knight did not suffer the same fate as Crawford, because as he was being marched to the Shawnee town where he was to be executed, he managed to overpower his guard and make his way back to Pennsylvania. He arrived there on July 4, 1782.

With the end of the Revolutionary War in 1783, British support to the warring Ohio Indians came to a halt, and the Indians were faced with the daunting option of carrying on the war against the Americans alone. The prospect of a savage and bloody war caused many of the Lenape chiefs to blame each other for their predicament. Since Captain Pipe was the preeminent war chief, he received much of the criticism, and even Buckongahelas publicly denounced Pipe as being incompetent. Even so, Pipe continued in his role as war chief, and resisted white expansion into Ohio.

It's not known exactly when Captain Pipe moved from the Tymochtee Creek area, but some accounts indicate he was in the area of the old town of Goschachgunk in 1787 and 1799. General Josiah Harmar encountered Captain Pipe on March 9, 1788, and described him thusly: "Yesterday old Pipe, with seven of his young men arrived at the garrison…. Their object is to dispose of their skins to a contractor. He is a manly old fellow, and much more of a gentleman than the generality of the frontier people."[20] The following month, April 1788, Pipe was reputedly camped with about seventy of his tribe at the mouth of the Muskingum River at present Marietta, Ohio.

Notwithstanding the sighting of Captain Pipe at Goschachgunk and at the mouth of the Muskingum, it's likely his principal village was still in the Sandusky River area. However, there are some indications that prior to 1787, he moved from Tymochtee Creek and established a village near the junction of the Broken Sword Creek and Sandusky River, which was simply called Pipe's Town.

13. *Charloe (c. 1770s–c. 1838).*
Now: Charloe, Paulding County *(41°7'52.68"N–84°26'6.98"W)*

The Ottawa village of Charloe at the site of present Charloe, in Paulding County, is another of the Ottawa towns, or more correctly a town of one of the Three Fires Confederacy, which were mainly composed of either Ottawa, Potawatomi, or Ojibwe Indians. Since the Ottawa were the largest group representing the Three Fires Confederacy in Ohio, most of the villages are thought to have been inhabited by Ottawa. However, they may very well have been Potawatomi or Ojibwe.

Charloe was likely established in the 1770s when most of the Three Fires Confederacy villages along the Maumee River were settled by Indians moving south out of present Michigan. (See Maumee River Ottawa Villages in this book.) According to writer Nevin O. Winter, "The largest Indian village ever located within the county [Paulding] was that of Charloe, which was situated on a beautiful site upon the left bank of the Auglaize. It was near the center of an Indian reserve, of four miles square, which was known as Oquanoxa's reserve. Here dwelt the chieftain of that name with several hundred Indians, who were a portion of the Ottawa tribe."[21] Winter continued that Charloe "was pleasantly located on a commanding bluff along the Auglaize River. It had been the site of a little Indian town, and received its name from the chief known as Charloe Peter. The Indians raised corn on the rich bottom land opposite the village. Their cemetery was just north of the town, and silver brooches, pipes and other trinkets have frequently been exhumed at Charloe from the graves."[22]

Like the Three Fires Confederacy towns along the Maumee, the Indians in the reserve lived in smaller settlements grouped around their principal village. Winter further stated that "when the first settlers arrived, there were several small bands of Indians who dwelt along the Auglaize or the Maumee, and the names of some of them, such as Totigose, Saucy Jack, Big Yankee Jim, Draf Jim, P. Ashway, Pokeshaw, and Wapacanaugh were familiar names. These Indians were generally peaceable and kindly disposed toward the settlers, excepting when under the influence of firewater brought in by the civilized race, … and the reservation was sold in 1820, when the chief and his followers took up their line of march toward the retiring sun."[23] Like most of the Ohio Indians, they moved west in hopes of finding a permanent homeland, and "the last remnant of the once powerful Ottawa tribe of Indians removed from this valley to lands beyond the Mississippi in 1838."[24]

15. Chillicothe (c. 1780–c. 1782).
Now: Piqua, Miami County (40°10'59.14"N–40°10'59.14"N)

After George Rogers Clark's destruction of the Shawnee towns of Chillicothe at Oldtown on the Little Miami River in 1780, most of the inhabitants relocated northwest to the abandoned Miami village of Pickawillany on the Great Miami River. It was hoped the additional thirty-five-mile distance would decrease their vulnerability from attacks by Kentuckians, and also provide them with better access to British weapons, supplies, and support from Fort Detroit. But British support tapered off with the surrender of General Cornwallis at Yorktown, Virginia, in October 1781, even though it would take almost two more years before the Revolutionary War officially ended.

In August 1782, a force of about 50 Loyalist rangers and 300 Indians led by Captain Willam Caldwell of Butler's Rangers crossed into Kentucky to attack Bryan Station at present Lexington, Kentucky. After a two-day siege, the raiders destroyed all of the station's cattle and burned all the crops before withdrawing back toward Ohio. A militia force of about 187 men under the command of Colonel John Todd, assisted by Lieutenant Colonel Daniel Boone, Colonel Stephen Trigg, and Major Hugh McGary set out after the raiders. On the morning of August 19, 1782, the Kentucky militia who had been following the Indians' trail reached the Licking River in Kentucky near a salt spring known as Lower Blue Licks. Colonel Todd, the militia commander, asked Daniel Boone's advice on how to proceed. Boone said he was suspicious of the obvious trail the Indians had left, and was concerned the frontiersmen were being enticed into an ambush. He advised against proceeding, and recommended they cross farther upstream to attack the rangers and Indians from the rear. Hugh McGary, who was a known hot-head, urged an immediate attack. He jumped on his horse and yelled something to the effect of, "Them that ain't cowards, follow me, and I'll show you where the yellow dogs are!"[25] That was enough to get all the officers and men to charge across the river. Daniel Boone reluctantly joined them, but was heard to say, "Come on! We are all slaughtered men."[26]

As Boone feared, Caldwell's force was concealed on the high ground across the river, and as the Kentuckians advanced up the hill, they were met with a withering fire at point-blank range. Todd and Trig were shot from their saddles and were among the first to be killed. The Kentuckians fled in panic as the pursuing Indians cut them down in hand-to-hand combat. Daniel Boone grabbed a riderless horse for his 23-year-old son Israel to escape, but before he could mount, Israel was shot through the neck and killed. The battle was an American disaster, with 72 Americans killed and 11 captured. The British Loyalists and Indians suffered seven killed and ten wounded. It was the worst defeat of the war for the Kentuckians. McGary, who was probably most responsible for the defeat, never got over it, and four years later, he murdered the 94-year-old Shawnee chief Moluntha, because he believed the old Indian had been at Blue Licks.

In November 1782, in retaliation for their defeat at Blue Licks, George Rogers Clark mounted another expedition against the Ohio Indians. Gathering his force at the Licking River in Kentucky, he marched to attack the Shawnee village of Chillicothe at present Old-town. The few Indians who still lived there had fled, so after destroying the town, Clark continued on to the newest Shawnee Chillicothe town at the abandoned Miami village of Pickawillany. Among Clark's force were Daniel Boone and Simon Kenton.

Shawnee scouts were aware of Clark's progress, and by the time the Kentuckians reached the village it was deserted except for a few stragglers. Clark's troops occupied the Shawnee town, while a detachment continued a few miles upstream to Louis Lorimer's trading post. Lorimer, or in some sources Loramie (1748–1812), was a Frenchman who supported the British and was on good terms with the Shawnee, because Lorimer's wife, Charlotte Bougainville, was half French and half Shawnee. Clarks's detachment looted Lorimer's store and burned it to the ground.

Clark delayed at Chillicothe/Pickawillany for four days, hoping to draw the Shawnee into a fight, but the Indians were content to snipe from the cover of the forest in attempting to lure the Kentuckians into an ambush. It almost worked when about 100 Kentuckians chased a small group of Shawnee but narrowly avoided being slaughtered when they wisely retreated at the first barrage from the hidden Indians.

On November 15, 1782, Clark burned the town and Indian food stores, declared his expedition a victory, and marched back to Kentucky. During his campaign his troops had only killed ten Indians, and the Kentuckians had lost three dead and several wounded.

The Shawnee did not rebuild their village near Piqua. Most of them moved about seventy-five miles northwest to join the Miami near present Fort Wayne, Indiana, where they established yet another Chillicothe outside of Ohio.

21. *Contuntuth (c. 1738–c. 1800),*
also Wyandot Town, Canoutout, Chanondet, Cantontia.
Now: Castalia, Erie County (41°24'0.19"N, 82°48'30.67"W)

As early as 1738, a group of Wyandot Indians associated with Orontony's breakaway faction moved into Ohio and traveled beyond Orontony's principal village at Junundat to settle near present Castalia, Ohio.[27] It would have been a desirable location, having several springs as well as an abundance of game and fertile land in the vicinity.

On January 3, 1761, Robert Rogers traveled southeast from Sandusky Bay, and wrote in his journal of how he "came to a small Indian town of about ten houses. There is a remarkable fine spring at this place, rising out of the side of a small hill with such force that it boils above the ground in a column three feet high. I imagine it discharges ten hogsheads of water in a minute."[28] Unfortunately, Rogers's mention of a gushing spring doesn't help pinpoint the specific location of the village since there were several very active springs within two or more miles of the center of Castalia. While Rogers mentioned a small Indian town

Section of Thomas Hutchins's 1764 map (Library of Congress, Geography and Map Division-2001695748).

of about ten houses in 1761, he doesn't designate their tribal affiliation. However, at that time in history, it would likely have been a community of Wyandots who did not follow Orontony to Conchaké in 1750. Sir William Johnson visited Fort Sandusky on September 22, 1761, and wrote that the fort "is about three miles from another village of Hurons [Wyandots]."[29] Castalia is a little more than three miles south of Fort Sandusky. Historian Charles A. Hanna also wrote that Johnson visited a Wyandot village that was "three miles south of Fort Sandusky."[30]

Other than these rather oblique references to "Wyandot Town" or towns named Contuntuth, Canoutout, Chanondet, Cantontia, or any Indian town specifically associated with the Castalia area, I've been unable to locate any documentation that provides more specific information other than the depiction of "Wyandot Town" on Thomas Hutchin's maps between 1764 and 1778.

Of historical interest, the town was the scene of an Indian attack that took place on June 2, 1813, during the War of 1812. According to local lore, Indians in the area were in the habit of sneaking in at night and pilfering corn from Docartus P. Snow's gristmill near the head of Cold Creek. Apparently, Snow devised a method of booby-trapping the approach to the mill, and after having been thwarted several times, the Indians decided to take revenge on the settlement there. On June 2, while the men were working in the fields, the Indians struck and carried away twelve women and children. During their escape, they killed and scalped two young boys, one girl, and Mrs. Snow, who could not keep up. Three months later, in September 1813, General William Henry Harrison recaptured Detroit from the British, and obtained the release of the surviving captives.

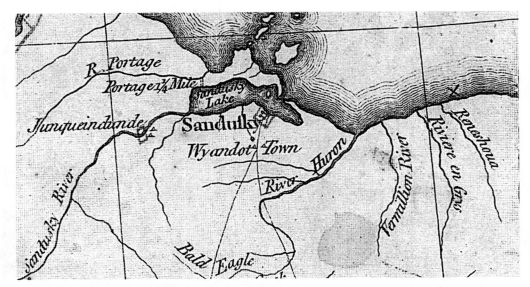

Section of Thomas Hutchins's 1778 map (Library of Congress, Geography and Map Division-74696155).

26. *Fort Sandoské (Fort Sandoski) (c. 1749–c. 1754).*
Now: Port Clinton, Ottawa County (41°29′56.71″N–82°55′11.81″W)

Fort Sandoské was located on the Marblehead Peninsula, about 1.8 miles south of present Port Clinton, Ohio, in Ottawa County. The fort was at the southern terminus of what was known as the deLéry Portage across the Marblehead Peninsula, which follows present Fulton Street between Lake Erie to the north and Sandusky Bay to the south. The portage not only shortened the travel distance from Fort Detroit to Sandusky Bay by more than fifteen miles, it also allowed travelers to avoid the more treacherous water route around the Marblehead Peninsula. The site of Fort Sandoské is marked by a stone obelisk with bronze plaques and was dedicated in 1912 by the Ottawa County Historical Society and the Ohio Historical Society.

FORT SITES

Near here the peninsula carrying place where earlier British traders may have had a post, French soldiers built in 1750 and 1751, a small palisaded fort called "Sandoski." Lt. DeLery reported that the fort was in ruins in 1754.

In September 1764, British soldiers under the command of Colonel John Bradstreet, while attempting to quell the Indians during Pontiac's Conspiracy, began to construct a fort ¾ of a mile west of the old French fort, but work was soon abandoned.

DE LERY PORTAGE

Near this point was the southern terminus of a French and Indian portage by which travelers crossed the peninsula to the mouth of the Portage River and Lake Erie.

The portage is named after French Lt. Joseph G. Chaussegros DeLery who described it in his journal and who used the crossing in 1754 and 1755 on his way to and from Detroit.

French and Indians traveling by canoe along the south shore of Lake Erie to or from the Sandusky-Scioto waterway, or between Fort Duquesne and Detroit used this carrying place to avoid the more dangerous water route around the peninsula.

Fort Sandoské should not be confused with the British Fort Sandusky that was built in 1761 about nine miles east-southeast across Sandusky Bay at the western outskirts of the present city of Sandusky.

Some sources indicate that English fur traders were active in the area from as early as 1699–1700, and in 1745, they supposedly constructed a small fortified trading post or blockhouse "among the Hurons on the north side of Sandusky Bay."[31] Of course, the French at Fort Detroit, which was less than 60 miles away, were not at all inclined to tolerate English "trespassers" encroaching on the French fur trade in New France, so in 1748 French troops were dispatched from

Paul Misencik at site of Fort Sandoské (author photograph).

Fort Detroit to evict them. Apparently, the location of the now vacated English post seemed to appeal to the French, so in 1749 they improved and strengthened the site, and named it Fort Sandoské.

The presence of Fort Sandoské was well known, but until the 20th century its precise location was in question. However, the discovery of Joseph Gaspard Chaussegros deLéry's journals at Montréal in 1906 helped identify the site of the fort. On April 22, 1754, deLéry set out from Quebec for Fort Detroit, leading an expedition of about 24 regular French soldiers and 60 militia. On August 24, 1754, deLéry reached the mouth of Sandusky Bay, which the French referred to as Lac [Lake] Dotsandoské. DeLéry's Journal entry for that date reads in part:

> I discovered a large body of water which I thought must be Lake Dotsandoské [Sandusky Bay]. I unfurled my flag as a signal to all the canoes following me; several had shipped water and had suffered greatly from the heavy wind. I saw all of them enter the lake, and on reaching the island [likely Johnson Island], they emptied the water from their canoes, and M. Péan changed his clothes which were soaked. I did not know where the portage was. I thought some trace must remain of the fort built there by the French in 1751, and later abandoned. To find it, I followed the northern coast of said lake which runs E. & W. After having covered about 3 leagues, I perceived a clearing where I landed at noon, and found the remains of the old fort.[32]

DeLéry discovered the portage path near the ruins of the fort and supervised carrying most of his canoes and equipment over the portage to the Lake Erie side. He reported the portage path to be "57 arpents long," which almost exactly equals the distance from Sandusky Bay to Lake Erie over the course of Fulton Street. An arpent is a French measurement equal to 64 yards or 59 meters.

In March 1755, deLéry departed Fort Detroit for Fort Duquesne, and crossed the DeLéry Portage on March 16. He reported in his journal that while crossing the portage, he was "walking in water all the way, as the portage was flooded at this season."[33]

Even before deLéry's journal was discovered in 1906, other historians had accurately described Fort Sandoské's location. One of those was the late Mr. Alfred T. Goodman, former secretary of the Western Reserve Historical Society. In July 1871, Goodman wrote, "As early as the year 1745 English traders penetrated as far as Sandusky, or 'St. Dusky,' and established a post on the north side of the bay near the carrying place or portage from the Portage River across the peninsula."[34]

There is no information why Fort Sandoské was only in use for a few years, but most likely the French fort-building expedition on the Allegheny and upper Ohio Rivers in 1753, and the subsequent opening of hostilities between France and England at Jumonville Glen and Great Meadows in 1754, placed a greater need for troops in western Pennsylvania instead of the little post on Sandusky Bay.

In 1764, as a result of Pontiac's Conspiracy, which had begun the previous year, British troops began to reconstruct another fort on the north shore of Sandusky Bay about three-quarters of a mile west of old Fort Sandoské. Their aim was to regain a strong British military presence on Lake Erie after the destruction of Fort Presque Isle at present Erie, Pennsylvania, and Fort Sandusky as well as the continuing siege of Fort Detroit. However, the Indian offensive in Pontiac's War began to lose traction, and work on the new fort was abandoned in October of 1764, about three weeks after it was begun.

27. *Fort Sandusky (1761–1763).*
Now: Sandusky, Erie County *(41°26'43.98"N–82°46'13.09"W)*

The French and Indian War did not formally end until the Treaty of Paris was signed on February 10, 1763, but combat operations ceased for the most part in America after the British captured Montréal on September 10, 1760. Major Robert Rogers, the celebrated leader of "Rogers' Rangers," was sent to take possession of Fort Detroit, and after traveling through Ohio in 1760, he mentioned to commander-in-chief General Jeffery Amherst that there was a lack of British fortified posts south of Lake Erie.[35] Whether Amherst acted on Rogers's advice or not, the general ordered Colonel Henry Bouquet at Fort Pitt to have a fort built on Sandusky Bay.

Amherst was contemptuous of Indians, and his establishment of Fort Sandusky was not only to maintain a British post between Fort Pitt and Fort Detroit, but also to impose new draconian measures on the Ohio tribes. Now that the war was essentially over, the British no longer needed the Indians as allies. Amherst's measures included severely restricting the sale and trade of guns, powder, and lead to the Indians, which created a hardship, since the natives had become dependent on firearms for hunting. He informed the Indians that all trade would have to be conducted at British forts to ensure his rules were followed, that the Indians would no longer be given gifts, and that liquor would no longer be available to them. The Indians were angered by Amherst's decrees, but were more shocked by the arrogant attitudes of the British who dealt with them, especially when contrasted with the previous sociability and camaraderie of the French. Most galling was Amherst's disregard for British treaties that promised a restriction on white incursions into Ohio. When the Indians protested, Amherst bluntly told them that if they did not obey, "they must not only expect the severest retaliation, but an entire destruction of all their nations, for I am firmly resolved whenever they give me an occasion, to extirpate them root and branch."[36]

The most complete history of the construction of Fort Sandusky comes from a series of letters between Lieutenant Elias Meyer and Colonel Henry Bouquet, Meyer's commanding officer at Fort Pitt. Meyer, with his detachment of about forty men,[37] had explicit orders from Bouquet dated August 12, 1761, that read in part, "You are hereby directed to take under your command and march tomorrow thirteen August [1761] a detachment of 1 Sub., two Sergt., one Dr., Two Corp. and thirty privates of the first Battn R.A.R. & proceed with convenient Dispatch to Sandusky Lake on the south side of which; and at the most convenient Place, you are to build a small Block House with a Palisade around it, to serve as a Halting Place for our Party going and coming from Detroit."[38]

On September 1, 1761, Meyer wrote to Bouquet: "I have decided on a place here, to build a blockhouse, which is three miles from a village which the savages call Canoutout Chanondet [Castalia], and where all the horses of the merchants unloaded and loaded the merchandise for Detroit. It is about in the middle of the small Lake Sandusky [Sandusky Bay]."[39]

The construction of Fort Sandusky was begun in September 1761, and reported complete on November 29, 1761. A historical marker erected in the present Venice neighborhood[40] at the western edge of the city of Sandusky claims the fort was located at the present intersection of Venice Road and Fremont Avenue.

On November 29, 1761, Meyer wrote to Bouquet reporting that "The Blockhouse, stockade … Banquettes, etc. were finished that day."[41] During the fort's construction, the site was visited on September 22, 1761, by Sir William Johnson, the British superintendent of all the Indians of the northern colonies. Johnson wrote, "I sent Mr. Croghan to the Indian town, and went down the lake in a little birch canoe to the place where the blockhouse is to be built by Mr. Meyer. This place is about three leagues from the mouth of Lake Sandusky, where it disembogues itself into Lake Erie."[42] Johnson's estimate of three leagues from the fort to the entrance of Sandusky Bay was obviously a rough guess. The straight-line distance from Fort Sandusky to the entrance to Sandusky Bay is at the most two leagues or less. However, even that is subject to some interpretation. A British league is normally about three miles on land and 3.42 miles at sea, but the distance may vary in some historical documents depending on the location and era.

It's only fair to point out that some sources contend that Fort Sandusky was located about 1.75 miles east of the Fort Sandusky historical marker. For comparison, we'll refer to the site at the historical marker as the Cold Creek site. The other

Fort Sandusky Site (author photograph).

possible location mentioned is an area near the mouth of Mills Creek. The late William Darlington stated in his book *Christopher Gist's Journal* that the Mills Creek site was the correct location, which was near the present intersection of West Monroe and Ohio Streets (41°28'45.54"N–82°44'11.19"W).

Other Mills Creek proponents base their contention on Lieutenant Thomas Hutchins's map of 1764. Since Hutchins visited the ruins of Fort Sandusky in 1764, a year after it had been destroyed by the Indians, it would appear to make the Mills Creek site more credible. However, when examining Hutchins's map, it can readily be seen that the scale and detail of the map make it difficult to determine with any certainty whether the map favors either the Cold Creek or the Mills Creek site. Note that Bald Eagle Creek shown on the map to the east of Fort Sandusky was one of the names by which the Huron River was called.

The idea that Fort Sandusky was sited at Mills Creek instead of Cold Creek may have been the result of grain mills on Cold Creek and references to the "mill tail race," which was a mill race diversion of Cold Creek to operate the mills. Although the Cold Creek mills had not been built during the brief existence of Fort Sandusky, subsequent writers used terms like "mill," "mill tail race," or "mill race" in conjunction with Cold Creek. An Erie County court decision dated 1893 mentions a mill and tail race in the judgment: "The said premises include within the boundaries the head spring and pond made thereby of Big Cold Creek, and also Big Cold Creek for a distance of one-half mile or more from said head spring and pond and also the *race* from said Cold Creek to the place where was located, until recently, the Castalia *mill* and pond, made by the dam erected at that point, and the *tail-race* from said dam and *mill* to where it joined again the waters of Big Cold Creek as they flow into Sandusky Bay." It continues, "That the water of Cold Creek and of said pond and *race* comes from said underground channel or course upward into said pond, and out through the

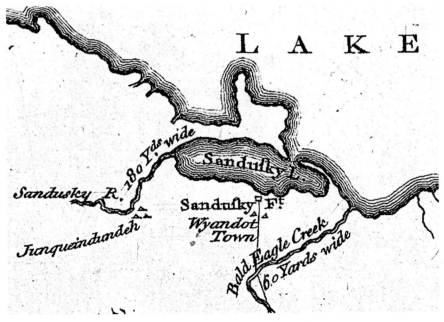

Section of Thomas Hutchins's 1764 map (Library of Congress, Geography and Map Division-2001695748).

channel of Cold Creek and said *race*, and uniting where said *tail-race* joins with Cold Creek flow into Sandusky Bay."[43]

The same court document mentions that the water of Cold Creek rises from a "spring in great volume, and is of a temperature of fifty-two degrees [F] at least in all seasons of the year, and is exceedingly clear; and for this reason said waters are especially adapted for the propagation and raising of valuable kinds of fish."[44] That further supports the Cold Creek site as the location of the fort, since a nearby, year-round freshwater source that never freezes over and is replete with fish would be an attractive benefit for a fort.

Charles E. Frohman, in his book *Sandusky's Yesterdays*, wrote, "[T]he location of British Fort Sandusky was on the south shore of Sandusky Bay, just west of the Mill Tail Race (Cold Creek) at Venice, about three miles west of the center of the city of Sandusky."[45] While Frohman correctly distinguishes the Mill Tail Race as associated with Cold Creek, other writers may have simply assumed that waterway descriptions containing the word "mill" referred to Mills Creek.

In 1764, a year after the destruction of Fort Sandusky, Colonel John Bradstreet led an expedition to Fort Detroit, accompanied by his chief engineer, Captain John Montresor, a skilled surveyor, mapmaker and keeper of extensive and elaborate journals. On September 18, 1764, Montresor wrote, "About 2 o'clock entered Sandusky Lake and arrived in the afternoon where our old fort stood that the Indians burned last year, a bad place for boats. The whole set sail and arrived at Thistle Creek about one mile and ¾ to the Eastward of it, but the water failing, returned and encamped ½ a mile to the westward of the old Fort."[46] I couldn't find any other reference to "Thistle Creek" in the Sandusky area, but Montresor stated that Thistle Creek was 1.75 miles east of the fort site. It's likely he was referring to Mills Creek when he mentioned Thistle Creek, since it is almost exactly 1.75 miles east of the Cold Creek site. The nearest creek to the east of Mills Creek is Pipe Creek, which is about 3 miles away.

Lieutenant Elias Meyer mentioned that the location of the fort was three miles from a village called Canoutout Chanondet (possibly Contuntuth), which some sources locate near present Castalia, Ohio. He could also have mistaken Canoutout or Chanodet for Junundat. There are many instances where the names of Indian villages were heard and transcribed differently, often giving the impression that there were more villages in an area than actually existed. However, Meyer likely traveled from Fort Pitt over the Great Trail, which would have come through the Castalia area, and the distance from Castalia to the Fort Sandusky historical marker is about 3.7 miles, so it's likely he was referring to Contuntuth at Castalia when he wrote Canoutout Chanondet.

Based on our research, we're of the opinion that the bulk of documentary evidence conclusively supports the Cold Spring site as the location of Fort Sandusky, but we suppose there are some who will continue to advocate for the Mills Creek site.

Fort Sandusky was captured by the Indians and destroyed less than two years after it was constructed. In 1763, the Ottawa chief Pontiac attempted to create a unified force of Indians in the trans-Allegheny region to expel the English by force. That uprising became known as Pontiac's Conspiracy. During the uprising, several English forts were attacked by the Indians and eight were captured. Fort Sandusky was the first to be taken. In 1763, Ensign Christopher Pauley (Pauli or Paully in some sources) of the 60th Regiment was in command of the small garrison of about 15 soldiers. On May 16, 1763, there were also about a dozen traders in the fort, and Pauley reported what happened at his court of inquiry:

Ensign Paully [*sic*] who commanded at Fort Sandusky informs the court that on the 16th of May, he was informed by his sentry at the Gate that Indians had come who wanted to speak to him. There were 4 Huron and 3 Ottawa Indians from his own area. He permitted them to come in, gave them some tobacco. After a short time, one of the Indians raised his head, which might have been a signal, and he was seized and bound and taken from his room. The sentry was dead in the gateway, and others massacred, and the Fort surrounded by Indians. The Sergeant, who had been planting in his garden, was there murdered. The merchants were all killed, and their stocks plundered. Paully was taken to Detroit but escaped from the Indians into the Fort on July third.[47]

According to legend, Pauley was told that when he arrived at Fort Detroit, which was still under siege by the Indians, he would be ceremoniously tortured and burned at the stake. However, before that happened, he was claimed by a squaw as a replacement for her husband, who had been killed in the fighting. Pauley stayed with the squaw for a couple of months before he was able to slip away and join the besieged garrison inside Fort Detroit.

After the siege of Fort Detroit was lifted in October of 1763, and Pontiac's Rebellion began to lose impetus, there was a brief consideration to rebuild Fort Sandusky, but serious support never materialized, and the rebuilding project was abandoned. After its brief existence as a military post, the ruins of Fort Sandusky were simply left to rot away.

9. *The Glaize (c. 1789–1794), includes: Captain Johnny's Town, Blue Jacket's Town, Black Snake's Town, Big Cat and Buckongahelas's Town, Tetapachksit's Town, Little Turtle's Town, Traders Town.*
Now: Defiance Area, Defiance and Henry Counties
(41°17'10.91"N–84°21'38.06"W)

The Glaize was a composite or multicultural Indian community located on the Maumee River centered around the mouth of the Auglaize River at present Defiance, Ohio. It was a composite community in the sense that it was composed of six Indian villages whose inhabitants were primarily Shawnee, Lenape, and Miami. It was multicultural in the sense that its population also included French, English and American residents.

The area around the confluence of the Auglaize and Maumee Rivers was a popular hunting area in the 18th century, but there were no permanent communities after the Beaver Wars until around 1789, when the first village was established under the Shawnee chief Kekewepelethy (Great Hawk), who was better known as Captain Johnny. The site was initially chosen because of its distance from white settlements and American military posts, and it became the headquarters for Indian resistance against white encroachment.

At the end of the American Revolution, the Ohio Indians learned that Britain, without consulting their Indian allies, signed a treaty with the United States, and ceded all land east of the Mississippi, north of Florida, and south of the Great Lakes to the Americans. The outraged Indians condemned the English king as treacherous and cruel for ceding land that was not his to give. The American viewpoint was that the lands were theirs by conquest since they had defeated the English and their Indian allies. The Ohio Indians, on the other hand, considered the American argument ridiculous, since they had not been defeated by the Americans even if the British had. The young Shawnee war chief Captain Johnny told the American diplomats that he and his people were not inclined to give up their land just because the Americans and British had signed a piece of paper in Paris.

The Indians quickly learned that the Americans meant to have their land, and as a flood of land-hungry whites poured over the Allegheny Mountains, the Indians realized they would have to fight to retain their territory. A council was held at Upper Sandusky in September 1783, and hundreds of representatives from most of the woodland tribes met to determine the best course of action. The famous Mohawk chief Theyendanegea (Joseph Brant) spoke for Indian unity and cooperation, and the Indians decided to form a confederation of tribes who would unify to resist white expansion into Indian lands. They decided that all decisions regarding peace and war with the Americans required the unanimous consent of all the representative tribes, and that only the Indian Confederacy had the authority to cede Indian land to the Americans.

As the Indians increased their attacks on white settlers, the American Army was sent to subdue them. The center of Indian resistance early in what became known as the Northwest Indian War was around Kekionga and the other Miami towns near present Fort Wayne, Indiana. In October 1790, a large force of 1,300 militia and 353 regulars under the command of General Josiah Harmar marched to attack Kekionga along with the Shawnee, Lenape, Miami, and other Indian villages in western Ohio. Harmar's force burned several villages, but the Indians regrouped under the Miami chief Little Turtle, and on October 20, 1790, they ambushed several hundred militia under Colonel John Hardin, killing most of them. On October 22, Harmar launched an attack, and was defeated by Little Turtle's warriors in what became known as "Harmar's Defeat," or what the Indians referred to as the "Battle of the Pumpkin Fields." It received that name because the steam rising from the scalped white skulls reminded the Indians of squash steaming in the autumn air. Harmar's force suffered almost 300 killed and 106 wounded.

In November 1791, the Americans launched another attack against the Miami towns at Kekionga. A force of about 2,000 men consisting of 600 regular troops, 800 six-month conscripts, and 600 militia under General Arthur St. Clair started out, but by the time they arrived in the Kekionga area, desertions and illness had whittled the force down to about 1,000 men and several women camp followers. On the evening of November 4, 1791, just as the troops stacked arms and lined up for their breakfast, about 1,100 Indians under Little Turtle, Blue Jacket, and Buckongahelas attacked and routed St. Clair's army. After a three-hour battle, the American force suffered the highest percentage casualty rate of an American Army unit to that time. Over 832 American soldiers and nearly all of the camp followers lost their lives in St. Clair's defeat, while the Indian casualties were estimated at 21 killed and 40 wounded.

After the two major attacks against Kekionga and the other nearby Miami towns, several of the chiefs decided to relocate their villages to the Auglaize River area about forty miles east of Kekionga. The Indians believed the new location was better situated, because it increased the distance to about ninety miles from the nearest American Army post at Fort Jefferson in present Darke County, Ohio. The move also allowed better communication between the Indian Confederation tribes in Ohio. Captain Johnny was the first of the Indian leaders to establish a village at the Glaize, and his village was located on the east side of the Auglaize River about a mile and a half south of the river's mouth (41°16'1.78"N–84°21'51.86"W). Between 1789 and 1792 other chiefs moved into the area, including the famous warriors Little Turtle of the Miami; Blue Jacket and Black Snake of the Shawnee; Big Cat, Buckongahelas, and Tetapacksit of the Lenape.

Though Captain Johnny was a renowned Shawnee warrior and chief, and was the first to move to the Glaize, the de facto headquarters of the Indian Confederation was the village of the more famous Chief Blue Jacket (41°17'23.78"N–84°20'3.35"W), which was established about 1792. The name Blue Jacket was simply a popular name or nickname used by white men, who had difficulty wrapping their tongues around Indian pronunciations. When Blue Jacket was a boy, he was named Sepettekenathé ("Big Rabbit"), and when he reached manhood his name became Waweyapiersenwaw ("Whirlpool"). Blue Jacket was one of the most illustrious Shawnee warriors, in a nation of outstanding warriors and distinguished leaders. His town was located on the north bank of the Maumee River about a mile downstream (east) of the mouth of the Auglaize. In 1792, Blue Jacket's Town had a population of about 300 people living in about forty bark-covered sapling frame dwellings. There were gardens and pasture lands behind the town, and on the south side of the Maumee was an almost unbroken communal cornfield that stretched about nine miles from opposite Black Snake's Town to Little Turtle's Town and south on the east bank of the Auglaize to Captain Johnny's Town.

Black Snake's Town, or simply Snake's Town, another Shawnee village, was located about nine miles east of the confluence on the north bank of the Maumee River, in the immediate vicinity of present Florida, Ohio (41°19'36.37"N–84°12'11.35"W). Black Snake or Shemeneto was a noted war chief who had been instrumental in the defeat of Colonel William Crawford in 1782. His biography is difficult to encapsulate, because there were several other notable Shawnee leaders who were also called "snake," which causes their profiles to overlap according to different accounts and sources.

Big Cat and Buckongahelas's Town was about four and a half miles southwest of the confluence on the west side of the Auglaize, near the intersection of present Ohio Route 111 and Hammersmith Road (41°14'17.48"N–84°24'15.15"W). The social chief or civic leader was Big Cat or Machingwe Pushis, and the war chief was Buckongahelas or Pachgantschihilas (c. 1720–1805), or "one whose movements are certain."

Reportedly adjacent to Captain Johnny's Town on the Auglaize was a Lenape village that was likely the town of Tetapachksit (41°16'12.92"N–84°22'24.75"W), also referred to in some sources by various names, such as "Grand Glaize King," "One who has been split," and "Branching Tree." Along with Big Cat and Buckongahelas, Tetapachksit was one of the three most influential Lenape leaders at the time. Other than accounts claiming that his town was located adjacent to Captain Johnny's Town, there is no other information regarding its specific site.

The sixth Indian community at the Glaize settlement was the Miami town of Little Turtle or Mihšihkinaahkwa (c. 1747–1812), which was situated on the north side of the Maumee River, near the mouth of the Tiffin River, about two and a half miles west of the confluence of the Maumee and Auglaize Rivers (41°16'54.31"N–84°24'6.79"W). Little Turtle was recognized as one of the most capable war leaders of the Indian Confederacy, largely as a result of his role in the stunning victory over St. Clair in 1791.

Also on the north bank of the Maumee, opposite the mouth of the Auglaize, was the solitary home of Coocoochee, a Mohawk medicine woman who, along with her husband, three sons and a daughter, had left their home on the Richelieu River near Montreal several years previous, to live with the Shawnee in Ohio. Two of her sons, Black Loon and White Loon, were warriors in Blue Jacket's Town, and the third son lived five or six miles upstream on the Auglaize.[48] Coocoochee's husband was killed in Harmar's attack on the Miami towns in 1790, and their daughter was married to the British trader George Ironside, who lived in the Glaize Traders Village. The Mohawk woman was not only knowledgeable about herbal medicine but was frequently consulted because of her reputed spiritual power and reputation as a seer. She was regularly visited by warriors before they took to the warpath, and "if the old woman predicted success, the warriors crossed the Maumee in their canoes, some of them standing erect cradling their muskets in their arms, in greater heart."[49]

The Traders Town was located on the point of land formed by the junction of the Maumee and Auglaize Rivers (41°17'10.91"N–84°21'38.06"W) and encompassed a cleared area "200 yards wide and a quarter of a mile long, bordered on the west and south by tall trees and hazel underbrush. At the north end of the clearing, half a dozen buildings had been erected for traders and for the British Indian Agency."[50] Several other French and English families had their homes along the Auglaize River, including a couple who had been captured during St. Clair's defeat in 1791. An estimated white population of fewer than fifty white individuals resided at the small Traders Village.[51]

The traders themselves were prominent frontier individuals, and they included the English trader George Ironside, who was married to Coocoochee's daughter; John Kinzie, silversmith and trader, who was married to a white woman captured by the Shawnee; Jacques Lasselle, who married Blue Jacket's daughter; and a French baker listed simply as Perault, who probably was John Baptiste La Plante, born at Isle Perault.[52] There was also Indian agent Alexander McKee and his assistant Mathew Elliott. James Girty, who was married to a Shawnee woman, also lived in the town, and he often shared his home with his more notorious brother Simon.

At its peak, the Glaize contained extensive pastures, gardens, cornfields, and outlying buildings, and the community had a combined population of about 2,000 that included small clusters of Nanticoke, Chickamauga, Cherokee, and Mingo Indians who had migrated into the area.

After the defeats of Harmar and St. Clair, the Americans were determined to subdue the Indian rebellion, and the Glaize became the primary focus. In 1793, General Anthony

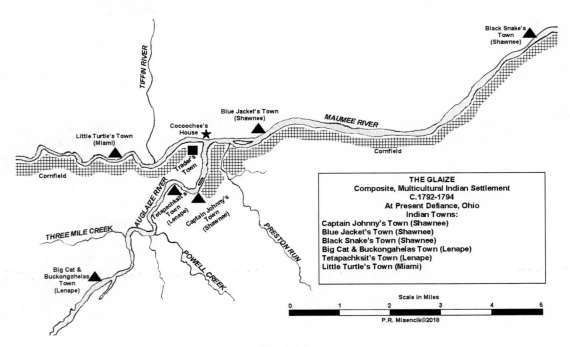

The Glaize.

Wayne, commanding the newly formed "Legion of the United States," launched an expedition against the Indians in northwest Ohio. Wayne's Legion was the first U.S. Army unit to receive basic training to turn recruits into professional soldiers. In 1793, Wayne marched north from Fort Washington at present Cincinnati, Ohio, with over 2,000 well-trained troops, and he built a chain of forts along the way.

They reached the Glaize in early August 1794 but found the towns virtually empty. A deserter from Wayne's force had warned the Indians, who then escaped down the Maumee River to regroup at the Maumee Rapids. Wayne's troops burned the homes at the Glaize and systematically destroyed what Wayne described as fifty miles of cornfields along the south bank of the Maumee. With that, the Glaize community ceased to exist. On August 9, Wayne began construction of Fort Defiance on the site of the Traders Town and completed construction on August 19.

Fort Defiance was used by Wayne for operations against the Indians even after the climactic Battle of Fallen Timbers on August 20, 1794. Following the Treaty of Greenville on August 3, 1795, the fort became a trading post, and during the War of 1812, Fort Defiance was used by William Henry Harrison as one of the westernmost outposts against the British and their Indian allies under Tecumseh.

34. *Junundat (Junandot) (c. 1739–c. 1800), also Ayonontout, Sunyendeand.*
Now: Wightmans Grove, Sandusky County
(41°25'22.04"N–83°3'5.36"W)

Based on extant maps, journals, and other sources that place the location of the Wyandot chief Orontony's town near the mouth of the Sandusky River, it was likely sited near the present tiny community of Wightmans Grove in Sandusky County. Wightmans Grove is the only community in the area, and it's not surprising that many of the old Indian village sites are located at or near present-day communities. What made the site desirable to the Indians certainly had the same attraction for the white settlers who displaced them: a good water supply, adequate materials for shelter, plenty of food and fuel, and land to plant crops. In many cases, the Indians cleared fields for crops, and otherwise improved the land, which made the area even more attractive to homesteaders.

Junundat was founded by the breakaway Huron or Wyandot leader Nicolas Orontony around 1739. Orontony's Wyandots moved from the Fort Detroit area to distance themselves from the aggressively belligerent Ottawa and other Three Fires Confederacy tribes in the area; however, their move was viewed by the French as a Wyandot defection to the English. In fact, the Wyandots were somewhat more disposed to trade with the English, whose merchandise was generally superior in quality, more plentiful, and less expensive. This was primarily due to the advanced state of the industrial revolution in England compared to France, and indeed the rest of Europe. The shorter British supply routes from England to the American interior gave the British an even greater trade advantage.[53]

Orontony established his village south of Sandusky Bay, near the mouth of the Sandusky River. In a letter dated August 10, 1751, from Marquis de la Jonquiere to Governor George Clinton of New York, Jonquiere refers to "Ayonontout," a Wyandot town on Sandusky Bay that in 1747 was selected by the rebel Huron chief as his stronghold. Jonquiere described the town as being near the "little lake of Otsanderket" (a misprint for "Otsand-esket," i.e. Sandusky). Further, Jonquiere said the town was "ten leagues of the town of Detroit,"[54] but his distance estimate is obviously incorrect. A French league was about 1.75 to 2.5 miles, which at most would have placed Junundat near the mouth of the Detroit River in present Michigan. Otherwise, the description appears to be identical to the location of Junundat as it was described on a 1755 map by Lewis Evans. Evans sited the town on the east side of the Sandusky River near its mouth. Some sources also use the names "Sunyende-and" or "Junqueindundeh" for Junundat, but Junqueindundeh or "Lower Sandusky" was another Wyandot town located at present Fremont, Ohio, approximately nine miles south or upstream of the mouth of the Sandusky River. Sunyendeand, on the other hand, appears to be associated with several Indian towns in the Sandusky River area, and most likely it is merely a corruption of Junundat. The captive James Smith wrote in his account, "I arrived at Sunyendeand, which was a Wyandot town, that lay on a small creek which empties into the little lake below the mouth of the Sandusky."[55] Smith's description of the location of Sunyendeand would place it close to the area where Junundat was likely located. Another entry in Smith's memoir supports the location of Sunyendeand as near the mouth of the Sandusky. He wrote of another visit, "When we came to the little lake at the mouth of the Sandusky we called at a Wyandot town that was then there, called Sunyendeand."[56] Based on Christopher Gist's journal, William M. Darlington (1782–1863) believed that Junundat was farther to the east of the mouth of the Sandusky River. He wrote that it is "probably on what is now called Cherry Island, in the marshes, between Green Creek and the Sandusky River, about two miles from the mouth of the latter. It now contains but a few acres of good land, above overflow, and is the most inaccessible of the islands in the vast Sandusky marshes, and only accessible by canoes or small boats."[57] It seems unlikely that Orontony would select such an inhospitable area for his village, especially since he wished to avail himself of the English trade.

The exact location of Junundat has not been definitively determined, and the changing geography of the area, including a fluctuating water level and shore erosion, further complicate matters. DeLéry said the town was below the mouth of the Sandusky River, and Frederick Webb's *Handbook of the American Indians North of Mexico* indicates that the town was located "On a small creek that empties into a little lake below the mouth of the Sandusky River."[58] That would place the location of Junundat near the present community of Wightmans Grove, Ohio.

Unfortunately for Orontony, Junundat and indeed Anioton were still near enough to Fort Detroit to allow the French to coerce and intimidate the wayward Wyandots. The French pressured Orontony's Wyandots to cease interaction with English traders and return to Fort Detroit, where the French would have more control over them. The French intimidation escalated, and in 1747, Orontony responded with open rebellion. He fortified the towns of Junundat and Anioton with palisades, and launched retaliatory attacks against the French. Emboldened by Orontony's resistance to French pressure, the Miami chief Memeskia at Pickawillany also joined the rebellion, in which French traders and troops were killed and Fort des Miamis at present Fort Wayne was burned to the ground.

The French were alarmed by Orontony's rebellion, because it not only interfered with their lucrative fur trade, but it also threatened French sovereignty in the Ohio territory. The French believed that the recalcitrant Indians would have to be brought under control before the British could take advantage of the erosion of French influence. The French responded with overwhelming force, and in September 1747, French reinforcements began to arrive

Wightmans Grove, Ohio, March 2016 (author photograph).

at Fort Detroit with plans to crush the rebellion before it expanded to other tribes. Rather than engage in a savage and unwinnable war against French troops, Orontony decided to abandon the area. In 1748, he moved his Wyandots about 105 miles southeast to the confluence of the Muskingum, Tuscarawas, and Walhonding Rivers at present Coshocton, Ohio, where he established his village called Conchaké. Orontony died at Conchaké around 1750, presumably from smallpox.

33. Junqueindundeh (Junquindundeh) (c. 1650–c. 1812), also Lower Sandusky, Wyandot Town, Dunkeindundeh.
Now: Fremont, Ohio, Sandusky County
(41°21'14.80"N–83°06'40.02"W)

From about 1750, Junqueindundeh ("it has a rock") was a Wyandot village that was situated on the west bank of the Sandusky river at present Fremont, Ohio. It was often referred to as Lower Sandusky because it was on the lower or downstream rapids of the Sandusky River, while the town of Upper Sandusky was located farther upstream about 36 miles south.

The Ohio mound-builder culture was the first aboriginal people to settle in the area, and they were followed by the Erie nation. Among anthropologists there is a consensus that the Erie were descended from the earlier mound-builder culture. The mighty Erie Confederation ruled most of Ohio until they were destroyed by the Iroquois during the Beaver Wars or Iroquois Wars of the mid–17th century.

For a period of almost eighty years, present Ohio was virtually devoid of permanent settlements, but around the late 1730s, tribes began to enter the area to establish their communities. Probably the first were the Wyandots under Nicolas Orontony, who led his breakaway faction south into Ohio from the Fort Detroit area in 1738 and established towns on Sandusky Bay. Soon after, in the 1740s, Piankashaw Miamis under the Miami chief Memeskia broke away from the French at Fort des Miamis at present Fort Wayne and established the new village of Pickawillany on the Great Miami River in western Ohio. The French viewed those moves as defections that threatened their sovereignty and control of the Ohio Indians, so they tried to use force to coerce the break-

Sign at Junqueindundeh, in present Fremont, Ohio (author photograph).

away tribes to return to the fold. The Indians fought back in what was known as Orontony's Rebellion, but as French troops poured into the area, Orontony realized he was faced with an unwinnable war. In 1748, Orontony led most of his people southeast to the Forks of the Muskingum, where he established the village of Conshaké. Not all of the Wyandots followed Orontony, however; some stayed in their village on Sandusky Bay, while others moved deeper into the interior of Ohio.

Around 1750, one band of Wyandots traveled south up the Sandusky River and established the town of Junqueindundeh at the first or lower falls upstream from the mouth of the Sandusky. The name, meaning "it has a rock," likely pertains to the twelve-foot falls that defined the area. The falls were where the Ballville Dam was constructed in 1913.

A rather fanciful and romanticized bit of folklore connected with Lower Sandusky is included in Henry Howe's book, *Historical Collections of Ohio*, which claims:

> Upon the Sandusky river, and near where the town of Lower Sandusky now stands, lived a band of Wyandots, called the Neutral Nation. They occupied two villages, which were cities of refuge, where those who sought safety never failed to find it. During the long and disastrous contests which preceded and followed the arrival of the Europeans, in which the Iroquois contended for victory, and their enemies for existence, this little band preserved the integrity of their territories and the sacred character of peace-makers. All who met upon their threshold met as friends, for the ground on which they stood was holy. It was a beautiful institution, a calm and peaceful island looking out upon a world of waves and tempests. This annexed is a note from the above.
>
> This Neutral Nation, so-called by Father Seguard, was still in existence two centuries ago, when the French missionaries first reached the upper lakes. The details of their history, and of their character and privileges, are meagre and unsatisfactory; and this is the more to be regretted, as such a sanctuary

among the barbarous tribes is not only a singular institution, but altogether at variance with that reckless spirit of cruelty with which their wars are usually prosecuted. The Wyandot tradition represents them as having separated from the parent stock during the bloody wars between their own tribe and the Iroquois, and having fled to the Sandusky river for safety. That they here erected two forts, within a short distance of each other, and assigned one to the Iroquois and the other to the Wyandotts and their allies, where their war parties might find security and hospitality, whenever they entered their country. Why so unusual a proposition was made and acceded to, tradition does not tell. It is probable, however, that superstition lent its aid to the institution, and that it may have been indebted for its origin to the feasts and dreams and juggling ceremonies which constituted the religion of the aborigines. No other motive was sufficiently powerful to restrain the hand of violence and to counteract the threat of vengeance.

An internecine feud finally arose in this Neutral Nation, one party espousing the cause of the Iroquois and the other of their enemies; and like most civil wars, this was prosecuted with relentless fury. Our informant says that, since his recollection, the remains of a red cedar post were yet to be seen, where the prisoners were tied previously to being burned.

The informant above alluded to by Gov. CASS we have reason to believe was Major B. F. STICKNEY, of Toledo, long an Indian agent in this region. That there may have been such a tradition among the Indians we are unable to gainsay, but of its truth we have doubts. Major STICKNEY, in a lecture (as yet unpublished), delivered Feb. 28, 1845, before the Young Men's Association, of Toledo, says:

"The remains of extensive works of defense are now to be seen near Lower Sandusky. The Wyandotts have given me this account of them. At a period of two centuries and a half since, or more, all the Indians west of this point were at war with all the Indians east. Two walled towns were built near each other, and each was inhabited by those of Wyandot origin. They assumed a neutral character, and the Indians at war recognized that character. They might be called two neutral cities. All of the west might enter the western city, and all of the east the eastern. The inhabitants of one city might inform those of the other that war parties were there or had been there; but who they were or whence they came, or any thing more, must not be mentioned. The war parties might remain there in security, taking their own time for departure. At the western town they suffered the warriors to burn their prisoners near it; but the eastern would not. (An old Wyandott informed me that he recollected seeing, when a boy, the remains of a cedar-post or stake, at which they used to burn prisoners.) The French historians tell us that these neutral cities were inhabited and their neutral character respected, when they first came here. At length a quarrel arose between the two cities, and one destroyed the inhabitants of the other. This put an end to all neutrality."[59]

It's difficult to determine whether there is any factual basis for Howe's tale, but most likely it is entirely fanciful. During the 19th century it was very common to romanticize or otherwise spice up tales, much in the fashion of James Fennimore Cooper's *Leatherstocking Saga*, and this is probably another example.

Aside from Howe's tale of the neutral sanctuary towns of Lower Sandusky, present Freemont has a rich and colorful Indian history. Although the Wyandots called their town Junqueindundeh, the village was almost equally well known as Lower Sandusky, and often simply as Wyandot Town. However, many Indian towns were shown on maps or even referred to in journals according to a tribal affiliation like "Wyandot Town," "Mingo Town," or "Shawnee Town," and that sometimes makes it difficult to ascertain specifically which town is being discussed. Even towns that are named for the chief or village leader are often shown on maps or described as being in different locations for the simple reason that after a period of time, the chief found it necessary to relocate his village elsewhere. As a result, it's necessary to identify the town and its location along with the specific time period it occupied that particular site.

Possibly the first white man who visited Junqueindundeh was James Smith (1737–1813), who was captured by Indians in Pennsylvania in 1755. Smith, a soldier with Braddock's ill-fated expedition, was captured by Caughnawaga Indians[60] prior to the battle on the Monongahela and was adopted by them. Smith lived with the Indians until he escaped in 1759, but during his years with the Indians he traveled extensively in the Ohio area and provided one of the first descriptions of the Sandusky River area, including what he called the Falls of the Sandusky at present Fremont.

In 1763, during Pontiac's Conspiracy, British troops under Captain James Dalyell arrived at the site of Fort Sandusky, where they found the mutilated bodies of the fort's garrison in the burned fort. In an act of revenge, after burying the dead, Dalyell led his troops up the Sandusky River to Junqueindundeh where he burned the village and destroyed the Indian cornfields.[61] However, at least one source surmises that the Wyandot village Dalyell and his men destroyed was at present Castalia instead of Junqueindundeh.[62] Dalyell then marched his troops to Fort Detroit to assist in breaking the Indian siege. On July 31, 1763, Dalyell was killed during the Battle of Blood Run when he led his troops in a sortie against Pontiac's village.

Junqueindundeh was rebuilt and the cornfields reestablished, and the town continued as a major Indian village on the Sandusky River. Documentary evidence indicates that during its existence, both the French and English had established trading posts there at various times.

The first time Junqueindundeh was depicted on a map was on Thomas Hutchins's map dated 1764, and the village was also shown on his 1778 map. For some reason, Hutchins erroneously placed Junqueindundeh on the east side of the Sandusky River. It's interesting to note that Fort Sandusky was depicted on both maps, even though Fort Sandusky was totally destroyed in 1763 during Pontiac's Conspiracy. Also of interest is the depiction of "Wyandot Town" near the location of present Castalia, Ohio, which was likely the Wyandot village of Contuntuth.

In 1764, toward the end of Pontiac's Rebellion, two parallel expeditions were launched against the Indians in Ohio. Colonel Henry Bouquet marched from Fort Pitt into central Ohio, while Colonel John Bradstreet led a force of 1,180 men west from Albany. Bradstreet's force traveled in watercraft along the southern shore of Lake Erie, and on September 18, 1764, they landed at the site of Fort Sandusky, where Bradstreet planned to meet and nego-

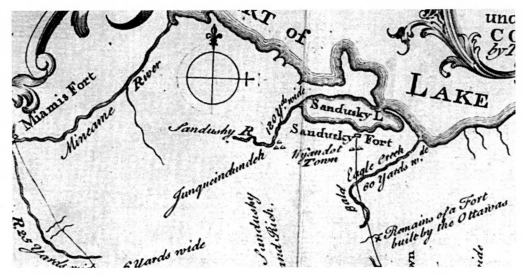

Section of Thomas Hutchins's 1764 map (Library of Congress, Geography and Map Division).

tiate with the Indians. When the Indians failed to appear, Bradstreet marched his force up the Sandusky River to the site of Junqueindundeh, and camped a mile below the falls on the site of the present Sandusky County Fairgrounds, where he again tried to negotiate with the Indians.[63] Bradstreet was accused of acting contrary to his orders, failing to act aggressively, mismanaging his campaign, and attempting to negotiate an independent peace treaty with the Indians. Even so, he was promoted to major general in 1772.

The military engineer Captain John Montresor accompanied Bradstreet, and on September 22, 1764, made the following observation: "I went to the Huron village (Junque-in-dundeh) and took a sketch of the bearings of that advantageous and beautiful situation and the meanderings of the river. Remarked, that the left of our encampment is contiguous to the remains of an old fort where the Delawares and some western Indians took post to shelter themselves against the Iroquois nearly one hundred years ago—this constructed in the form of a circle 300 yards in circumference, one-half defended by the river and a remarkable hollow or gully which covers the left and parts of our encampments."[64] Montresor was mistaken in identifying the earthworks as the remains of a Delaware or Lenape fort from the time of the Iroquois Wars of the mid–17th century. Not only were the Lenape not in the vicinity of Lower Sandusky at the time of the Beaver Wars, but the mounds were much older than that period. Most likely, Montresor referred to ancient mound-builder earthworks that were in the area. According to the *Archeological Atlas of Ohio*, one such large circular, reverse "C"-shaped earthwork was located on the east side of the Sandusky River in Ballville Township south of Fremont.[65] The earthwork was likely

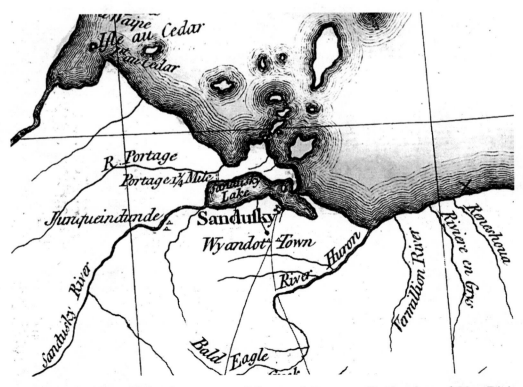

Section of Thomas Hutchins's 1778 map (Library of Congress, Geography and Map Division-74696155).

destroyed by the construction of the Ballville Dam project in 1913, and subsequent development in the area.

Ohio's first permanent white settlers made their home at Junqueindundeh. James Whittaker (1756–1804) and Elizabeth Foulks (1768–1833) were captured as children in Pennsylvania by the Wyandots in 1774 and 1776 respectively. James was eighteen when he was taken, and Elizabeth was eight. They were brought to Junqueindundeh, where they both adapted to the Indian way of life and were adopted and raised by an Indian family. James and Elizabeth fell in love, were married around 1781 or 1782, and the Wyandots gave them a tract of about 1180 acres along the Sandusky River. They raised eight children, and the house they built was supposedly the first European-style home in Ohio. James died in 1804 at the age of 48 and Elizabeth passed away in 1833 at the age of sixty-five.

In 1778 the frontiersmen Daniel Boone and Simon Kenton were brought at different times to Junqueindunduh as captives. In 1780, Captain Samuel Brady, a frontier scout, spent at least one night on the large island in the Sandusky River adjacent to Junqueindundeh, from where he observed the Indians racing their horses along the river. The island is now called "Brady's Island." The west bank of the river was not only used by the Indians as a race course; it was in effect the center of their town where council meetings were held, and also where captives were forced to run the gantlet.[66]

Running the gantlet was a fairly common ordeal that prisoners were forced to endure. It consisted of the Indians in two long lines facing each other about three or four yards apart, and a prisoner was forced to run the distance while the Indians beat him with sticks, clubs, rocks, or all sorts of other weapons. It was not unusual for a captive to be killed during the ordeal. In some cases, the prisoners were paraded through several villages, and they would be forced to run the gantlet at each one. Often captives who exhibited qualities of stoicism, bravery, strength, athleticism, agility, and speed, were adopted into the tribe, and the others at best became slaves, or were tortured to death. In his book, Colonel James Smith described his experiences in running the gantlet, as well as observing prisoners from Braddock's defeat being burned to death.

In October 1781, the Moravian missionaries David Zeisberger, John Heckewelder, William Edwards, and Gottlob Sensemann were kept in the town as prisoners on the way to Fort Detroit, where they were tried by the British as spies. After their trial they were acquitted and released.

On September 7, 1783, the Mohawk chief Thayendanegea (1743–1807), also known as Joseph Brant, spoke at the "Sandusky Council," which was held at Junqueindundeh. The meeting was attended by Wyandot, Lenape, Shawnee, Cherokee, Ojibwe, Ottawa, and Mingo representatives. Thayendanegea expressed

Site of Junqueindundeh gantlet and race course (author photograph).

his opinion that no peace would be possible unless the Muskingum and Ohio Rivers were designated as boundaries against white incursions in accordance with the 1768 Treaty of Fort Stanwix. The treaty specified the boundary between Indian lands to the west and the British colonial lands to the east. The boundary began at Fort Stanwix at present Rome, New York, and proceeded south and west to the confluence of the Ohio and Kanawha Rivers, and from there along the Ohio River to its confluence with the Tennessee River.

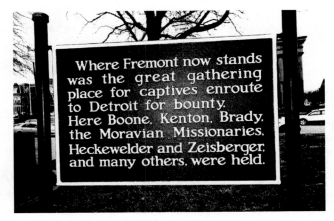

Sign on the Fremont Town Square (author photograph).

In March 1781, the Second Continental Congress, and its successor organization the Confederation Congress, adopted the Articles of Confederation, which was a rather anemic agreement that was meant to frame the new national government. On the frontier, the document failed to address the increasing flood of settlers and land speculators into what was supposed to be territory reserved for the Indians. During the colonial period, over 300 treaties were signed with the Indians, most of which had to do with land acquisition that guaranteed land for the Indians. However, after the Revolutionary War, other than some feeble initiatives in favor of honoring the previous treaties, the fledgling U.S. government did not have the power nor the will to prevent land-hungry white settlers and entrepreneurs from streaming into the Indian territory. In effect, Congress simply looked the other way while the Indian lands were being taken over. As a result, it wasn't long before Thayendanegea's prediction of an Indian war came true.

During the Indian War in Ohio, which effectively ended in 1794 with the Battle of Fallen Timbers, the chief at Junqueindundeh or Lower Sandusky was Tarhe, also known as "The Crane" (1742–1818). Tarhe fought in Lord Dunmore's War in 1774, and later fought to stem the expansion of white settlers into the Ohio area. He took part in the Battle of Fallen Timbers on August 20, 1794, and after the Indians' defeat, he signed the Treaty of Greenville. Later, Tarhe refused to join the confederation of Indians in Tecumseh's War (1810–1813), and instead urged the Wyandots to honor the Treaty of Greenville they had signed in 1794. During the War of 1812, Tarhe, who was in his seventies, allied himself with the Americans against the British, and took part in the Battle of the Thames in 1813. That was the battle in which Tecumseh was killed. Tarhe died in 1818 at the age of seventy-eight on the Wyandot reservation at Upper Sandusky.

After Ohio became a state in 1803, settlers flooded into the area, including the northern section that was to be preserved as Indian lands under the Treaty of Greenville. That included the Sandusky River area around Junqueindundeh, which was attractive to settlers. For a while the U.S. government considered removing the white settlers by force, but that never happened, and as white settlements sprang up and expanded, the Indians were displaced. The Indians attempted to fight back, but by the end of the War of 1812, the day of the free Indian in Ohio was over. The last Indian preserve in Ohio was the large Wyandot reservation at Upper Sandusky about thirty-seven miles south of Junqueindundeh on the Sandusky River. In 1842, the Wyandots were removed to a new reservation in the Kansas Territory. The following year, the new white settlement of Upper Sandusky was founded at the upper falls of the Sandusky River, and it became the county seat of Wyandot County.

44. *Maumee River Ottawa Villages (c. 1770s–c. 1834), including Tontoganee (Tontogany, Tonedog-o-ney), Nawash Village, Anpatonajowin, Kinjoino's Town.*
Now: Tontogany, Wood County (41°27′35.61″N–83°45′16.91″W)

There were several villages in the vicinity of the Maumee River rapids, southwest of Toledo near present Waterville, Ohio. While most sources identify them as Ottawa (Odowa) towns, some in fact were populated by Potawatomi (Bodowdomi), or Ojibwe (Chippewa), who were the three main divisions of what was known as the "Three Fires Confederacy." The Ottawa were perhaps the most dominant nation of the Confederacy, and by the latter third of the 17th century, they were so important to the French fur trade that it was common practice to refer to any Algonquin from the Lake Huron and Lake Michigan area as an Ottawa. Their original homeland was mainly on Manitoulin Island in present Ontario, and also in Michigan and Wisconsin, but by the late 17th century, they were established in the Fort Detroit area, and in the 18th century, they began to establish villages in present northwest Ohio along the Maumee River. The Ottawa were composed of five branches, divisions, or septs, which were the Keinouche (Pickerel), Kiskakon (Bear), Nassawaketon (Fork People), Sable, and Sinago (Gray Squirrel). In addition, they were also subdivided into numerous local bands or clans.

Unfortunately, the specific ethnicity of the villages has been for the most part lost, and while some of the villages may have had Potawatomi or Ojibwe inhabitants, in many sources they are regarded as Ottawa towns. A few Ottawa established villages farther east, like Ogoutz at present Sandusky, Ohio, and Ottawa Town on the Cuyahoga River. The easternmost Ottawa town was located at Venango in western Pennsylvania. The name Ottawa comes from the Algonquin word "Adawe," which means "to trade," but like many Indians, the Ottawas refer to themselves in their own language as "people" or "Anishinabe." During the French and Indian War, they were early allies of the French, and participated in Washington's defeat at Great Meadows on July 4, 1754, and Braddock's defeat on the Monongahela on July 9, 1755.

After the French and Indian War, they were part of Pontiac's ill-fated 1763 uprising, which was an attempt to drive the white English settlers out of present Michigan, Ohio, and western Pennsylvania. During the American Revolutionary War, they allied with the British as their best option of preventing white settlement incursions west of the Allegheny Mountains. Shortly before and during the American Revolutionary War, Ottawa or Three Fires Confederacy tribes began to establish communities in Ohio, and most were located in the area of the Maumee River from present Toledo to the junction of the Blanchard and Auglaize Rivers near present Dupont, Ohio.

One of the earliest Ottawa villages in Ohio was called Tushquegan, which took its name from the chief, who is variously referred to in different sources as K'Oarty, McCarty, Equshawa, and Aqushawa. The town was established around the time of the American

Revolutionary War on the south bank of the Maumee River in present Toledo, Ohio. Chief Tushquegan allied with the British during the Revolutionary War, and hoped the British would support the Indians' efforts to exclude white settlements in Ohio and Michigan.

In 1822, the Presbyterians established the Maumee Indian Mission on the east bank of the Maumee River opposite present Missionary Island.[67] The mission was abandoned in 1834, and because of the mission records, we're able to list several of the Indian villages in the area.

Tontoganee, or sometimes "Tontogany" and "Tonedog-o-ney," which translates to "The Dog," was named for its village chief. The town was located at the mouth of Tontogany Creek on the Maumee River, and should not be confused with the present town of Tontogany about 2.8 miles south of the old town site. It's not known when the village was established, but most likely it was abandoned when the majority of Ottawa were removed to Kansas around 1833–1834.

Nawash's Town on present Indian Island almost directly across from Tontoganee was established around 1819. This village was populated by Ojibwe or Chippewa Indians, under their chief Nawash, also known as Naiwash, Naiwasha, or Neywash. Nawash was a Saugeen Ojibwe war chief who fought beside the Shawnee chief Tecumseh during Tecumseh's War of 1810, and during the War of 1812. Like the rest of the Indian towns in that area, it was likely abandoned around 1833–1834.

Some sources indicate that there was a village called Petonquet's Town[68] on Station Island, which is now called Missionary Island. However, there is very little supporting documentation regarding its specific location. The village of Waugau, named after its chief, was located at Wolf Rapids on the Maumee River, near present Grand Rapids, Ohio. There was also a village called Agushawas at Blanchard's Fork, which was the name of the confluence of the Blanchard and Auglaize Rivers less than a mile south of present Dupont, Ohio. Like most of the Ottawa or Three Fires villages in the vicinity, they were established either before or during the Revolutionary War, or in the early 1800s, just prior to the War of 1812.

With the loss of British support after the Revolutionary War, the Indians fought on by themselves in a vain attempt to preserve their Ohio homeland. That period was known as the Northwest Indian War, which raged from 1785 through the Indian defeat at Fallen Timbers on August 20, 1794. The subsequent Treaty of Greenville on August 3, 1795, forced the Indians to concede most of present Ohio, leaving them with a section of Northwest Ohio that lay within a line down the Cuyahoga and Tuscarawas Rivers to Fort Laurens at present Bolivar, Ohio, then west to Fort Loramie on the Great Miami River, and then west-northwest to Fort Recovery on the Wabash River. The area reserved for the Indians included the Ottawa towns in northwestern Ohio, but the Indian defeat caused a breakdown of tribal authority. In 1807, other Three Fires Confederacy tribes including Ottawa, Ojibwe, and Potawatomi, along with some Wyandot, ceded seven million acres in southeast Michigan for $3,300 in cash, an $800 annuity for eight years, and a 28,000-acre reservation on the Maumee above Roche de Bœuf, near present Waterville, Ohio.

After the British and Indian defeat in Tecumseh's War and the War of 1812, the Americans considered the Ohio Indians to be vanquished enemies. The Treaty of Fort Meigs in September 1817 forced the Ottawa to cede the bulk of their Ohio lands in return for two small reservations that were 34 square miles in total at Blanchard's Creek and the Little Auglaize River. Even those small parcels were taken way with the Indian Removal Act of 1830. Most of the Ohio Ottawas and their related Three Fires Confederacy tribes relocated to present Kansas in 1833–1834.

27. Ogontz (Ogantz) (c. 1784–c. 1812).
Now: Sandusky, Erie County (41°27'20.96"N–82°42'53.32"W)

Ogontz, according to most sources, was the chief of several families of Christian Ottawa Indians and French families who settled within the present Sandusky city limits. The location of his settlement was in the northeast area of the present city between Columbus Avenue and the mouth of Pipe Creek. An entry in the book *Historical Collections of Ohio* may be more specific, because it states: "The lodge of Ogontz was on the site occupied by the national bank on Columbus Avenue, between Market and Water Streets."[69]

The name is somewhat unusual in that it simply refers to an Indian's name, and doesn't really convey the idea that there may have been a village associated with it, as in "Captain Pipe's Town" or "White Eyes' Town." However, there were indeed several Indian and at least a few white French-Canadian families living in Ogontz's community.

Most of what is known of Ogontz comes from an article in *The Firelands Pioneer, June 1863*[70] by Joseph M. Root (1807–1879)[71] who heard the story from Benajah Wolcott (1764–1832), originally of Danbury, Connecticut. Wolcott was one of the first settlers in the Firelands,[72] and according to Root, Wolcott said he was well acquainted with Ogontz, and first met him immediately after Ogontz had killed another Ottawa chief in self-defense. After the killing, Ogontz took in the dead chief's son and raised him as his own, even though he knew the son would eventually kill him in revenge for the death of his father.

Ogantz told Wolcott that he originally came from the far north, and his parents died when his village was devastated by smallpox. Orphaned, he was raised by French Catholic missionaries, and was educated near Québec, where he received training as a priest and a missionary. After completing his education, and prior to the American Revolution, Ogontz was sent to the Fort Detroit vicinity, where he preached in nearby Canada among the Ottawa Indian villages and French-Canadian families who lived in the area.

When the Revolutionary War ended, Ogontz had a dislike for the British government in Canada, so he persuaded two groups of Ottawa Indians and some French-Canadian settlers to move with him south to the Sandusky Bay area. Ogontz said that he agreed be their "Father or Priest."[73] They arrived in the Sandusky area in 1784, and Ogontz stipulated that the French and Indians should live separately, with the French settling on Marblehead Peninsula, while the Indians established their village in what is now the city of Sandusky.

During the Ohio Indian Wars between 1785 and 1794, some of the people who came with Ogontz were fearful of being caught up in the wars and decided to return to Canada, but most remained at Sandusky. They were worried they would be attacked either by the hostile Indians or white troops. Ogontz cautioned them not to arouse the wrath of either side by taking sides in the conflict, so they followed his advice and were not molested during the wars. Supposedly, Ogontz later remarked that it was a good thing the Indians were defeated, because if they had won, they probably would have taken revenge on Ogontz and his community for not supporting them during the wars.

According to Wolcott, Ogontz said that about fifteen years prior, he gave up the priesthood, because he was frustrated that he could not influence the Indians more. He said the Indians found it easier to be Catholics than to be Christians, meaning they accepted the forms of Catholicism, but not the laws of Christianity. He said that his preaching was becoming more of an imposition, so he quit the priesthood and instead became a chief of one of the two bands of Ottawas in his community. The man he killed was the chief of the other Ottawa band.

Ogontz was worried that a new war was developing between the Americans and British, and that the western Lake Erie area would become a battleground, so when the war started in 1812, Ogontz led his community north into Canada. After the war, he returned to Ohio with many of his followers, and they formed a new settlement near the Maumee River. In 1817, as he predicted, Ogontz was killed by his adopted son, in revenge for the death of the boy's father several years before.[74]

Interestingly, the *Encyclopedia of Cleveland History*, maintained by Case Western Reserve University, tells a different version of Ogontz. It states: "OGONTZ (OGANTZ) was the leader of a band of Ottawa Indians encamped near the mouth of the Cuyahoga River during the first few years of Cleveland's settlement [Cleveland was founded in 1796]. The Ottawas usually spent the winter months on the west side of the river, migrating in the spring to the Sandusky area. Ogontz, although not known for his friendliness, was nonetheless tolerant of the white settlers and encouraged trade with them. As white settlement increased in the first years of the 1800s, the Ottawas resettled further west, mainly in the Sandusky area. Ogontz, by white accounts, was last seen there in 1811.[75]

Comparing both versions, the only commonality was that Ogontz and his band of Ottawas had a community in the Sandusky area at least until around 1811.

49. *Ottawa Village (c. 1770s–c. 1821).*
Now: Findlay, Hancock County (41°2′25.98″N–83°39′3.30″W)

American Indians established a town in and around present Findlay, Ohio. Apparently the first to settle in the area were Ottawa Indians who entered Ohio from Michigan and first settled along the Maumee. They extended their villages upstream along the Maumee and Auglaize Rivers to the Blanchard River. "The Ottawas had a small village on the site of Findlay, which stretched along the river within the present limits of the city."[76] They likely established their village in the 1770s. After the September 29, 1817, Treaty of the Maumee Rapids ceded all remaining Indian lands in Ohio to the U.S. government, certain reservations were set aside for the Indians who remained in Ohio. Some Ottawa remained in the area after 1817, but they were joined by Wyandots who took up residence in and around old Fort Findlay. Fort Findlay was constructed during the War of 1812 on the south bank of the Blanchard River near the present intersection of South Main Street and West Front Street.

The last Indians departed around 1821 when the first town lots were laid out for the city of Findlay.

15. *Pickawillany (c. 1745–1752), also Tawixtwi Town, Pick Town.*
Now: Piqua, Miami County (40°10′59.14″N–84°15′3.45″W)

The village was located near the confluence of Loramie Creek and the Great Miami River, approximately 2.25 miles north of present Piqua, Ohio. It was established by Miami Indians,[77] who were occasionally referred to by others as "Twightwees" (sandhill crane). It's not recorded exactly when Pickawillany was established, but around the mid–1740s, a group of breakaway Miamis left Quiskakon, the major Miami town situated at the confluence of the Maumee, St. Joseph, and St. Mary's Rivers at present Fort Wayne, Indiana. In some accounts, Quiskakon (cut tail) was also referred to as Kiskakon, or Kekionga (blackberry patch).[78]

The leader of the breakaway Miamis was Memeskia, a member of the Piankashaw[79] Miami group. For some reason the French referred to Memeskia as La Demoiselle, meaning damselfly or young lady, but because of his staunch British loyalty the English called him "Old Briton."

Ever since French explorers penetrated the area in the 17th century, the lands west of the Allegheny Mountains were considered to be the property of France, and indeed the territory was called "New France." And to enforce their monopolistic control of the Ohio fur trade, the French constructed Fort St. Phillipe des Miamis at Quiskakon. The fort was simply called Fort Miamis or Fort des Miamis. It was thought that French troops at Fort Miamis and Fort Detroit would be able to coerce the Indians into maintaining loyalty to the French while preventing English traders from trespassing into the area.

In spite of the French efforts, increasing numbers of English fur traders ventured into New France, and even more troublesome to the French was the fact that the Indians preferred English trade merchandise. The French were aware of the erosion of their fur trade monopoly, but they were at a loss for ways to effectively compete with the English. After his 1749 expedition among the Ohio Indians, which included a visit to Memeskia at Pickawillany, Captain Pierre Joseph Céloron de Blainville reported to Governor-General Jacques-Pierre de Taffenel de la Jonquiére, Marquis de la Jonquiére, that his expedition alone was not sufficient to secure the exclusive allegiance of the Indians, nor to deter the flood of Englishmen into the Ohio area. He reported that even the once-loyal Miamis were being won over by the British with their inexpensive and plentiful trade goods, and the Miamis were even influencing neighboring tribes, including the once staunchly loyal Wyandots of the Huron Confederacy. He added, "All I can say is that the nations of these localities are very badly disposed towards the French, and are entirely devoted to the English. I do not know in what way they can be brought back." He continued, "If our traders were sent there for traffic, they could not sell their merchandise at the same price as the English sell theirs, on account of the many expenses they would be obliged to incur."[80]

The primary reason that Memeskia left Quiskakon was simply to take advantage of the more lucrative and desirable trade with the English fur merchants. He concluded that the most expedient way to escape French control was to relocate, so he led his band of Piankashaw Miamis about 75 miles southeast to the Great Miami River, where he established Pickawillany. The shrewd chief strategically situated his town near the juncture of several major Indian trails, which provided easy access to all of the principal towns and villages in the Ohio area. That convenient location certainly contributed to Pickawillany's rapid growth as one of the most important trading hubs in what is now Ohio.

A contemporary description of Pickawillany stated that the "town, immediately became a place of importance to the factors[81] [fur traders]. A number of houses were erected for the accommodation of goods and peltries. These were ordinary log cabins, the trading being carried on below, while an 'upper story' or 'loft' was used to stow skins and combustible material."[82] Once the traders established their presence in the Miami town, they made improvements to protect their investment. The same account states, "Having obtained permission from the Indians, the English in the fall of 1750, began the erection of a stockade, as a place of protection, in case of sudden attack, both for their persons and property. When the main building was completed, it was surrounded with a high wall of split logs, having three gateways."[83] Christopher Gist visited the town in 1751, and he wrote in his journal that Pickawillany was one of the "strongest Indian towns on this continent." Inside the stockade, the traders dug a well, "which furnished an abundant supply of fresh water during the fall, winter, and spring, but failed in the summer. At this time Pickawillany contained four hundred Indian families, and was the residence of the principal chief of the Miami Confederacy."[84]

Describing Memeskia as the "principal chief of the Miamis" is subject to discussion. By the end of 1750, he was perhaps the de facto principal chief, and English traders referred to him as the "Piankashaw King," or the "Great King of the Miamis." However, prior to 1750, Le Pied Froid (Cold Foot) at Quiskakon was deemed to be the principal chief, and Le Gris (The Gray) of the Pepikoika band was the war chief. By 1750, due to Pickawillany's popularity, the village had grown considerably in size and importance, and Memeskia was indeed a powerful chief in his own right. Through 1750 more and more Indians slipped away from their Illinois and Indiana villages to resettle at Pickawillany despite Pied Froid's pleading. That made Pickawillany's importance as a major Indian village superior to that of Quiskakon, and Memeskia's importance as a leader greater than Pied Froid. As a side note, Pied Froid remained loyal to the French, and continued to live at the much-diminished Quiskakon, where he died from smallpox during the winter of 1750–51.

Memeskia's refusal to submit to the French fur-trade monopoly, and the successful growth of Pickawillany as a major English trading hub, irked the French authorities. Rather than stationing troops along the Alleghenies to interdict and seal off the Ohio area from further English encroachment, Governor-General Jonquiére instead decided to chasten and make an example of the recalcitrant tribes who traded with the English. In 1751, he ordered Céloron, who was now commandant at Fort Detroit, to punish the wayward Pickawillany Miamis. Céloron tried to assemble a force of Ottawa, Ojibwe, and Adirondack Indians from the Fort Detroit area, but was unable to muster a sufficient force. Only a group of Adirondacks decided to go it alone, but they were warned off by the warlike Ottawas, who were on friendly terms with the Miamis.

Another attempt to punish the Pickawillany Indians was launched later that year, and about 50 Nippissings and a few warriors from other tribes set out for Memeskia's village. The war party reached Fort Sandoské, where they were met by Ottawa and Ojibwe warriors who threatened them if they harmed the Miamis. Most turned back, but a greatly reduced number continued to Pickawillany, where they found the town mostly empty. An Ottawa woman had raced ahead and warned the town of the approaching raiders. The Nippissings vented their frustration by killing and scalping a Miami man and woman before they returned to Fort Detroit. In retaliation, the angered Miamis killed and scalped two unfortunate French traders who happened to be in the vicinity.

Governor-General Jonquiére died in March 1752 and was succeeded by Charles Le Moyne de Longueuil. Longueuil had a long, distinguished military career, and was inclined to deal more severely with the recalcitrant Miamis at Pickawillany than his predecessor Jonquiére did. Longueuil directed Céloron, who was still commandant at Fort Detroit, to take decisive punitive action against Pickawillany, because the town represented the most flagrant defection from French authority. The action was to be so severe that it would not only force the Pickawillany Miami back into the French fold but would also serve as an unmistakable warning to the other tribes that the French would not tolerate any shift in allegiance toward the English.

Céloron chose Charles Michel Langlade to lead the force against Pickawillany, and if he wanted to severely chastise the Miamis, he couldn't have chosen better. Langlade's father was a French fur trader and his mother was an Ottawa woman who was the sister of Nissowaquet, a noted war chief whom the French called La Fourche (The Fork). Young Charles had been educated by the Jesuits, but it was his mother's Ottawa culture that Charles more readily absorbed. When Langlade was ten, his uncle Nissowaquet took him as a member of a war party against the Chickasaws. Before leaving, Langlade's father told him, "You must go with your uncle, but never let me hear of your showing any marks of cowardice."[85] Apparently young Charles acquitted himself satisfactorily, because he earned the respect of the Ottawa war chiefs, who accorded him the title "Auke-wing-eke-taw-so" (defender of his country). Langlade embraced the Ottawa way of life and was highly respected as a leader and an exceptionally brave and fierce warrior. Various writings described him as honest, ambitious, diplomatic, charming, and courageous, while others portrayed him as egocentric, self-seeking, and possessing a cruel streak.

On Sunday morning, June 21, 1752, just after sunrise, Langlade and his friend, the Ottawa war chief Pontiac, with a strong force of over 250 Ottawa and Ojibwe Indians and some Canadian militia, struck Pickawillany. At the time of the attack, most of the defenders were away hunting, and the invaders swept through the town without much opposition. Many of the inhabitants were killed before they could escape into the woods and a large number were wounded or captured, including Memeskia and five English traders who were in the village. Thirteen of Memeskia's warriors were killed and scalped after they were captured, and Memeskia and one of the traders were ritually killed, boiled and eaten. It's not certain whether Memeskia was ritually cannibalized as a sign of respect for his personal qualities, or whether Langlade's raiders meant to shock the Ohio Indians with a horrific example of what could happen to other defectors from French allegiance.

After the devastating attack, Pickawillany ceased to exist as an Indian village, much less a vibrant trading hub. The Pennsylvanian William Trent, who had been sent with gifts from Virginia Lieutenant Governor Dinwiddie, arrived several days after the attack, and found two French flags flying over the almost deserted village. Some of the surviving Indians scattered into the forest, but most returned to Quiskakon. Pickawillany lay virtually deserted for several years until 1769, when the French-Canadian trader Peter Loramie established a trading post in the immediate vicinity that was called Loramie's Station. During the Revolutionary War, Loramie sided with the British, and his station served as a base of operations for spying and partisan activities against the Americans. In 1780, the Shawnee, who were allied with the British, occupied Pickawillany after their villages in the south had been destroyed, but in 1782 George Rogers Clark destroyed the Shawnee village at Pickawillany and burned Loramie's Station to the ground. They were never rebuilt.

12. Pipe's Town (c. 1787–c. 1795), also Pipetown, Captain Pipe's Town.
Now: Harpster, Wyandot County (40°46'0.00"N–83°11'11.52"W)

Around 1787, Captain Pipe relocated from Tymochtee Creek south to the Little Sandusky River just downstream of its confluence with Broken Sword Creek,[86] about six and a half miles southeast of Upper Sandusky, Ohio, and about one and a third miles west of the old Captives' Town, where the Christian Indians spent the winter of 1781–82. The Northwest

Indian War had begun two years previous, and in October 1786, General Benjamin Logan led a force of 800 Kentuckians up the Great Miami River. They destroyed several Shawnee and Lenape villages, including the towns of Buckongehelas and Blue Jacket. Captain Pipe relocated his village south of the primary Lenape and Wyandot villages around Upper Sandusky to help guard against a large-scale attack from Kentucky. To the southeast of their main village at Upper Sandusky, the Wyandots were in a village called Wyandot Town. The Lenape at Pipe's Town were part of the Indian coalition who continued the fight to preserve their homeland in Ohio, but apparently, Captain Pipe felt no animosity toward the Lenape who chose not to join them, including the Christian Indians who resided in the Moravian villages.

During the America Revolution, Pipe mistrusted the avowed neutrality of the Christian Indians, and recommended their removal from the Tuscarawas River to Captives' Town on the Sandusky River to keep them from mischief. In 1786, the Moravian missionaries and their Christian community returned from their forced exile, stopping for about ten months at a temporary village called Pilgerruh on the Cuyahoga River. While at Pilgerruh, David Zeisberger heard from the commander at Fort Pitt that the Indians in the vicinity of the Tuscarawas were still hostile, and the Moravians and their Christian Indians would be in great danger if they returned to that area. Zeisberger yielded to Butler's advice, and in March 1787, he decided the Christian Indian congregation would relocate to the Petquotting River, which is now called the Huron River, and establish a new community there called New Salem.

Surprisingly, when Captain Pipe and the Lenape Indians on the Sandusky River learned that the Moravians and Christian Indians were relocating west, he, along with Welendawecken and Pomoacan, invited David Zeisberger to establish his mission community in the vicinity of their Lenape towns along the Sandusky River, where they would be protected. Zeisberger demurred and continued to his original destination on the Petquotting (Huron) River. However, the threat of attack from militant Indians followed the Christian community, and in January 1791, Zeisberger wrote in his diary, "We heard very bad and dangerous news on the part of the ill-disposed Indians, of their wicked designs against us."[87] On January 8, Zeisberger sent messengers to Captain Pipe to ascertain the validity of the Indian threat to New Salem, and they returned four days later with a disturbing message. Captain Pipe advised the Christian community to leave New Salem in the spring, and he also admitted that he was going to move farther west.[88] The Moravian community decided to seek refuge in Canada, but apparently Captain Pipe changed his mind and remained in his village on the Sandusky River.

After 1791, it's difficult to follow Captain Pipe's movements, because his son Tahunqueecoppi was also called Captain Pipe, and some events that young Captain Pipe took part in were attributed to his father. Various years are listed for Captain Pipe's death. David Zeisberger's diary notes that Captain Pipe died in 1794, and Dr. Henry C. Shetrone maintains that "Hopocan," or Captain Pipe, died at his town near Upper Sandusky the year before the signing of the 1795 Treaty of Greenville.[89] The 1794 date of Captain Pipe is also accepted by many other historians.

After the death of Captain Pipe in 1794, and the Treaty of Greenville the following year, the residents of Captain Pipe's Town dispersed. Some of the Indians remained in the area living as single families or very small groups, while the majority joined the refugees from the Glaize in present Indiana or in small settlements in the northwest corner of Ohio.

52. *Pluggy's Town (c. 1772–1778), also Mingo Town.*
Now: Delaware, Delaware County (40°18'23.20"N–83°3'41.66"W)

Around 1772, an expatriate Iroquoian Mohawk named Plukkemehnotee, who was also known as Tecanyatereighto, but most often referred to by whites as "Pluggy," established a village at present Delaware, Ohio. His town was situated at present Mingo Park on the horseshoe bend of the Olentangy River. The name Pluggy stemmed from the whites' difficulty in pronouncing Plukkemehnotee. Prior to moving to Ohio, Pluggy took part in the French and Indian War, and fought on the side of the British. Like some of the Six Nations, he left the Iroquois homeland and relocated to present Ohio where the expatriate Iroquois became known as Mingos.

The relentless expansion of white settlements into areas that had been guaranteed by the British Crown as Indian land caused many Ohio tribes to attack white settlements, which led to Lord Dunmore's War. That bloody war was fought from May through October 1774 and culminated with the Treaty of Camp Charlotte after the Indian defeat at the Battle of Point Pleasant. While the treaty caused a cessation of Indian attacks for a time, many of the Shawnee and other disaffected tribes decided to carry on their attacks to try to stop white incursions onto their lands. Several members of Pluggy's family, including women and children, had been killed by white frontiersmen, which incited Pluggy and his band to join those who were carrying on the fight. In fact, by 1775, most of the attacks on white settlements were carried out by Pluggy's band of irreconcilable warriors. In 1776 and 1777, the 2nd Continental Congress considered sending a punitive expedition against Pluggy's village, but the idea was abandoned for fear of inciting a general Indian uprising in the west. On March 13, 1777, the Virginia Assembly also ordered a punitive expedition against Pluggy's Town, but it was cancelled a month later on April 12, 1777.[90] Pluggy's aggressiveness attracted warriors from other tribes including Ojibwe, Wyandot, Ottawa, and Mingo, with the result that Pluggy's Town grew to be quite large. At its peak, there were an estimated 600 or more residents living in log cabins, bark-covered huts, and longhouses, and the town even had a resident French blacksmith.

Pluggy allied with the British faction during the American Revolutionary War, and Henry Hamilton, who was lieutenant-governor of Canada and commander at Fort Detroit, supplied Pluggy and his warriors with guns, ammunition and supplies. Hamilton gained the sobriquet "the hair-buyer," because Americans claimed he paid Indians for American scalps. Hamilton denied he was involved in that practice and was known to have cautioned the Indians to avoid harming women, children and innocent men. He told them they should confine their attacks to legitimate combatants. While there is no documentary evidence that Hamilton actually paid for scalps, it's a fact that the British supplied the Indians with what were described as "scalping knives," and Hamilton was known to accept gifts of scalps from returning war parties. That would indicate that on some level, he was aware and willing to accept that segment of brutal frontier warfare.

Pluggy was a formidable force along the border as he and his warriors raided American homesteads and settlements along the Ohio River in present Pennsylvania, West Virginia, and Kentucky. On Christmas Day 1776, he launched an attack against American settlements in Kentucky, including Harrod's Town at present Harrodsburg, and later that afternoon, his war party ambushed a group of men who were going after gunpowder. On December 29, Pluggy's war party attacked McClelland's Station, at present Georgetown, Kentucky, which contained about thirty families. After several hours of siege, during which a number of defenders were killed, including the town's founder John McClelland, the Indians withdrew toward Ohio.

They were followed by a group of frontiersmen from McClelland's Station who attacked the Indian war party, and during the engagement Pluggy was shot and killed. Legend has it that his warriors carried off Pluggy's body and buried him on a bluff overlooking a nearby spring, and for many years, people claimed they could hear Pluggy shouting his death cry.

Pluggy's village remained at present Delaware after Pluggy's death, and for a time one of its residents was the famous Mingo Chief Logan. However, the successes of American campaigns, like those under George Rogers Clark, forced the Indians to relocate north and west, where most joined other communities in northwest Ohio and around Fort Detroit.

67. Shawnee Town (Shawneetown) (c. 1774–c. 1833).
Now: Lima, Allen County (40°42'19.90"N–84°9'5.13"W)

Shawnee Town was located in present Lima, Ohio, southeast of the junction of the Ottawa River and the Little Ottawa River near the intersection of present Shawnee Road and Fort Amanda Road. It was about ten and a half miles north of the principal Shawnee village of Wapogkonneta on the Auglaize River in present Wapakoneta, Ohio.

It was established around 1774 by militant Shawnee who relocated from the upper Scioto River during Lord Dunmore's War of 1774, and who later sided with the British during the American Revolution. After the Revolutionary War, and during what became known as the Northwest Indian War of 1785–1795, most of the Shawnee continued to fight against American expansion into Ohio. The Shawnee town of Wapogkonetta, and Shawnee Town at present Lima, were ravaged by General Benjamin Logan in August of 1794, but after the Treaty of Greenville in August 1795, many of the Shawnee returned and rebuilt their villages in western Ohio.

In 1811, they once again went to war against the Americans in what was known as Tecumseh's War. Many of the Ohio Shawnee joined Tecumseh against the Americans and allied with the British during the War of 1812. In 1817, the Treaty of Fort Meigs forced the Shawnee to cede all of their lands to the U.S. government, and they were given three reservations in Ohio to share with the Mingo: one at Wapogkonetta; another at present Lewiston, Ohio; and the third, known as the Hog Creek Reservation, in present Lima, Ohio. Although the Shawnee got along well with their white neighbors, in 1830 President Andrew Jackson signed the Indian Removal Act, which forced the Native American tribes to relocate west of the Mississippi River. Around 1833, the Shawnee left their reservation lands in Ohio.

The area around present Heritage Park in Lima was the location of the last Shawnee reservation in Ohio. A council house was erected in 1790 and was used for celebrations, funerals, religious ceremonies, and important meetings. The council house stood until 1834, when it was torn down by the Hover family, who then owned the property.

60. Upper Sandusky (c. 1750–c. 1843),
also Wyandot Old Town, Old Town, Half-King's Town, Dunquat's Town.
Now: Upper Sandusky, Wyandot County
(40°49'34.24"N–83°16'50.74"W)

Upper Sandusky was established about 1747 by Wyandot Indians who were part of Nicholas Orontony's rebellion against the French and their restrictive fur trade monopoly.[91]

That year French troops poured into Fort Detroit to crush Orontony's rebellion before it spread to the other Ohio Indians. Faced with a savage and likely unwinnable war, Orontony abandoned his villages along the south shore of Sandusky Bay and led most of his followers about 105 miles southeast to the confluence of the Muskingum, Walhonding, and Tuscarawas Rivers, at present Coshocton, Ohio, where they established the town of Conshaké.

Not all of the Wyandots followed Orontony to Conshaké. Some traveled south up the Sandusky River, and established the village of Junqueindundeh at present Fremont, Ohio. Junqueindundeh was situated at the lower falls of the Sandusky River, which explains why many sources refer to the town as "Lower Sandusky." Incidentally, the name Sandusky comes from the Wyandot "Sa-un-dus-te," which translates to "water within pools," "cold water," or "pure water."

One band of Wyandots considered Junqueindundeh as still being too near to the French at Fort Detroit, and they continued about 40 miles south of Junqueindundeh to the upper reaches of the Sandusky River, where they established the village of "Upper Sandusky." The location of the Wyandot village was on the site of present Upper Sandusky on the west side of the river, and it is often referred to as "Wyandot Old Town" or simply "Old Town." Various sources locate the Indian town on the east side of the Sandusky River, and other sources place it as much as five miles north. There were in fact several peripheral Indian villages at various times in that area of Wyandot County, which may have caused some of the confusion as to the location of the original Wyandot town. For example, for a time, Tarhe, also known as "The Crane," maintained his own village about five miles north-northeast of Upper Sandusky.

Upper Sandusky became an important town almost immediately after it was established, mainly because of its location on the Sandusky River, and at the junction of several major trails. The trails were the Scioto Trail or Warriors Path, Wappatomica Trail, Black Swamp Trail, Killbuck Trail, and the Watershed

Monument marking site of Crane Town or Tarhe Town where Tarhe died in 1818 (40°53'43.38"N-83°14'36.96"W) (author photograph).

Trail, which provided access to most Indian villages in Ohio as well as routes into Indiana, Kentucky, West Virginia, Pennsylvania, and Michigan.

The Wyandots viewed Ohio as their new homeland, and they realized their best chance of maintaining that homeland was to keep the voraciously land-hungry British from establishing a permanent foothold in the area. When the French were defeated in 1763, the Wyandots joined the Ottawa chief Pontiac's rebellion in 1763–1764, which was an abortive effort to expel the British from the trans-Allegheny region. Then, during the American Revolution and the War of 1812, the Wyandots considered an alliance with the British against the Americans as their best hope for preserving Ohio as an Indian homeland.

One of the notable chiefs at Upper Sandusky was Dunquat (also known as Pomoacan or Petawontakas). Dunquat was head of the Wyandot, and while the term "chief" is almost universally accepted as a designation for the leader of a community of Indians, Wyandot leadership was more sophisticated than traditional chiefdoms. Leaders were chosen for their ability to wisely influence and negotiate as well as for their leadership in war. During the American Revolutionary War, Dunquat allied with the British, and was regarded as a "Half-King," or one of the leading voices of the Wyandots. Half-king is a British-coined term, which meant Dunquat was representative or spokesperson of the council, and indeed many sources simply refer to Dunquat as half-king. That can be confusing, since several Indian leaders also carried the half-king designation. Perhaps the most famous half-king was the Seneca chief Tanacharison, who represented the Iroquois Council and interacted with young George Washington in 1753–1754. Dunquat is best known for his role in the forced removal of the Moravian missionaries and Christian Indians from the towns along the Tuscarawas River to Captives' Town in 1781. Although he was a Wyandot, Dunquat once unexplainably intimated he was Iroquois, which may simply have meant that as half-king he interacted between the Wyandots and the Iroquois Council.

Incidentally, the Wyandots at Upper Sandusky accepted fugitive slaves, and by 1800 there was a community of African Americans living in close proximity to the Wyandot village. The black community included one white man named Wright, who was married to an African-American woman.

The Wyandots were traditionally regarded as particularly fierce warriors. According to legend, Captain William Wells, also known as Apekonit (Carrot Top), who was the son-in-law of Little Turtle of the Miami, was asked by General Anthony Wayne to bring back a prisoner from Upper Sandusky for intelligence-gathering purposes. Wells, who had been captured at a young age and raised by the Indians, replied, "He could bring in a prisoner, but not from Sandusky, because there were none but Wyandots at Sandusky, and they would not be taken alive."[92]

Another famous person associated with Upper Sandusky was the frontiersman Simon Girty (1741–1818). Girty was considered by many Americans to be a villainous renegade, who terrorized American settlements along the Ohio frontier. That nefarious reputation was enhanced by author Zane Grey, who made Girty the chief villain in his books about the Ohio frontier, *The Spirit of the Border* and *The Last* Trail. Certainly, Girty and his brothers were in sympathy with the Indians who wanted to preserve Ohio as an Indian homeland. In fact, the Girtys were probably more Indian in nature than white, but their wicked reputation is probably undeserved. In 1756, when Simon Girty was fifteen, he and his brothers Thomas, James, and George were captured by Indians. Thomas escaped, but Simon was adopted and raised by the Ohio Mingos, James by the Shawnee, and George by the Lenape. The brothers were repatriated during Bouquet's expedition in 1764, but they had almost fully assimilated into the Indian culture. Soon after their repatriation, the three left their white homes and returned to live among the Indians. Simon Girty spoke eleven different languages, including English, French and several different Indian dialects, which prompted the British to appoint him as an Indian agent for the Ohio Indians. In addition, Girty often served as interpreter at various meetings and councils between Indian factions and between Indians and whites. In 1778, Girty was living among the Wyandots at Upper Sandusky[93] when the famous American frontiersman Simon Kenton (1756–1836) was brought into the town as a prisoner. Kenton was condemned to be tortured and burned at the stake, but Girty and Kenton had been close friends some time before, and when Girty recognized Kenton, he interceded and was able to spare Kenton's life.

In 1781, the British and their Indian allies believed the Moravians and their Christian Indians along the Tuscarawas River were in fact forwarding information to the Americans that was harmful to the British. Based on the writings of David Zeisberger, the Moravians may have in fact been more sympathetic to the American cause, but outwardly they tried to maintain a strict neutrality. Unfortunately, in time of war, that's a difficult position when everyone is assumed to support one side or the other. It's simply a case of "If you're not with us, you must be against us," or as the Oneida Half-King Scarouady once said, "You can't live in the woods and be neutral."[94]

In the summer of 1781, the influential chiefs along the Sandusky River, including Captain Pipe and the Wyandot Dunquat, persuaded Major William DePeyster at Fort Detroit to relocate the Moravians and the "praying Indians" to the Sandusky River area, where they could be closely watched. So in August of that year, a combined force of about 300 Indians, including Wyandot, Shawnee, Ojibwe, and Ottawa warriors led by Loyalist Captain Matthew Elliott (1739–1814), appeared at the Moravian villages and escorted the inhabitants back to the Sandusky River. The group arrived at Upper Sandusky around October 1, 1781, and were told to establish a village about six and a half miles southeast near the mouth of Broken Sword Creek on the Sandusky River. Because they had been forced to relocate, the Moravians named their new village "Captives' Town." (See Captives' Town.)

In 1782, Colonel William Crawford, who was a personal friend of George Washington, led a punitive mission against the Indians along the Sandusky River to retaliate for Indian raids against American settlements. The main thrust of Crawford's expedition was against the Wyandot village at Upper Sandusky. Crawford and his troops penetrated Upper Sandusky and stopped for water at a spring, which is now called "the old Indian spring" on the property of the Elk's Lodge at East Wyandot Avenue and North 4th Street. Coincidentally, British author Charles Dickens visited the site in 1842, and drank from the same spring.

On June 4, 1782, Crawford and his army of about 500 militiamen moved about two and a half miles north from Upper Sandusky and encountered a force of between 350 and 600 Wyandot and Indians. The fighting centered around a grove of trees near the present intersection of Ohio 67 (Tarhe Trail) and Township Route 121. During the fight, Captain Pipe's warriors outflanked the Americans and drove them into defensive positions in and around the grove of trees, which became known as "Battle Island." The Americans had clearly lost the initiative. During a lull, Simon Girty approached the American positions with a white flag and asked them to surrender. But the Americans thought they inflicted more casualties than they actually had, and they believed the Indians were losing the stomach for the fight. That belief was reinforced the next day, when the Indians sniped at the Americans from long range. In fact, the Indians were waiting for British reinforcements that arrived that afternoon. British agent Alexander McKee arrived with 140 Shawnee under Chief Blacksnake, and the additional warriors were able to complete the encirclement of the American positions. The Americans had no alternative but to attempt a stealthy withdrawal under cover of darkness, but they were discovered, and the retreat turned into a disorganized rout.

Colonel Crawford lost contact with the main body, and he and a small group followed the Sandusky River to the south and southeast. On June 7, Crawford and Dr. John Knight were discovered by Lenape Indians under Chief Wingenund and taken prisoner. The two men were marched to the Lenape village on Tymochtee Creek near present Crawford, Ohio, and on June 11, 1782, Crawford was stripped, beaten, horribly tortured and burned at the stake. Simon Girty was present when Crawford was tortured and killed. Four years earlier in 1778, Girty had saved Simon Kenton from a similar fate, but though Crawford begged him to intercede, Girty was unable to spare Crawford's life. While prisoners were often exchanged or adopted, Crawford was killed in retaliation for his role in the destruction of

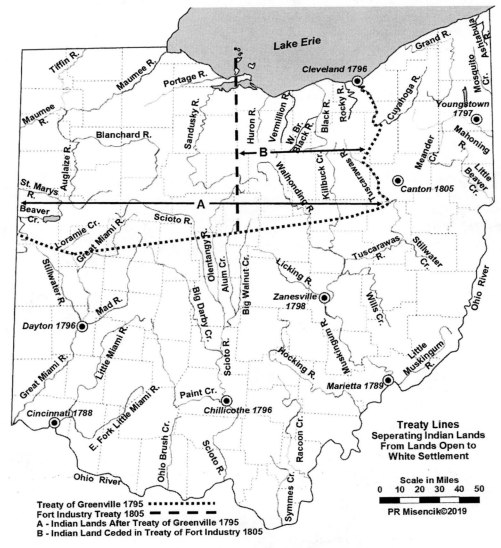

Ohio Indian lands as a result of 1805 Treaty of Fort Industry.

two Indian villages during Lord Dunmore's War (1774), and his supposed participation in the attack and massacre of the Moravian Indians three months earlier at Gnadenhütten.[95]

After the American Revolutionary War, the British ceded all lands east of the Mississippi River to the Americans, excepting Canada and Spanish possessions in Florida. In the Treaty of Paris, little or no effort was made to protect the homelands of the Indians. In fact, even before the Revolutionary War ended, a tidal wave of settlers poured into the area. The Indians fought back, and after each of the Indians wars, treaties were signed that guaranteed a homeland for the Indians, but none stemmed the flow of whites onto Indian lands. Most whites viewed the Indian treaties as meaningless, because Indians were considered little more than forest animals without any more legal status than the birds, bears, or deer.

The British made a minor effort to formalize an Indian homeland in the Treaty of Ghent (1814), which ended the War of 1812, but the effort never gained traction. The Land Ordinance of 1785, along with the treaties of Greenville in 1795, and Fort Industry in 1805, signaled the beginning of the end of Indian homelands in Ohio. The Land Ordinance of 1785 set up a standardized system for whites to purchase land in the undeveloped areas, which included most of the remaining Indian treaty lands. The Land Ordinance partitioned land into six-by-six-mile squares called townships, which were further subdivided into one-by-one-mile square sections of 640 acres, and the Indians were required to relocate onto specific township reserves. In addition, the Fort Industry Treaty moved the eastern boundary of the Indian reserve west approximately 62 miles from the Cuyahoga River, or 120 miles from the Pennsylvania state line. That adjustment took more than a half-million acres of Ohio land away from the Indians.

The Treaty of Fort Meigs in 1817 forced the Indians to cede all of their remaining Ohio lands in northwest Ohio, and in return the tribes were allocated specific reserves. The Wyandots under Dunquat received a twelve-mile square equal to four townships surrounding Upper Sandusky, called "The Grand Reserve." In addition, the Wyandots were granted a separate one-mile-square cranberry bog near Broken Sword Creek. However, within twenty-six years, even those small reserves were taken from the Indians.

The end of the Indian reserves in Ohio was a result of Andrew Jackson's Indian Removal Act of 1830, which directed that all eastern Indians be relocated west of the Mississippi River. By 1840, the only Indian communities in Ohio were the Wyandots in the Upper Sandusky area, who refused to move. The U.S. government exerted pressure upon them to comply, and on July 12, 1843, the last of the Wyandots in Ohio at Upper Sandusky departed for Kansas.

8. Wakatomika #2 (c. 1775–1786), also Wapatomica, Waketomika, Waketameki.
Now: Bellefontaine, Logan County (40°18'31.15"N–83°42'9.56"W)

After the destruction of Wakatomika on the Muskingum River during Lord Dunmore's War in 1774, Kisinoutha led his community of Shawnee about ninety miles west to the Mad River, where they established a new village also called Wakatomika. The town was situated on the west bank of the Mad River on present County Route 5, less than two-tenths of a mile northeast of its intersection with County Route 29.

With the move to the Mad River, the Mekoche chief Kisinoutha, who had previously advocated for peace with the Americans, began to shift to the more militant philosophy of the western Shawnee. After years of treaty violations, they concluded that it was impractical to remain neutral. The final straw for the Shawnee occurred when American Colonel Brodhead bluntly told the Mekoche chiefs that they would have to demonstrate their friendship to the Americans by taking up the hatchet against the British and their Indian allies. Brodhead's ultimatum stunned the Shawnee, who still hoped to tread a peaceful path between the warring factions, but when Kisinoutha and Nimwha, the two strongest remaining proponents of peace, died that winter, most of their people concluded that neutrality was no longer an option, and they joined the militant faction on the side of the British. The American authorities immediately denounced the Wakatomika Shawnee as treacherous rebels and called them a banditti of savages.

Wakatomika became one of the centers for the warring Shawnee, and a jumping-off point for raids into Kentucky and along the Virginia frontier. In 1778, the noted frontiersman Simon Kenton was captured on one of the raids. His face was painted black, and he was pronounced cut-ta-ho-tha, which meant that he would be ritually tortured and burned to death. On the way to Upper Sandusky, he was forced to run the gantlet at Wakatomika. Fortunately for Kenton, he impressed the Indians with his bravery, and by stoically enduring other tortures. At Upper Sandusky he was spared from death and adopted by a motherly squaw whose own son had been killed, but within the year Kenton escaped and made his way back to Kentucky.

Now that the Shawnee were fully engaged, the war chiefs took over leadership of the Shawnee, and in 1781, the Pekowi war chief Aquitsica at Wakatomika traveled to Fort Detroit to ask the British for assistance against the Americans. The Shawnee launched bloody attacks against the Kentucky settlements, but by the early 1780s, the white population of Kentucky had grown to nearly ten thousand, and any hope of reclaiming Shawnee lands south of the Ohio River were gone forever. Worse, the Kentuckians launched devastating raids against the Shawnee settlements in Ohio, and not only burned Shawnee villages, but also destroyed their crops in a war of attrition.

When the Revolutionary War ended in 1783, British assistance to the Shawnee abruptly ceased, but the Shawnee grimly continued the fight for their homeland. American emissaries castigated the Shawnee, telling them the war was over, and as being on the losing side they must stop fighting. The Shawnee scoffed at the American demand, and said they had not been defeated, so they saw no reason to quit fighting. The young Wakatomika war chief Kekewepelethy or Captain Johnny added, "You seem to grow proud, because you have thrown down the King of England, but neither he nor his tribespeople were ready to give away their land just because George III had signed a piece of paper across the ocean."[96]

However, the pacifistic Mekoche hokimas once again tried to take control, and the old chief Moluntha, who succeeded Kisinoutha as the ceremonial hokima, sought to enter peace talks with the Americans. The most vocal opposition to Moluntha and the peace faction were the militant Shawnee at Wakatomika, which by now had become a mixed Shawnee and Mingo community. Once again, the Shawnee Nation was divided, but the issue was further complicated by a third faction who were tired of the constant wars and opted to distance themselves from the aggressively land-hungry white men by relocating west of the Mississippi River.

In 1784, the Wakatomika war chief Aquitsica died, and was succeeded by his close ally and equally militant chief Waweyapiersenwaw or Blue Jacket. The war chief at Wakatomika was Peteusha, who sided with Blue Jacket and also refused to negotiate with the Americans. Through the summer of 1786, Wakatomika Shawnee joined Blue Jacket's Indians in attacks against the American settlements along the Ohio River and in Kentucky. When the Kentuckians retaliated, their strength and numbers overwhelmed the war-weary Shawnee. In October 1786, in the opening stage of what would be known as the Northwest Indian War, Colonel Bejamin Logan raised a large force of Kentucky militia, and without official authorization, marched against the Shawnee towns on the Great Miami and Mad Rivers. His attack destroyed many of the Shawnee towns, along with the crops the Indians needed to survive the winter, and Wakatomika was one of the primary targets. The result was that over one thousand Shawnee were forced to retreat north to the Maumee and St. Mary's Rivers, where they were closer to their Miami Indian allies, and where they would hopefully gain support from the British in Canada.

63. *Wapogkonetta (c. 1774–1831), also Wapaghkanetta, Wapahkanetta, Wapakonákunge, Wapoghoognata, Wappaukenata, Warpicanata, Wauphauthawonaukee, and others.*
Now: Wapakoneta, Auglaize County (40°34'8.08"N–84°11'38.16"W)

Wapogkonetta was a Shawnee village on the Auglaize River at present Wapakoneta in Auglaize County, Ohio. It was established around 1774 by Shawnee who had relocated from the upper Scioto River area. The name means "white jacket," and was supposedly named after the Shawnee chief who initially established the village. The village was located on the Auglaize Trail that ran from present Defiance, Ohio, to its junction with the Miami Trail at Loramie's Store in present western Shelby County.

The inhabitants of Wapogkonetta were militant Shawnee who fought white European incursions into Kentucky and Ohio during the Northwest Indian War (1785 to 1795). The town was destroyed in October 1786 by a strong force of Kentuckians under General Benjamin Logan. After the defeat of the Indians at the Battle of Fallen Timbers in August 1794, General Anthony Wayne allowed the tribes to resettle their old village sites. As a result, Catahecassa, known as "Black Hoof" (c. 1740–1831), who was the principal chief of the Shawnee, reestablished the village of Wapogkonetta at its old site, and at the time the town was the principal Shawnee village.

Following the 1795 Treaty of Greenville, Catahecassa realized the Indians had no hope of defeating the Americans and reclaiming their land, so he encouraged the Shawnee to adopt a white style of living. As a result, they established cattle herds, a gristmill, and a sawmill, and farmed over two hundred acres in the area.

Catahecassa's Village refused to support Tecumseh's uprising in 1808, and they remained neutral during the War of 1812. In 1826, most of the villagers relocated to Kansas, with only a very few remaining at Wapogkonetta. Catahecassa died at Wapogkonetta in 1831.

Eleven

Towns and Posts of Southwest Ohio

"We must protect the forest for our children, grandchildren and children yet to be born. We must protect the forests for those who can't speak for themselves such as the birds, animals, fish and trees."—Chief Edward Moody

3. Beaver's New Town (1750s–1830s), also Hockhocking, Assinink, Assünnünk, Assünink, Ach-sin-sink, Standing Stone.
Now: Lancaster, Fairfield County (39°42'44.60"N–82°36'28.77"W)

Most of the Lenape supported Pontiac's Rebellion of 1763–1764, and when the tide turned in favor of the British, Tamaqua (Beaver or King Beaver) decided to move his village farther west from present Bolivar, Ohio, to a location beyond the reach of British troops. Tamaqua led the Lenape about 90 miles southwest, where they established their village at the head of the Hockhocking River, now called the Hocking. His town was near Standing Stone, which is now called Mount Pleasant at present Lancaster, Ohio.[1] The town was situated near the intersection of the Ohio–Standing Stone Trail, the Belpre Trail, and the Coshocton Trail.

The death of Shingas the previous winter elevated Tamaqua to the sole leadership of the Lenape village, and though the new town was called Hock-

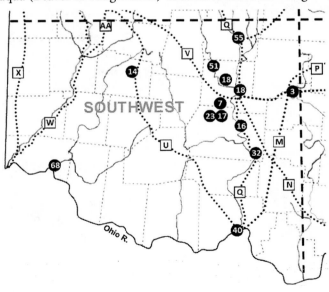

Numbers may represent more than one community in fairly close proximity.

215

hocking, it was also predictably referred to as Beaver's New Town. Apparently, a few Lenape families lived in the vicinity from an earlier time, because Christopher Gist visited the site in 1751, and he mentioned encountering Delaware or Lenape Indians who lived there. His journal entry for Saturday, January 19, 1751, reads, "W 15 M, to Hockhockin a small town with only four or five Delaware [Lenape] families."[2] Historian William Darlington expanded on Gist's journal entry with the following note:

> January 19—Hockhockin, now Lancaster, Fairfield County, the "Standing Stone" or Ach-sin-sink of the Delawares [Lenape], is a rocky eminence near the town. Visited by the Rev. David Jones in 1773. He mentions in his journal 'February 9th, at the Standing Stone. This town consists chiefly of Delaware Indians. It is situated on a creek called Hock-hock-in. Hack-hack is a Delaware word, and signifies a gourd with a neck; also applied to bottles. Hockhocking from the shape of the creek, resembling that of a bottle.' John Brickell's account: he was for five years a prisoner among the Delawares in Ohio. Marked Hockhocking or French Margaret's town on Evans' Map of the Middle Colonies, 1755. Mitchell's ditto, Pownall's of 1776 ditto. French Margaret was a daughter of Madame Montour. It is probable she resided here at one time.[3]

With regard to Darlington's comment, we can't be certain what relation the French Margaret mentioned here was to Madame Montour. See the "French Margaret's Town" entry in this book.

Lieutenant Thomas Hutchins apparently visited Hockhocking in 1763 or 1764, and mentioned the town in his description of the route from Fort Pitt:

> The path leads through Level, Rich Land for 3 miles, to Licking Creek, 30 yards wide, at which is A good ford.[4] Then through Level wet Land, but Not Swampy, and Shrubby only in some places, 28 miles to the Beaver's New Town, on A branch of Hockhocking River, about a half A Mile above the Ford. This Town had, last Spring [1763?], about 15 Houses in it, and Consisted of thirty Warriors and near 80 women & Children; but as the Indians some distance from it purposed Moving to it immediately, it's very probable the Warriors there now are more Numerous than they were then. Their Houses are close to each other, and their Cornfields are between the Town and the Path.[5]

Tamaqua died around 1769–1770, and was succeeded by Welepachtschiechen, who was better known as Captain Johnny. At the beginning of the Revolutionary War, a number of Christian Lenape from the Tuscarawas and Muskingum area moved to Hockhocking, or Assünnünk, as the Moravian missionaries referred to it.[6] Their intention was to distance themselves from possible major military actions.[6] By 1776, the Shawnee had also established a village called Shawnee Town, a short distance southwest of the Lenape village of Hockhocking. In 1777, Captain Johnny decided to return to the Tuscarawas River, where he and several of his followers joined the Christian Indians in the Moravian settlements. He was among those murdered by Pennsylvania militia in the infamous Gnadenhütten Massacre on March 8, 1782.

The end of the Revolutionary War brought a flood of settlers and land speculators into the area guaranteed to the Indians by the 1768 Fort Stanwix Treaty, which essentially defined the Indians' homeland as west of Fort Stanwix, at present Rome, New York, and north of the Ohio River. In 1785, the Indians were forced to accept the more onerous Treaty of Fort MacIntosh, which took additional Indian lands in southern and eastern Ohio and confined the Indians to the northwestern corner of the present state. The treaty area was a line that ran roughly from the Cuyahoga and the Tuscarawas Rivers to Fort Laurens at present Bolivar, Ohio, then west to Pickawillany on the Miami River. From there the line continued to present Fort Wayne and then to Lake Erie, where it followed the shoreline east to the Cuyahoga River.

Hockhocking at Standing Stone was outside the new Indian area, which marked the end of the Indian villages there. The Ohio Indians fought to hold onto their land, but after they were defeated at the Battle of Fallen Timbers in 1794, they were forced to make further land concessions in the 1795 Treaty of Greenville. Most of the Lenape moved west, and some settled in the multinational settlement of the Glaize on the Maumee River. After the War of 1812, few Lenape remained in Ohio, and the Indian Removal Act of 1830 forced the relocation of all Indians to the unsettled areas west of the Mississippi River. The last Indian villages were vacated when the Wyandots were forced off their reserve at Upper Sandusky in 1843.

7. Blue Jacket's Town #1 (c. 1758–c. 1777).
Now: Williamsport, Pickaway County (39°30'37.13"N–83° 6'26.22"W)

In a nation of noted warriors, Blue Jacket (c. 1743–1810), or Waweyapiersenwaw (Whirlpool) was the most renowned Shawnee war leader in the Northwest Indian War (1785–1795), and he was the predecessor war chief of the famous Shawnee leader Tecumseh. In 1778, British Lieutenant-Colonel Henry Hamilton described him as a young chief of about thirty-five.

The first mention of Blue Jacket was in the journal of Baptist missionary David Jones, who visited Blue Jacket's Town in January 1773. It's important to note that as a relatively young man of about thirty, he was prominent enough that whites referred to his village as Blue Jacket's Town. Some sources indicate that Blue Jacket was born in present Ross County, but since the Scioto villages weren't established until around 1758, it's more likely that he was born at Lower Shawnee Town at present Portsmouth, Ohio. Not much is known of his parentage or family members except that he had a sister and he referred to someone as "brother." That person was Musquaconocah or Red Pole. Red Pole, who was slightly younger, also became a chief and noted orator. The Shawnee often used the term "brother" to recognize a blood relationship, such as first cousins, but Blue Jacket used the term in a way that implied they were half-brothers who shared the same mother.[7] The sept of a Shawnee was inherited from the father, and since Blue Jacket was a Peckowe and Red Pole was a Mekoche, they would have had different fathers, so most likely their mother had two husbands. The closeness of the two half-brothers resulted in a unique power-sharing situation whereby the two brothers controlled the two main leadership positions of the Shawnee nation. The Peckowe Blue Jacket became the senior war chief, and Red Pole as a Mekoche was the hokima, or civil leader in times of peace.

When Shawnee children were born, they were given a name, and in adulthood the Shawnee were permitted to choose their own name. Blue Jacket was named Sepettekenathe, or Big Rabbit, which he used until about 1776, and then he chose the name Waweyapiersenwaw, or Whirlpool. However, for some unknown reason he was generally referred to as Blue Jacket. There is no documentation regarding how that name came to be associated with him.

Blue Jacket had two wives. His first was a white woman named Margaret Moore, who had been captured when she was about nine during the French and Indian War. She was adopted and raised in the Shawnee towns and became the wife of Blue Jacket. They had a son named Joseph, and when she was pregnant with her second child, she visited her family. Margaret was on good terms with Blue Jacket, but her family persuaded her to stay with them, and Margaret's daughter Nancy was born in the white settlements. Blue Jacket's second wife was a half-French and half-Shawnee woman who was the daughter of French trader Jacques Dupéront Baby and his Shawnee wife. The girl was raised by the Shawnee, and though she understood French, she could only speak Shawnee. Blue Jacket and his second wife had at least four children, Jim Blue Jacket, Mary Louise, Sally, and George Blue Jacket.[8]

In January 1773, David Jones described Blue Jacket's Town as being located on the east bank of Deer Creek and north of a large plain. He said the creek was clear and beautiful and would have been useful for mills and healthful for the inhabitants. He said the buildings in Blue Jacket's Town were constructed of logs, and there were about twelve of them. According to Jones, Blue Jacket's Town was near the Scioto Trail, about three miles west-northwest of Pickoweekee (Pecowick), which would place it just east of Deer Creek almost astride the county line separating present Ross and Pickaway Counties, about 2.3 miles east of present Clarksburg, Ohio.

With the start of the American Revolutionary War in 1775, the Shawnee were undecided whether to remain neutral or ally themselves with the British. Not many Shawnee were in favor of supporting the American cause, since most of the of settlers pouring onto Indian lands were from Virginia and Pennsylvania. At first, Blue Jacket sided with the neutral or peace-seeking faction, who believed friendship and diplomacy with the Americans was the best way to preserve their lands. In 1776, Blue Jacket accompanied Cornstalk and other peace-seekers to the Muskingum River, where they considered relocating their villages near the neutral Lenape. However, by 1777, Blue Jacket opted to enter the war on the side of the British, and later that year, he abandoned his village on Deer Creek and relocated some seventy miles northwest to his new village at present Bellefontaine, Ohio, in Logan County.

16. *Chillicothe (c. 1750s–c. 1778).*
Now: *Chillicothe, Ross County (39°22'40.00"N–82°58'40.05"W)*

There is little documentary evidence that a Shawnee town called Chillicothe was located in the present Ohio city of Chillicothe, Ohio. The closest Indian community would have been just north of the present city. Robert White McFarland wrote in *The Chillicothes*: "Chillicothe—Now called Hopetown, three miles north of the present city of that same name in Ross County. When I lived in Chillicothe over half a century ago, this village was usually called 'Old Town,' in reference to the old Indian village. The present city of Chillicothe does not occupy the site of an Indian town of this name."[9] Historian Charles Hanna also refers to the town, but only in reference to McFarland. He writes: "According to Mr. R.W. McFarland, a fourth Chillicothe stood on the east side of the Scioto, three miles north of the present town of Chillicothe, the county seat of Ross County, and on the site now occupied by the village of Hopetown."[10] Hopetown is an unincorporated community in Ross County, Ohio. No other information concerning a Shawnee village in this vicinity has been found.

17. *Chilicothe (c. 1758–1787),*
also Upper Chillicothe, Old Chillicothe, Lower Shawnee Town.
Now: *Frankfort, Ross County (39°24'5.80"N–83°10'51.44"W)*

The Shawnee most often named their villages according to the predominant sept of the town's inhabitants. The word Chillicothe was a corruption of Chalahgawatha, and when it was used in the context of the name of a village, it simply meant "principal place of the Chalahgawathas." Other Shawnee towns like Maqueechaick, or Macacheek, refer to the principal town of the Mekoches sept, Piqua the town of the Pekuwe sept, and likewise Kispoko for the Kispokotha sept. Since the Shawnee relocated for various reasons, it's understandable that there were several Shawnee villages in Ohio with the same name. When the Chalahgawatha Shawnee moved, they simply designated their new principal village as Chillicothe. That was the case with Chillicothe on the Ohio or Lower Shawnee Town at present Portsmouth, Ohio. In 1758, the Shawnee abandoned the town to relocate farther up the Scioto River, where another Chillicothe was established. In addition, white frontiersmen from Kentucky often raided Shawnee villages in Ohio, which prompted the residents to relocate to a new Chillicothe in order to distance themselves from their adversaries. The same was true of the other septs, like the Pekowis and their Piqua towns.

The Shawnee referred to their town at the mouth of the Scioto at present Portsmouth as Chillicothe, but white men called it Lower Shawnee Town, and it was shown as such on most maps. Confusing to many historians was the fact that after the Shawnee established new villages up the Scioto River, whites referred to the old Shawnee village at Portsmouth as "Old Lower Shawnee Town," and the new principal Chalahgawatha village on the upper Scioto as "Lower Shawnee Town," which had been the name of the village at the mouth of the Scioto River. The two locations were shown that way on Thomas Hutchins's map of 1778, although he spells them "Old Lower Shawanoe T." and "Lower Shawanoe T.," respectively. The village at present Frankfort was sometimes referred to as "Upper Chillicothe" and "Old Chillicothe."

There is some confusion among historians regarding which of the Upper Scioto towns were called Chillicothe, because some sources indicate that Kispoko, at present Westfall, Ohio, was called Chillicothe. Since the towns were generally named after the sept of its inhabitants, it stands to reason that Kispoko would have Kispokotha residents, while Chillicothe would be a town of Chalahgawatha residents. Much of that confusion stems from the relatively close proximity of the Shawnee towns to each other in that area. So, a community of Chalahgawatha Shawnee that was near a Kispokotha town could cause some confusion.

The Chillicothe we are discussing here was situated between Oldtown Run and the North Fork of Paint Creek at present Frankfort, Ohio. According to Baptist missionary David Jones, the Indians called Paint Creek Alamoneetheepeeca, which according to Jones meant "Paint Creek." Jones visited the town on Friday, February 22, 1773, and wrote that a trader named John Irwine, who resided in a neighboring Shawnee town, kept a storehouse at Chillicothe. According to Jones, a gunsmith from Lancaster, Pennsylvania, named Moses Henry lived at Chillicothe among the Shawnee. Henry was married to a white woman who as a young girl had been captured by the Shawnee, and Henry chose to live in her village. Jones said, "Mr. Henry lives in a comfortable manner, having plenty of good beef, pork, milk, &c."[11] He also described the town thusly: "Chillicaathee [*sic*] is the chief town of the Shawanee Indians—it is situated north of a large plain adjacent to a branch of Paint Creek. This plain is their corn-field, which supplies great part of their town. Their houses are made of logs, nor is there any more regularity observed in this particular than in their morals, for any man erects his house as fancy directs."[12] Jones mentioned an ancient earthwork from the Ohio mound-builder culture to the north of the Indian town: "North of this town are to be seen the remains of an old fortification, the area of which may be fifteen acres, and appears to have gates at each corner. It lies near four square, and in the middle likewise. From the west middle gate, went a circular entrenchment including about ten acres."[13] That earthwork was described in *The Archeological Atlas of Ohio*, which reads, "A typical work of the square-and-circle combination formerly existed at the eastern edge of the city of Chillicothe and another of similar type was located at the town of Frankfort."[14]

Jones met the chief he called Othaawaapeelethee,[15] or Yellow Hawk. Yellow Hawk (c. 1728–c. 1817) belonged to the Thawikilas sept, and moved from Alabama to Ohio in 1755. He fought for the French during the French and Indian War and was at Braddock's Defeat in 1755. He fought on the side of Cornstalk through the Ohio Indian Wars from 1755 through Lord Dunmore's War in 1774,[16] but after the defeat at Point Pleasant, Yellow Hawk returned to Alabama to distance himself from possible white reprisals.

David Jones met Yellow Hawk in February 1773, fifteen months prior to Lord Dunmore's War. Being a member of the Thawikila sept, it's unlikely that Yellow Hawk was the principal chief at Chillicothe, since it was primarily a Chalahgawatha town. He may have resided in a nearby Thawikila town, or possibly chose to live among the Chalahgawathas. Neucheconneh was likely the hokima or village leader at Chillicothe, since he had been one of the principal chiefs at Lower Shawnee Town on the Ohio River. Cottawamago (also Mkahdaywaymayqua) or Blackfish (c. 1729–1779) may also have been a chief there until he moved west to join the Indians allied with the British after the start of the Revolutionary War. Other prominent chiefs in the area, like Hokolesqua or Cornstalk, and Waweyapiersenwaw or Blue Jacket, had their own towns. Nimwha, who some sources indicate was the brother of Cornstalk and Nonhelema, was likely the chief of the Chalahgawatha village called Chillicothe that was adjacent to Kispoko, but not to be confused with Chillicothe at present Frankfort, Ohio.

Jones ran afoul of Yellow Hawk during their meeting, and he described the encounter thusly:

> This Indian is one of their chiefs, and esteems himself as a great speaker and very wise: and this may be justly said of him, that he is saucy enough.... After common formalities were past, he told me he wanted to know my business among them; for he understood that I was no trader. First, informed him from whence I came, and that my chief business was to instruct them from God, for his mind was revealed to us, &c.—That I had a great desire for many years to see my brothers the Indians—now wanted to talk with them, and was in hopes that he would allow me an opportunity. He replied that he thought something of that nature was my business. Then he proceeded to make a long speech, not with a very pleasant countenance, nor the most agreeable tone of voice, and replied to the effect, viz. 'When God, who at first made us all, prescribed our way of living, he allowed white people to live one way, and Indians another way'; and as he was one of the chiefs of this town, he did not desire to hear me on the subject of religion, for he was resolved not to believe what might be said, nor pay any regard to it. And he believed it would be the mind of the other Indians.... He said that they had lived a long time as they now do, and liked it very well, and he and his people would live as they had done.[17]

Jones began to argue and harangue, and Yellow Hawk became angry at Jones's insulting breech of etiquette. That prompted some warriors present to approach Jones with the intention of killing him, but his life was saved by some Shawnee "Peace Women" who didn't want to cause an incident that might result in reprisals. Jones apparently didn't learn from that experience, because a short time later, he enraged the Indians a second time, and as a warrior rose to tomahawk him, he was saved by two or three squaws, one of whom was "Blinking Woman," a noted person of the Shawnee, who stepped in and saved Jones.[18]

Because there were several Shawnee villages scattered in the area of the Scioto River between present Chillicothe and Circleville, journals and accounts of white visitors make it difficult to determine exactly which village they were mentioning. Often, they erroneously use the name of a neighboring village, or they use a generic term like "Shawnee Town." Also, since the villages were in fairly close proximity to one another, Indians from one village, including the chiefs, would visit neighboring towns, and when the chiefs are mentioned, it's difficult to determine if they were from that village or visitors from a neighboring town.

As far as can be determined, Chillicothe at present Frankfort was a viable Shawnee community from about 1758 until about 1778, when a schism divided the Shawnee along the Scioto between those who wanted war and those who advocated peace. Those who wanted to fight moved west to join the other Indian allies of the British along the Great Miami, Little Miami, and Mad Rivers. Those who wished for peace relocated east near the Lenape under White Eyes at the Forks of the Muskingum. However, after the deaths of peace advocates Nimwha and Kisinoutha the following winter, many of the Shawnee at the Forks of the Muskingum joined their more militant tribesmen at the Little Miami and Mad River settlements. Several Shawnee, along with members of other Indian nations, remained in the Scioto village through the end of the American Revolutionary War, but in 1787, the town was attacked and destroyed by Americans during the Northwest Indian War.

14. *Chillicothe (c. 1775–c. 1807), also Old Chillicothe, Old Town.*
NOW: OLDTOWN, GREENE COUNTY (39°43'49.00"N–83°56'16.00"W)

Another Chillicothe established in Greene County around 1775 at the start of the American Revolutionary War was one of several Shawnee villages in Ohio with that name. Chillicothe used in the context of a town or village means "principal village of the Chalahgawatha sept," and Chillicothe at Oldtown became the principal city of the more militant faction of Shawnees, who opted to fight against white expansion into Ohio and Kentucky. Its chief was the famous Chalahgawatha war chief Blackfish (c. 1729–1779), who was also known as Cottawamago and Mkahdaywaymayqua. Blackfish's town was located at present Oldtown in Greene County, Ohio, less than one-half mile southeast of the confluence of the Little Miami River and Massies Creek, and about three miles north of the center of present Xenia, Ohio.

Blackfish was one of first leaders to relocate west to the Miami and Mad Rivers, where he was encouraged and supplied by British agents to carry out raids on American settlements in Kentucky. The Shawnee had long considered Kentucky as their private hunting ground, and their fight to defend it from American encroachment resulted in Lord Dunmore's War of 1774. At the end of Lord Dunmore's War, the Indians were forced to agree to the Treaty of Camp Charlotte, which ceded Kentucky to the whites; however, the more militant Shawnee and Mingo refused to accept the terms of the treaty.

In November 1777, Blackfish launched a winter raid against the Kentucky settlements, and on February 7, 1778, they captured the famous frontiersman Daniel Boone (1734–1820) and several others who were making salt at Blue Licks on the Licking River in Kentucky, about sixty miles from Boonesborough. The captives were taken back to Chillicothe at present Oldtown, where they were forced to run the gantlet between two lines of Indians who were armed with sticks, stones and even weapons. At Chillicothe the gantlet stretched from the top of present Sextons Hill to the Shawnee council house, a distance of 30 rods, or 165 yards. After the ordeal, Boone and some of the prisoners were adopted into the tribe, while the other captives were sent to Fort Detroit. Boone was reputedly adopted by Chief Blackfish himself, although historian John Sugden indicates that he was adopted by another Shawnee family. Boone bided his time and was able to gain a measure of freedom. In June of 1778, he learned that the Shawnee were planning another attack on Boonesborough, so he escaped and traveled the 160 miles in five days to warn the residents. Blackfish and his Shawnees attacked Boonesborough in September 1778 but were unable to subdue the town after a ten-day siege. The following June, Colonel John Bowman led the Kentuckians, including Boone, in an attack on Chillicothe. They were repulsed by the Shawnee, but the attacking Kentuckians managed to lay waste to much of the town. Blackfish was wounded in the leg during the fight and died from the resultant infection.

The noted frontiersman Simon Kenton was also captured by the Shawnee in 1778, but unlike Daniel Boone, Kenton was condemned to death. His face was painted black, and he was pronounced cut-ta-ho-tha, which meant that he would be ritually tortured and burned to death. Impressed with Kenton's endurance and bravery, Pierre Drouillard, an interpreter for the British, saved his life, and Kenton was adopted by a motherly squaw whose own son had been killed. Within the year, Kenton escaped and made his way back to Kentucky, where he enlisted as a scout with George Rogers Clark's expedition against Fort Sackville at present Vincennes, Indiana. In 1793–1794, Kenton fought in the Ohio Indian War under General "Mad" Anthony Wayne.

Chillicothe at Oldtown, often referred to as Old Chillicothe was perhaps the most famous of the Chalahgawatha or Chillicothe villages. Local legend maintains that the famous war chief Tecumseh (1768–1813) was born there, although that's unlikely since he was born several years before Chillicothe at Oldtown was established. Most likely, he was born in Kispoko, a Shawnee village on the upper Scioto River.

Chillicothe at Oldtown was attacked and burned again in 1780, by George Rogers Clark and the Kentucky militia, although some sources indicate the Shawnee burned their village and crops to deny the Kentuckians food and plunder. In 1782, the Indians soundly defeated the Kentuckians at the Battle of Blue Licks, and in November 1782, George Rogers Clark led a retaliatory attack on Chillicothe. This time they completely destroyed the town along with four other Shawnee villages. The Shawnee gamely rebuilt, but many families moved north to the old Miami town of Pickawillany, where they established yet another Chillicothe. Chillicothe at Oldtown remained a village, although it continued to diminish through the Ohio Indian Wars of 1785–1795. Some stayed, but most of its inhabitants moved north to the Glaize at the confluence of the Maumee and Auglaize Rivers, and some Shawnee abandoned Ohio altogether. Local historians claim that Chillicothe at Oldtown was occupied until about 1807.

18. *Chillicothe (c. 1758–c. 1778), also Kispoko.*
Now: Westfall, Ross County (39°33′24.54″N–83°0′1.41″W)

This village was reportedly adjacent to the Shawnee village of Kispoko, but there is little evidence to support that claim. Traditionally, the Shawnee tended to group according to their septs, so for the most part, Kispoko would have Kispokotha inhabitants, and a town called Chillicothe would primarily be inhabited by Chalahgawathas. In 1903, Robert White McFarland wrote in *The Chillicothes*: "Chillicothe—Also often called 'Old Chillicothe.' This was about four miles down the river from Circleville, and was on the west side of the Scioto, at or very near the village of Westfall. All histories which give accounts of 'Lord Dunmore's War,' including the battle of Point Pleasant, when they say 'Chillicothe,' means this one at Westfall."[19] Like Lower Shawnee Town at the mouth of the Scioto River at present Portsmouth, it's likely that Kispoko and Chillicothe were conjoined or in very close proximity to one another, with one section having Kispokotha and the other having Chalahgawatha residents.

The Pickaway Plains, which was the area south of Circleville, east of the Scioto River and west of Scippo Creek, was considered the richest body of land in Ohio.[20] It was described as a lush area, having few trees or brush, but covered with prairie grass that sometimes grew higher than a man. Chillicothe at present Westfall was the chief village and rendezvous point for the allied tribes during Lord Dunmore's War in 1774, and after the Indians' defeat at the Battle of Point Pleasant, the American Army established Camp Charlotte at nearby Scippo Creek, where they dictated their terms in what is known as the Treaty of Camp Charlotte. The Mingo Chief Logan (c. 1723–1780),[21] who fought in Dunmore's War, refused to attend the Camp Charlotte meeting. Instead, he took lodging at Chillicothe at present Westfall, and delivered his famous oration under a great elm tree, thereafter known as "Logan Elm." The tree was one of the largest elm trees recorded. It stood 65 feet tall and

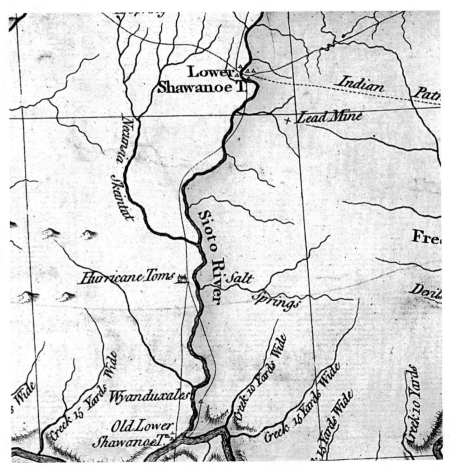

The 1778 Thomas Hutchins map section with Lower Shawanoe T. on both sides of the Scioto River at present Westfall, Ohio. The town comprised the Kispokotha village of Kispoko and the Chalahgawatha village of Chillicothe (Library of Congress, Geography and Map Division-74696155).

had a trunk circumference of 24 feet. Its crown spread 180 feet. The tree was weakened by Dutch Elm Disease and was toppled and died during a storm in 1964. The site is at present Logan Elm State Park.

> I appeal to any white man to say, if ever he entered Logan's cabin hungry, and he gave him not meat; if ever he came cold and naked, and he clothed him not. During the course of the last long and bloody war, Logan remained idle in his cabin, an advocate for peace. Such was my love for the whites, that my countrymen pointed as they passed, and said, Logan is the friend of the white men. I have even thought to live with you but for the injuries of one man. Col. Cresap, the last spring, in cold blood, and unprovoked, murdered all the relations of Logan, not sparing even my women and children. There runs not a drop of my blood in the veins of any living creature. This has called on me for revenge. I have sought it: I have killed many: I have fully glutted my vengeance. For my country, I rejoice at the beams of peace. But do not harbor a thought that mine is the joy of fear. Logan never felt fear. He will not turn on his heel to save his life. Who is there to mourn for Logan? Not one."[22]

During the Revolutionary War, the Shawnee along the Scioto River were divided over whether to remain neutral or join in the fight. The neutral faction suffered a severe setback in 1777 when the popular chief Cornstalk was murdered along with his son and two other Shawnee while on a peace mission to Fort Randolph. The wanton killing motivated the more militant Shawnee to move west to the Little Miami, Great Miami, and Mad Rivers to join the Indians who were allied with the British. The remaining Shawnee on the Scioto felt vulnerable to the hostile Indians in the west, so in the early months of 1778, more than 200 Shawnee led by Nonhelema, the Grenadier Squaw, and chiefs Nimwha and Kisinoutha left their Scioto River villages and relocated to be near the Lenape town of White Eyes at the Forks of the Muskingum. However, after the deaths of peace advocates Nimwha and Kisinoutha the following winter, many of the Shawnee at the Forks of the Muskingum joined their more militant tribesmen at the Little Miami and Mad River settlements. Several Indian families opted to remain in their Scioto River settlements, but those villages were nowhere near their original size. Frontiersmen, traders, and missionaries said that some villages consisted of as few as five homes.

On January 21, 1785, Wyandot, Ojibwe, and Ottawa representatives signed the Treaty of Fort McIntosh, which restricted the Indians to a small area of northwestern Ohio. The Shawnee did not take part in the treaty negotiations but were forced to accept its terms a year later on January 31, 1786, when they signed the Treaty of Fort Finney. Even so, many Ohio Indians opted to fight for their lands, and in 1787, Chillicothe at present Westfall was destroyed by Kentucky militia.

Even those Indians who relocated to the new treaty area would not keep those lands. The Indian Removal Act of 1830 forced all the Indians out of Ohio, and the Indian reserves that had been guaranteed by treaty were opened to white settlement. The last Indian village in Ohio was vacated in 1843.

18. Cornstalk's Town (c. 1758–c. 1778).
Now: Circleville, Pickaway County (39°32'5.52"N–82°57'44.69"W)

After the Shawnee abandoned Lower Shawnee Town at the mouth of the Scioto River, they established several towns upstream on the Scioto in the area between present Chillicothe and Circleville, Ohio. Hokolesqua or Cornstalk[23] (c.1720–1777) was a prominent Mekoche leader, both a hokima, or civil chief, and a war chief.[24] After their resettlement to the upper Scioto, Cornstalk and Kisinoutha ("big wolf") were recognized as the primary leaders of the Shawnee nation.

Cornstalk established his town on the north bank of Scippo Creek about two and a half miles northeast of its junction with the Scioto River. Cornstalk's sister Nonhelema (c. 1720–1786), who was also a Shawnee chief, had her village almost directly across Scippo Creek opposite Cornstalk's Town. Nonhelema was reputedly six foot, six inches tall, and because of her great height was often referred to as "The Grenadier Squaw" or "The Grenadier," in reference to the customary height of 18th-century British grenadiers. One source indicates that Cornstalk was also the brother of the Shawnee chief Nimwah;[25] however, I couldn't locate any definitive evidence to support that. The close relationship between Cornstalk, Nonhelema, and Nimwah may have led observers to confuse them for siblings.

Cornstalk was described as tall, distinguished, a great orator, and particularly brave and skilled as a war leader. He reportedly fought on the side of the French during the French and Indian War, and joined the Indian confederation in the fight during Pontiac's 1763 Rebellion. During Lord Dunmore's War in 1774, Cornstalk was one of the principal war chiefs, and after the Indians' defeat at the Battle of Point Pleasant, he represented the Shawnee at the signing of the Treaty of Camp Charlotte. After agreeing to the terms of the treaty, Cornstalk felt honor-bound to adhere to its terms, and as a result, he opposed war against the Americans. He maintained that peaceful position even though white settlers continuously encroached onto Indian lands that were guaranteed by the treaty.

When the American Revolutionary War began in 1775, the majority of the Shawnee initially remained neutral in the white man's war. However, other Ohio Indian nations took an active role, mostly allying themselves with the British, because they considered the Americans the more dangerous threat to usurp their lands in Ohio. Cornstalk was convinced that waging war against the Americans would be devastating for the Shawnee, and advocated diplomacy as the best course of action. Along with his sister Nonhelema and most of the other Mekoche hokimas, he campaigned strongly against becoming involved in the war

By 1777, in spite of the efforts by Cornstalk and the other hokimas, most Shawnee were convinced that war was the only way to defend their land. It was apparent that the previous treaties were meaningless to the white people, since increasing numbers were settling on land that had been guaranteed to the Indians. Cornstalk and the hokimas still advocated peace, but the militant Shawnee began to consider the hokimas and even Cornstalk as traitors, derisively calling them "Virginians." Some of the Shawnee went so far as to threaten the peace-talkers' lives, and Cornstalk sadly mused that his people would not listen to him, and even threatened to do away with him.

The disagreement between the Shawnee advocating peace and those pressing for war grew so intense that it caused a rupture in Shawnee society. The militant faction abandoned their homes on the Scioto River and moved west along the Little Miami, Great Miami, and Mad Rivers to join the tribes supporting the British. The Shawnee who remained along the Scioto were in a precarious no-man's land, and were suspected by both the British and the Americans of supporting the other side. Cornstalk advocated relocating east to the Muskingum River to live among the Lenape, who seemed to be successfully negotiating the perilous path of neutrality.

However, in November 1777, disaster struck when Cornstalk, along with his son Elinipsco, a chief named Red Hawk, and a warrior called Petella, visited Fort Randolph at present Point Pleasant, West Virginia. The four were on a peace mission to inform the

Americans that they planned to relocate east to live among the peaceful Lenape on the Muskingum. While they were en route, a hostile Mingo war party killed and scalped a militiaman outside the fort, and when Cornstalk and his group arrived, the enraged garrison murdered the four Indians in revenge.

In spite of the death of Cornstalk at the hands of the Americans, Nimwah and Nonhelema still advocated neutrality, and in the early months of 1778, they left their towns on the Scioto River to lead seventeen families of more than 200 Shawnee to join the Lenape at Goschachgunk at the Forks of the Muskingum.

23. *Crooked Nose's Town (c. 1773–c. 1777),*
also Wockchaalli, Waccachalla
Now: Frankfort, Ross County (39°26'11.67"N–83°13'17.66"W)

According to Baptist missionary David Jones, who visited the Scioto River area in 1773, there was a Shawnee village located on the east side of Paint Creek or on one of its tributaries about three miles west-northwest of the Shawnee village of Chillicothe. Some sources erroneously use present Chillicothe, Ohio, as the starting reference, but during the time of Jones, the city did not exist. Rather, the Chillicothe that Jones visited in 1773 was located at present Frankfort, Ohio.

There is not much information regarding a Shawnee leader named Crooked Nose or Wockachaalli, but that's not entirely surprising since David Jones's spelling was often unique. However, Jones seems to have been accurate in his descriptions regarding the general location of Indian villages, even though his names or spelling may not be identifiable. Frank Wilcox, in his book *Ohio Indian Trails*, and William C. Mills in his book *The Archeological Atlas of Ohio*, both indicate there was a town called Waccachalla in that vicinity, but they don't offer any other information regarding its ethnicity or its chief. Even so, I believe it's safe to assume that this was the same town David Jones visited in 1773.

Some sources indicate the village was populated by Indian relatives of British Indian agent and fur trader Alexander McKee (c. 1735–1799). McKee's father Thomas was an Irish immigrant and his mother was either a white captive of the Shawnee or a Shawnee Indian woman. During the French and Indian War, McKee was a lieutenant in the Pennsylvania forces, and in 1760 he entered the Indian department as an assistant to George Croghan. After Alexander McKee's mother died, his father took Margaret Tecumsapah Opessa as his wife. She was the granddaughter of Cornstalk. To keep it all in the family, Alexander took Margaret's younger sister Sewatha Sarah Straighttail as his wife. Apparently, the sisters came from an illustrious family. They were the great-granddaughters of Pride Opessa, who signed the original treaty with William Penn in 1701, and Margaret and Sewatha's sister was Methotaske Mary Opessa, the mother of Tecumseh.[26] Through his wife and stepmother, Alexander became fluent in the Shawnee language and customs, and he developed a lifelong personal relationship with all of the Ohio Indian tribes.

David Jones wrote of his visit in his journal:

Saturday 23, [1773] In company with Mr. Irwine went to see captain McKee, who lives three miles west and by north of Chillicaathee in a small town called *Wockachaalli*, which signifies Crooked Nose's Place. Here the captain's Indian relatives live, and some others. This seems only a new town, not having much ground cleared. 'Tis situated east of a creek, which I suppose to be a branch of Paint Creek.

Some of the Indians of this town have a large number of the best horses in the nation; not are they worse supplied with cattle, so they chiefly live by stock. Returned that same evening to Chillicaathee.[27]

While most of the Shawnee settlements along the Scioto River were established around 1758, Jones observes in his journal that Crooked Nose's Town was in 1773 apparently a newer town, because not much ground had yet been cleared for crops. It's also difficult to determine the predominant Shawnee sept of the inhabitants. The three sisters Margaret, Sewatha, and Methotaske, if indeed were granddaughters of Cornstalk, would likely have been Mekoche Shawnee. However, Methotaske, the mother of Tecumseh, would have had a Kispokotha husband, since that was Tecumseh's sept.

A look at Alexander McKee's timeline may give us some sense of the time Crooked Nose's Town existed. McKee originally lived at what is now McKees Rocks near the Forks of the Ohio, and in fact, George Washington visited him there in 1770. Because of his family connections, McKee was appointed Indian Agent for Pennsylvania. However, as the friction between the American colonies and Great Britain grew heated, many of the rebellious Americans vented their anger at McKee. To escape the hostility of his American neighbors, McKee relocated to the Shawnee village near the Scioto River. It wasn't until some time later that he formally sided with the English at Fort Detroit and formed a close relationship with Matthew Elliot and the Girty brothers, Simon, James, and George. That time frame would be compatible with David Jones's estimation that Crooked Nose's Town was newly established in 1773. Around 1777–1778, most of the militant Shawnee living in the area of the Scioto River relocated west to join the British cause. Since McKee was already in the service of the English, it's likely he relocated at that time.

3. French Margaret's Town (Margaret's Town) (c. 1751–?).
Now: Lancaster, Fairfield County (39°44'1.41"N–82°36'46.06"W)

French Margaret's Town on the Hocking River, which the Indians called Hockhocking, was located at present Lancaster, Ohio. The town was thought to have been named after Margaret Montour of the illustrious Montour family of Pennsylvania. The grande dame of the family was Madame Montour (1667 or c. 1685–c. 1753), a well-known interpreter and local leader. It's believed that Madame Montour was Isabelle, or Elizabeth, a Métis[28] whose parents were Pierre Couc *dit* Lafleur (1627–1690) and Marie Miteoamegoukoué (1631–1699), a Christian Algonquin woman. Madame Montour claimed she had been captured, adopted, and raised by the Iroquois around 1694, when she was about ten years old. Another group of historians, Jon W. Parmenter and Nancy L. Hagedorn, contend that Madame Montour was in fact Isabelle's niece, and was born around 1685 in an Indian village near Sorrel, Québec. According to Parmenter and Hagedorn, her father was Louis Couc Montour, who was the brother of Isabelle (or Elizabeth) Couc, and her mother was Madeleine, a western Abenaki woman. Historian William A. Hunter claims that Madame Montour was a Métis named Elizabeth Couc, who was born in 1667 in an Indian village near Troi-Rivières (Three Rivers, Québec). The names Elizabeth and Isabelle were used interchangeably by the French at that time.

The confusion of trying to delineate the Montour family tree is evident from the difficulty in defining Madame Montour's lineage. What makes it even more difficult is that Iroquois kinship customs often portrayed a woman's niece as her daughter. Unfortunately, there were so many Montours active in frontier politics that it's difficult to ascertain which

Montours were descended from various family members, or who were associated with specific events. With that in mind, we cannot be certain whether "French Margaret" was the daughter or niece of Madame Montour.

In the 1740s, French Margaret Montour became the leader of "French Margaret's Town," an Indian village near the mouth of Lycoming Creek on the Susquehanna River at present Williamsport, Pennsylvania. The last recorded documentation regarding French Margaret is a notation in the Moravian records that in July 1754, "French Margaret, her Mohawk husband, and two grandchildren, travelling in semi-barbaric state, with an Irish groom and six relays of pack horses, halted a few days at Bethlehem [Pennsylvania] on their way to New York. During her stay she attended divine worship, expressed much gratification at the music and singing, and was pleased to find sisters who were conversant with French."[29] French Margaret never returned to her village on Lycoming Creek.[30]

The previous paragraphs make it doubtful that Margret Montour was associated with French Margaret's Town on the Hocking River in Ohio. In addition, accounts of frontiersmen Christopher Gist and William Trent along with the Moravian missionary John Heckewelder indicate that they visited "French Margaret's Town on the Hockhocking" during the time Margaret Montour resided in her village on Lycoming Creek over 300 miles away. In addition, there is no evidence that Margaret Montour ever visited the place, much less lived there. Even so, some sources maintain that the town was named after Margaret Montour, and that she resided there, but they offer no evidence to support that claim. For example, William M. Darlington, in his notes to Christopher Gist's journal of 1750–51, states that Hockhocking or French Margaret's town—depicted on Evans's 1755 map of the middle colonies, Mitchell's 1755 map, and Pownall's 1776 map—was named for French Margaret, the daughter of Madame Montour, and that it was probable she resided there at one time.[31] Darlington does not list any supporting evidence to support that claim. He makes a further leap of conjecture regarding the old name of Sugar Creek, a stream in Tuscarawas County Ohio. Gist wrote that on December 9, 1751, his trail crossed Margaret's Creek. Darlington expanded on that entry by writing, "The trail crossed it [Margaret's Creek] in the present Franklin Township, Tuscarawas County, near Strasburgh [Strasburg]." He added, "This stream was named for Margaret Montour, usually called 'French Margaret,' the daughter of Madame Montour. This stream was afterwards called Sugar Creek; it empties into the Tuscarawas at Dover."[32] Again, there is no evidence that Margaret Montour traveled west of her home along Lycoming Creek or ever resided in Ohio.

So, who was the French Margaret that the town on the Hockhocking was named after? We've ascertained that it likely wasn't Margaret Montour, because at the time Gist and William Trent visited Hockhocking in 1751 and 1752, Margaret Montour was living along Lycoming Creek in north-central Pennsylvania. Indian custom did not include naming a town in honor of someone who didn't live there. Towns were normally named according to a local geographic feature or the town's location, like "Standing Stone," or "Upper Sandusky." They were also named for the chief or principal leader, like "Beaver's Town," "White Eye's Town," or "White Woman's Town." Often when a chief relocated a town, the name of the town moved with the village, hence there might be references to more than one town by the same name as the chief relocated his village. In those cases, it's important to look at the dates associated with each town's location. By the same token, when a chief died or was replaced, the town took on the name of the new chief. In some cases, the town was named after the particular tribe of Indians who resided there, like "Mingo Town," or "Lower Shawnee Town."

Quite likely, French Margaret's Town on the Hocking was named after a different Margaret, who probably spoke French. Margaret Montour was associated with the Iroquois, but there are several indications that the town on the Hocking was a Lenape or Delaware Indian village. Christopher Gist specifies in his journal entry dated January 19, 1751, that he traveled "W [west] 15 M [miles] to Hockhockin a small town with only four or five Delaware Families."[33] John Heckewelder's book *The Travels of John Heckewelder in Frontier America* has the notation: "Hockhocking (French Margaret's Town): A Delaware Indian town at what is now Lancaster, Ohio, on the headwaters of the Hocking River." The Montour family was essentially Iroquois, and it is very unlikely that the Lenape (Delaware) would have accepted an Iroquois as chief or headperson of their village. At this time the identity of French Margaret of Hockhocking is not known, nor when the town ceased to exist.

18. *Grenadier Squaw's Town (c. 1758–1778), also Nonhalema's Town.*
NOW: CIRCLEVILLE, PICKAWAY COUNTY (39°32'2.39"N–82°57'32.33"W)

Nonhelema (c. 1720–1786) was the sister of the Mekoche Chief Hokolesqua or Cornplanter. She was remarkable in that she stood six feet, six inches tall, was reportedly an attractive woman, and well-proportioned for her height. Because of her tall stature, she was often referred to as "The Grenadier Squaw" or "The Grenadier," because British grenadiers were selected from among the tallest of the British troops, and their high hats made

Grenadier Squaw's Town was situated on the slightly higher ground where the present farm buildings are located. The tree line in background borders Scippo Creek. Cornstalk's Town was immediately across Scippo Creek opposite Grenadier Squaw's Town (author photograph).

them appear even taller. In addition to being the sister of a prominent chief, Nonhelema was a respected village leader and warrior in her own right, having fought against Colonel Henry Bouquet's army at the Battle of Bushy Run in August 1763. She was fluent in four languages and was a trusted advisor to Cornstalk. After the Shawnee moved from Lower Shawnee Town on the Ohio River in 1758, she established her village on the south side of Scippo Creek almost directly across from her brother's village less than one-half mile east of present U.S. 23.

Not much is known of Nonhelema's early life, other than she had three husbands and at least two other relationships with white men that produced children. Her three husbands were Shawnee. There is no record of the names or details of her first two husbands, but her third husband was the Shawnee chief Moluntha (c. 1692–1786), who was about twenty-eight years her senior. There are also no records of children she may have had by her three Indian husbands. However, she produced a son named Thomas McKee (1770–1814) by British Indian Agent Colonel Alexander McKee (c. 1735–1799), and she had another son named Tamanatha[34] (c. 1778–?) from her union with American Colonel Richard Butler (1743–1791. Ironically, Tamanatha and his father General Butler fought on opposite sides during Saint Clair's defeat at the Battle of the Wabash on November 4, 1791. Richard Butler, who was a major general at the time, was killed in the battle.[35]

It's probable that Nonhelema took part alongside her brother in Lord Dunmore's War of 1774, and was present at Camp Charlotte[36] for the treaty negotiations that ended the war. While at Camp Charlotte, Nonhelema was accompanied by a young woman called Fannie or Fawney, whom many assumed was her daughter. However, no other information confirming that Nonhelema had a daughter has been found.

According to the terms of the Treaty of Camp Charlotte, the Shawnee ceded their claim to Kentucky, and promised not to molest settlers traveling on the Ohio River. After signing the treaty, Cornstalk felt honor-bound to respect its terms, and Nonhelema fully supported him. They both opposed war against the Americans, even though white settlers continuously moved onto Indian Lands that were guaranteed by the treaty.

When the American Revolutionary War began in 1775, Cornstalk, Nonhelema and other influential Shawnee leaders convinced most of the Shawnee to remain neutral. However, other Ohio Indians quickly allied with the British, believing it was their best hope to stop the flood of American settlers onto their lands. Cornstalk believed that war against the Americans would be devastating to the Shawnee, so he and his sister Nonhelema, along with many Mekoche hokimas, campaigned that the Shawnee should rely on diplomacy to maintain their homeland in Ohio.

However, by 1777, most Shawnee were convinced that war was their only option, since the white people ignored the previous treaties. In addition, the militant Shawnee began to consider the "peace talkers" like Cornstalk and Nonhelema as traitors, derisively calling them "Virginians." Some of the Shawnee went so far as to threaten their lives, and Cornstalk sadly mused that his people would not listen to him but had threatened to do away with him.

The result of the schism among the Shawnee was that most of the Indians who advocated war moved west to the Little Miami, Great Miami, and Mad Rivers to join the British war effort. Cornstalk on the other hand advocated moving east to the Forks of the Muskingum to be near the Lenape villages, where the Lenape seemed to successfully negotiate the precarious path of neutrality. The problem of neutrality in time of war is that both warring factions are suspicious of the true allegiance of the neutral party.

In November 1777, Cornstalk, along with his son Elinipsco and two other Shawnee leaders, traveled on a peace mission to Fort Randolph at present Point Pleasant, West Virginia. Cornstalk wanted to affirm his neutrality and inform the fort's commander that he planned to relocate to the Forks of the Muskingum. However, during the mission, hostile Mingos killed and scalped a militiaman outside the fort, and in revenge, the enraged garrison killed Cornstalk, his son, and the other two Shawnee.

Even after Cornstalk's murder, Nonhelema and the Mekoche hokimas still advocated a peace strategy, though Nonhelema did not remain neutral in the strictest sense. She warned the American commander at Fort Randolph of an impending attack, even though the garrison was responsible for her brother's murder. When she learned that Fort Donnally, at present Fort Donnally, West Virginia, was going to be attacked, she disguised Phillip Hammond and John Prior as Indians, and sent the two American frontiersmen 160 miles to warn the garrison. In retaliation, a militant faction of Shawnee destroyed Nonhelema's cattle and horse herds.

During the early months of 1778, more than 200 Shawnee, led by Nonhelema, Nimwha and the Mekoche hokima Kisinoutha, left their Scioto River settlements to join the Lenape at the Forks of the Muskingum at present Coshocton, Ohio. That essentially marked the end of Cornstalk's Town and Grenadier Squaw's Town along Scippo Creek.

In 1780, she served as a guide and interpreter for Colonel Augustin de la Balme (1733–1780), who commanded an ill-fated expedition against Fort Detroit, and against the British-allied Indians in present Indiana. During a battle northwest of present Fort Wayne, Indiana, Miami Indians under Chief Little Turtle soundly defeated the Americans, and la Balme was killed in the fight.

In 1785, Nonhelema petitioned Congress for a land grant of 1,000 acres in Ohio as a reward for her efforts to facilitate peace between the Shawnee and the Americans, and also for her work as an interpreter and guide for the American Army. Instead, Congress awarded her a pension of daily rations, along with an annual allocation of clothing and blankets.

In 1786, during the Ohio Indian Wars, General Benjamin Logan led his militia troops from Kentucky into Ohio, and they took Nonhelema and her husband Moluntha into custody. Nonhelema was about sixty-six and Molunta about ninety-four at the time. Logan issued orders that none of the Indian captives should be molested or harmed in any way. One officer, Hugh McGary, had been a major in the Kentucky militia during the 1782 Battle of Blue Licks, in which the Kentuckians had been soundly defeated by British Loyalists and their Indian allies. McGary received much of the blame for the defeat and was still smarting four years later. Old Moluntha was sitting and cutting tobacco for his pipe when McGary walked up and asked him, "Were you at Blue Licks?" Moluntha either didn't understand the question or was hard of hearing, and the old Indian only repeated, "Blue Licks." Enraged, McGary took his tomahawk and buried it in Moluntha's head, killing him instantly. As he prepared to take another swing, Nonhelema rushed to stop McGary, but he swung his tomahawk at her and cut off three of her fingers. General Lyle and frontiersman Simon Kenton witnessed the cold-blooded murder, and both men rushed to kill McGary, but were stopped by troops. McGary was relieved of his command and court-martialed for murder, but his punishment was a mere one-year suspension.

Following the attack by McGary, Nohelema was transported to Fort Pitt, and for the short while she was in detention there, she occupied her time by compiling a dictionary of Shawnee words and phrases. She was released in December 1786 and died shortly after, but the cause, date, and place of her death are not known. There is no gravesite listed for Non-

Sally Misencik at Nonhelema monument (author photograph).

helema the Grenadier Squaw, but she has a fine stone monument in Logan Elm State Park, about 1.7 miles south of her old village on Scippo Creek.

The inscription reads: "Grenadier Squaw was Chief of the largest Indian Shawnee village located on the south bank of Scippo Creek upon the Pickaway Plains in 1774. Born about 1720, Non-hel-e-ma, sister of Chief Cornstalk, was named 'Grenadier Squaw' by white traders because of her imposing stature, regal bearing and unflinching courage. She spoke three languages, serving as peacemaker and interpreter between Indians and whites. Because of her friendships, she accepted Christianity. After the peace treaty in 1774, she was disowned by her people and became a homeless exile."

Despite the inscription, there is nothing to substantiate the assertion that Nonhelema was ever a homeless exile or that she became a Christian. Unlike the Lenape, most Shawnee preferred to retain their old religious beliefs, and few chose to be baptized as Christians.

32. *Hurricane Tom's Town (c. 1750–c. 1764),*
also Salt Lick Town, Harriskintom.
Now: Richmond Dale, Ross County (39°11′14.20″N–82°50′3.81″W)

A 1755 map by Thomas Evans shows a village called Hurricane Tom's Town astride the Scioto Trail on the west side of the Scioto River approximately opposite the mouth of what is labeled Salt Springs, likely today's Salt Creek, which joins the Scioto River less than a mile southwest of present Richmond Dale, Ohio. Interestingly, another map dated 1755, by British mapmaker John Mitchell, shows an Indian village called "Harriskintom" on the east side of the Scioto River in the vicinity of Salt Creek, which is likely a reference to Hurricane Tom's Town, and perhaps provides a clue to the origin of the name, which may have been a corruption of Harriskintom. However, the location of the town on Mitchell's map is probably erroneous, since most sources indicate it was on the west side of the Scioto River.

In 1751, the village was visited by Christopher Gist, who wrote in his journal, "24th [January]—went south fifteen miles [from Maguck], to a town called 'Hurricane Tom's—town' on the south west of Scioto creek, consisting of five or six families." Gist continues: "25th—went down on south east side of the creek, four miles to Salt Lick Creek."[37] Using Gist's measurements, it's difficult to place the location of Hurricane Tom's Town with any degree of accuracy, because "fifteen miles from Maguck" and "four miles from Salt Lick Creek" leaves a gap of about eight miles in which the town could have been sited. In fact, different sources place the site of Hurricane Tom's Town as far south as present Piketon, Ohio, or north to almost within the present Chillicothe city limits.

In a letter dated May 31, 1764, from Colonel Henry Bouquet to Sir William Johnson, Bouquet mentioned the Shawnee Salt Lick Town on the Scioto River, which was likely a reference to Hurricane Tom's Town.[38] The same source also states: "On highway route number 23, which follows the Scioto River from Circleville to Portsmouth, it is 17 miles from the Pickaway Plains to Chillicothe, Ohio." Gist traveled 15 miles, according to his own estimate, from Maguck to Hurricane Tom's Town located near present Chillicothe, Ohio.

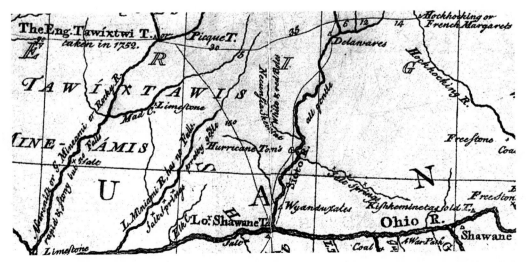

Section of 1755 Evans map showing Hurricane Tom's Town (Library of Congress, Geography and Map Division-75693767).

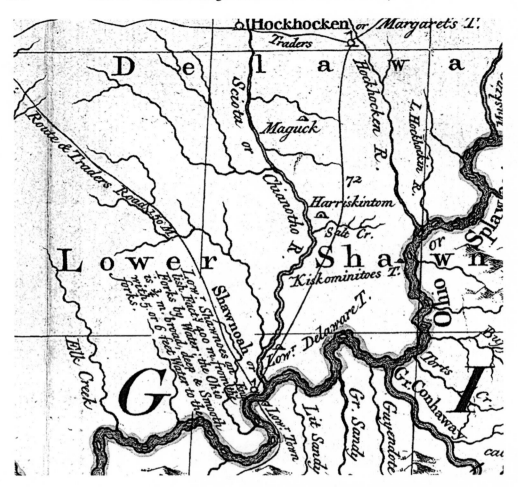

Section of 1755 Mitchell map showing Harriskintom (Library of Congress, Geography and Map Division-74693187).

Whatever Hurricane Tom's real name was, he must have been something of a renegade, because extant records indicate that from 1750 to 1756, the English trusted him for a quantity of trade goods that he defaulted on, and it was reported that he was the leader of a gang of Indian warriors who robbed a Pennsylvania trader by the name of Pat Mullen of almost £100 worth of buckskins.[39] An article in the Thursday, September 5, 1940, edition of the *Marion [Ohio] Star* read:

> Modern methods of installment paying were yet unknown to mid-eighteenth century Ohio country Indians, but Hurricane Tom was one of the Indians at the Shawnee town at the mouth of the Scioto river who managed to obtain considerable credit from the early traders. Hurricane Tom's accounts were turned over to the Pennsylvania colonial secretary when he defaulted. Although not a chief, Hurricane Tom was a Shawnee of importance, as borne out by records indicating that when he moved north some 50 miles to the mouth of Paint Creek on the Scioto, a large band of Indians followed and established Hurricane Tom's town. Existence of the town is given further credence by an entry in Christopher Gist's journal, locating the town to be about two and a half miles below the present site of Chillicothe on the west bank of the Scioto. Hurricane Tom's band joined the general Indian uprising in 1749. That year traders lost their goods to Indian raids, in addition to losses sustained by selling goods on credit to tribesmen.[40]

It's obvious that the article was embellished with statements that are not supported by evidence. For example, it's not certain who Hurricane Tom was, what nation he belonged to, or why he was called "Hurricane Tom." As mentioned earlier, it most likely was a variation of his Indian name that was corrupted into something more pronounceable by English traders. Some sources maintain that he may have been a French trader, but those claims have been largely discounted. Most sources identify him as a Shawnee, but some maintain he was Lenape, which is debatable, since few Lenape had moved farther west than the Muskingum and Tuscarawas River areas before the 1770s. The article placed Hurricane Tom at Lower Shawnee Town at the mouth of the Scioto, then claimed the Indian relocated to the mouth of Paint Creek south of present Chillicothe. However, most sources locate Hurricane Tom's Town near the mouth of Salt Creek on the Scioto River. The claim that a large number of Indians were with Hurricane Tom when he established his town is questionable, since Christopher Gist claimed that in 1751 the town consisted of only about five or six families.

During their research on the Ohio Mound Builder culture, archaeologists Olaf Prufer and Ellen Andors concluded that the Morrison Village Site on the west bank of the Scioto River in Franklin Township, Ross County, Ohio, was the location of Hurricane Tom's Town, which was visited by Christopher Gist in 1751. For some reason, Prufer identified it as a Delaware (Lenape) town without any supporting evidence. Carbon 14 dating of some of the more recent vegetal matter, debris, and other artifacts found in fire and refuse pits established a date no earlier than about 1744, so it was concluded that the town was established not much sooner than Gist's visit in 1751. By the same token, there was no evidence or even references to the town by travelers other than Bouquet's oblique reference to "Shawnee Salt Lick Town" in 1764. Most likely the village was a small Shawnee community that was established shortly before Gist's arrival and ceased to exist around the mid–1760s.

18. *Kispoko (Kispoko Town) (1758–c. 1786), also Lower Shawnee Town.*

Now: Westfall, Pickaway County (39°33′31.89″N–82°59′55.70″W)

Kispoko was one of several Shawnee towns established on the Upper Scioto River around 1758. The Shawnee supported the French during the French and Indian War, and Lower Shawnee Town at present Portsmouth on the Ohio was abandoned because of its increased vulnerability after the British captured Fort Duquesne in 1758. When the village was first established, Lower Shawnee Town was a grand experiment where a large number of Shawnee lived together in one cohesive community. However, it was soon evident that a very large town created a strain on the available resources of game, fish, firewood, and farmland, so when they relocated, they decided to establish smaller communities grouped in a general area, which provided sufficient cohesiveness for effective interaction without stripping the immediate area of necessary communal resources.

The first town established upstream on the Scioto River was called Kispoko, and as indicated by its name, it was mainly inhabited by Kispokothas, one of the five Shawnee septs or divisions. The five septs were the Chalahgawathas, Mekoches, Pekowis, Kispokothas, and Thawikilas.

Some sources indicate that Kispoko was populated by Chalahgawathas, but that was not the case, because Shawnee traditionally resided together according to their particular sept. Pucksinwa (dancing tail panther), who was the father of the famous war chief Tecumseh (shooting star or crouching panther) was a Kispokotha from Kispoko, and like all Shawnee, he was born into his father's sept. Incidentally, there are differences of opinion regarding Tecumseh's mother Methotaske (laying eggs in the sand). Some sources indicate she was a granddaughter of the Mekoche chief Cornstalk, while others say she was a Creek Indian. Both may be true. If she was adopted by the Shawnee, she would have been fully accepted as a member of the family, or Cornstalk's Mekoche family, in that particular case.

One explanation regarding the confusion of the town's predominant sept is that another Shawnee town named Chillicothe or Old Chillicothe, populated by Chalahgawathas, was reputedly established across the river on the east side of the Scioto,[41] which, because of its close proximity, may have caused confusion regarding the predominant sept at Kispoko. The Thomas Hutchins map dated 1778 shows Lower Shawanoe Town as being on both sides of the Scioto River, but the town on the east side may have been the Chalahgawatha town of Chillicothe.

By 1760, Kispoko was one of several Shawnee villages in that area of the Scioto, with each one, for the most part, populated according to a particular sept or division. However,

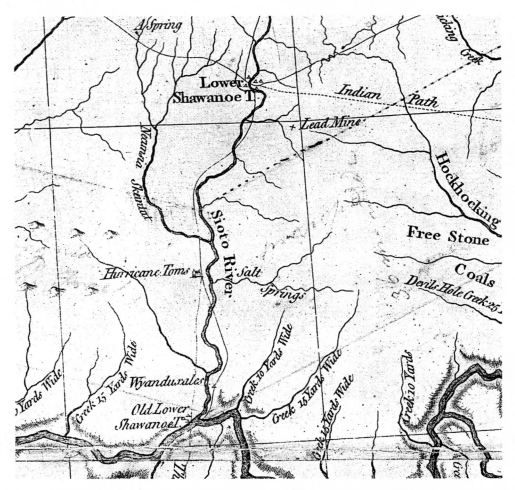

Section of 1778 map by Thomas Hutchins showing Old Lower Shawanoe Town (present Portsmouth) and Lower Shawanoe Town (Kispoko) at Westfall and towns on both sides of the Scioto River (Library of Congress, Geography and Map Division-74696155).

by the early 1770s, those villages underwent additional fragmentation as groups of people, regardless of their particular sept, preferred to live in the village of a leader whose charisma appealed to them. As a result, there were numerous tiny Shawnee hamlets, each consisting of as few as four or five dwellings, that were made up of members of different septs.

Prior to the French and Indian War, Indian relationships with the English were not as congenial as they were with the French. While the French were jealously protective of their claim of ownership of the trans-Allegheny region, and tried to interdict Indian trade with the British, they generally got along well with the Indians, and more importantly did not systematically usurp Indian lands for white settlements. The British, on the other hand, had a strong racist bias, which inclined them to consider the Indians as a separate, lesser order. That bias, coupled with their blatant appropriation of Indian lands for white settlements, guaranteed that the British and Indians would not peacefully coexist. Even so, the Shawnee assiduously tried to remain neutral during the growing competition between the French and the English.

The tipping point, however, was the Lancaster Treaty of 1744, in which the British colony of Virginia purchased from the Iroquois all the land "to the setting sun." To the Iroquois, the term simply meant to the crest of the Allegheny Mountains behind which the sun set, but the English interpreted the sale more broadly and claimed the land beyond the Alleghenies. The Indians in Ohio were not party to the sale and questioned the Iroquois's right to sell their land. The Iroquois, of course, claimed the land by right of conquest over the Erie in the previous century, but the feisty Shawnee did not feel obligated to abide by the Treaty of Lancaster since they were not party to its negotiation. No longer able to maintain their neutrality, the Shawnee openly sided with the French during the French and Indian War.

After the French were defeated, and the English took possession of former New France, the Shawnee remained hostile to the British, and most joined in Pontiac's Rebellion in 1763. All the while, English settlements continued to sprout up in Shawnee lands, which prompted the Shawnee to ask the French for aid and support against the English. The principal Shawnee civil chief[42] or "hokima" in the Scioto region was Hokolesqua,[43] or Cornstalk, a Mekoche, who had his village at Cornstalk's Town on Scippo Creek, about two and a half miles southeast of Kispoko. While it was not an ironclad custom, the Mekoches traditionally assumed leadership or hokima roles in the Shawnee nation in times of peace, while the war chiefs generally came from the Pekowi, Chalahgawathas, and Kispokotha septs.

Attacks by white frontiersmen, primarily from Kentucky, and retaliatory raids by the Indians, resulted in the extremely bloody Lord Dunmore's War, which lasted from May to October 1774. The war ended with the British victory at the Battle of Point Pleasant, and the Shawnee were forced to cede all land south of the Ohio River. Cornstalk led the Indians during the battle, and he signed the Treaty of Camp Charlotte that ended the war. Henceforth, Cornstalk felt honor-bound to abide by its terms. The future war Chief Weyapiersenwah or Blue Jacket took part in the Battle of Point Pleasant, and Pucksinwah, the father of Tecumseh, was one of the Shawnee warriors killed in the battle.

The American Revolutionary War began the following year 1775, and for the Shawnee it was the beginning of what would be called "The Twenty Years' War" for Shawnee survival in the Ohio region. In June 1775, two months after the skirmishes at Lexington and Concord that began the American Revolutionary War, messengers from Fort Detroit arrived at the Shawnee villages on the Scioto telling the Indians that it was in their interests to join the British in the fight against the rebellious Americans. The following month, July 1775, Virginia representatives also visited the Ohio Indians, asking them not to support the British and to adhere to the terms of the Camp Charlotte Treaty. The Virginians had been the chief usurpers of Indian land, and consistently violated treaty after treaty. In 1775, The Shawnee chief Kisinoutha complained that the Virginians regularly crossed the Ohio, killed Indians and drove off their game.[44] Another chief commented that the Virginians were "coming in the Middle of us like Crazey People."[45] Correctly reading the mood of the Shawnee, the Virginians recognized the irony, and refrained from asking for active Shawnee support against England.

Even so, the war created differing opinions among the Shawnee regarding whether it was in their best interests to stay neutral or support one side or the other. Not only did the various Indian nations represented in Ohio have differing opinions, but they became factionalized within the different societies, and even within individual villages.

Not certain of the best course of action, the Shawnee remained neutral in 1775 and 1776. Under Mekoche hokima leadership, they relied on diplomatic measures to try to protect their lands. The Mekoche hokimas, along with the war chiefs, tried to develop a strategy that would both keep them out of the war and preserve their lands in Ohio and Kentucky. It was an impossible task, but nevertheless in August of 1776, when British Lieutenant Governor Henry Hamilton offered a war belt to the Shawnee to bring them into the war against the Americans, the chiefs refused to accept it. In addition to proclaiming their neutrality, the Ohio Indians sent representatives to both the British and Americans demanding that both sides stay out of the Ohio Country.

One group of Indians, however, did not remain neutral. The Mingo war chief Pluggy, who had his village at present Delaware, Ohio, relentlessly carried on the fight against the Americans.[46] Their fight had little to do with the Revolutionary War, but rather was a fight to protect and defend their land from encroaching white settlements. Not surprisingly, warriors from several different Ohio nations flocked to join Pluggy.

By 1777, the Shawnee realized they would have to fight for their land. Regardless of previous treaties that guaranteed an Indian homeland in Ohio, more and more settlers entered the area. The Mekoche hokimas still advocated peace, and they denounced their militant tribesmen as foolish and short-sighted. In retaliation, the militant Shawnee derisively called the hokimas "Virginians." Even prominent chief Cornstalk, who advocated adherence to the Treaty of Camp Charlotte, sadly mused that "his people would not listen to him, but had threatened to do away with him."[47] The factional dispute among the Shawnee grew to the extent that it created a schism between those who advocated peace and those who believed war was their only option. The factions split from one another when the militant Shawnee abandoned their homes on the Scioto to relocate west along the Little Miami, Great Miami, and Mad Rivers.

The Mekoche hokimas who remained along the Scioto River tried to maintain their peace strategy, but it suffered a severe setback in November 1777, when the hokima Cornstalk, his son Elinipsco, a chief named Red Hawk, and Petella, a warrior, went to visit Fort Randolph at present Point Pleasant, West Virginia, on a peace mission. While they were en route, Mingo warriors from Pluggy's band killed an American militiaman outside the fort, and when Cornstalk and his party arrived, they were killed in revenge. During the winter of 1777–1778, more than 200 Shawnee, led by Cornstalk's sister Nonhelema, Nimwha, and the Mekoche hokima Kisinoutha, left their Scioto River settlements to join the neutral Lenape at the Forks of the Muskingum at present Coshocton, Ohio.

From 1779 through the end of the Revolutionary War, the Americans were able to devote more men and military resources to subdue the warlike Ohio Indians. Unfortunately for those Indians who tried to facilitate peace, the American expeditions did not differen-

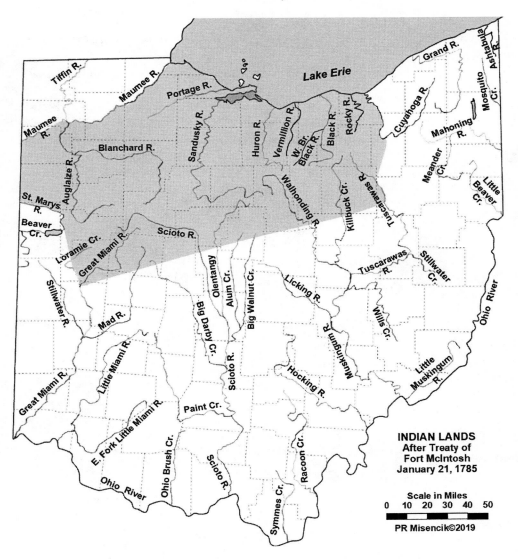

Ohio Indian lands remaining after the Treaty of Fort McIntosh, 1785.

tiate between Indians who were peaceful and those who were hostile, and many peaceful villages were attacked, and the inhabitants massacred as at Gnadenhütten in 1782. Even so, some villages like Kispoko continued to exist along the Scioto River, although most had diminished to only a handful of inhabitants.

The end came for the Scioto River Towns on January 21, 1785, when Wyandot, Ojibwe, and Ottawa representatives signed the Treaty of Fort McIntosh, which restricted the Indians to a small area of northwestern Ohio. The Scioto settlements, including Kispoko, were outside the area reserved for the Indians. The Shawnee did not take part in the treaty negotiations but were forced to accept its terms a year later when they signed the Treaty of Fort Finney on January 31, 1786. All Ohio Indians were required to relocate to the treaty area, but even that would not last. The Indian Removal Act of 1830 forced Indian communities out of Ohio, with the last leaving the state in 1843.

68. *Le Baril (c. 1700–c. 1770).*
NOW: CINCINNATI, HAMILTON COUNTY *(39°6'47.97"N–84°25'59.61"W)*

The Miami Indian village of Le Baril was thought to have been established near the mouth of the Little Miami River on the Ohio River around the beginning of the 18th century. It's known that a Miami village was located there in 1733, and Céloron de Bienville's expedition visited the town in 1749. Céloron wrote in his journal, "The 28th [August, 1749] We camped at the mouth of riviére Blanche [White River], where we found a small band of Miamis with their chief, named le Baril [the Barrel]. They had established themselves there a short time before, and formed a village of 7 or 8 cabins, a league[48] distant from the river."

Father Joseph Pierre de Bonnecamp, a French Jesuit who accompanied Céloron, indicated the village of Le Baril was on the west side of the Little Miami River. However, the

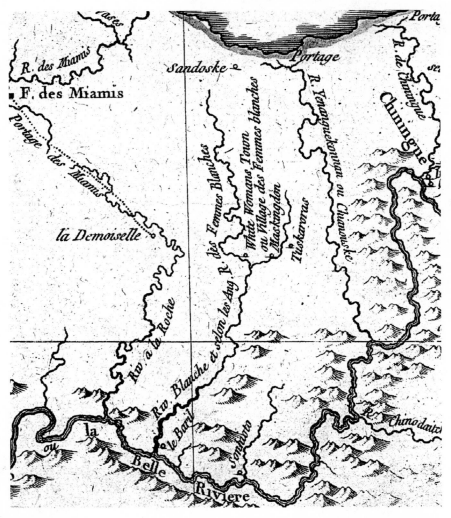

Section of 1755 map by Jacques-Nicolas Bellin showing Le Baril near mouth of the Little Miami River, which the French referred to as Rivière Blanche (Library of Congress, Geography and Map Division-73695755).

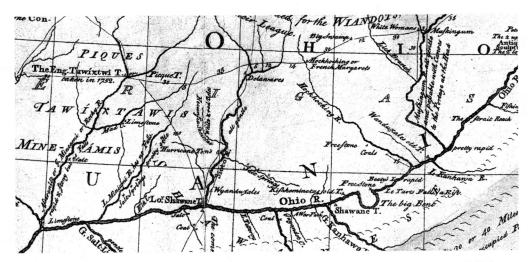

Section of 1755 Evans map showing southern Ohio rivers, but no mention of Le Baril (Library of Congress, Geography and Map Division-75693767).

town of Le Baril is shown on the east side of the Little Miami River on Jacques-Nicolas Bellin's 1755 map above. At the time the French called the Little Miami the Rivière Blanche or White River. As can be seen, Bellin confused the Little Miami with the Muskingum River, and incorrectly assumed the river forked into the Muskingdon (Muskingum) to the east and Rivière des Femmes Blanches or River of the White Women (Walhonding River) to the west. The error was first made by Jean Baptiste Bourguignon d'Anville in his 1746 map, when he applied the name Rivière des Femmes Blanc to the Muskingum, and on his 1755 map when he erroneously called the Sandusky River the White River. John Mitchell, the English cartographer, copied the mistake, as did Bellin on his 1755 map. Whether the village was on the east or west side of the Little Miami is not conclusively known, but since Father Bonnecamp actually visited the town, his placement of the village on the on the west side of the river appears more credible. Also, his placement of other Indian villages along the Ohio River are correct. The 1755 map by Lewis Evans was perhaps the first map that correctly differentiated between the rivers; however, Evans's map does not show the town of Le Baril.

There is no explanation why the town was named Le Baril or "the barrel," but some sources surmise it referred to the shape of the chief. There is no documentation that indicates when the village of le Baril ceased to exist, but it's unlikely that it continued to exist after Lord Dunmore's War of 1774, and most probably the inhabitants relocated some years prior.

40. *Lower Shawnee Town (c. 1734–1758),*
also Chillicothe, Sonionto, Sinhioto, Chalahgawatha,
St. Yotoc, Scioto Town.
NOW: PORTSMOUTH, SCIOTO COUNTY (38°43′57.94″N–83°1′4.40″W)

Lower Shawnee Town was established at the confluence of the Ohio River and Scioto River at present Portsmouth, Ohio, about 1734, and it was the first major Shawnee town established west of Pennsylvania since the Beaver Wars of the previous century. The village was located on the west bank of the Scioto and on the north side of the Ohio River, but a sizable portion of the village also extended across to the south bank of the Ohio. Hemmed in by the French to the west, the English to the east, the Iroquois to the northeast, and hostile tribes to the south, Neucheconneh, who was referred to as the "King of the Shawnee," decided to concentrate his people in one location for mutual strength and defense. Neucheconneh, along with Coyacolinne and Layparewah, who were also influential leaders, invited Shawnees from as far away as the Carolinas, Kentucky, and the Wyoming Valley in Pennsylvania to join them on the Ohio River.

The Shawnee village was commonly called Lower Shawnee Town and was generally shown as such on various maps; however, the Shawnee themselves referred to it by different names. One was Chalahgawatha, or "principal place of the Chalahgawathas," since their chief Neucheconneh was a member of the Chalahgawatha sept. The name gradually changed to Chillicothe, but it was only the first of several Chillicothes in Ohio as the Shawnee relocated for various reasons. As a result, Lower Shawnee Town was sometimes referred to as "Chillicothe on the Ohio."

The location of Lower Shawnee Town was advantageous, because it was at the confluence of two major waterways and the junction of four major Indian trails: the Kanawha

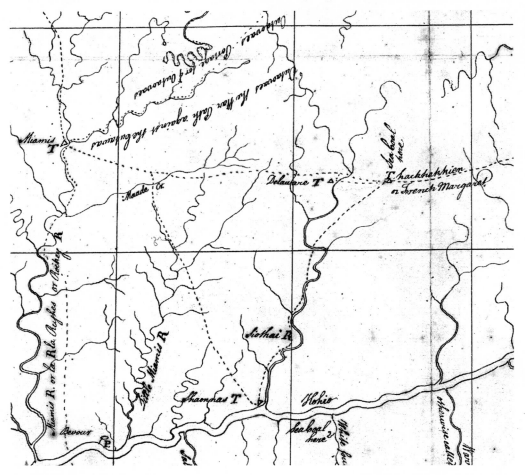

John Patten 1753 map section showing "Shaonnas T" (Library of Congress, Geography and Map Division-gm71002324).

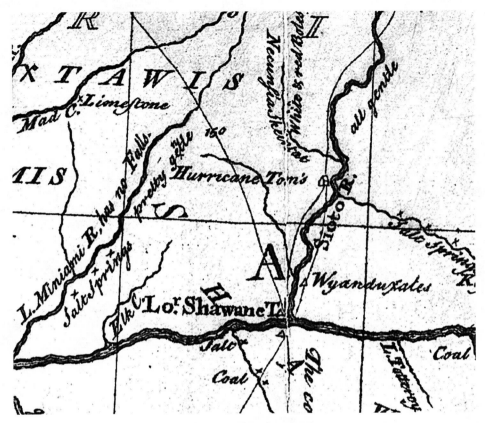

Section of 1755 Lewis Evans map showing Lor. Shawane T (Library of Congress, Geography and Map Division-75693767).

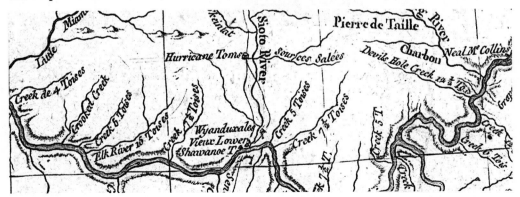

Section of 1781 French map showing Vieux (Old) Lower Shawanoe T (Library of Congress, Geography and Map Division-gm71002166).

Trail, the Pickawillany Trail, the Scioto Trail, and the Great Warriors Path leading south to the Catawba country. As such, the town quickly became a major rendezvous point and trading hub for both English and French fur traders. The town's location put it on the path of several military expeditions, as well as explorers, entrepreneurial land speculators, and fur traders. In 1739, a French force of 123 French troops and 319 Indians under the command of Baron de Longueuil passed through lower Shawnee Town on their way to New Orléans. George Croghan, the "King of the Pennsylvania traders," along with Andrew Montour, visited the town in November 1748 on the way to Pickawillany.

However, the most notable visit was in August 1749, when Captain Pierre Joseph Céloron de Blainville led a French force of 216 troops and about 30 Indians on an expedition to bury lead plates and nail the French coat of arms to trees proclaiming French ownership of the Ohio territory. When Céloron's party arrived at Lower Shawnee Town, they were fired upon by the Shawnee, who believed they were being invaded. Fortunately, a cease-fire was called before anyone was killed or seriously wounded, but even so, the Shawnee were not welcoming in any sense. The Indians were resentful of Céloron's claim of French ownership of their land, and their antipathy toward the French was likely aggravated by the presence of a large number of North Carolina fur traders. Céloron considered confiscating the English traders' goods before sending them packing, but he was forced to reconsider when it became apparent the Shawnee would take umbrage if he mistreated and evicted their guests. In addition, the Englishmen were not only numerous, but they appeared to be tough, well-armed, and ready to defend themselves. Faced with the possibility of a fight that would undoubtedly result in unacceptable casualties, Céloron opted to give the North Carolinians a letter to give to their governor protesting their trespass on French land.

The town was also visited by frontiersman Christopher Gist in 1751, and he described it as a considerable settlement of about forty houses and 300 warriors living on the Kentucky side of the Ohio, and about one hundred houses on the Ohio Side. It was estimated that the town consisted of between 1,200 and 1,500 residents, comprised mainly of Shawnee, but there were also several Lenape and Mingo residents. To emphasize that the town was indeed their Chillicothe or principal town as well as the center of their spiritual and political community, the Shawnee constructed a huge council house more than ninety feet long in the center of their village. As the town grew, it came to be recognized as the Shawnee center of power, and "the place of residence of the principal men of that nation."[49]

Early on, the village leadership recognized the disturbing effects of alcohol on Indian communities, and in the late 1730s, the chiefs Neucheconneh, Coyacolinne, and Laypareawah prohibited rum at Lower Shawnee Town. They appointed four men to seek out alcohol in the town and "Stave all the Rum or strong Lickquors."[50]

In 1753, a massive flood destroyed Lower Shawnee Town, but the redoubtable Shawnee immediately rebuilt. However, this time they established their city on higher ground on the east side of the Scioto River, where present Portsmouth is located.

Lower Shawnee Town welcomed English as well as French fur traders, which particularly irritated the French authorities, who viewed the English trespass as a threat to French sovereignty. That feeling was intensified after Céloron's visit in 1749, and Pierre Jacques de Taffenel, the governor of New France, even considered having the town destroyed as a punitive measure. A more insidious threat to the Shawnee was the formation of the "Ohio Company" by a group of Virginians in 1747. The Ohio Company was a land speculation venture started by a group of wealthy Virginia planters who petitioned the king and received a land grant of half a million acres in the Ohio River Valley. A provision of the land grant was that the land would be settled within seven years. Of course, the Shawnee viewed the arbitrary appropriation of their land with alarm, and in August 1752, when Virginia representatives visited the town, the Shawnee insultingly hoisted the French flag. To further impress upon the English how far their relationship had deteriorated, the Shawnee scornfully returned a British flag that had previously been given them.

Relations with the English deteriorated further when a party of Shawnee, including the influential Shawnee chief Lawachkamicky, who happened to be traveling through South Carolina, was imprisoned after a local colonist was killed. It was the chief's bad fortune to be in the area at the time. The situation worsened when Lawachkamicky inexplicably died in prison, which further convinced the Shawnee that the British had broken the alliance.

The rift between the Shawnee and the English colonists was a major factor in the Shawnee decision to support the French during the French and Indian War. Between 1755 and 1757, the Shawnee carried out particularly destructive attacks against English colonial settlements in Pennsylvania, Virginia, and Maryland. During those years, between fifteen hundred and two thousand colonists were killed, and about one thousand were taken prisoner. The raids were so devastating that the British concluded a Treaty at Easton in 1758 that guaranteed Indian lands west of the Alleghenies. That treaty was violated almost immediately when, in November 1758, the British captured Fort Duquesne at the Forks of the Ohio and replaced it with Fort Pitt and its associated settlement of Pittsburgh.

By 1758, a combination of factors concerned the leaders of Lower Shawnee Town regarding the viability of maintaining their principal town at its location on the Ohio River. The large population of the community critically strained the local resources, such as game, firewood, and farmland. Probably more important at the time was its location, which increased the town's vulnerability to English attack. As a result, it was decided to abandon the location and establish a new community farther up the Scioto River. However, instead of settling in one massive town like Lower Shawnee Town, the leaders decided to establish a number of smaller communities along the river; they would be more sustainable, yet close enough for mutual strength. By the end of 1758, Lower Shawnee Town was virtually abandoned, and its Shawnee population resettled along both banks of the Scioto River south of present Circleville, Ohio.

Kispoko was often confusingly referred to and shown on maps as Lower Shawnee Town, because for a short period of time it was the most downstream Shawnee village on the Scioto River. To differentiate between the two, the original Lower Shawnee Town at the mouth of the Scioto was often referred to as "*Old* Lower Shawnee Town." Adding to the confusion, the Kentuckians sometimes incorrectly referred to Kispoko as Upper Chillicothe.

18. *Maguck (Magueck) (c. 1750–c. 1778),*
also Magung, Maqueechaick.
Now: Circleville, Pickaway County (39°32'49.23"N–82°58'20.86"W)

Maguck wasn't a very large town by Indian standards, but its importance lay in the fact that it was located at or very near the junction of several major Indian trails that crisscrossed Ohio. It sat astride the major north-south Scioto Trail that ran between Sandusky Bay to the mouth of the Scioto River, where it connected with the Warriors' Path to the south. It was also at the junction of the Belpre Trail, Kanawha Trail, Shawnee-Miami Trail, and other lesser thoroughfares. In January 1751, frontiersman Christopher Gist visited the town for four days, and his journal recorded that visit: "Sunday 20 [1751]. The Snow began to grow thin, and the Weather warmer; set out from Hockhockin S .5 M, then W 5 M, then SW 5 M, to the Maguck a little Delaware [Lenape] Town of about ten Families by the N Side of a plain or clear Field about 5 M in Length NE & SW & 2 M broad, with a small Rising in the Middle, which gives a fine Prospect over the whole Plain, and a large Creek on the

N Side of it called Sciodoe Creek [Scioto River]."[51] Darlington expands on Gist's reference: "January 20—Maguck. In the Pickaway plains, between Scippo Creek and the Scioto River, in Pickaway County and township, three and one-half miles south of Circleville; 'the small rising in the middle' was called 'Black Mountain' by the natives."[52] The Black Mountain that Darlington refers to is a small hill immediately southwest of the intersection of U.S. 23 and Radcliffe Road.

In 1752, on his way to Pickawillany, William Trent received word that the town had been attacked, so he stopped at other Indian villages to gather more information. He arrived at Maguck on July 3, 1752, and his journal reads, "3d. We got to Meguck, where we heard much the same news, which made us conclude to go to the lower Shawnees town with the goods, that we might know the certainty." A footnote on the same page reads: "A Delaware [Lenape] town of ten families, fifteen miles southwest of Hockhocken."[53] Actually, the distance from the Hocking River, which was then called the Hockhocking, is about twenty-one miles.

Two maps that show Maguck are John Mitchell's 1766 map, and Thomas Pownall's "corrected and improved" version of Lewis Evans's 1755 map. Both maps place Maguck farther east of the Scioto River than the town's actual location.

Hanna attempts to plot the location of Maguck by using Gist's estimated distances. Maguck, "according to Gist's distances, was fifteen miles southwest of Hockhocking. The distance between Lancaster, Ohio, and Circleville, today by the Cincinnati & Muskingum

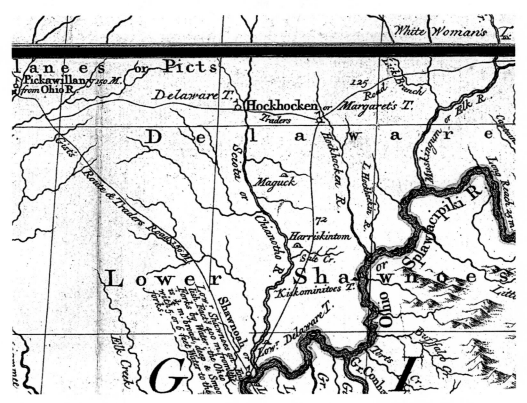

Section of 1755 John Mitchell map showing Maguck (Library of Congress, Geography and Map Division-74693187).

Valley Railroad, is twenty-one miles; so that Maguck was quite that far from Hockhocking." Hanna further states that "the site of Pickawillany is distant from the site of Maguck some sixty-eight miles west, and forty-five miles north; or about eighty-one miles on a direct line."[54] Based on the information above, the location of Maguck would be west of present U.S. 23 between Dupont and Radcliffe roads.

Interestingly, the historian Charles A. Hanna refers to it as "'Maguck' or 'Maqueecha-ick,' a town of Shawnee origin."[55] That is understandable due to the number of Shawnee villages that were established in the area after 1758, when the Shawnee relocated from Lower Shawnee Town at the mouth of the Scioto River. However, Christopher Gist and William Trent personally visited the town in 1751 and 1752, respectively, and they certainly would have known the difference between Lenape and Shawnee. It's possible that some Shawnee lived with the Lenape, or the Lenape name of the village was similar to Maguck, which is associated with the Mekoche Shawnee. Indeed, the town is spelled several different ways in different sources, including "Maqueechaick,"

To add some confusion to whether Maguck was a Shawnee town at some time in its history, a letter was written by Captain Edward Ward to Sir William Johnson on May 2, 1764. Ward wrote: "Yesterday I received a letter from Lieut. Hutchins from Fort Pitt in five days to inform me that a few days ago, one Hicks (a renegade and a scoundrel) came into Fort Pitt from the Indians who informs him that for certain my cousin Major Thomas Smallman is a prisoner with the Shanney's [Shawnees] at a place called Magguck."[56] As a side note, Small-man was among the prisoners surrendered to Bouquet on November 9, 1764.[57]

Additional information regarding Maguck is lacking, particularly the years the town was established and when it was finally abandoned. One source indicates that around 1750, the Wyandots permitted the Lenape to establish villages in south-central Ohio, which would

Section of Thomas Pownall's 1776 "corrected version" of Lewis Evans's 1755 map showing Magung [Maguck] (Library of Congress, Geography and Map Division-74693076).

likely have included Maguck.[58] There is no information regarding the chief or head-person of the village, or the time period when it was occupied by Lenape and when the Shawnee may have taken over the town. Most likely, it was abandoned sometime around 1778, when many of the Indians in that area of the Scioto River either moved farther west to become allies of the British or moved east in an attempt to remain on peaceful terms with the Americans.

7. Pecowick (Pickoweeke) (c. 1758–c. 1774).
NOW: CLARKSBURG, ROSS COUNTY (39°28'29.44"N–83°4'19.79"W)

Pecowick, as the name implies, was a town primarily inhabited by members of the Pekowis sept of Shawnee. Several sources indicate that a town named Pecowick or Pickoweeke was located between present Chillicothe and Circleville on the west side of the Scioto River, but documentation that identifies the precise location has not been found. In 1773, Baptist missionary David Jones visited the village and gave us some clues that help us deduce the approximate location. On Tuesday, January 11, 1773, David Jones, along with a Mr. Butlar and Mr. Nailar, camped at the confluence of Paint Creek and the Scioto River, south of present Chillicothe, Ohio. According to Jones, the Shawnee called Paint Creek Alamoneetheepeeca, which "takes its name from some kind of paint that is found in or about it."[59] Jones's journal continued:

> Tuesday 12 [January 1773], … set out for Pickaweekee [Pecowick] in company with my Indian friend, whose name is *Cutteway*, his wife and some others. It may be well thought that my journey was solitary, for three words of the Shawannee language were not known by me, and as little English by my fellow-traveler; so that we could converse none by the way. The day being cold induced me to ride fast, so that about two o'clock we came to the town. About one mile from the town my Indian friend cast off, and his part of his load, and leaving the women behind, made signs for me to ride on with him. Perhaps the reason of his conduct was, lest we should be molested by drunken Indians; for when they are intoxicated, their abuses are not confined to white people, but they will even rob Indians. Drawing near the town, many thoughts arose about the event, for to me it was not known that there was one white man in town; but all anxiety was removed by seeing Mr. Joseph Nicholas, a former acquaintance from Fort Pitt. With kindness he received and entertained me with such refreshments as the situation afforded. While we were refreshing ourselves Mr. John Irwine came in, and invited me home with him. Mr. Irwine's chief habitation is a small town, situated W.N.W. of Pickaweeke about three miles. By the English it is called Blue Jackets Town, an Indian of that name residing there. Before this is described, it is proper to take notice of Pickaweeke—it is situated south of a brook that, east of the town, empties into Deer Creek. It takes its name from a nation of Indians called Picks [Pekowis]. Some of them being the first settlers—the word signifies 'the place of the "Picks." Now it consists of about one hundred souls, being a mixture of Shawannees and other nations, so that it is called a Shawannee town. It is the most remarkable town for robbers and villains, yet it pretends to have its chief men, who are indeed very scoundrels guilty of theft and robbery without any apology or redress. Some of these took four or five mares from Mr. McMechen on Ohio, nor was there any prospect of redress. Leaving this, went with Mr. Irwine to his habitation [Blue Jacket's Town]. This town is situated east of Deer Creek, and north of a large plain.[60]

It's difficult to determine the location of Pecowick just from David Jones's description; however, by combining it with some other information we may have more of a clue. Several sources place the town in the northern section of present Ross County, so that would indicate that Pecowick was between present Andersonville and Clarksburg, Ohio. Frank Wilcox sites Pecowick at present Yellowbud, Ohio, on Yellowbud Creek, which is at the northern edge of Ross County, but that doesn't agree with David Jones's description of the town as being on the south side of a stream that runs into Deer Creek, since Yellowbud Creek has no confluence with Deer Creek. However, two locations fit that description. Waugh Run enters Deer Creek about four miles west of the Scioto, and Hay Run enters Deer Creek two miles farther west. Both would have suitable sites for a village south of the creeks west of where they enter Deer Creek.

From the journal of David Jones, we know that Blue Jacket's Town was about three miles to the west-northwest of Pecowick on the east side of Deer Creek. From its confluence with Waugh Run, Deer Creek is oriented approximately west-northwest for about two miles to its junction with Hay Run, then it veers slightly northwest about 1.25 miles to the Ross County Line, where it turns almost due north. To satisfy Jones's assertion that Blue Jacket's Town was about three miles west-northwest of Pecowick and be on the east side of Deer Creek, the only possible location could be south of the confluence of Waugh Run and Deer Creek. Any other location would place Blue Jacket's Town almost due north of Pecowick.

Whether Pecowick was a town populated by thieves and renegades as asserted by Jones is open to question. The Pekowis Shawnee sept was a more militant branch of the Shawnee, since they were known by their war chiefs to be opposed to the Mekoches sept that traditionally provided hokimas, or civic chiefs who generally led the nation in times of peace. Jones had a history of insulting the Shawnee with his ignorance of tribal etiquette, and narrowly escaped death on at least two occasions when chiefs refused to allow him to preach in their village. The Shawnee in general were very satisfied with their spirituality, and unlike the Lenape, they were not inclined to change. They may have rebuffed his missionary effort at Pecowick, which caused Jones to regard them and their chief as scoundrels and reprobates.

Most likely, the town was established in 1758 at the time of the Shawnee exodus from Lower Shawnee Town at present Portsmouth, Ohio. As the name implies, it was inhabited mainly by members of the Peckowis sept, since Shawnee primarily grouped according to hereditary septs. Interestingly, Blue Jacket's Town, about three miles away, was also primarily a Pekowis village, because Blue Jacket, or Waweyapiersenwaw (whirlpool), was a Peckowis Shawnee. Shawnee often followed a leader based on his charisma, wealth, bravery, or any number of personal reasons, which would account for different towns of the same sept within relatively close proximity to one another.

Jones stated that Kishshinottisthee, or Hardman, was the chief of Blue Jacket's Town, but Hardman was a Mekoche Shawnee, and at that time he was the principal hokima or civil chief of the Shawnee in the area. His town was Wakotomica on the Muskingum River at present Dresden, Ohio. His temporary residence at Blue Jacket's Town was likely a result of a close relationship between the Mekoche hokima and the prominent Peckowis war chief Blue Jacket.

By the winter of 1776–1777, a serious breach was developing between the Shawnee who believed war was inevitable if they were to retain their land in Ohio, and those who wanted to pursue their goals through peaceful diplomacy. Mekoche chiefs like Hardman and Cornstalk wanted to take the Shawnee east to the Muskingum River to join with the Lenape and form a neutral bloc in order to avoid involvement in the American Revolutionary War. The militant Shawnee advocated moving west to the Little Miami and Great Miami Rivers to join the war in support of the British. Blue Jacket initially considered siding with the peace faction, but in 1777, he decided to join the militants. It's not known for certain which direction the residents of Pecowick decided to go, but if they were undecided, it's likely the murder of the peace-seeking Cornstalk at Fort Randolph convinced them to join the militant Shawnee in the west. By 1778, most of the Shawnee in the Scioto River area, including the inhabitants of Pecowick and Blue Jacket's Town, had dismantled their towns and relocated.

51. *Puckshenose's Town (c. 1770s–c. 1795).*
Now: Orient, Pickaway County (39°47′30.57″N–83°10′1.99″W)

Puckshenose's Town was shown on Crevecœr's 1787 map on the west side of Paint Creek on the Scioto Plains about a mile south of present Harrisburg, Ohio, in Pickaway County. Historian Charles Hanna surmised the town was named after Pucksinwah, the father of Tecumseh, but Pucksinwah was killed during the 1774 Battle of Point Pleasant in Lord Dunmore's War, so his tenure as village chief would have been relatively short.

The name of the village could also indicate it was inhabited by Pekowis Shawnee, which would make it unlikely to have been Pucksinwah's town, since Pucksinwah was a Kispokotha Shawnee, and Shawnees traditionally grouped according to their septs. To further muddy the waters, there was a Shawnee chief named Buckshenoath, who was mentioned in a letter dated April 19, 1756, from Edward Shippen to Governor Morris. Shippen wrote. "Buckshenoath, a great man, a Shawnese Captain."[61] However, there is no supporting evidence other than a similarity of names to indicate that Buckshenoath could have established a town in Ohio that was named after himself.

The Shawnee who lived in Puckshenose's Town most likely relocated there in a progression of moves beginning in 1758 from Lower Shawnee Town at the mouth of the Scioto River, to Peckowik near present Clarksburg, Ohio, and then to Puckshenose's Town around 1774–1775. With the end of the Revolutionary War, the influx of white settlers into Ohio increased dramatically, and the Northwest Indian War was raging. Those villagers who still remained along the Scioto River were particularly vulnerable to American military action from both the east and the south. Most likely, they would have relocated west to the Little Miami and Mad River areas to distance themselves from the Americans. At any rate, they would have been forced to move after the 1795 Treaty of Greenville, which confiscated the land on which their village stood.

55. *Salt Lick Town (c. 1770–c. 1785),*
also Big Salt Licks Town, Mingo Town.
Now: Columbus, Franklin County (39°57′44.71″N–83°0′31.51″W)

The area around the confluence of the Scioto and Olentangy Rivers at present Columbus, Ohio, contained several Indian villages within a relatively small area, and in general they were collectively referred to as Salt Licks Town or Mingo Town. The primary thoroughfares during the 18th century were the rivers and the trails, and present Columbus, Ohio, sits astride the mighty Scioto Trail, and the Scioto and Olentangy Rivers. While other Indian nations certainly had villages in the area, the first recorded villages there were established by the expatriate Iroquois, known as Mingo. The first permanent Mingo village in Ohio was called Mingo Town or Crow's Town at present Mingo Junction south of Steubenville, Ohio. Around 1770, groups of more militant Mingo migrated west to join the Shawnee and the militant Lenape faction in their fight against the Virginians who had moved into Kentucky. One group under the warlike chief Pluggy established his community on the Olentangy River about twenty-four miles north at present Delaware, Ohio. Another group established three towns in close proximity to each other along the Scioto River in present Columbus. Not surprisingly, all three towns were often referred to as Mingo Town, which was the case with most of the Mingo villages in Ohio.

The largest village was on the south side of the Scioto River near the Franklin County Veterans Memorial, where U.S. 40 crosses the Scioto. In the 18th century, there were several salt springs in the area,[62] and the town was variously referred to as Salt Licks Town, Big Salt Lick Town, and of course Mingo Town. A second Mingo village, simply referred to as Mingo Town, was located less than three-quarters of a mile southwest at the west end of the Interstate 70 bridge. A third Mingo community was established less than two miles south-southeast of Salt Lick Town, on the east side of the Scioto River at the present intersection of Greenlawn Avenue and South Front Street. That village was also referred to as Mingo Town.

In 1774, Shawnee, Mingo, and Lenape skirmishes with the Kentuckians erupted into a savage and bloody conflict known as Lord Dunmore's War. The war raged from May through October 1774 and ended with the defeat of the Indians at the Battle of Point Pleasant. The victorious Virginians met some of the defeated chiefs at Camp Charlotte in October 1774 and negotiated the Treaty of Camp Charlotte, which required the Indians to abandon their claim to lands south and east of the Ohio River. Several chiefs refused to attend the meeting at Camp Charlotte, including the Mingo, who vowed to carry on the fight.

Because of the refusal of the Mingo to admit defeat, Lord Dunmore, Royal Governor of Virginia, sent a force to punish them by destroying their villages at the "Forks of the Scioto," which meant the area of the junction of the Scioto and Whetstone in present Columbus, Ohio.[63] The Olentangy River at the time was often referred to as the Whetstone. In 1871, Mr. Joseph Sullivant gave an address to the Franklin County Pioneer Society and talked about the attack:

> There were three Indian encampments or villages in this vicinity, one on the high bank near the old Morrill House, one and a half miles below the city, from which the party was sent out to capture my father and his party, on Deer Creek, in 1795; one at the west end of the Harrisburg bridge; and the principal one on the river below the mouth of the Whetstone, near the Penitentiary[64] where formerly stood Brickell's cabin, and now [1871] stands Hall and Brown's warehouse. The location of these villages I had from John Brickell, Jeremiah Armstrong and Jonathon Alder, who had been captives among the Indians. Alder was my visitor in my boyhood, at my father's house and afterwards at mine, and I had many of the incidents of his life, as related by himself, which afterwards, at my suggestion, were written out. In his boyhood Alder had been captured in Virginia by a marauding party of Indians, was brought into Ohio and adopted into a tribe, and when grown up married and lived among them. He lived on Big Darby, died there, and was well known to our earliest settlers. In one of the personal narratives to which I have alluded he told me he had heard from the older men of the tribe that in the fall of 1774, when all the male Indians of the upper village except a few old men, had gone on their first fall hunt, one day about noon the village was surprised by the sudden appearance of a body of armed white men who immediately commenced firing upon all they could see. Great consternation and panic ensued, and the inhabitants fled in every direction. One Indian woman seized her child of five or six years of age, and rushed down the bank of the river and across to the wooded island opposite, when she was shot down at the farther bank. The child was unhurt among the shower of balls, and escaped into the thicket and hid in a large hollow sycamore standing near the middle of the island, where the child was found two days afterward when the warriors of the tribe returned, having been summoned back to the scene of disaster by runners sent for the purpose. This wooded and shady island was a favorite place for us boys when we went swimming and fishing, especially when we were lucky enough to hook.[65]

William Crawford was the commander of the expedition, and he described the attack in a letter to George Washington:

> Lord Dunmore ordered myself and two hundred and forty men to set out in the night. We were to march to a town about forty miles distant from our camp, up the Scioto, where we understood the whole of the Mingoes were to rendezvous the next day in order to pursue their journey. This intelligence came by John Montour, son of Captain Montour, whom you formerly knew.
>
> Because of the number of Indians in our camp we set out of it under pretense of going to Hockhocking for more provisions. Few knew of our setting off anyhow, and none knew where we were going to until next day. Our march was performed with as much speed as possible. We arrived at the town called Salt Lick Town the ensuing night, and at daybreak we got around it with one-half our force, and the remainder were sent to a small village half a mile distant.
>
> Unfortunately, one of our men was discovered by an Indian who lay, out from the town some distance, by a log which the man was creeping up to. This obliged the man to kill the Indian. This happened before daylight, which did us much damage, as the chief part of the Indians made their escape in the dark; but we got fourteen prisoners, and killed six of the enemy, wounding several more. We got all of their baggage and horses, ten of their guns, and two hundred white prisoners. The plunder sold for four hundred pounds sterling, besides what was returned to a Mohawk Indian who was there. The whole of the Mingoes were ready to start, and were to have set out the morning we attacked them. Lord Dunmore has eleven prisoners, and has returned the rest to the nation. The residue are to be returned upon his lordship's demand.[66]

Interestingly, there is very little written in history books, and no public markers or monuments concerning the attack, which in essence was a massacre of women, children and some old men. However, if there is such a thing as karma, seven years later, Crawford was forced to pay dearly at Captain Pipe's Town after he was taken prisoner by the vengeful Indians.

The Mingo villages continued to exist after Crawford's attack, and in July 1775, the Virginian Captain James Wood, accompanied by Simon Girty, traveled from Fort Pitt to invite the Ohio Indians to meet the Virginia commissioners and negotiate a treaty. After stopping at several villages, they traveled from Upper Sandusky "up the Sandusky and down the Olentangy branch of the Scioto to Pluggy's Town, which stood on the site of present Delaware, Ohio. From here they went to Big Salt Licks Town, on the west bank of the Scioto, near Columbus, about opposite the site of the Ohio Penitentiary."[67]

The Treaty of Fort McIntosh in 1785 marked the end of the Indian villages around present Columbus, Ohio. According to the terms of the treaty, the Indians were restricted to an area of northwestern Ohio bounded by the Cuyahoga and Tuscarawas Rivers to Fort Laurens at present Bolivar, Ohio, then west to Pickawillany at present Piqua, Ohio. The area around present Columbus was outside that treaty area, and the Mingo were forced to relocate farther north and west.

70. Shawnee Town (dates unknown).
Now: Darbyville, Pickaway County (39°42'39.69"N–83°7'55.79"W)

A village called Shawnee Town on Paint Creek was depicted on a map in *The Archeological Atlas of Ohio*; however, the book contains no other information regarding the town. The map depicts the village about a mile and a third northwest of present Darbyville, Ohio, on the west side of Paint Creek, however, a study of other 18th-century maps and documents does not indicate a Shawnee town in that vicinity. If in fact a Shawnee community existed in that vicinity, it was likely a transient village or one of the many small four- or five-family communities that remained after the majority of Shawnee migrated farther west.

3. *Standing Stone (c. 1750s–c. 1795), also Assinink, Beaver's New Town, French Margaret's, Hockhocking, Shawnee Town, Tarhe Town.*
NOW: LANCASTER, FAIRFIELD COUNTY (39°43'29.58"N–82°35'40.32"W)

Standing Stone gets its name from the 250-foot-high sandstone bluff that overlooks present Lancaster, Ohio, from the north side of the city. The hill, now known as Mount Pleasant, is part of Lancaster's Rising Park.

Passing near Standing Stone are the Hocking River, once called Hockhocking, along with several large tributary streams, which made the area a desirable location for Indian settlements. In fact, from the 1750s through the 1795 Treaty of Greenville, which restricted the Indians to the northwest section of present Ohio, it was almost continuously the site of Indian villages. These included Hockhocking (Lenape), French Margaret's Town[68] (Lenape), Beaver's New Town[69] (Lenape), and Assinink ("stony place"; Lenape).

There was no defined convention for naming Indian villages, and often the same village was referred to by different names, depending on the sources. Some villages were designated by tribal name, such as "Mingo Town," "Shawnee Town," or "Ottawa Town," while others were referred to by the name of their principal leader, such as "Shingas's Town," "White Eyes Town," and "Blue Jacket's Town." Other towns were identified by a geographical feature, like "Standing Stone," "Cuyahoga Town," and "Hockhocking." In the case of villages named for their principal leader or particular tribal identification, those names were often carried with them when the community relocated. That resulted in a succession of villages with the same name; for example, Captain Pipe's Town, Chillicothe, and Mingo Town.

Standing Stone, now called Mount Pleasant (author photograph).

Rather than describe in detail all of the various iterations of towns that were located in the vicinity of Standing Stone, they are listed separately.

3. Tarhe Town (c. 1790–c. 1800), also Crane Town, Wyandot.
Now: Lancaster, Fairfield County (39°42′44.60″N–82°36′28.77″W)

Reportedly, the Wyandot chief Tarhe ("The Crane"; 1742–1818) located his village in the vicinity of Standing Stone around 1790. When visited by scouts from Marietta in 1790, Tarhe Town or Crane Town was said to have contained about 100 wigwams and some 500 souls. Tarhe was nicknamed "The Crane" by the British, and "La Grue" (Crane) by the French, likely in reference to his slender build and reputed height of six feet, four inches. Tarhe, a member of the Porcupine Clan, was born near Fort Detroit in 1742, and in 1754, at the age of thirteen or fourteen, fought against Braddock on the Monongahela. In 1763, he joined Pontiac in the Ottawa chief's abortive rebellion, and later fought in Lord Dunmore's War in 1774. He consistently fought the expansion of white settlements into the Ohio area, and took part in the Battle of Fallen Timbers on August 20, 1794. After the Indians' defeat at Fallen Timbers, he signed the Treaty of Greenville. Later, Tarhe refused to join the confederation of Indians in Tecumseh's War (1810 to 1813), and instead urged the Wyandots to honor the Treaty of Greenville that they signed in 1794. During the War of 1812, Tarhe, who was in his seventies, allied with the Americans against the British, and took part in the Battle of the Thames in 1813. That was the battle in which Tecumseh was killed. Tarhe died in 1818 at the age of seventy-eight on the Wyandot reservation at Upper Sandusky. He was regarded as a brave and exceptional warrior, but apparently exceptional warriors were common among the Wyandot, and Tarhe was not chosen to be the "Ron-Tun-Dee" (War Pole), or head war chief. He was, however, sufficiently esteemed as a wise and influential leader to be considered the sachem or titular head of the Wyandot nation.

Isaac Zane, the brother of Ebenezer Zane, who founded Lancaster, Ohio, was the husband of Tarhe's sister Myerrah, "White Crane." Isaac (1753–1816) was captured at the age of nine by the Wyandots in 1762, and he spent most of his life among the Wyandot, achieving prominence. According to some sources, Isaac and Myerrah settled at the confluence of the Licking and Muskingum Rivers, where the town of Westbourne, later Zanesville, Ohio, was established around 1799.[70]

29. Three Legs Town (dates unknown), also Three Ledges, The Ledges.
Now: Uhrichsville, Tuscarawas County (40°24′49.35″N–81°22′51.72″W)

Three Legs Town was located on the east side of Tuscarawas River approximately one mile south of the mouth of Stillwater Creek, between Midvale and Uhrichsville, Ohio, in Tuscarawas County.

Frank Wilcox states that the Moravian Trail "arrived at Old Schoenbrunn, four miles above the end of the Yellow Creek Route, which reached the Tuscarawas via the Stillwater at Midvale, where there was a community known as Three Legs Town."[71] The name immediately causes the reader to question whether the town was actually named after an Indian leader who had three legs.

In his book, Charles Hallowell Mitchener alleges the following:

> Tradition says it was named after a chief who first resided there by the name of "Three Legs," because of the fact that he had an extra leg. His father was said to be the great Shawnese chief Blackhoof, and his mother a Cherokee of great beauty from the south—the climate having imparted to her all the ingredients of beauty incident to southern women of a later day. Blackhoof had brought her up into the Sciota country, and while out one day gathering wild plums she was attacked by a wounded buffalo, limping on three legs, but succeeded in escaping from him. In proper time she gave birth to a boy, who like the beast, had three legs, and when he learned to walk, limped with one leg dangling after him.... On reaching the age of manhood and being unable to follow the chase or go to war, he was offered a chiefship and privilege to select his place of abode in this valley. He chose the mouth of Gehelemukpechuk (Stillwater), for the reason that immense quantities of fish were caught there—as they are caught there at this day in larger quantities than at other places along the river. Three Legs, being an invalid, could not expect to, nor did he ever, become chief over a large town, but those who settled near him were old braves who had spent their energies, and sat down at Three Legs town to pass the residue of their lives fishing, smoking, and giving advice to young warriors.[72]

Indeed, many maps and sources indicate the name "Three Legs" in the area of where Stillwater Creek flows into the Tuscarawas River, but whether they refer to an Indian town or merely a landmark is open to question. Other than Mitchener's "Legend of Three Legs Town on the Stillwater," there isn't any other definitive documentation of a village or the Indians who may have lived there.

It's more likely that "Three Legs" is a corruption of "The Ledges," or "Three Ledges," which denotes the place as a landmark designating the head of navigation on the Tuscarawas River for vessels like bateaux or barges that are larger and heavier than canoes. That

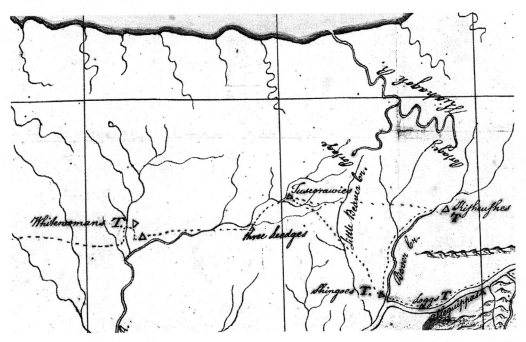

Section of John Patten map of 1753 (Library of Congress, Geography and Map Division-gm71002324).

concept is reinforced by Jedidiah Morse in the 1797 *American Gazetteer*, where he wrote that the river "is navigable by large bateaux and barges to the Three Legs, 100 miles from its mouth."[73] "The Three Legs" seems to imply a geographical location rather than the name of an Indian chief's village. There is some thought that early mapmakers may have attempted to abbreviate the word "Ledges" with "Legs.,"[74] and the name stuck. By the same token, a misspelling or misunderstanding may have changed "the" into "three."

A 1752 map drawn by frontiersman John Patten, designated the spot on the map as "Three Leedges," apparently meaning Three Ledges.

For further reinforcement, John Heckewelder's journal mentions layers of sandstone on the side of a hill in the area, and a search of old topographical charts reveal ledges close to the river in the vicinity of Stillwater Creek. A visit to the site in 2016 reveals a steep ridge with rocky outcroppings along the east side of the Tuscarawas River west of present Uhrichsville, Ohio, and south of Midvale, Ohio. There are also several very shallow areas on the Tuscarawas at that point, which would certainly impede any river traffic other than a light canoe. That supports the location as being the head of navigation on the river.

So what about the three-legged Indian chief who founded his town here? Did he really exist? The author Charles Hanna summarily dismisses the legend by stating that "Mitchener's 'legends' however, are nearly all pure fiction, and not worthy of serious consideration."[74]

Afterword

The Ohio Indians are gone now. They came to Ohio to establish a new homeland, and though they signed treaty after treaty guaranteeing their right to remain, those treaties were constantly violated by land-hungry European and American settlers. The Indians desperately fought back in a forlorn effort to defend their homes and communities but were consistently driven farther west and north until the 1805 Treaty of Fort Industry relegated them to a small corner of northwest Ohio. Even that didn't last. On March 30, 1830, President Andrew Jackson signed the Indian Removal Act, which in effect negated the previous Indian treaties, and opened Indian lands for white settlement. Even worse, the Indians were required to relocate onto federal territories west of the Mississippi River. The forced exodus referred to as the "Trail of Tears" was strongly enforced by both President Andrew Jackson and his successors.

The Wyandot were the last to leave Ohio in July 1843 when they were ousted from their reserve at Upper Sandusky. After that time, the Wyandot, Shawnee, Miami, Lenape, Mingo, Ottawa, and other nations that represented Ohio's 18th-century patchwork of Native American cultures no longer had towns or villages of their own within the state. Sadly, all we have to remember them by are their beautiful, melodic names of rivers, streams, towns, and landmarks, along with some prehistoric mounds and petroglyphs.

Their villages and trails have been overgrown, excavated, built upon or paved under, and the Indians' way of life has given way to 21st-century "progress." It's a pity that only in a few isolated areas of the state we can still wander forested pathways and imagine the paradise that once was Ohio. Things change rapidly, because only five or so decades earlier we could find traces of old Indian trails, see a few of the surviving curiously bent trail marker trees, scoop a cup of water to drink from a remote stream or river, and marvel at an idyllic spot where a community of Indians established their village. Where once we walked a plowed field after a spring rain and picked up a handful of flint arrowheads, finding even one in today's world is a rare occurrence indeed. Only in adventure stories like Zane Grey's *Spirit of the Border*, *The Last Trail*, and *Betty Zane*, or Alan Eckert's marvelous tale *The Frontiersmen*, can we get an indication of Ohio's frontier past.

We hope this book will reinvigorate some of that history, particularly with regard to those refugee tribes who tried to establish their homeland in Ohio during the 18th century and planned to remain "as long as the grass grows, and the rivers flow." They fought the good fight, abided by the treaties they signed, and refused to give up in the face of incredible odds. The Lenape Chief White Eyes negotiated with the American Congress in an attempt to make Ohio an Indian state, which would have been the fourteenth of the United States, and though Congress tentatively agreed to the concept, it never came to pass. After the Revolutionary War, a young Shawnee chief named Welepachtschiechen, also known as Captain Johnny, told the Americans who came to evict the Shawnee that he and his people were not inclined to give up their land just because George III had signed a piece of paper across the ocean. We owe it to White Eyes and Welepachtschiechen, and indeed all the Ohio Indians, to remember them and honor their place in the history of the state.

Chapter Notes

Chapter One

1. Huron was a pejorative French term meaning "lout" or "ruffian" from the French *hure* (bristling hair). That was in reference to the tribe's distinctive hair style. The Huron referred to themselves as Wendat, "people of the peninsula" or "people of the island." Wendat became corrupted into Wyandot or Wyandotte, and though the name refers to the same people, the term Wyandot is generally used to denote the Huron living in Michigan and Ohio.
2. Frederick Webb Hodge, ed., *Handbook of American Indians North of Mexico*, Part 1 (New York: Rowman and Littlefield, 1965), p. 430.
3. *Ibid.*
4. Paul R. Misencik, *George Washington and the Half-King Chief Tanacharison: An Alliance That Began the French and Indian War* (Jefferson, NC: McFarland, 2014), pp. 49–50.
5. *Ibid.*, p. 19.

Chapter Two

1. Richard White, *The Middle Ground: Indians, Empires, and Republics in the Great Lakes Region, 1650–1815* (Cambridge: Cambridge University Press, 1991), p. 193.
2. *Ibid.*
3. *Ibid.*, p. 195.
4. Some sources claim that Angouriot and Orontony were the same person.
5. Misencik, p. 19.
6. Fort Sandoské was intermittently in use until about 1754, when it was abandoned.
7. Misencik, pp. 29–30.
8. *Ibid.*
9. White, p. 203.
10. *Ibid.*
11. Misencik, pp. 31–32.
12. Theodore Besterman, ed., *The Complete Works of Voltaire*, tome 101 (Banbury, Oxfordshire, UK: Voltaire Foundation, 1971), Correspondence XVII, 1968, Letter D7215.
13. Voltaire, *Candide* (Mineola: Dover, 1991), p. 64.
14. Literally "runner of the woods," an independent, entrepreneurial French-Canadian woodsman, trapper and trader, who lived among the Indians and learned their ways.
15. Misencik, p. 39.
16. *Ibid.*

Chapter Three

1. Sami Lakomäki, *Gathering Together: The Shawnee People through Diaspora and Nationhood, 1600–1870* (New Haven: Yale University Press, 2014), p. 15.
2. Jerry E. Clark, *The Shawnee* (Lexington: University Press of Kentucky, 1993), p. 3.
3. *Ibid.*, p. 13.
4. Lakomäki, pp. 17–18.
5. *Ibid.*, p. 26.
6. *Ibid.*
7. Michael N. McConnell, *A Country Between: The Upper Ohio Valley and Its People, 1724–1774* (Lincoln: University of Nebraska Press, 1992), p. 59.
8. Charles A. Hanna, *The Wilderness Trail*, vol. 1 (New York: G.P. Putnam's Sons, 1911), p. 302.

Chapter Four

1. C.A. Weslager, *The Delaware Indians: A History* (New Brunswick: Rutgers University Press, 1972), p. 31.
2. From ancient Greek, derived from *phratria* meaning "brotherhood." It was in essence a social division in a Greek society.
3. D.G. Brinton, *The Lenâpé and Their Legends* (Philadelphia: Brinton, 1885), p. 36.
4. Weslager, p. 45.
5. Brinton, p. 39.
6. Weslager, pp. 41–42.
7. Frank G. Speck, "The Delaware Indians as Women: Were the Original Pennsylvanians Politically Emasculated?" *Pennsylvania Magazine of History and Biography* 70, No. 4 (October 1946): p. 378.
8. *Ibid.*
9. Weslager, p. 156.

10. *Ibid.*, p. 158.
11. *Ibid.*
12. *Ibid.*
13. *Ibid.*, p. 157.
14. Around 1722, the Tuscarora were accepted as the sixth nation of the Iroquois League.
15. Weslager, p. 198.
16. *Ibid.*
17. "Large bull thistles."
18. Venetian Zuan Chabotto, or more popularly Giovanni Caboto, an Italian navigator and explorer commissioned by HenryVII of England to explore and discover new lands.
19. Misencik, p. 45.
20. *Ibid.*, p. 53.
21. *Ibid.*, p. 182.
22. Also referred to in some sources as: Na-taut-whale-mund, Neattawatways, Netahutque-maled, Netodwehement.
23. McConnell, p. 203.

Chapter Five

1. McConnell, p. 19.
2. Hodge, p. 867.
3. McConnell, p. 77.
4. Hanna, p. 348.
5. *Ibid.*
6. C. Hale Sipe, *The Indian Chiefs of Pennsylvania* (Butler: Ziegler Printing Co, 1927), p. 261.
7. Hodge, p. 772.
8. The Logan Elm stood near Circleville in Pickaway County, Ohio, and was one of the largest elms recorded. It was 65 feet tall, had a trunk circumference of 24 feet, and a crown of 180 feet. Weakened by Dutch Elm Disease, the tree died from storm damage in 1964.
9. Thomas Jefferson, *Notes on the State of Virginia* (Richmond: J.W. Randolph, 1853), pp. 68–69.
10. McConnell, *A Country Between*, p. 71.
11. *Ibid.*

Chapter Six

1. Frank Wilcox, *Ohio Indian Trails* (Cleveland: The Gates Press, 1934).
2. William C. Mills, *Archeological Atlas of Ohio* (Columbus: Fred J. Heer, 1915).
3. Frank Wilcox, *Ohio Indian Trails*, 3rd ed., edited by William A. McGill (Kent: Kent State University Press, 2015).
4. The "perch" is an Anglo-Saxon unit of length typically measuring 5½ yards or 16½ feet, or 5.0292 meters. It was a common land measure in England between the 9th and 14th centuries. Although the perch was abolished in the United Kingdom in 1963, it still survives in some areas of the United States.
5. Daniel Agnew, *Fort McIntosh: Its Times and Men* (Pittsburgh: Myers, Shinkle & Co., 1893), p. 13.
6. James Smith, *An Account of the Remarkable Occurrences in the Life and Travels of Col. James Smith During His Captivity with the Indians in the years 1755. '56. '57, '58, & '59* (Lexington: John Bradford, 1799).

Chapter Seven

1. Earl P. Olmstead, *Blackcoats Among the Delaware: David Zeisberger on the Ohio Frontier* (Kent: Kent State University Press, 1991), p. 5.
2. In English texts, it is often spelled Gnadenhütten, because English does not always use the umlaut (ü). I'll try to be consistent, but some sources show the umlaut and others don't. Often, œ will be used in lieu of an ö, as in schœn for schön (beautiful). In German, the letter "a" sometimes has an umlaut (ä). If the umlaut is not used, it will be simply depicted as "a."
3. Olmstead, *Blackcoats*, pp. 6–7.
4. August C. Mahr, "Practical Reasons for Algonkian Indian Stream and Place Names," *The Ohio Journal of Science* 59(6): 365 (November 1959): p. 371, https://kb.osu.edu/bitstream/handle/1811/4658/V59N06_365.pdf (Accessed January 20, 2019).
5. Decorated beaded belts (now often referred to as "wampum belts" were commonly used as tangible records or symbols of peace, friendship, or alliance.
6. John Brand Mansfield, *The History of Tuscarawas County, Ohio* (Chicago: Warner, Beers & Co., 1884), p. 273.
7. *Ibid.*
8. *Ibid.*
9. In German the word for "beautiful" is "schön," but written English does not use the umlaut, so "oe" is used in place of "ö," and schön is written as schoen.
10. The site is immediately south of present Harry Clever Field Airport at New Philadelphia, Ohio
11. Edmund De Schweinitz, *The Life and Times of David Zeisberger: The Western Pioneer and Apostle of the Indians* (Philadelphia: J.B. Lippencott, 1871), pp. 375–376.
12. Earl P. Olmstead, *David Zeisberger: A Life Among the Indians* (Kent: Kent State University Press, 1997), pp. 205–206.
13. *Ibid.*, p. 194.
14. *Ibid.*, p. 274.
15. This rule was later added during the Revolutionary War.
16. De Schweinitz, pp. 378–379.
17. *Ibid.*, p. 277.
18. Mansfield, pp. 276–277.
19. At this time, the settlements were the reoccupied Gnadenhütten, New Schoenbrunn, and Salem. The original Schoenbrunn had been abandoned in 1777, and Lichtenau was abandoned in 1780.
20. Olmstead, *David Zeisberger*, p. 39.
21. J.T. Holmes, *The American Family of Rev. Obadiah Holmes* (Columbus: Ulan Press, 1915), p. 169.
22. *Ibid.*, p. 199.
23. William Henry Rice, *David Zeisberger and His Brown Brethren* (Bethlehem: Moravian Publications Concern, 1908), p. 42.

24. Elizabeth Cobbs and Edward Blum, eds., *Major Problems in American History*, vol. 1: *to 1877* (Boston: Centage, 2015), p. 187.

25. See Goschachgunk in this book.

26. N.N. Hill, *History of Coshocton County, Ohio: Its Past and Present, 1740–1881* (Newark: A.A. Graham & Co.), p. 230.

27. *Ibid.*

28. William J. Bahmer, *Centennial History of Coshocton County, Ohio*, vol. 1 (Chicago: S.J. Clarke, 1909), p. 47.

29. Mansfield, p. 284.

30. *Ibid.*, p. 286.

31. Bahmer, pp. 228–230.

32. *Ibid.*

33. William E. Hunt, *Historical Collections of Coshocton County (Ohio), 1764–1876* (Cincinnati: Robert Clarke & Co., 1876), p. 7.

34. Mansfield, p. 285.

35. Weslager, p. 314.

36. Douglas Hurt, *The Ohio Frontier: Crucible of the Old Northwest, 1720–1830* (Bloomington: Indiana University Press, 1996), p. 81.

37. Olmstead, *David Zeisberger*, p. 39.

38. See Gnadenhütten section.

39. Mansfield, p. 285.

40. *Ibid.*, p. 286.

41. *Ibid.*

42. *Ibid.*, p. 287.

43. *Ibid.*

44. *Ibid.*, p. 289.

45. At this time, the Moravian settlements were the reoccupied Gnadenhütten, New Schoenbrunn, and Salem. The original Schoenbrunn had been abandoned in 1777, and Lichtenau was abandoned in 1780.

46. Olmstead, *David Zeisberger*, p. 39.

47. *Ibid.*, p. 43.

48. *Ibid.*

49. *Ibid.*

50. *Ibid.*, p. 48.

51. Rice, p. 42.

52. David Sanders Clark, "The Moravian Mission of Pilgerruh," in *Transactions of the Moravian Historical Society* 12, No. 2 (1940): pp. 53–79.

53. *Ibid.*, pp. 53–54.

54. *Ibid.*, p. 60.

55. *Ibid.*, p. 58.

56. *Ibid.*, p. 59.

57. Olmstead, *Blackcoats*, p. 71.

58. Clark, "Moravian Mission," p. 59.

59. Olmstead, *Blackcoats*, p. 71.

60. Clark, "Moravian Mission," p. 59.

61. *Ibid.*, pp. 64–65.

62. *Ibid.*, pp. 62–63.

63. Breakneck Creek empties into the Cuyahoga River in Franklin Township northeast of present Kent, Ohio.

64. Clark, "Moravian Mission," p. 69.

65. James Smith, *An Account of the Remarkable Occurrences in the Life and Travels of Col. James Smith During His Captivity with the Indians in the years 1755, '56, '57, '58, & '59* (Lexington: John Bradford, 1799), p. 26.

66. See the Pilgerruh section in this chapter.

67. Eugene F. Bliss, translator, *Diary of David Zeisberger: A Moravian Missionary Among the Indians of Ohio*, vol. 1 (Cincinnati: Robert Clarke & Co., 1885), p. 332.

68. *Ibid.*, p. 335.

69. *Ibid.*, pp. 335–336.

70. *Ibid.*, p. 340.

71. The French trader was possibly John Baptiste Flammand, a Quèbec-born trader. See section on Joseph du Shattar's trading post.

72. Olmstead, *Blackcoats*, p. 76.

73. *Ibid.*, p. 84.

74. *Ibid.*, p. 85.

75. A village near present Fort Wayne, Indiana.

76. Olmstead, *Blackcoats*, p. 85.

77. Bliss, p. 158.

78. Olmstead, *Blackcoats*, p. 117.

79. Mansfield, p. 309.

80. *Ibid.*, p. 310.

81. *Ibid.*

82. *Ibid.*

83. *Ibid.*

Chapter Eight

1. Misencik, p. 182.

2. Paul A.W. Wallace, ed., *The Travels of John Heckewelder in Frontier America* (Pittsburgh: University of Pittsburgh Press, 1958), p. 41.

3. Lewis Evans (c. 1700–1756), Welsh surveyor and geographer, who worked principally in British America.

4. Hanna, p. 334.

5. *Ibid.*, p. 335.

6. Weslager, p. 244.

7. Hanna, pp. 185–86.

8. Misencik, p. 182.

9. Wilcox, *Ohio Indian Trails*, p. 120.

10. Nicholas Cresswell, *The Journal of Nicholas Cresswell, 1774–1777* (New York: The Dial Press, 1924), pp. 108–110.

11. *Ibid.*, pp. 114–115.

12. Hanna, p. 2.

13. *Ibid.*, p. 192.

14. *Ibid.*

15. William M. Darlington, *Christopher Gist's Journals with Historical, Geographical and Ethnological Notes* (Pittsburgh: J.R. Wedlin & Co., 1893), p. 37.

16. *Ibid.*, p. 39.

17. See White Woman's Town section in this book.

18. Russell H. Booth, *The Tuscarawas Valley in Indian Days, 1750–1797* (Cambridge: Gomber House Press, 1994), p. 8.

19. William Trent, *Journal of Captain William Trent From Logstown to Pickawillany, A.D. 1752* (Cincinnati: Robert Clarke & Co., 1871), p. 85.

20. *Ibid.*

21. Sylvester K. Stevens and Donald H. Kent, eds.,

Journal of Chaussegros de Léry (Harrisburg: Pennsylvania Historical Commission, 1940), pp. 104–105.

22. Booth, p. 24.

23. Nicholas B. Wainwright, *George Croghan: Wilderness Diplomat* (Chapel Hill: University of North Carolina Press, 1959), p. 15.

24. Charles Whittlesey, *Early History of Cleveland, Ohio* (Cleveland: Fairbanks, Benedict & Co., 1867), pp. 131–132.

25. Also Na-taut-whale-mund, Neattawatways, Netahutquemaled, Netodwehement, and New Comer.

26. As of August 2017, there is an Akron, Cuyahoga Falls, and Summit County Metro Parks initiative to remove the Gorge Dam at a projected cost of 70 million dollars.

27. Mahr, p. 371.

28. There was legend, most likely started around 1876, that New Comer's Town was named because of an event that occurred at White Woman's Town, in which Mary Harris killed her husband Eagle Feather, and blamed it on a recent white captive who was called "The New Comer." New Comer fled to Netawatwees village, but was recaptured, brought back to White Woman's Town, and executed. The town to which she fled was henceforth called "New Comer's Town." Although Christopher Gist witnessed the killing of a white captive woman at Conchaké, the legend is false, and neither Mary Harris nor anyone else murdered her husband. For more information see "White Woman's Town."

29. McConnell, p. 202.

30. *Ibid.*, p. 203.

31. *Ibid.*

32. Booth, pp. 288–290.

33. McConnell, p. 212.

34. *Ibid.*

35. *Ibid.*

36. *Ibid.*

37. *Ibid.*, p. 213.

38. Booth, , maps 7a, 7b.

39. Olmstead, *David Zeisberger*, p. 175.

40. Sipe, p. 410.

41. Weslager, p. 297.

42. Weslager, pp. 296–297.

43. Hill, p. 411.

44. *Ibid.*, pp. 296–297.

45. Booth, Jr., p. 273.

46. Herman Wellenreuther and Carola Wessel, eds., *The Moravian Mission Diaries of David Zeisberger, 1772–1781* (University Park: Pennsylvania State University Press, 2005), p. 481.

47. Often referred to as John Killbuck (1737–1811), whose paternal uncle was Netawatwees. See Killbuck Town.

48. Mansfield, p. 286.

49. In various sources Paxomet is also referred to as Captain Thomas Armstrong, Tom Armstrong, or Thomas Steen (Steene) Armstrong.

50. Abraham J. Baughman, *History of Ashland County, Ohio*, vol. 1 (Chicago: S.J. Clarke, 1909), p. 167.

51. *Ibid.*, p. 168.

52. John Heckewelder, *History, Manners, and Customs of The Indian Nations Who Once Inhabited Pennsylvania and the Neighboring States* (Philadelphia: Historical Society of Pennsylvania, 1881), p. 143.

53. *Ibid.*

54. *Ibid.*, p. 144.

55. George W. Hill, *History of Ashland County, Ohio, With Illustrations and Biographical Sketches* (Cleveland: Williams Brothers, 1880), p. 54.

56. *Ibid.*

57. *Ibid.*

58. *Ibid.*

59. Hanna, pp. 332–333.

60. A.G. Rober, ed., *Ethnographies and Exchanges: Native America, Moravians, and Catholics in Early North America* 96, No. 1 (June 2009): p. 159.

61. Ermine Wheeler-Voegelin, David A. Horr, Helen Hornbeck Tanner, *Indians of Northern Ohio and Southeastern Michigan: An Ethnohistorical Report (American Indian Ethnohistory: North Central and Northeastern)* (Garland Publishing, 1974), p. 193.

62. In various sources Paxomet is also referred to as Captain Thomas Armstrong, Tom Armstrong, or Thomas Steen (Steene) Armstrong.

63. Weslager, p. 295.

64. Cresswell, p. 108.

65. *Ibid.*

66. *Ibid.*

67. Siegrun Kaiser, *Die Munsee: Migrationsgeschichte und Ethnische Identität* (Franfurt am Main: Johann Wolfgang Goethe-Universität, 2003), p. 205.

68. *Ibid.*, p. 228.

69. Booth, p. 284.

70. *Ibid.*, p. 285.

71. *Ibid.*

72. *Ibid.*, p. 284.

73. *Ibid.*

74. *Ibid.*, p. 285.

75. Samuel Kercheval, *A History of the Valley of Virginia* (Winchester: Samuel H. Davis, 1833), p. 100.

76. Hodge, p. 688.

77. Larry L. Miller, *Ohio Place Names* (Bloomington: Indiana University Press, 1996), pp. 122–123.

78. David A. Stallman, *Our Home Town Holmesville, Ohio* (Sugarcreek, OH: Carlisle Printing, 2001), p. 112.

79. *Ibid.*, p. 12.

80. Booth, p. 283.

81. Hurt, p. 44.

82. James G. Wilson and John Fiske, eds., *Appleton's Cyclopædia of American Biography*, vol. 4 (New York: D. Appleton & Co., 1888), p. 5.

83. Hanna, p. 342.

84. *Ibid.*, p. 200.

85. Hanna, pp. 370–371.

86. Wilcox, *Ohio Indian Trails*, p. 78.

87. Lucius V. Bierce, *Historical Reminiscences of Summit County* (Akron: T. & H.G. Canfields, 1854), p. 39.

88. *Ibid.*, p. 120.

89. www.villageofsilverlakeohio.com/coppacaw. html, last accessed on August 27, 2017.

90. Case Western Reserve Encyclopedia of Cleveland History, *Stigwanish*, https://case.edu/ech/ articles/s/stigwanish/ (last accessed August 2, 2017).

91. Hutchinson may have been referring to either Yellow Creek east of present Hammondsville, Ohio, or the West Fork of the Little Beaver, near Glasgow, Pennsylvania.

92. Hanna, p. 196.

93. Mills, p. ix.

94. Wilcox, *Ohio Indian Trails*, p. 126.

95. Michael McDonnell, *Masters of Empire: Great Lakes Indians and the Making of America* (New York: Hill and Wang, 2015), p. 143.

96. *Ibid.*, p. 144.

97. Kathryn Zabelle Derounian, ed., *Women's Indian Captivity Narratives* (New York: Penguin Books, 1998), pp. 144–145.

98. James E. Seaver, *The Life of Mary Jemison* (New York: Harper & Brothers, 1918), p. 41.

99. *Ibid.*, pp. 355–357.

100. Reuben Gold Thwaites, *Early Western Travels, 1748–1846* (Cleveland: Arthur H. Clark Co., 1904), p. 128.

101. Hanna, vol. 2, p. 41.

102. *Ibid.*, p. 141.

103. Wilcox, *Ohio Indian Trails*, pp. 148ff.

104. Hill, *History of Coshocton County*, p. 520.

105. Hanna, vol. 2, p. 208.

106. *Ibid.*, p. 21.

107. Plain Township is one of sixteen townships in Wayne County, and located west of Wooster, Ohio.

108. Approximately 2.3 miles east of the center of Wooster.

109. Mohican John's Lake is now called Odell Lake, and it is actually in Holmes County, between Big Prairie and Lakeview, just south of the Wayne County line.

110. Henry Howe, *Historical Collections of Ohio in Two Volumes*, vol. 2 (Cincinnati: Krehbiel & Co., 1907), p. 832.

111. On the Rocky Fork about 3 miles southeast of Mansfield.

112. Howe, p. 832.

113. Rogers referred to the stream as Maskongam (Muskingum), and did not differentiate between the various tributaries of the Muskingum. Rogers apparently was on the Jerome Branch of Lake Fork of the Mohican.

114. Hanna, vol. 2, p. 185.

115. *Ibid.*, p. 206.

116. *Ibid.*, p. 209.

117. *Ibid.*, p. 68.

118. B.F. Bowen, *History of Wayne County, Ohio*, vol. 1 (Indianapolis: B.F. Bowen & Co., 1910), p. 87.

119. Zuck, Ohio, is an extinct town that the GNIS (Geographic Names Information Service) classifies as a "populated place." It appears to have been in existence as a town from 1880 until 1903, and was named after Stephen Zuck, who owned the local mill.

120. Wilcox, *Ohio Indian Trails*, pp. 147–148.

121. Weslager, p. 295.

122. Cresswell, p. 108.

123. Wilcox, *Ohio Indian Trails*, p. 120.

124. James B. Holm, ed., *Portage Heritage* (Kent: Commercial Press, 1957), p. 21.

125. Hanna, vol. 1, p. 349.

126. Whittlesey, p. 137.

127. Olmstead, *Blackcoats*, p. 71.

128. Wilcox, *Ohio Indian Trails*, p. 84.

129. Mills, p. viii.

130. Wallace, p. 346.

131. Howard Henry Peckham, *Pontiac and the Indian Uprising* (Detroit: Wayne State University Press, 1947), p. 60.

132. Lewis Cass (1782–1866), American military officer, politician, and statesman.

133. Peckham, p. 60.

134. Bierce, p. 39.

135. *Ibid.*

136. Peter Cherry, *The Western Reserve and Early Ohio* (Akron: R.L. Fouse, 1921), p. 200.

137. *Ibid.*, p. 163.

138. Wilcox, *Ohio Indian Trails*, p. 64.

139. *Ibid.*, p. 120.

140. Holder of an administrative office responsible for finances.

141. Simone Vincens, *Madame Montour and the Fur Trade (1667–1752)* (Québec: Amérique, 1979), p. 229.

142. Hanna, vol. 1, p. 350.

143. Hodge, p. 420.

144. Wallace, p. 435.

145. Hurt, p. 68.

146. *Ibid.*

147. *Ibid.*

148. *Ibid.* p. 69.

149. *Ibid.*

150. Wilcox, *Ohio Indian Trails*, p. 120.

151. Evert O. Hutchins, *The Hutchins Family of Allegan County, Michigan* (Skokie: Imprints Inc., 1961), p. 81.

152. John R. Wise, supr., *The Indian School Journal* 10 (November 1909) (Chilocco: U.S. Indian School, 1909), p. 26.

153. Some sources show his name as "de Shattar."

154. Marjorie Wilkins Campbell, *The North West Company* (New York: St. Martin's Press, 1957).

155. The name officially became "Cleveland" when the city was incorporated in 1836.

156. Whittlesey, p. 132.

157. John Leith, *A Short Biography of John Leith, With a Brief Account of His Life Among the Indians* (Cincinnati: Robert Clark & Co., 1883), p. 65.

158. Caughnawaga refers to Christianized Indians, who were mostly Mohawks, with other nations represented. They were usually referred to as "French Praying Indians" or French Mohawks." The name refers to the Jesuit-run Caughnawaga village near Montréal and a later town on the Mohawk River near present Fonda, New York.

159. Jacob Richards Dodge, *Red Men of the Ohio Valley: An Aboriginal History of the Period Commenc-*

ing A.D. 1650. and Ending At the Treaty of Greenville, A.D. 1795; Embracing Notable Facts and Thrilling Incidents in the Settlement by the Whites of the States of Kentucky, Ohio, Indiana, and Illinois (Springfield: Ruralist, 1860), p. 76.

160. Heckewelder, p. 93.
161. Bowen, p. 87.
162. Smith, *An Account*, p. 13.
163. Hanna, p. 187.
164. *Ibid.*, p. 21.
165. Hodge, p. 944.
166. Sources indicate several different spellings of his name.
167. The school was renamed Princeton University in 1896.
168. Booth, p. 273.
169. Wellenreuther and Wessel, p. 481.
170. Joseph H. Bausman, *History of Beaver County, Pennsylvania*, vol. 1 (New York: Knickerbocker Press, 1904), p. 32.
171. Christianized Indians, many of whom were Iroquois, who generally favored the French side. Their principal village was on the south shore of the St. Lawrence River opposite Lachine, Quebec.
172. The 22 men included ten Deerfield men, five garrison soldiers, and seven men from neighboring Hadley who saw the flames from the burning buildings, and rushed to Deerfield.
173. Emma Lewis Coleman, *New England Captives Carried to Canada between 1677 and 1760 During the French and Indian Wars*, vol. 2 (Portland: The Southworth Press, 1925), p. 87.
174. Old or Julian calendar. The British used the Julian calendar until midnight on September 2, 1752, when they switched to the Gregorian calendar used today. Overnight, they advanced the calendar 11 days to September 14.
175. Hanna, pp. 148–149.
176. Evan Haefeli and Kevin Sweeney, *Captors and Captives: The 1704 French and Indian Raid on Deerfield* (Amherst: University of Massachusetts Press, 2003), p. 224.
177. George F. Smythe and C.H. Mitchner, "Legend of the White Woman, and Newcomerstown," *Ohio Archaeological and Historical Quarterly* 33, pp. 283–300.
178. Ruben Gold Thwaites and Louise Phelps Kellogg, *The Revolution on the Upper Ohio, 1775–1777* (Madison: Wisconsin Historical Society, 1908), pp. xvii, 46ff.

Chapter Nine

1. Wilcox, *Ohio Indian Trails*, p. 191.
2. William Smith, *Bouquet's Expedition* (Carlisle: Applewood Books, 1907), p. 123.
3. Hanna, p. 267, n. 1.
4. Wilcox, *Ohio Indian Trails*, p. 261.
5. Mills, p. ix.
6. *History of Butler County, Pennsylvania* (Chicago: Waterman, Watkins & Co., 1883), p. 12 n‡.

7. Darlington, p. 42.
8. *Ibid.*, p. 43.
9. John Jennings, "Journal from Fort Pitt to Fort Chartres in the Illinois Country, March-April, 1766," *The Pennsylvania Magazine of History and Biography* 31, No. 2 (1907): p. 146.
10. Hodge, p. 956.
11. Hanna, p. 195.
12. *Ibid.*, p. 198.
13. Booth, p. 80.
14. *Ibid.*, p. 300.
15. Weslager, p. 228.

Chapter Ten

1. White, pp. 194–96.
2. Misencik, pp. 14–20.
3. A French league was about 1.75 to 2.53 miles, while an English league was about 3 miles on land and 3.452 at sea (3 nautical miles). A league was originally figured as the distance a man could walk in an hour.
4. Stevens and Kent, p. 101.
5. Hanna, p. 320.
6. See Junundat.
7. Misencik, pp. 28–29.
8. The meaning of the name Muskingum is unclear. Most likely Delaware "mooskinkum," meaning "Elk's eye."
9. John Sugden, *Blue Jacket, Warrior of the Shawnees* (Lincoln: University of Nebraska Press, 2000), p. 54.
10. *Ibid.*
11. "The Fort McIntosh Treaty Journal," Timothy Pickering Papers, LIX, 122–123, Massachusetts Historical Society, Boston.
12. Reginald Horseman, "American Indian Policy in the Old Northwest, 1783–1812," *The William and Mary Quarterly* 18, No. 1 (January 1961): p. 39.
13. Weslager, p. 315.
14. *Ibid.*, p. 330.
15. Edward Butts, *Simon Girty, Wilderness Warrior* (Toronto: Dundurn, 2011), p. 150.
16. *Ibid.*
17. John Knight and John Slover, *Indian Atrocities: Narratives of the Perils and Sufferings of Dr. Knight and John Slover Among the Indians During the Revolutionary War* (Cincinnati: U.P. James, 1867), pp. 22–26.
18. Parker B. Brown, "The Search for the Colonel William Crawford Burn Site," *Western Pennsylvania Historical Magazine* 68, No. 1 (January 1985).
19. Phillip W. Hoffman, *Simon Girty, Turncoat Hero: The Most Hated Man on the Early American Frontier* (Franklin: Flying Camp Press, 2008), p. 175.
20. William Barholt, *Hopocan (Capt. Pipe), The Delaware Chieftain* (Akron: Summit County Historical Society, 1966), p. 11.
21. Nevin O. Winter, *A History of Northwest Ohio* (Chicago: Lewis Publishing Co., 1917), p. 529.
22. *Ibid.*, p. 532.

23. *Ibid.*, p. 529.

24. *Ibid.*, p. 198.

25. Robert Morgan, *Boone: A Biography* (Chapel Hill: Algonquin Books, 2007), p. 319.

26. John Mack Faragher, *Daniel Boone* (New York: Henry Holt & Co., 1993), p. 219.

27. Hunt, p. 14.

28. Hanna, p. 184.

29. William Stone, *The Life and Times of Sir William Johnson, Bart.*, vol. 2 (Albany: J. Munsell, 1865), p. 466.

30. Hanna, p. 321.

31. M. Kristina Smith, *Lost Sandusky* (Charleston: The History Press, 2015), pp. 14–15.

32. Stevens and Kent, p. 54.

33. *Ibid.*, p. 96.

34. Lucy Elliot Keeler, "Old Fort Sandoski of 1745 and the Sandusky Country," reprinted from *Ohio Archaeological and Historical Publications* 17 (1908): p. 368.

35. William L. Clement, *The Journal of Major Robert Rogers* (Worcester: American Antiquarian Society, 1918), pp. 46–47.

36. Murray N. Rothbard, *Conceived in Liberty* (Auburn: Ludwig von Mises Institute: 2011), p. 784.

37. Charles E. Frohman, *Sandusky's Yesterdays* (Columbus: Ohio Historical Society, 1968), p. 10.

38. *Ibid.*, p. 11.

39. *Ibid.*, p. 10.

40. The hamlet of Venice sprang up quickly after its beginning in 1817. While Sandusky had no more than a few log cabins, Venice was the largest Ohio settlement west of Cleveland. However, Sandusky developed its own industry and shipping port and eclipsed Venice, which began to languish for several reasons, including the shallowness of the water, which prevented large vessels from using its port. Venice remained an independent hamlet until it was annexed by the city of Sandusky in 1963.

41. Frohman, p. 8.

42. Stone, p. 466.

43. "Water Course—Pleading—Estoppel," *Reports of Cases Argued and Determined in Circuit Courts of Ohio*, vol. 8, Ohio Circuit Decisions (Norwalk: The American Publishers, 1898), pp. 693–694.

44. *Ibid.*, p. 694.

45. Frohman, p. 18.

46. *Ibid.*, pp. 12–13.

47. *Ibid.*, p. 19.

48. Helen Hornbeck Tanner, "The Glaize in 1792: A Composite Indian Community," *Ethnohistory* 25, No. 1 (Winter 1978): p. 21.

49. Sugden, p. 131.

50. Tanner, p. 25.

51. *Ibid.*

52. M. Agnes Burton, *Collections and Researches Made by the Michigan Pioneer and Historical Society*, vol. 20 (Lansing: Wynkoop Hallenbeck Crawford Co., 1912), p. 698.

53. Misencik, p. 14–20.

54. Hanna, vol. 1, pp. 320–21.

55. Smith, *An Account*, p. 44.

56. *Ibid.*, p. 100.

57. Darlington, p. 110.

58. Hodge, p. 637.

59. Howe, vol. 2, p. 522.

60. Caughnawaga refers to Christianized Indians, who were mostly Mohawks, with other nations represented. The name refers to the Caughnawaga village site on the Mohawk River near present Fonda, New York.

61. Hurt, p. 49.

62. Frohman, p. 19.

63. Basil Meek, ed., *Twentieth Century History of Sandusky County, Ohio, and Representative Citizens* (Chicago: Richmond-Arnold, 1909), p. 71.

64. *Ibid.*

65. Mills, p. 72.

66. Original spelling from the earlier English word "gantlope," which in turn comes from the Swedish "gatlopp." Gauntlet is an alternative spelling, but its meaning primarily refers to an armored glove.

67. At the time, Missionary Island was referred to as "Station Island."

68. According to at least one source, Petonquet's Town was also called Anpatonajowin or Kin-jo-i-no's Town.

69. Howe, p. 522.

70. *The Fire Lands Pioneer*, vols. 4, 5, 6, and 7 (Norwalk: 1863, 1864, 1865, and 1866), pp. 25–30.

71. Root (1807–1879): mayor of Sandusky 1832–1833, prosecuting attorney of Huron County in 1837, Ohio State Senate 1840–1841, U.S. House of Representatives 1845–1851, Presidential Elector 1860, U.S. Attorney 1861, Ohio State Senate 1869, Democratic delegate to the State constitutional convention 1873, and Judge of Erie County 1875. His home was reputedly a "safe house" on the Underground Railroad.

72. The Firelands (Fire Lands) or Sufferer's Lands was a large tract in Ohio that was intended a restitution for the residents of the Connecticut towns of Danbury, Fairfield, Greenwich, Groton, New Haven, New London, Norwalk, and Ridgefield, whose homes had been burned by the British between the years 1779 and 1781.

73. *The Fire Lands Pioneer*, p. 28

74. David M. Strothers and Patrick M. Tucker, *The Fry Site: Archaeological and Ethnohistorical Perspectives of the Maumee River Ottawa of Northwest Ohio* (Morrisville, NC: Lulu Press, 2006), p. 64.

75. *Case Western Reserve Encyclopedia of Cleveland History*, "Ogontz (Ogantz)," https://case.edu/ech/articles/o/ogontz-ogantz/ (last accessed August 25, 2017).

76. Winter, p. 430.

77. Meaning "people who live on the peninsula."

78. Misencik, pp. 29–30.

79. A sub-group of Miami Indians, who generally lived in what is now western Indiana and Ohio.

80. Misencik, p. 32.

81. Defined here as "fur trader." By definition, "factor" denotes one who transacts business for another, such as a broker.

82. Trent, p. 40.

83. *Ibid.*, p. 43.
84. *Ibid.*
85. Misencik, p. 39.
86. *The History of Wyandot County Ohio* (Chicago: Leggett Conway & Co., 1884), p. 290.
87. Olmstead, *Blackcoats*, p. 84.
88. *Ibid.*, p. 85.
89. Henry C. Shetrone, *The Indian in Ohio* (Columbus: F.J. Heer, 1918), p. 188.
90. Thwaites and Kellogg, pp. xvii, 247.
91. See Junundat, Anioton, and Contuntuth sections in this book,
92. David Carver Caldwell and Peggy Anderson Caldwell, *Long Ago Tales of Our Family* (Morrisville, NC: Lulu Press, 2016), p. 132.
93. Cecil B. Hartley, *The Life and Times of Colonel Daniel Boone* (New York: Perkins Book Co., 1902), p. 228–235.
94. Misencik, pp. 49–50.
95. See Gnadenhütten section this book.
96. Lakomäki, p. 114.

Chapter Eleven

1. Weslager, p. 244.
2. Darlington, p. 42.
3. *Ibid.*, p. 116.
4. Near the present crossing point of Brownsville Road (Ohio 668) over the Licking River at the former town of Claylick, Ohio (now Heath, Ohio.)
5. Hanna, vol. 2, pp. 194–195.
6. Wellenreuther and Wessel, p. 490, n1364.
7. Sugden, p. 26.
8. *Ibid.*, p. 32.
9. Robert White McFarland, "The Chillicothes," *Ohio Archaeological and Historical Publications* 11 (1903): pp. 230–231.
10. Hanna, vol. 1, p. 146.
11. David Jones, *A Journal of Two Visits Made to Some Nations of Indians on the West Side of the River Ohio, in the Years 1772 and 1773* (Burlington, VT: Isaac Collins, 1774), p. 40.
12. *Ibid.*, p. 40–41.
13. *Ibid.*, p. 41.
14. Mills, p. 71.
15. In some sources as Othawapeeleethi and Hathaawapeleethi.
16. Don Green, *Shawnee Heritage II: Selected Lineages of Notable Shawnee* (Morrisville, NC: Lulu Press, 2009), p. 363.
17. Jones, pp. 46–47.
18. Lakomäki, p. 94.
19. McFarland, p. 230.
20. Howe, vol. 2, pp. 401–403.
21. There is some question regarding Logan's Mingo name. He was the son of Shikellamy, who had two sons named Logan: Logan Elrod and Logan the Orator. Logan the Orator, whom we are discussing, was variously called Tahgahjute, Technechdorus, Soyechtowa, and Tocanioadorogon.
22. Howe, vol. 2, p. 406.

23. In some sources, Cornstalk is referred to as Hokolesqua, Hokoleskwa, colesqua, Keigh-tugh-qua, and Wynepuechsika.
24. Some sources erroneously indicate that he was a Chalahgawatha.
25. Lakomäki, p. 105.
26. Some sources indicate that Methotaske was a Creek Indian who had been adopted by the Shawnee, which would not have been unusual. As such, she would have been fully accepted as a member of the family.
27. Jones, p. 41.
28. Person of mixed Native American and European ancestry.
29. John F. Meginness, ed., *History of Lycoming County, Pennsylvania 1892* (Lycoming: Heritage Books, 2008), p. 31.
30. *Ibid.*, p. 31.
31. Darlington, p. 116.
32. *Ibid.*, p. 104.
33. *Ibid.*, p. 42.
34. Also known as Captain Butler and Tamanatha Butler.
35. The battle, also known as Saint Clair's Defeat and "Battle of a Thousand Slain," was a stunning Indian victory. American casualties out of a force of about a thousand men were 656 killed or captured and 277 wounded. The Indian casualties out of about 1,100 were 21 killed and 61 wounded.
36. Camp Charlotte, a temporary military camp, was located on the south bank of Scippo Creek, immediately north of the intersection of Ohio 56 and Ohio 159 at present Leistville, Ohio.
37. Samuel Preston Hildreth, *Pioneer History: Being an Account of the First Examinations of the Ohio Valley, and the Early Settlement of the Northwest Territory; Chiefly From Original Manuscripts* (Cincinnati: H.W. Derby & Co., 1848), p. 30.
38. Lois Mulkearn, ed., *George Mercer Papers Relating to the Ohio Company of Virginia* (Pittsburgh: University of Pittsburgh Press, 1954), pp. 495–96, n112.
39. Hildreth, p. 30.
40. Gilbert F. Dodds, "Anecdotes of Ohio," *Marion [Ohio] Star*, Thursday, September 5, 1940.
41. McFarland, pp. 230–231.
42. Hokimas were the civil chiefs or "peacetime" chiefs. According to Shawnee tradition, in time of war the hokimas stepped aside for the military leaders or war chiefs to take over leadership.
43. In some sources, Colesquo, Hokolesqua, Keightughqua, or Wynepuechsika.
44. Lakomäki, p. 105.
45. *Ibid.*
46. See Pluggy's Town section in this book.
47. Lakomäki, p. 109.
48. At the time a French league equaled 4,452.2 meters or 2.76 statute miles.
49. Lakomäki, p. 55.
50. *Ibid.*
51. Darlington, p. 42.
52. *Ibid.*, p. 116.

53. Alfred T. Goodman, ed., *Journal of Captain William Trent from Logstown to Pickawillany, A.D. 1752* (Cincinnati: Robert Clarke & Co., 1871), p. 86.

54. Hanna, vol. 1, p. 279.

55. *Ibid.*, p. 148.

56. George T. Fleming, *History of Pittsburgh and Environs From Prehistoric Days to the American Revolution* (New York: The American Historical Society, 1922), p. 484.

57. *Ibid.*

58. Hurt, p. 17.

59. Jones, p. 36.

60. *Ibid.*, pp. 36–37.

61. Israel Daniel Rupp, *The History and Topography of Dauphin, Cumberland, Franklin, Bedford, Adams, and Perry Counties* (Lancaster: Gilbert Hills, 1846), p. 317.

62. Alfred Emory Lee, *History of the City of Columbus, Capital of Ohio*, vol. 1 (New York: Munnsell & Co., 1892), p. 149.

63. The Penitentiary was located bounded by Spring Street, Neil Avenue, West Street, and Maple Street in downtown Columbus. It was in operation from 1834 until 1984, and was demolished in 1998.

64. Lee, pp. 97–98.

65. C.W. Butterfield, *The Washington-Crawford Letters Concerning Western Lands* (Cincinnati: Robert Clarke & Co., 1877), p. 56.

66. Hanna, vol. 2, p. 210.

67. Not to be confused with French Margaret Montour. See French Margaret's Town in this book.

68. Tamaqua, also known as King Beaver. He was the brother of Shingas. See Beaver's New Town in this book.

69. In 1799, Ebenezer Zane and John McIntire platted the town and opened an inn and ferry across the Muskingum. Ebenezer Zane called the town Westbourne, but in 1801, the town name was officially designated as Zanesville. Some sources claim the town was named after Isaac, while others claim it was named in honor of Ebenezer.

70. Wilcox, *Ohio Indian Trails*, p. 104.

71. C.H. Mitchener, ed., *Ohio Annals—Historic Events in the Tuscarawas and Muskingum Valleys* (Dayton: Thomas W. Odell, 1876), pp. 219–20.

72. Booth, p. 253.

73. *Ibid.*

74. Hanna, vol. 2, pp. 148–149.

Bibliography

Agnew, Daniel, *Fort McIntosh: Its Times and Men* (Pittsburgh: Myers, Shinkle & Co., 1893).

Bahmer, William J., *Centennial History of Coshocton County, Ohio*, vol. 1 (Chicago: S.J. Clarke, 1909).

Barholt, William, *Hopocan* (*Capt. Pipe*), *The Delaware Chieftain* (Akron: Summit County Historical Society, 1966).

Baughman, Abraham J., *History of Ashland County, Ohio*, vol. 1 (Chicago: S.J. Clarke Publishing, 1909).

Bausman, Joseph H., *History of Beaver County, Pennsylvania*, vol. 1 (New York: Knickerbocker Press, 1904).

Besterman, Theodore, ed., *The Complete Works of Voltaire*, tome 101 (Banbury, Oxfordshire, UK: Voltaire Foundation, 1971), Correspondence XVII, 1968, Letter D7215.

Bierce, Lucius V., *Historical Reminiscences of Summit County* (Akron: T.&H.G. Canfields, 1854).

Bliss, Eugene F., translator, *Diary of David Zeisberger: A Moravian Missionary Among the Indians of Ohio*, vol. 1 (Cincinnati: Robert Clarke & Co., 1885).

Booth, Russell H., *The Tuscarawas Valley in Indian Days, 1750–1797* (Cambridge: Gomber House Press, 1994).

Bowen, B.F., *History of Wayne County, Ohio*, vol. 1 (Indianapolis: B.F. Bowen & Co., 1910).

Brinton, D.G., *The Lenâpé and Their Legends* (Philadelphia: Brinton, 1885).

Brown, Parker B., "The Search for the Colonel William Crawford Burn Site," *Western Pennsylvania Historical Magazine* 68, No. 1 (January 1985).

Burton, M. Agnes, *Collections and Researches Made by the Michigan Pioneer and Historical Society*, vol. 20 (Lansing: Wynkoop Hallenbeck Crawford Co., 1912).

Butterfield, C.W., *The Washington-Crawford Letters Concerning Western Lands* (Cincinnati: Robert Clarke & Co., 1877).

Butts, Edward, *Simon Girty, Wilderness Warrior* (Toronto: Dundurn, 2011).

Caldwell, David Carver, and Peggy Anderson Caldwell, *Long Ago Tales of Our Family* (Morrisville, NC: Lulu Press, 2016).

Campbell, Marjorie Wilkins, *The North West Company* (New York: St. Martin's Press, 1957).

Case Western Reserve Encyclopedia of Cleveland History, "Ogontz (Ogantz)," https://case.edu/ech/articles/o/ogontz-ogantz/, last accessed August 25, 2017.

Chafe, Wallace L., *Handbook of the Seneca Language* (Albany: University of the State of New York, 1963).

Cherry, Peter, *The Western Reserve and Early Ohio* (Akron: R.L. Fouse, 1921).

Clark, David Sanders, "The Moravian Mission of Pilgerruh," in *Transactions of the Moravian Historical Society* 12, No. 2 (1940).

Clark, Jerry E., *The Shawnee* (Lexington: University Press of Kentucky, 1993).

Cleland, Hugh, *George Washington in the Ohio Valley* (Pittsburgh: University of Pittsburgh Press, 1955).

Clement, William L., *The Journal of Major Robert Rogers* (Worcester: American Antiquarian Society, 1918).

Cobbs, Elizabeth, and Edward Blum, eds., *Major Problems in American History*, vol. 1: *To 1877* (Boston: Centage, 2015).

Coleman, Emma Lewis, *New England Captives Carried to Canada between 1677 and 1760 During the French and Indian Wars*, vol. 2 (Portland: Southworth Press, 1925).

Cresswell, Nicholas, *The Journal of Nicholas Cresswell, 1774–1777* (New York: The Dial Press, 1924).

Darlington, William M., *Christopher Gist's Journals with Historical, Geographical and Ethnological Notes* (Pittsburgh: J.R. Wedlin & Co., 1893).

Derounian, Kathryn Zabelle, ed., *Women's Indian Captivity Narratives* (New York: Penguin Books, 1998).

De Schweinitz, Edmund, *The Life and Times of David Zeisberger: The Western Pioneer and Apostle of the Indians* (Philadelphia: J.B. Lippencott. 1871).

Dodds, Gilbert F., "Anecdotes of Ohio," *Marion [Ohio] Star*, Thursday, September 5, 1940.

Dodge, Jacob Richards, *Red Men of the Ohio Valley: An Aboriginal History of the Period Commencing A.D. 1650 and Ending at the Treaty of Greenville, A.D. 1795; Embracing Notable Facts and Thrilling Incidents in the Settlement by the Whites of the States of Kentucky, Ohio, Indiana, and Illinois* (Springfield: Ruralist, 1860).

Faragher, John Mack, *Daniel Boone* (New York: Henry Holt, 1993).

The Fire Lands Pioneer, vols. 4, 5, 6, and 7 (Norwalk: 1863, 1864, 1865, and 1866).

Fleming, George T., *History of Pittsburgh and Environs from Prehistoric Days to the American Revolution* (New York: The American Historical Society, 1922).

"The Fort McIntosh Treaty Journal," Timothy Pickering Papers, LIX, 122–123, Massachusetts Historical Society, Boston.

Foster, Emily, ed., *The Ohio Frontier: An Anthology of Early Writings* (Lexington: University Press of Kentucky, 2000).

Frohman, Charles E., *Sandusky's Yesterdays* (Columbus: Ohio Historical Society, 1968).

Galbreath, C.B., ed., *Expedition of Celoron to the Ohio Country in 1749* (Columbus: F.J. Heer, 1921).

Goodman, Alfred T., ed., *Journal of Captain William Trent from Logstown to Pickawillany, A.D. 1752* (Cincinnati: Robert Clarke & Co., 1871).

Green, Don, *Shawnee Heritage II: Selected Lineages of Notable Shawnee* (Morrisville, NC: Lulu Press, 2009).

Haefeli, Evan, and Kevin Sweeney, *Captors and Captives: The 1704 French and Indian Raid on Deerfield* (Amherst: University of Massachusetts Press, 2003).

Hanna, Charles A., *The Wilderness Trail*, vols. 1 and 2 (New York: G.P. Putnam's Sons, 1911).

Hartley, Cecil B., *The Life and Times of Colonel Daniel Boone* (New York: Perkins Book Co., 1902).

Heckewelder, John, *History, Manners, and Customs of the Indian Nations Who Once Inhabited Pennsylvania and the Neighboring States* (Philadelphia: Historical Society of Pennsylvania, 1881).

Hildreth, Samuel Preston, *Pioneer History: Being an Account of the First Examinations of the Ohio Valley, and the Early Settlement of the Northwest Territory; Chiefly from Original Manuscripts* (Cincinnati: H.W. Derby & Co., 1848).

Hill, George W., *History of Ashland County, Ohio, With Illustrations and Biographical Sketches* (Cleveland: Williams Brothers, 1880).

Hill, N.N., *History of Coshocton County, Ohio: Its Past and Present, 1740–1881* (Newark: A.A. Graham & Co.).

History of Butler County, Pennsylvania (Chicago: Waterman, Watkins & Co., 1883).

The History of Wyandot County, Ohio (Chicago: Leggett, Conway & Co., 1884).

Hodge, Frederick Webb, ed., *Handbook of American Indians North of Mexico*, parts 1 and Part 2 (New York: Rowman and Littlefield, 1965).

Hoffman, Phillip W., *Simon Girty, Turncoat Hero: The Most Hated Man on the Early American Frontier* (Franklin: Flying Camp Press, 2008).

Holm, James B., ed., *Portage Heritage* (Kent, OH: Commercial Press, 1957).

Holmes, J.T., *The American Family of Rev. Obadiah Holmes* (Columbus: Ulan Press, 1915).

Horseman, Reginald, "American Indian Policy in the Old Northwest, 1783–1812," *The William and Mary Quarterly* 18, No. 1 (January 1961).

Howe, Henry, *Historical Collections of Ohio in Two Volumes*, vol. 2 (Cincinnati: Krehbiel & Co., 1907).

Hunt, William E., *Historical Collections of Coshocton County (Ohio), 1764–1876* (Cincinnati: Robert Clarke & Co., 1876).

Hurt, Douglas, *The Ohio Frontier: Crucible of the Old Northwest, 1720–1830* (Bloomington: Indiana University Press, 1996).

Hutchins, Evert O., *The Hutchins Family of Allegan County, Michigan* (Skokie, IL: Imprints, 1961).

Jefferson, Thomas, *Notes on the State of Virginia* (Richmond: J.W. Randolph, 1853).

Jennings, John, "Journal from Fort Pitt to Fort Chartres in the Illinois Country, March-April, 1766," *The Pennsylvania Magazine of History and Biography* 31, No. 2 (1907).

Jones, David, *A Journal of Two Visits Made to Some Nations of Indians on the West Side of the River Ohio, in the Years 1772 and 1773* (Burlington, VT: Isaac Collins, 1774).

Kaiser, Siegrun, *Die Munsee: Migrationsgeschichte und Ethnische Identität* (Frankfurt am Main: Johann Wolfgang Goethe-Universität, 2003).

Keeler, Lucy Elliot, "Old Fort Sandoski of 1745 and the Sandusky Country," reprinted from *Ohio Archaeological and Historical Publications* 17 (1908).

Kercheval, Samuel, *A History of the Valley of Virginia* (Winchester: Samuel H. Davis, 1833).

Knight, John, and John Slover, *Indian Atrocities: Narratives of the Perils and Sufferings of Dr. Knight and John Slover Among the Indians During the Revolutionary War* (Cincinnati: U.P. James, 1867).

Lakomäki, Sami, *Gathering Together: The Shawnee People through Diaspora and Nationhood, 1600–1870* (New Haven: Yale University Press, 2014).

Lee, Alfred Emory, *History of the City of Columbus, Capital of Ohio*, vol. 1 (New York: Munnsell & Co., 1892).

Leith, John, *A Short Biography of John Leith, With a Brief Account of His Life Among the Indians* (Cincinnati: Robert Clark & Co., 1883).

Library of Congress, Geography and Map Division, Washington, D.C.

Mahr, August C., "Practical Reasons for Algonkian Indian Stream and Place Names," *The Ohio Journal of Science* 59(6): 365 (November 1959): p. 371, https://kb.osu.edu/bitstream/handle/1811/4658/V59N06_365.pdf (Accessed January 20, 2019).

Mansfield, John Brand, *The History of Tuscarawas County, Ohio* (Chicago: Warner, Beers & Co., 1884).

McConnell, Michael N., *A Country Between: The Upper Ohio Valley and Its People, 1724–1774* (Lincoln: University of Nebraska Press, 1992).

McDonnell, Michael, *Masters of Empire: Great Lakes Indians and the Making of America* (New York: Hill and Wang, 2015).

McFarland, Robert White, "The Chillicothes," *Ohio Archaeological and Historical Publications* 11 (1903).

Meek, Basil, ed., *Twentieth Century History of Sandusky County, Ohio, and Representative Citizens* (Chicago: Richmond-Arnold Pub., 1909).

Meginness, John F., ed., *History of Lycoming County, Pennsylvania 1892* (Lycoming: Heritage Books, 2008).

Miller, Larry L., *Ohio Place Names* (Bloomington: Indiana University Press, 1996).

Mills, William C., *Archeological Atlas of Ohio* (Columbus: Fred J. Heer, 1915).

Misencik, Paul R., *George Washington and the Half-King Chief Tanacharison: An Alliance That Began the French and Indian War* (Jefferson: McFarland, 2014).

Mitchener, C.H., ed., *Ohio Annals—Historic Events in the Tuscarawas and Muskingum Valleys* (Dayton: Thomas W. Odell, 1876).

Morgan, Robert, *Boone: A Biography* (Chapel Hill: Algonquin Books, 2007).

Mulkearn, Lois, ed., *George Mercer Papers Relating to the Ohio Company of Virginia* (Pittsburgh: University of Pittsburgh Press, 1954).

Olmstead, Earl P., *Blackcoats Among the Delaware: David Zeisberger on the Ohio Frontier* (Kent: Kent State University Press, 1991)

_____, *David Zeisberger: A Life Among the Indians* (Kent: Kent State University Press, 1997).

Peckham, Howard Henry, *Pontiac and the Indian Uprising* (Detroit: Wayne State University Press, 1947).

Pickaway Plain—https://www.raremaps.com/gallery/detail/47190/a-map-of-the-ancient-indian-towns-on-the-pickaway-renick, last accessed Aug. 10, 2018.

Rice, William Henry, *David Zeisberger and His Brown Brethren* (Bethlehem: Moravian Publications Concern, 1908).

Rober, A.G., *Ethnographies and Exchanges: Native America, Moravians, and Catholics in Early North America* 96, No. 1 (June 2009).

Rothbard, Murray N., *Conceived in Liberty* (Auburn: Ludwig von Mises Institute, 2011).

Rupp, Israel Daniel, *The History and Topography of Dauphin, Cumberland, Franklin, Bedford, Adams, and Perry Counties* (Lancaster: Gilbert Hills, 1846).

Seaver, James E., *The Life of Mary Jemison* (New York: Harper & Brothers, 1918).

Shetrone, Henry C., *The Indian in Ohio* (Columbus: F.J. Heer, 1918).

Sipe, C. Hale, *The Indian Chiefs of Pennsylvania* (Butler: Ziegler Printing Co, 1927).

Smith, James, *An Account of the Remarkable Occurrences in the Life and Travels of Col. James Smith During His Captivity with the Indians in the years 1755. '56. '57, '58, & '59* (Lexington: John Bradford, 1799).

Smith, M. Kristina, *Lost Sandusky* (Charleston: The History Press, 2015).

Smith, William, *Bouquet's Expedition* (Carlisle: Applewood Books, 1907).

Smythe, George F., and C.H. Mitchner, "Legend of the White Woman, and Newcomerstown," *Ohio Archaeological and Historical Quarterly* 33, pp. 283–300.

Speck, Frank G., "The Delaware Indians as Women: Were the Original Pennsylvanians Politically Emasculated?" *Pennsylvania Magazine of History and Biography* 70, No. 4 (October 1946).

Stallman, David A., *Our Home Town Holmesville, Ohio* (Sugarcreek, OH: Carlisle Printing, 2001).

Steckley, John L., *The Eighteenth-Century Wyandot: A Clan-Based Study* (Waterloo: Wilfrid Laurier University Press, 2014).

Stevens, Sylvester K., and Donald H. Kent, eds., *Journal of Chaussegros de Léry* (Harrisburg: Pennsylvania Historical Commission, 1940).

Stone, William, *The Life and Times of Sir William Johnson*, vol. 2 (Albany: J. Munsell, 1865).

Strothers, David M., and Patrick M. Tucker, *The Fry Site: Archaeological and Ethnohistorical Perspectives of the Maumee River Ottawa of Northwest Ohio* (Morrisville, NC: Lulu Press, 2006).

Sugden, John, *Blue Jacket, Warrior of the Shawnees* (Lincoln: University of Nebraska Press, 2000).

Tanner, Helen Hornbeck, "The Glaize in 1792: A Composite Indian Community," *Ethnohistory* 25, No. 1 (Winter 1978).

Thwaites, Reuben Gold, *Early Western Travels, 1748–1846* (Cleveland, Arthur H. Clark Co., 1904).

Thwaites, Ruben Gold, and Louise Kellogg Phelps, *The Revolution on the Upper Ohio, 1775–1777* (Madison: Wisconsin Historical Society, 1908).

Trent, William, *Journal of Captain William Trent From Logstown to Pickawillany, A.D. 1752* (Cincinnati: Robert Clarke & Co., 1871).

Vincens, Simone, *Madame Montour and the Fur Trade (1667–1752)* (Québec: Amérique, 1979).

Voltaire, *Candide* (Mineola, NY: Dover Publications, 1991).

Wainwright, Nicholas B., *George Croghan: Wilderness Diplomat* (Chapel Hill: University of North Carolina Press, 1959).

Wallace, Paul A.W., ed, *The Travels of John Heckewelder in Frontier America* (Pittsburgh: University of Pittsburgh Press, 1958).

"Water Course—Pleading—Estoppel," *Reports of Cases Argued and Determined in Circuit Courts of Ohio*, vol. 8, Ohio Circuit Decisions (Norwalk: The American Publishers, 1898).

Wellenreuther, Herman, and Carola Wessel, eds., *The Moravian Mission Diaries of David Zeisberger, 1772–1781* (University Park: Pennsylvania State University Press, 2005).

Weslager, C.A., *The Delaware Indians: A History* (New Brunswick: Rutgers University Press, 1972).

Wheeler-Voegelin, Ermine, David A. Horr, and Helen Hornbeck Tanner, *Indians of Northern Ohio and Southeastern Michigan: An Ethnohistorical Report* (*American Indian Ethnohistory: North Central and Northeastern*) (Garland Publishing, 1974).

White, Richard, *The Middle Ground: Indians, Empires, and Republics in the Great Lakes Region, 1650–1815* (Cambridge: Cambridge University Press, 1991).

Whittlesey, Charles, *Early History of Cleveland, Ohio* (Cleveland: Fairbanks, Benedict & Co., 1867).

Wilcox, Frank, *Ohio Indian Trails* (Cleveland: The Gates Press, 1934).

_____, *Ohio Indian Trails*, 3rd ed., edited by William

A. McGill (Kent: Kent State University Press, 2015).

Wilson, James G., and John Fiske, eds., *Appleton's Cyclopædia of American Biography*, vol. 4 (New York: D. Appleton & Co., 1888).

Winter, Nevin O., *A History of Northwest Ohio* (Chicago: Lewis Publishing Co., 1917).

Wise, John R., supr., *The Indian School Journal* 10 (November 1909) (Chilocco: U.S. Indian School, 1909).

www.villageofsilverlakeohio.com/coppacaw.html, last accessed on August 27, 2017.

Index

Numbers in *bold italics* indicate pages with illustrations